LOEB CLASSICAL LIBRARY

FOUNDED BY JAMES LOEB 1911

EDITED BY

JEFFREY HENDERSON

# MACROBIUS

# II

LCL 511

# MACROBIUS

## SATURNALIA

### BOOKS 3–5

EDITED AND TRANSLATED BY

ROBERT A. KASTER

HARVARD UNIVERSITY PRESS
CAMBRIDGE, MASSACHUSETTS
LONDON, ENGLAND
2011

*First published 2011*



Library of Congress Control Number 2010924777
CIP data available from the Library of Congress

ISBN 978-0-674-99671-7

*Composed in ZephGreek and ZephText by
Technologies 'N Typography, Merrimac, Massachusetts.
Printed on acid-free paper and bound by
The Maple-Vail Book Manufacturing Group*

# CONTENTS

# ABBREVIATIONS

| | |
|---|---|
| *CA* | J. U. Powell, ed. *Collectanea Alexandrina*. Oxford, 1925 |
| *CAG* | *Commentaria in Aristotelem Graeca*. 23 vols. Berlin, 1882–1909 |
| *CCAG* | *Catalogus Codicum Astrologorum Graecorum*. 12 vols. Brussels, 1898–1924 |
| *CIL* | *Corpus Inscriptionum Latinarum*. 17 vols. Berlin, 1862– |
| *CGF* | G. Kaibel, ed. *Comicorum Graecorum Fragmenta*. Vol. 1, fasc. 1. Berlin, 1899 |
| *CPG* | F. G. Schneidewin and E. L. von Leutsch, ed. *Corpus paroemiographorum Graecorum*. Vol. 1. Göttingen, 1839 |
| *EGM* | R. Fowler, ed. *Early Greek Mythography*. Vol. 1. Oxford, 2000 |
| *FCRR* | H. Scullard. *Festivals and Ceremonies of the Roman Republic*. Ithaca, NY, 1981 |
| *FGrH* | F. Jacoby, ed. *Die Fragmente der griechischen Historiker*. 4 parts. Leiden, 1957– |
| *FHG* | C. and T. Müller, ed. *Fragmenta Historicorum Graecorum*. 5 vols. Paris, 1878–1885 |
| *FLP*² | E. Courtney, ed. *The Fragmentary Latin Poets*. 2nd ed. Oxford, 2003 |

| | |
|---|---|
| *FPL*[3] | J. Blänsdorf, ed. *Fragmenta Poetarum Latinorum*. 3rd ed. Stuttgart, 1995 |
| *GG* | *Grammatici Graeci*. Leipzig, 1867– |
| *GL* | H. Keil, ed. *Grammatici Latini*. 7 vols. (with a supplement edited by H. Hagen). Leipzig, 1855–1880 |
| *GRF* 1 | H. Funaioli, ed. *Grammaticae Romanae Fragmenta*. Leipzig, 1907 |
| *GRF* 2 | A. Mazarino, ed. *Grammaticae Romanae Fragmenta Aetatis Caesareae*. Turin, 1955 |
| *HRR* | H. Peter, ed. *Historicorum romanorum reliquiae*. 2nd ed. 2 vols. Leipzig, 1914 |
| *IAH* | F. P. Bremer, ed. *Iurisprudentiae Antehadrianae*. 2 vols. Leipzig, 1898–1901 |
| *IAR*[6] | P. E. Huschke, ed. *Iurisprudentiae Anteiustinianae Reliquiae*. 6th ed. E. Seckel and B. Kübler. 2 vols. Leipzig, 1908–1911 |
| *ICUR* | J. B. de Rossi, ed. *Inscriptiones Christianae Urbis Romae*. 2 vols. Rome, 1861–1888 |
| *IG* | *Inscriptiones Graecae*. 14 vols. Berlin, 1873– |
| *IGBulg* | G. Mikhailov, ed. *Inscriptiones Graecae in Bulgaria repertae*. Serdica, 1956– |
| *ILS* | H. Dessau, ed. *Inscriptiones Latinae Selectae*. 3 vols. Berlin, 1892–1916 |
| *Inscr. It.* | *Inscriptiones Italiae*. 13 vols. Rome, 1931– |
| *ISmyrna* | *Die Inschriften von Smyrna*. 2 vols. Bonn, 1982–1900 |
| *LALE* | R. Maltby. *Lexicon of Ancient Latin Etymologies*. Leeds, 1981 |

| | |
|---|---|
| Lausberg | H. Lausberg. *Handbook of Literary Rhetoric*. Trans. M. T. Bliss, A. Jansen, D. E. Orton. Ed. D. E. Orton and R. D. Anderson. Leiden, 1998 |
| *LIMC* | *Lexicon Iconographicum Mythologiae Classicae*. 8 vols. Zürich, 1981– |
| *LSJ*[9] | H. G. Liddell and R. Scott. *Greek-English Lexicon*, 9th ed. Rev. by H. S. Jones, with a revised supplement. Oxford, 1996 |
| *LTUR* | E. M. Steinby, ed. *Lexicon Topographicum Urbis Romae*. 6 vols. Rome, 1993–2000 |
| *LTUR Sub.* | A. La Regina, ed. *Lexicon Topographicum Urbis Romae: Suburbium*. 5 vols. Rome, 2001– |
| *MRR* | T. R. S. Broughton. *Magistrates of the Roman Republic*. Vols. 1–2: New York, 1951; Vol. 3 (supplement): Atlanta, 1986 |
| *OGIS* | W. Dittenberger, ed. *Orientis Graeci Inscriptiones Selectae*. 2 vols. Leipzig, 1903–1905 |
| *ORF*[2] | E. Malcovati, ed. *Oratorum Romanorum Fragmenta*. 2nd ed. Turin, 1955 |
| Otto | A. Otto. *Die Sprichwörter und sprichwörtlichen Redensarten der Römer.* Leipzig, 1890 |
| *PCG* | R. Kassel and C. Austin, ed. *Poetae Comici Graeci*. 8 vols. Berlin, 1983– |
| *PEGr* | A. Bernabé, ed. *Poetae Epici Graeci*. Stuttgart, 1996– |
| *PLRE* | A. H. M. Jones, J. R. Martindale, and J. Morris, ed. *Prosopography of the Later Roman Empire*. 3 vols. Cambridge, 1971–1992 |
| *PMGr* | D. Page, ed. *Poetae Melici Graeci*. Oxford, 1962 |

| | |
|---|---|
| *RS* | M. Crawford, ed. *Roman Statutes*. 2 vols. London, 1996 |
| *SRPF*[3] | O. Ribbeck, ed. *Scaenicae Romanorum poesis fragmenta*. 3rd ed. 2 vols. Leipzig, 1897–1898 |
| *SRRR* | F. Speranza, ed. *Scriptorum Romanorum de re rustica reliquiae*. Messina, 1974– |
| *SVF* | J. von Arnim, ed. *Stoicorum veterum fragmenta*. 4 vols. Leipzig, 1903–1924 |
| *TLL* | *Thesaurus Linguae Latinae*. Leipzig, 1900– |
| *TrGF* | B. Snell and R. Kannicht, ed. *Tragicorum Graecorum Fragmenta*. 5 vols. Göttingen, 1971–2004 |

# SATURNALIA

# <LIBER TERTIVS>[1]

1 < . . . > violatum, cum se nosset multa[2] caede pollutum:
tu genitor cape sacra manu patriosque Penates:
me bello e tanto digressum et caede recenti
adtrectare nefas, donec me flumine vivo
abluero.

2. post Caietae quoque nutricis sepulturam, quo potissimum navigans adpellitur quam ad eam partem per quam

. . . fluvio Tiberinus amoeno . . .
in mare prorumpit,

ut confestim in ipso Italiae limine fluviali unda ablutus possit quam purissime

. . . Iovem Phrygiamque ex ordine matrem

invocare? 3. quid quod Euandrum aditurus per Tiberim

[1] *add. edd., inscript. caret* ω
[2] violatum . . . multa *om.* α

---

[1] Morning of the second day, 18 December, in the house of Virius Nicomachus Flavianus. The apportionment of "roles" at Book 1.24.16–21 allows us to identify the speaker as Praetextatus, who had promised to claim "our Virgil" as "the supreme pontiff"; the first part of his exposition has been lost, as have those of

# <BOOK THREE>[1]

< . . . > violated, since he knew that he had been polluted by 1
much bloodshed (*A*. 2.717–20):

> You, my father, take up the holy objects and ancestral Penates:
> since I have come fresh from the bloodshed of this great battle,
> it is unlawful for me to handle them until I have cleansed myself
> in a flowing stream.

2. So too, after burying his nurse, Caieta, where could he more properly sail and put in to shore than the region where (*A*. 7.30, 32)

> . . . the Tiber's pleasant stream . . .
> bursts forth into the sea,

so that on the very threshold of Italy he might be cleansed by the river water and so invoke, with perfect ritual purity,

> . . . Jupiter and the Phrygian mother one after the other

(*A*. 7.139)?

3. Consider the fact that when Aeneas is going to visit

Eustathius, on philosophy and astronomy, and Flavianus, on augural law (in that order: 1.24.24).

navigat, quod eum esset reperturus Herculi sacra celebrantem, ut sic purificatus sacris posset hospitalibus interesse? 4. hinc[3] et Iuno ipsa conqueritur non magis quod Aenean contigisset contra suum velle in Italiam pervenire quam quod optato potiretur Thybridis alveo, quia sciret eum hoc amne purificatum posse sacra etiam sibi rite perficere; nam ne supplicari quidem sibi ab eo vellet. 5. nunc quoniam purificationem ad sacra superorum pertinentem deorum in Vergiliana observatione monstravimus, videamus utrum et circa inferorum deorum cultum proprietatem moris idem poeta servaverit.

6. 'Constat dis superis sacra facturum corporis ablutione purgari, cum vero inferis litandum est, satis actum videtur si aspersio sola contingat. de sacris igitur superorum ait Aeneas,

> . . . donec me flumine vivo
> abluero.

7. at Dido cum sacra dis inferis instituit ait,

> Annam, cara mihi nutrix, huc siste sororem:
> dic corpus properet fluviali spargere lympha,

et alibi,

> sparserat et latices simulatos fontis Averni;

8. nec non cum Misenum sepulturae mandari refert:

[3] hinc R[2]$\epsilon$: hic $\omega$

---

[2] Cf. A. 8.59–61, 84–85.

Evander—and in fact will find him celebrating the rites of Hercules—he sails along the Tiber, so that he might thus be purified before attending his host's rites. 4. Hence, too, Juno's bitter complaint, provoked as much by the fact that he reached "the Tiber's longed-for channel" (*A.* 7.303) as by the fact that he had succeeded in reaching Italy against her will: for she knew that once he was purified by the river he could also sacrifice to her acceptably[2]—and she did not even want to receive his supplication. 5. Since I've now shown the care Virgil takes in treating the ritual purity appropriate to the rites of the heavenly gods, let's see whether the poet also observed due custom in treating the rites of underworld's gods.

6. 'It's agreed that someone intending to sacrifice to the heavenly gods washes his body clean, whereas to sacrifice acceptably to the gods of the underworld it is considered enough merely to sprinkle oneself. Thus Aeneas says, with reference to the heavenly gods' rites (*A.* 2.719–20),

> . . . until I have cleansed myself
> in a flowing stream.

7. But when Dido intends to sacrifice to the gods of the underworld, she says (*A.* 4.634–35*),

> My dear nurse, bring my sister here to me:
> tell her to quickly sprinkle her body with river water,

and elsewhere (*A.* 4.512),

> and she had sprinkled the waters of a make-believe
> Avernus.

8. So also when he recounts the funeral of Misenus (*A.* 6.229–30*):

idem ter socios pura circumtulit unda,
spargens rore levi.

sed et cum facit Aenean apud inferos ramum Proserpinae consecraturum, ita infert:

occupat Aeneas aditum corpusque recenti
spargit aqua.

2 'Verborum autem proprietas tam poetae huic familiaris est ut talis observatio in Vergilio laus esse iam desinat. nullis tamen magis proprie usus est quam sacris vel sacrificialibus verbis. 2. et primum illud non omiserim, in quo plerique falluntur:

. . . extaque salsos
porriciam in fluctus . . .

non ut quidam "proiciam," aestimantes dixisse Vergilium proicienda exta, quia[4] adiecit "in fluctus." sed non ita est. 3. nam et ex disciplina haruspicum et ex praecepto pontificum verbum hoc sollemne sacrificantibus est, sicut Veranius ex primo libro Pictoris ita dissertationem huius verbi est executus: "exta porriciunto, dis danto,[5] in altaria

[4] quia S: qui *ω*
[5] dis danto S: dis dando *α*F, distanto *β* (distato B[1])

---

[3] The reading *porriciam* favored by M. is acknowledged by Serv. on this verse and found in one 8th-cent. Virgilian MS. All other early MSS of Virgil read *proiciam*; modern editors are split, but *porriciam* is favored by the use of the same verb in the proverbial expression "between the slaying and the offering [*porrecta*]," cf. 1.16.3 n.

[4] Refs. to "Pictor" here and §11 perhaps result from a confu-

Three times, too, he circled his companions with pure water,
sprinkling them with a light dew,

and when he shows Aeneas intending to dedicate the bough to Proserpina in the underworld, he introduces him with these words (*A.* 6.635–36*):

Aeneas reaches the entry-way and sprinkles his body with fresh water.

'Now, this poet of ours knows precise and proper usage so intimately that attentiveness in such matters ceases to be a cause for praise in his case. Yet he used no terminology more precisely than the language of sacred rites or sacrifices. 2. To start with, let me not fail to mention a passage where many go astray (*A.* 5. 237–38*): 2

. . . and the entrails I shall
offer up [*porriciam*] into the briny waves. . . .

Not "cast forth" [*proiciam*], the reading favored by some people who judge that Virgil said the entrails should be "cast forth" because he added "into the waves."[3] But that is not correct. 3. According to both soothsayers' doctrine and pontiffs' rule, "offer up" is the traditional word for those conducting a sacrifice: thus Veranius' explication of the word (fr. 9 *GRF* 1:432), drawing on Pictor's[4] first book (fr. 4 *IAH* 1:11 = fr. 2 *IAR*[6]), "May they offer up entrails, may they give them to the gods, onto the *altaria* ['high altar'] or

sion of Q. Fabius Pictor, Rome's first historian, and Q. Fabius Maximus Servilianus, historian and author of a work on religious law cited at 1.16.25.

aramve focumve eove quo exta dari debebunt." 4. "porricere" ergo, non "proicere" proprium sacrifici verbum est, et quia dixit Veranius, "in aram focumve eove quo exta dari debebunt," nunc pro ara et foco mare accipiendum est cum sacrificium dis maris dicatur. 5. ait enim,

Di quibus imperium est pelagi, quorum aequore[6] curro,
vobis laetus ego hoc candentem in litore taurum
constituam ante aras voti reus extaque salsos
porriciam in fluctus et vina liquentia fundam.

ex his docetur in mare rite potuisse porrici exta, non proici.

6. Constituam ante aras voti reus.

'Haec vox propria sacrorum est, ut reus vocetur qui suscepto voto se numinibus obligat, damnatus autem qui promissa vota iam solvit. sed de hoc non opus est a me plura pro-

[6] aequore ω, *codd. nonnull. Verg.*: aequora *codd. cett. Verg., Tib.*

---

[5] Varro (*Divine Antiquities* lib. 5 fr. 65) distinguishes among *altaria* (for the "heavenly gods," *di superi*), *arae* (for the "terrestrial gods," *di terrestres*) and *foci* (for the "gods of the underworld," *di inferi*), with sim. distinctions drawn at Livy 1.32.9, Paul. Fest. p. 27.1–3, DServ. on *A.* 5.54, Lact. Plac. on Stat. *Theb.* 4.459–60 (diff. Serv. on *A.* 2.515).

[6] Cf. *E.* 5. 80 (to the deified Daphnis), "You too will condemn (*damnabis*) men with their vows," on which Serv. says: "That is, when as a god you have begun to benefit humankind, you will oblige them to pay their vows, which keep people bound and, as it were, condemned (*damnatos*) until they are paid." For *reus* cf. Fest. p. 336.5–6; M. uses Virgil's phrase, *voti reus*, at 1.12.31.

*ara* ['altar'] or *focus* ['hearth'][5] or wherever the entrails ought to be given." 4. "To offer up" is the proper term for sacrifice, then, not "to cast forth," and in view of the fact that Veranius said "onto the altar or hearth or wherever the entrails ought to be given," the sea should be understood to serve as an altar and hearth in the present passage, where a sacrifice is dedicated to the gods of the sea. 5. For Virgil says (*A.* 5.235–38):

> Gods whose dominion is the deep, on whose level surface I speed,
> joyfully on this shore shall I make a gleaming white bull stand
> before your altars, answerable for my vow, and the entrails I shall
> offer up into the briny waves, and I shall pour out clear-flowing wine.

From these lines we learn that entrails could be "offered up" into the sea in a ritually proper way, not "cast forth."

> 6. Make . . . stand before your altars, answerable for my vow . . . (237*)

'This is the technical language of sacred rites: the person who incurs an obligation to divine powers by undertaking a vow is said to be "answerable" [*reus*] for it, the person who now discharges the vow he promised is said to have been "condemned" to do so.[6] But there is no need for me to say

ferri; cum vir doctissimus Eustathius paulo ante hanc partem plenius exsecutus sit.

7. 'Est profundam scientiam huius poetae in uno saepe reperire verbo, quod fortuito dictum vulgus putaret. multifariam enim legimus quod litare sola non possit oratio nisi ut is qui deos precatur etiam aram manibus adprehendat. 8. inde Varro Divinarum libro quinto dicit aras primum "asas" dictas, quod esset necessarium a sacrificantibus eas teneri—ansis autem teneri solere vasa quis dubitet?—commutatione ergo litterarum "aras" dici coeptas, ut "Valesios" et "Fusios" dictos prius, nunc "Valerios" et "Furios" dici. 9. haec omnia illo versu poeta exsecutus est:

talibus orantem dictis arasque tenentem
audiit omnipotens.

nonne eo additum auditum[7] credideris, non quia orabat tantum, sed quia et aras tenebat? nec non cum ait,

[7] auditum *transposui, post* tenebat *collocavit* ω

---

[7] In a part of Book 3 now lost, on Virgil's knowledge of astrology and "all of philosophy," cf. 1. 24. 18.

[8] For the contrast with "ordinary readers" (sim. §7 below), cf. the proper goal of reading described at 1.24.12–13.

[9] Cf. Terent. Scaur. *GL* 7.13.13–14.

[10] The original term for "altar" was indeed *asa*—the intervocalic *s* later becoming *r*, as Varro said, by a process called rhotacism—and it was not unreasonable to suspect a link between *asa* and *ansa*, since many words spelled with an internal or terminal *ns* in Varro's day had earlier been spelled with *s* (e.g., *consul* vs. *cosul*; the *n* between the vowel and *s* was not pronounced). But the point

more on this subject, since that exceptionally learned man Eustathius pursued this subject more fully a little earlier.[7]

7. 'We can often discover our poet's profound learning in a single word that ordinary readers suppose was used at random.[8] For example, we find it written in many places that speech alone cannot propitiate the gods unless the person praying also takes hold of the altar with his hands. 8. That is why Varro, in the fifth book of his *Divine Antiquities* (fr. 66), says that altars [*arae*] were first called *asae*,[9] because people offering sacrifice had to grasp them—and who would doubt that vessels are usually grasped by means of handles [*ansae*]?—and that by a change of letters they began to be called *arae*, just as people once called the "Valesii" and "Fusii" are now called the "Valerii" and "Furii."[10] 9. The poet covered all this ground in the following verse (*A*. 4.219–20†):[11]

> As with such words he prayed and grasped the altar,
> the All-Powerful One paid heed. . . .

Surely you accept that "paid heed" was added, not because he was merely praying, but because he was also grasping the altar? And so too when Virgil says (*A*. 6.124),

of the rhetorical question that introduces *ansae* is obscure, and the sequence of thought in the passage was perhaps condensed or garbled by M. when he derived it from his likely source, Aelius Donatus. In any case, *asa*, which is cognate with Engl. "ash," is unrelated to *ansa*.

11 Cf. also Serv. on *A*. 6.124.

talibus orabat dictis arasque tenebat,

item,

tango aras, medios ignes ac[8] numina testor,

eandem vim nominis ex adprehensione significat.

10. 'Idem poeta tam scientia profundus quam amoenus ingenio non nulla de veteribus verbis, quae ad proprietatem sacrorum noverat pertinere, ita interpretatus est ut mutato verbi sono integer intellectus maneret. 11. nam primo pontificii iuris libro apud Pictorem verbum hoc positum est, "vitulari": de cuius verbi significatu Titius ita retulit, "vitulari est voce laetari"; Varro etiam in libro quinto decimo Rerum divinarum ita refert quod pontifex in sacris quibusdam vitulari soleat, quod Graeci *παιανίζειν* vocant.[9] 12. has tot interpretationis ambages quam paucis verbis docta elegantia Maronis expressit:

. . . laetumque choro paeana canentes!

nam si vitulari est voce laetari, quod est *παιανίζειν*, nonne in cantu laeti *παιᾶνος* enarratio verbi perfecta servata est? 13. et ut huic vocabulo diutius immoremur, Hyllus libro quem de dis composuit ait Vitulam vocari deam quae laetitiae praeest. 14. Piso[10] ait Vitulam Victoriam nominari.

[8] ac] et *Verg.* [9] *παιανίζειν* vocant V (ΠΑΙΑΝΙΖΕ invocant O): itaianize invocant BL, ita ianicein v. M (-izein) F (-Φzein) δ, ita ΠΑΙΑΝΙΖΕΙΝ v. C, *om.* α (*spat. relict.*)

[10] Piso J²S: poso ω (post F, *om.* B¹)

---

[12] The author and work are not otherwise known; Mommsen's conjecture that the name should be restored as (Julius) Hyginus (cf. 3.4.13) was rejected by Funaioli (*GRF* p. 537).

> With such words he was praying and grasping the altar,

or again (*A.* 12.201),

> I set my hand on the altar and call to witness the divine powers
> in the midst of the flames,

he indicates that this same force of the word [*arae* < *a*(*n*)*sae*] derives from the act of grasping.

10. 'Our poet—with knowledge as profound as his talent is beguiling—also took some archaic words that he knew belonged to the proper usage of sacred ritual and so construed them that the meaning remained intact though a given word's sound was changed. 11. For example, in the first book of Pictor's *Pontifical Law* we find the word *vitulari* (fr. 5 *IAH* 1:11 = fr. 1 *IAR*[6]): Titius glossed its meaning thus, "*vitulari* means 'vocally rejoice'" (fr. 3 *GRF* 1:556); Varro, too, in the fifteenth book of his *Divine Antiquities* (fr. 223), reports that in certain rites a pontiff is accustomed to *vitulari*, which the Greeks term "singing a paean." 12. How economically, how learnedly, how neatly Maro conveyed all these interpretive obscurities! (*A.* 6.657)

> . . . and singing a joyous paean in a chorus!

If *vitulari* means "vocally rejoice," which in turn is the same as "sing a paean" [παιανίζειν], is not the verb perfectly interpreted by "singing a joyous paean"? 13. And to dwell on this word a bit longer: in his book *On the Gods* (cf. fr. 23 *GRF* 1:537) Hyllus says that the goddess of joy is called Vitula;[12] 14. Piso says (fr. 45) that Victory is named

cuius rei hoc argumentum profert, quod postridie nonas Iulias re bene gesta, cum pridie populus a Tuscis in fugam versus sit—unde Populifugia vocantur—post victoriam certis sacrificiis fiat vitulatio. 15. quidam nomen eius animadversum putant quod potens sit vitae tolerandae, ideo huic deae pro frugibus fieri sacra dicuntur, quia frugibus vita humana toleratur. unde hoc esse animadvertimus quod ait Vergilius,

> cum faciam vitula[11] pro frugibus, ipse venito,

ut "vitula" dixerit pro vitulatione, quod nomen esse sacrificii ob laetitiam facti superius expressimus. 16. meminerimus tamen sic legendum per ablativum,

> cum faciam vitula pro frugibus, . . .

id est cum faciam rem divinam non ove, non capra, sed vitula, tamquam dicat "cum vitulam pro frugibus sacrificavero" [quod est cum vitula rem divinam fecero].[12]

[11] vitula *ω*, *Serv.*, *GL 5.643.35*: vitulam G$\pi$O(*an* O$^2$?)A$^1$ (*corr.* B$^2$A$^2$), *codd. Verg.*, *Non.*, *Prisc.* [12] quod . . . fecero *seclusi*

---

[13] A connection is made between *vitulari* and *victoria* already at Ennius 339 *SRPF*$^3$ 1:73 = fr. 381 Jocelyn. [14] The *Poplifugia* was celebrated on July 5 (so the remains of inscribed calendars, cf. *Inscr. It.* 13,2:476–77: M. joins other literary sources in mistaking the date); our sources' conflicting explanations for the festival suggest that its true origin had been forgotten (*FCRR* 159). For the "success" enjoyed on 8 July, cf. 1.11.36–40, on the "Caprotine Nones." [15] The point turns on the repeated phrase *vitam tolerare*, "to sustain life": analyzed selectively, in the manner of ancient etymologies, the phrase could be taken to yield the goddess' name, VI*tam* TOL*er*A*re* > Vitula.

Vitula,[13] and in proof adduces the fact that—when the Roman people enjoyed a success on 8 July, after the Etruscans had put them to flight the day before (hence that day's name, 'Flight of the People')—there was exuberant rejoicing [*vitulatio*] after the victory, accompanied by specific rites.[14] 15. Some people reckon that the goddess' name suggested itself because she has life-sustaining power, and for this reason sacred rites are said to be performed for her in return for the harvest, since it is through the harvest that human life is sustained.[15] It is for this reason, we remark, that Virgil says (*Ecl.* 3.77*),

> When I make an offering with a calf [*vitula*] for the harvest, may you come,

using "a calf" [*vitula*] in place of "exuberant rejoicing" [*vitulatio*], which as I explained previously is the name of the sacrifice performed for some joyous reason. 16. Still, let us bear in mind that we should read this phrase with the ablative case,[16]

> When I make an offering with a calf (*vitula*) for the harvest, . . . "

that is, when I perform the religious rite not with a sheep, not with a goat, but with a calf, as though to say "when I shall sacrifice a calf for the harvest."

16 All the ancient and early medieval MSS of Virgil in fact read *vitulam*, the objective case expected after the verb meaning "do" or "make" (*faciam*), though the case makes no sense here: the instrumental ablative ("by means of . . . "), adopted by all editors, is found only in M., in Servius' commentary on the line, and a few other grammatical texts.

17. 'Pontificem Aenean vel ex nomine referendorum laborum eius ostendit. pontificibus enim permissa est potestas memoriam rerum gestarum in tabulas conferendi, et hos annales appellant et quidem[13] maximos quasi a pontificibus maximis factos. unde ex persona Aeneae ait,

. . . et vacat annales tantorum[14] audire laborum.

3 'Et quia inter decreta pontificum hoc maxime quaeritur, quid sacrum, quid profanum,[15] quid sanctum, quid religiosum, quaerendum utrum his secundum definitionem suam Vergilius usus sit et singulis vocabuli sui proprietatem suo more servaverit.

2. 'Sacrum est, ut Trebatius libro primo de religionibus refert, "quicquid est quod deorum habetur": huius definitionis poeta memor ubi sacrum nominavit, admonitionem deorum paene semper adiecit:

sacra Dionaeae matri divisque ferebam,

item,

13 et quidem *Willis*: equidem *ω*
14 vacat . . . tantorum] vacet . . . nostrorum *Verg.*
15 quid prophanum [*sic*]A^m^, *om. ω*

17 Compiled and publicly posted by the *pontifex maximus* down to the end of the 2nd cent. BCE, the *annales maximi* provided a yearly record of Rome's magistrates and of events affecting the city; they were published in 80 books during the Gracchan era by the *pontifex maximus* P. Mucius Scaevola.

18 With the following discussion, based on Trebatius, compare the distinctions drawn among *sacrum, sanctum*, and *religiosum* at Fest. p. 348.33–350.12.

17. 'He shows that Aeneas is a pontiff even from the term he uses for the narrative of his labors: for the pontiffs were empowered to record the events of history, and this record was called the "annals"—in fact, the "supreme annals," as if compiled by the supreme pontiffs.[17] For that reason the poet says, in the character of Aeneas (*A.* 1.373†),

> . . . and there is time free to hear the annals of great
> labors.

'In the pontiffs' edicts it is a matter of greatest concern to determine what is "sacred" (*sacrum*), what "profane" (*profanum*), what is "holy" (*sanctum*), what "filled with religious scruple" (*religiosum*): we should therefore inquire whether Virgil used each of these terms according to its proper definition and maintained the precise force of each word in his customary way.[18] 3

2. 'The "sacred," as Trebatius says in his first book *On Religious Scruples*, is "whatever is considered to belong to the gods" (fr. 1 *IAH* 1:404 = fr. 1 *IAR*[6]). Mindful of this definition, our poet almost always added mention of the gods when he used the term "sacred" (*A.* 3.19):

> I was making sacred offerings to my mother,
> daughter of Dione, and the gods,

or again (*A.* 4.638†),

sacra Iovi Stygio, quae rite incepta parabam,[16]

item,

. . . tibi enim, tibi, maxima Iuno
mactat sacra ferens . . .

3. 'Profanum omnes paene consentiunt id esse quod extra fanaticam causam sit, quasi porro a fano et a religione secretum. cuius significatus exemplum exsecutus est, cum de luco et aditu inferorum sacro utroque loqueretur:

". . . procul, o procul este profani,"
conclamat vates, "totoque absistite luco."

4. eo accedit quod Trebatius profanum id proprie dici ait quod ex religioso vel sacro in hominum usum proprietatemque conversum est, quod apertissime poeta servavit cum ait,

"Faune, precor, miserere," inquit, "tuque optima ferrum
Terra tene, colui vestros si semper honores,
quos contra Aeneadae bello fecere profanos."

dixerat enim,

[16] parabam] -avi *Verg.*

---

[19] Ancient scholars commonly, and correctly, offer an etymology along theses lines: see *LALE* 499.

> . . . things sacred to Stygian Jupiter, which I was
> making ready in due order,

or again (*A.* 8.84–85†),

> . . . indeed, he brings things sacred to you—to
> you, greatest Juno—
> and makes a solemn offering . . .

3. 'Virtually everyone agrees that the "profane" is that which lies beyond the concerns of a holy precinct, that is to say, "set farther (*porro*) apart from a holy precinct (*fanum*) and religious scruple."[19] Virgil succeeded in providing an example of this meaning in speaking about a grove and the entrance to the underworld, each of which was "sacred" (*A.* 6.258–59):

> ". . . Away, profane ones, be ye far away,"
> the seer cries out, "and stand apart wholly from this
> grove."

4. Note also that Trebatius says (*ibid.*) the term "profane" is used precisely of something that has ceased to be "sacred" and "filled with religious scruple" and has passed into the use and ownership of human beings—and our poet very plainly preserved this sense in saying (*A.* 12.777–79†),

> "Take pity, Faunus, I pray," he said, "and you, fairest
> Earth, hold tight
> That weapon, if I have always carefully tended your
> honors,
> Which Aeneas' men in contrast have profaned."

For the poet had just previously said (*A.* 12. 770–71),

sed stirpem Teucri nullo discrimine sacrum
sustulerant . . .

unde ostendit proprie profanatum, quod ex sacro promiscuum humanis actibus commodatum est.

5. "'Sanctum est,'" ut idem Trebatius libro decimo religionum refert, "interdum idem quod sacrum idemque quod religiosum, interdum aliud—hoc est nec sacrum nec religiosum—est." 6. quod ad secundam speciem pertinet:

sancta ad vos anima atque istius inscia[17] culpae
descendam. . . .

non enim sacro aut religioso eius anima tenebatur, quam sanctam, hoc est incorruptam, voluit ostendere, ut in illo quoque:

. . . tuque, o sanctissima coniunx,
felix morte tua. . . .

in quo castitatis honorem incorruptae uxoris amplexus est: unde et sanctae leges, quae non debeant poenae sanctione corrumpi. 7. quod autem ad priorem speciei definitionem de sancto attinet, id est ut non aliud sit quam sacrum aut religiosum:

[17] inscia ω, *codd. vett. Verg.*: nescia (*metri causa*) *codd. recc. Verg., alii alia*

---

[20] "Holy laws" (*leges sanctae*) were compacts sworn by members of the plebs early in the Republic stipulating that anyone who violated them would be "accursed" (*sacer*): for laws carrying a divine sanction of that sort, any merely human punishment would be inappropriate.

But the Trojans, drawing no distinctions, had destroyed
the sacred tree . . .

and he showed thereby that "profaned" is properly applied to something once "sacred" that has indiscriminately been made to serve human purposes.

5. "'The term 'holy,'" Trebatius also reports, in his tenth book *On Religious Scruples*, "is sometimes the same as 'sacred' and 'filled with religious scruple,' sometimes different—that is, neither 'sacred' nor 'filled with religious scruple'" (fr. 9 *IAH* 1:406 = fr. 7 *IAR*[6]). 6. The following pertains to the second category (*A*. 12.648–49†):

I shall go down to meet you with a spirit that is holy and ignorant
Of such wrong-doing. . . .

That is, Turnus' soul was not bound by anything "sacred" or "filled with religious scruple": he wanted to make plain that it was "holy," which is to say, "untainted." So also in the following (*A*. 11.158–59†):

. . . And you, oh most holy wife,
Lucky you were to have died . . . ,

where Evander focused on the honor of chastity that belonged to his uncorrupted wife. Hence, too, "holy laws," which should not be corrupted by any tie to penal sanction.[20] 7. As for the first category of Trebatius' definition of "holy," according to which it is the same as "sacred" or "filled with religious scruple," consider this (*A*. 2.682–83):

ecce levis summo de vertice visus Iuli
fundere lumen apex . . .

et paulo post,

nos pavidi trepidare metu crinemque flagrantem
excutere et sanctos restinguere fontibus ignes.

hic enim "sanctos" ac si "sacros" accipiemus, quia divinitus contigerunt. item,

. . . tuque, o sanctissima vates
praescia venturi . . . :

non aliud nisi "sacram" vocat, quam videbat et vatem et deo plenam et sacerdotem.

8. 'Superest ut quid sit religiosum cum Vergilio communicemus. Servius Sulpicius religionem esse dictam tradidit quae propter sanctitatem aliquam remota ac seposita a nobis sit, quasi a relinquendo dicta, ut a carendo caerimonia. 9. hoc Vergilius servans ait,

est ingens gelidum lucus prope Caeretis[18] amnem
religione patrum late sacer . . . ,

et adiecit quo proprietatem religionis exprimeret,

18 Caeretis] -itis *Verg.*

---

21 Gellius (4.9.8) attributes the same explanation to Masurius Sabinus (see "Index of Persons"), who could have derived it from Sulpicius. For other ancient etymologies of *religio* and *religiosus*, deriving the terms from *relegere* ("to review/recount") or *religare* ("to bind/constrain"), see *LALE* 523; for *caerimonia* < *carere*, cf. Aug. *Retractationes* 2.37.2 (cited at *LALE* 93).

Behold, from the crown of Iulus' head a delicate
tongue of flame
Seemed to spill its light . . . ,

and shortly after (*A.* 2.685–86†),

In a panic we trembled with dread, trying to drive
the flame
From his hair and douse the holy fires.

Here we will understand "holy" as though it were "sacred," since the fires were of divine origin. Or again (*A.* 6.65–66),

. . . And you, oh most holy seer,
Who already know what is to come . . . :

it is no different from calling "sacred" a woman whom he saw to be a seer, and possessed by the god, and a priestess.

8. 'It remains to take counsel with Virgil on the meaning of "filled with religious scruple." Servius Sulpicius has recorded (fr. 3 *IAH* 1:241 = fr. 14 *IAR*[6]) that "religious scruple" [*religio*] is the term attached to something that a certain holiness makes remote and apart from us, as though the term were derived from "to leave behind" [*relinquere*], as "reverence" [*caerimonia*] is derived from "to be in want of" [*carere*].[21] 9. Virgil observes this usage when he says (*A.* 8.597–98),

There is an enormous grove near Caere's icy stream,
Held sacred far and wide by the scruple of
generations . . . ,

and to convey fully the proper sense of "religious scruple" he added (*A.* 8.598–99),

. . . undique colles
inclusere cavi et nigra nemus abiete cingit,[19]

quae res utique faciebat lucum a populi communione secretum. et ut relictum locum ostenderet non sola adeundi difficultate, adiecit et sanctitatem:

Silvano fama est veteres sacrasse Pelasgos,
agrorum[20] pecorisque[21] deo . . .

10. secundum Pompeium Festum "religiosi sunt qui facienda et vitanda discernunt." hinc Maro ait,

. . . rivos deducere nulla
religio vetuit . . . ;

quod autem ait "deducere" nihil aliud est quam "detergere." nam festis diebus rivos veteres sordidatos detergere licet, novos fodere non licet. 11. in transcursu et hoc notandum est, quod et ipse velut praeteriens sub unius verbi significatione proiecit. cavetur enim in iure pontificio ut—quoniam oves duabus causis lavari solent, aut ut curetur scabies aut ut lana purgetur—festis diebus purgandae lanae gratia oves lavare non liceat, liceat autem si curatione scabies abluenda sit. 12. ideo hoc quoque inter concessa numeravit:

balantumque gregem fluvio mersare . . .

19 cingit] -gunt *Verg.* 20 agrorum] arvorum *Verg.*
21 pecorisque J², *Verg.*: pecorique ω, pecorumque A²C²

---

22 Cf. Fest. p. 348.22–24, 366.2–4. With the substance of §§10–12 cf. 1.7.8, 15.21, 16.12; on streams, cf. also Cato *On Agriculture* 2.4, on sheep, Col. 2.21.2.

. . . hollow hills on every side
enfold it, and darks woods encircle it with silver firs,

circumstances that expressly set the grove apart from the people's possession. Moreover, to make plain that the place was not abandoned [*relictum*] just because it was difficult of access, he also added the fact that it was "holy" (*A.* 8.600–601):

Tradition has it that the ancient Pelasgians hallowed
it to Silvanus,
God of fields and the herd . . .

10. According to Pompeius Festus, those who can distinguish the things they ought to do from the things they ought to avoid are "filled with religious scruple."[22] Accordingly, Maro says (*G.* 1.269–70*†),

. . . no religious scruple has forbidden
drawing down the streams. . . .

By "drawing down" he just means "clearing out": for on holidays [*dies festi*] it is permitted to clear out old streambeds that have become silted up, but not to dig new ones. 11. I should note in passing this point, too, which the poet himself also made by the way, relying on a single word's suggestiveness. Pontifical law stipulates that—whereas sheep are usually washed for two reasons, either to treat their mange or to clean their wool—on holidays it is not permitted to wash them to clean their wool, but washing is permitted if their mange can be cleared up by the treatment. 12. That is why our poet counted the following among the permitted activities (*G.* 1.272):

And dipping the bleating flock in the current . . .

quod si huc usque dixisset, licita et vetita confuderat, sed adiciendo "salubri" causam concessae ablutionis expressit.

4 'Nomina etiam sacrorum locorum sub congrua proprietate proferre pontificalis observatio est. ergo delubrum quid pontifices proprie vocent et qualiter hoc nomine Vergilius usus sit requiramus. 2. Varro libro octavo Rerum divinarum delubrum ait alios aestimare in quo praeter aedem sit area adsumpta deum causa, ut est in Circo Flaminio Iovis Statoris, alios in quo loco dei simulacrum dedicatum sit, et adiecit, sicut locum in quo figerent candelam "candelabrum" appellatum, ita in quo deum ponerent nominatum "delubrum." 3. his a Varrone praescriptis intellegere possumus id potissimum ab eo probatum, quod ex sua consuetudine in ultimo posuit, ut a dei dedicato simulacro delubrum coeperit nuncupari. 4. Vergilius tamen utramque rationem diligenter est exsecutus. ut enim a postrema incipiamus, observavit delubrum nominaturus aut propria[22] deorum nomina aut ea quae dis accommodarentur inserere:

> at gemini lapsu delubra ad summa dracones
> effugiunt . . . ,

[22] propria S: proprie ω

---

[23] The Circus Flaminius was a large plaza built by C. Flaminius (censor 220 BCE) near the Tiber at the southern edge of the Campus Martius; the temple of Jupiter Stator was built by Q. Metellus Macedonicus after his triumph in 146.

[24] Cardauns assigns the fragment, with its fanciful etymology, to *Divine Antiquities* Book 6 ("on sacred buildings"), not Book 8 ("on holy days"); the same lore is cited in DServ. at *A.* 2.225 (cf.

Now, if he had stopped there, he would have failed to distinguish what was permitted from what was forbidden, but by adding "health-giving" to "current" he made plain why the cleansing was permitted.

'The diligence worthy of a pontiff also entails using the names of sacred places with fitting precision. Let us try to find out, then, what pontiffs properly call a "shrine" [*delubrum*] and how Virgil used the same term. 2. According to Varro, in the eighth book of his *Divine Antiquities* (lib. 6 fr. 70) some people judge that a "shrine" includes, besides the temple building, the open space taken over for the gods' use, as in the case of Jupiter Stator's shrine in the Circus Flaminius,[23] while others take it to be the place where a god's image has been dedicated; to this Varro added that just as the place where a candle is inserted is called a "*candelabrum*," so the places where a god [*deus*] is located is called a "*delubrum*."[24] 3. In this formulation of Varro's, we can take it that he particularly endorsed the alternative that he put last, in his customary fashion, namely that the term "*delubrum*" is derived from the dedication of a god's image. 4. Still, Virgil carefully exploited both senses of the term. To start from the second: he made sure that when he was about to use the word "shrine" he inserted either the gods' proper names or terms used for gods, for example (*A*. 2.225–26†), 4

But the twin serpents make their escape, slithering up
to shrines on the city's heights, . . .

4.56), where the book number is certainly corrupt. For other ancient etymologies, see *LALE* 181.

et ut mox simulacrum nominaret subtexuit,

> . . . saevaeque petunt Tritonidis arcem,
> sub pedibusque deae clipeique sub orbe teguntur,

item,

> nos delubra deum miseri, quibus ultimus esset
> ille dies . . .

5. illam vero opinionem de area, quam Varro praedixerat, non omisit:

> principio delubra adeunt, pacemque per aras
> exquirunt . . .

et mox,

> . . . aut ante ora deum pingues spatiatur ad aras.

quid enim est "spatiatur" quam "spatio lati itineris obambulat"? quod adiciendo ante aras ostendit aream adsumptam deorum causa. ita suo more velut aliud agendo implet arcana.

6. 'De dis quoque Romanorum propriis, id est Penatibus, aspersa est huic operi non incuriosa subtilitas. Nigi-

---

[25] I.e., Athena, so called either because she was born from Zeus' head by the river Triton ([Apollod.] *Library* 1.3.6, DServ. A. 2.171) or because she was the daughter of Poseidon and Lake Tritonis in North Africa (Hdt. 4.180.5, Paus. 1.14.6, cf. Aesch. *Eum.* 293, Pomp. Mela 1.36, DServ. ibid.).

[26] §§6–12 are based on Cornelius Labeo (cf. Mastandrea 1977, 112–17), who in turn relied upon Nigidius Figulus (Nigid. fr. 69 overlaps with DServ. on *A.* 1.378, Arnob. 3.40.1) and Varro (who overlaps with DServ. ibid.).

and, not to delay naming the relevant image, he added (*A.* 2.226–27),

> . . . they head for cruel Tritonis'[25] citadel
> and take shelter beneath the goddess' feet and the circle of her shield.

Or again (*A.* 2.248–49):

> We [wreathe] the shrines of the gods—wretches, whose last day
> that day was . . .

5. Yet he did not overlook the view concerning open space that Varro cited first: for example (*A.* 4.56–57†),

> First they approach the shrines and seek the gods' peace
> among the altars. . . .

to which he soon adds (*A.* 4.62),

> . . . or before the eyes of the gods she paces about near their rich altars.

For does not "pace about" mean simply "walk about over the expanse of a broad thoroughfare"? And by adding "near their altars" he shows that the space was taken over for the gods' use. Thus Virgil in his usual manner develops a point about cult by the way, as it were.

6. 'Fine observations on the gods who are wholly the Romans' own—the Penates—are also carefully interspersed in our poet's work.[26] For example, in the nine-

dius enim De dis libro nono decimo requirit num di Penates sint Troianorum Apollo et Neptunus, qui muros eis fecisse dicuntur, et num eos in Italiam Aeneas advexerit. Cornelius quoque Labeo libro de dis Penatibus eadem existimat. hanc opinionem sequitur Maro cum dicit,

sic fatus meritos aris mactabat[23] honores,
taurum Neptuno, taurum tibi, pulcher Apollo.

7. Varro Humanarum secundo Dardanum refert deos Penates ex Samothrace in Phrygiam, et Aeneam ex Phrygia in Italiam detulisse. qui sint autem di Penates in libro quidem memorato Varro non exprimit. 8. sed qui diligentius eruunt veritatem Penates esse dixerunt per quos penitus spiramus, per quos habemus corpus, per quos rationem animi possidemus, esse autem medium aethera Iovem, Iunonem vero imum aera cum terra et Minervam summum aetheris cacumen; et argumento utuntur quod Tarquinius, Demarati Corinthii filius, Samothracicis religionibus mys-

[23] mactabat (*sic et Non*. 320.24)] -tavit *Verg*.

---

[27] Cf. DServ. on *A*. 1.378, 2.325, 3.12, 148, Serv. on *A*. 8.679. Dardanus founded the line of Trojan kings: the Samothracian origin given him here points to the tradition that made him a son of Zeus and Atlas' daughter Electra. Awareness of the alleged link between the Penates and the Samothracian Great Gods (below) is perhaps implied by Marcellus' dedication to the latter of spoils from the sack of Syracuse (211 BCE: Plut. *Marc*. 30.6).

[28] In fact, probably Varro himself, see fr. 205 (*Divine Antiquities* Book 15): Varro was evidently not named by Labeo, the common source of M., DServ. on *A*. 2. 296 ("some people"/ *nonnulli*), and Arnob. 3.40 ("nor were there lacking those who . . . "/

teenth book of his *On the gods*, Nigidius asks (fr. 69) whether "Penates" is the Trojans' name for Apollo and Neptune, who are said to have built Troy's walls, and whether Aeneas carried them to Italy. Cornelius Labeo, too, takes the same view in his book on the Penates (fr. 12b Mast.), which Maro follows when he says (*A.* 3.118–19†),

> So he spoke and set about paying the due honor of sacrifice on the altars,
> A bull to Neptune, a bull to you, fair Apollo.

7. In the second book of his *Human Antiquities* (fr. 8), Varro says that Dardanus brought the Penates from Samothrace to Phrygia, and that Aeneas brought them from Phrygia to Italy;[27] yet he does not there make plain who the Penates are. 8. But those who do a more diligent job of unearthing the truth[28] have said that the Penates are the gods who allow us to breathe deeply [*penitus*] and to have both our physical being and our mind's rational capacity.[29] Moreover, they say that Jupiter is fiery air in the middle, Juno the lower atmosphere (along with the earth), and Minerva the ether's very pinnacle,[30] and in support of this view they adduce the fact that Tarquinius, the son of Demaratus of Corinth and an initiate in the mystery-

*nec defuerunt qui* . . . ), all presenting substantially the same account.

29 The more common ancient etymology for the Penates links them to *penetralia* (cognate with *penitus*), denoting the inner recesses of a house or temple: *LALE* 462f.

30 Pinnacle: cf. 1.17.70n.

tice imbutus, uno templo ac sub eodem tecto numina memorata coniunxit. 9. Cassius vero Hemina dicit Samothracas deos eosdemque Romanorum Penates proprie dici *θεοὺς μεγάλους, θεοὺς χρηστούς, θεοὺς δυνατούς*. noster haec sciens ait,

cum sociis natoque, Penatibus et magnis dis,

quod exprimit *θεοὺς μεγάλους*. 10. sed et omnia haec nomina cum in uno de supra dictis numinibus servat, doctrinam procul dubio suam de omni hac opinione confirmat. cum enim ait,

Iunonis magnae primum prece numen adora,

*τὴν μεγάλην* nominavit;

adsit laetitiae Bacchus dator et bona Iuno,

*τὴν χρηστήν*;

. . . dominamque potentem,

*τὴν δυνατήν*. 11. eodem nomine appellavit et Vestam,

---

[31] The mystery-cult of the Great Gods of Samothrace is first attested at Hdt. 2.51–52; the earliest physical evidence of ritual activity in the sanctuary dates to the mid-7th cent. BCE. The gods, called the *Kabeiroi* in the literary sources, were variously identified with the Dioscuroi (the "common opinion" acc. to Varro *Latin Language* 5.58) or the Penates (as here) or heaven and earth (Varro ibid.).

[32] Acc. to the dominant tradition, Rome's fifth king, Tarquinius Priscus the son of Demaratus, vowed the temple of Jupiter Optimus while at war with the Sabines; the temple, which contained a central shrine to Jupiter flanked by smaller shrines of

religions of Samothrace,[31] brought together the three divinities just mentioned in one and the same temple.[32] 9. Now, Cassius Hemina says (fr. 7) that the Samothracian gods and the corresponding gods of the Romans—the Penates—are properly called (in Greek) "great (*megaloi*) gods," "good (*khrêstoi*) gods," and "mighty (*dynatoi*) gods."[33] Fully aware of this, our poet says (*A.* 3.12†),

> With my companions and son, with the Penates and the great gods,

which translates *megaloi*. 10. Indeed, given that he uses all the relevant epithets in speaking of one of the aforementioned gods, we can be sure that he thereby attests his knowledge of the doctrine overall. For when he says (*A.* 3.437†),

> First beseech in prayer the divinity of great Juno,

he calls her *megalê*; when he says (*A.* 1.734†),

> May Bacchus attend, the giver of joy, and good Juno,

he calls her *khrêstê*; and when he says (*A.* 3.438),

> . . . and the mighty mistress,

he calls her *dynatê*. 11. He also applied the same epithet

Juno and Minerva, was completed by Rome's last king, Tarquinius Superbus, and dedicated (acc. to tradition) in the first year of the Republic, 509 BCE.

33 Cf. DServ. on *A.* 1. 378, where the same three examples based on Virgil are given; see also the Servian citations in §7n. above and Tert. *On Spectacles* 8.4 (prob. drawing on Varro, cf. *Latin Language* 5.58, *Logist*. fr. 39).

quam de numero Penatium aut certe comitem eorum esse manifestum est, adeo ut et consules et praetores seu dictatores, cum adeunt magistratum, Lavinii rem divinam faciant Penatibus pariter et Vestae. 12. sed et Vergilius ubi ex persona Hectoris dixit,

> sacra suosque tibi commendat Troia Penates,

mox adiecit:

> sic ait et manibus vittas Vestamque potentem
> aeternumque adytis effert penetralibus ignem.

13. addidit Hyginus in libro quem de dis Penatibus scripsit vocari eos θεοὺς πατρῴους. sed nec hoc Vergilius ignoratum reliquit:

> di patrii, servate domum, servate nepotem,

et alibi,

> patriique Penates.

5 'Nec minus de sacrificiorum usu quam de deorum scientia diligentiam suam pandit. cum enim Trebatius libro primo de religionibus doceat hostiarum genera esse duo, unum in quo voluntas dei per exta disquiritur, alte-

---

[34] DServ. offers virtually the same account at *A.* 2.296, save in stating that the magistrates perform the rites on leaving office (*abeunt* vs. *adeunt*). The Penates were associated very closely with Lavinium, Aeneas' settlement in Latium (cf. Varro *Latin Language*. 5.144, Serv. on *A.* 3.12), and the "rites of the Penates performed for the Roman people at Lavinium" are attested by Asconius (p. 21.8, cf. Val. Max. 1.6.7).

[35] Hyginus' work on the Penates is otherwise unattested.

[36] Cf. DServ. on *A.* 4.56.

to Vesta, who is plainly one of the Penates, or at any rate their companion: that is why on entering their magistracy both consuls and praetors or dictators offer sacrifice at Lavinium to the Penates together with Vesta.[34] 12. But Virgil, too, speaking in the character of Hector, said (*A.* 2.293),

> Troy entrusts to you her sacred objects and her Penates,

and soon added (*A.* 2.296–97†):

> So he spoke and with his own hands brought forth from the shrine's
> Inmost part the priestly fillets, mighty Vesta, the eternal flame.

13. 'In the book that he wrote on the Penates Hyginus added that they are called (in Greek) the "ancestral (*patrôioi*) gods"[35]—nor did Virgil leave this fact unacknowledged (*A.* 2.702):

> Ancestral (*patrii*) gods, protect my house, protect my grandson,

and elsewhere (*A.* 2.717, 4.598, 5.63),

> ancestral penates.

'He also reveals his attention to detail in matters of 5
sacrificial practice, no less than in theology. For example, in Book 1 of *On Religious Scruples* Trebatius tells us (fr. 3 *IAH* 1:405 = fr.3 *IAR*[6] = fr. 1 *GRF* 2:394–95) that there are two sorts of sacrificial victim,[36] one whose entrails are inspected to discern the god's will, one whose life-spirit

rum in quo sola anima deo sacratur, unde etiam haruspices animales has hostias vocant, utrumque hostiarum genus in carmine suo Vergilius ostendit. 2. et primo quidem illud quo voluntas numinum per exta monstratur:

mactat[24] lectas de more bidentes,

et mox:

. . . pecudumque reclusis
pectoribus inhians spirantia consulit exta.

3. alterum illud in quo hostia animalis dicitur, quod eius tantum anima sacratur, ostendit, cum facit Entellum victorem Eryci mactare taurum. nam ut expleret animalis hostiae causas, ipso usus est nomine:

"hanc tibi, Eryx, meliorem animam pro morte
Daretis."

et ut nuncupata vota signaret, ait "persolvo," quod de voto proprie dicitur, utque ostenderet persolutum dis, signavit dicens,

sternitur exanimisque tremens procumbit humi bos.

4. videndum etiam ne et illam hostiam ostendat animalem:

24 mactat (*cf. 3.12.10, sic et Arus. GL 7:493.25*)] -tant *Verg.*

[*anima*], by itself, is consecrated to the god—whence soothsayers, too, call these "spirit victims" [*animales*]. Virgil shows both kinds of victim in the *Aeneid*. 2. First, the case in which the gods' will is shown by the entrails (*A.* 4.57):

> She slaughters the two-year-old sheep chosen
> according to custom.

and soon thereafter (*A.* 4.63–64),

> . . . with the animals' chests split open
> she pores, open-mouthed, over the still-pulsing
> entrails.

3. He shows the second sort of case—where the animal is called a "spirit victim" because only its life-spirit is offered up—when he has Entellus slaughter a bull to Eryx in victory. To make fully apparent why the victim is so called, he uses the precise term (*A.* 5.483*):

> This life-spirit [*anima*] to you, Eryx, a better one, in
> place of Dares' death . . .

and to show that this was a formal vow, he says, "I pay out" [*persolvo*], the verb properly used of a vow, and to show that the payment to the gods was accomplished, he made the point explicit, saying (*A.* 5.481),

> The bull falls to the ground, laid low and quivering,
> its life-spirit gone [*exanimis*].

4. 'We must consider, too, whether the following passage also shows us a spirit-victim (*A.* 2.116–19†):

sanguine placastis ventos et virgine caesa,
cum primum Iliacas, Danai, venistis ad oras:
sanguine quaerendi reditus animaque litandum
Argolica. . . .

nam et "animam," id est hostiae nomen, posuit et "litare," quod significat sacrificio facto placasse numen.

5. 'In his ipsis hostiis, vel animalibus vel consultatoriis, quaedam sunt quae iniuges vocantur, id est quae numquam domitae aut iugo subditae sunt. harumquoque noster poeta sic meminit:

nunc grege de intacto septem mactare iuvencos
praestiterit, totidem lectas de more bidentes;

et ut iniuges evidentius exprimeret, adiecit:

. . . et intacta totidem cervice iuvencos.

6. '"Eximii" quoque in sacrificiis vocabulum non poeticum *ἐπίθετον* sed sacerdotale nomen est. Veranius enim in pontificalibus quaestionibus docet "eximias" dictas hostias quae ad sacrificium destinatae eximantur e grege, vel quod eximia specie quasi offerendae numinibus eligantur. hinc ait,

---

[37] Cf. also (D)Serv. on *A*. 4.50.

[38] Cf. Paul. Fest. p. 101.7.

[39] Cf. Paul. Fest. p. 72.3–4.

You calmed the winds with a slaughtered maiden's blood,
when first you came, Greeks, to Ilium's shores:
with blood you must seek your return, an Argive's life-spirit
must be offered in propitiation . . . ,

for he used both "life-spirit," to denote the victim, and "offer in propitiation" [*litare*], which indicates that he placated a god by making the sacrifice.[37]

5. 'Among these victims, whether the "spirit" sort or those used to seek the gods' will, there are some, called "unyoked," that have not been tamed or put to the yoke.[38] Our poet makes mention of them in these terms (*A.* 6.38–39*),

Now it would be better to slay seven bullocks from an untouched
herd, and as many two-year-old sheep chosen according to custom;

and to make more apparent that he means "unyoked" animals, he added (*G.* 4.540* = 551),

. . . and as many bullocks with necks untouched.

6. 'The word "choice" [*eximii*], too, when used of offerings, is not a poetic epithet but a term of priestly art.[39] In his *Pontifical Investigations* Veranius tells us (fr. 4 *GRF* 1:431 = fr. 8 *IAH* 2.1:8 = fr. 4 *IAR*[6]) that victims are called "choice" when they're marked out for sacrifice and removed from the herd, or because they're selected for their "choice" appearance, as worthy of being offered to the gods. That's why Virgil said (*G.* 4.538 = 550),

quattuor eximios praestanti corpore tauros,

ubi quod eximuntur "eximios," quod eliguntur "praestanti corpore" dicendo monstravit.

7. "'Ambarvalis" hostia est, ut ait Pompeius Festus, quae rei divinae causa circum arva ducitur ab his qui pro frugibus faciunt. huius sacrificii mentionem in Bucolicis habet ubi de apotheosi Daphnidis loquitur:

haec tibi semper erunt, et cum sollemnia vota
reddemus nymphis et cum lustrabimus agros,

ubi "lustrare" significat "circumire": hinc enim videlicet et nomen hostiae adquisitum est, ab ambiendis arvis, sed et in Georgicorum libro primo:

terque novas circum felix eat hostia fruges.

8. observatum est a sacrificantibus ut si hostia quae ad aras duceretur fuisset vehementius reluctata ostendissetque se invitam altaribus admoveri, amoveretur quia invito deo offerri eam putabant. quae autem stetisset oblata, hanc volenti numini dari aestimabant. hinc noster:

---

[40] Cf. also Serv. on *E.* 3.77. The Ambarvalia, a movable feast usually held in May, was a ritual of purification in which the victim, as M. indicates, was led around the boundaries of the fields before being sacrificed; cf. *FCRR* 124–25.

[41] *lustrum* was the general term for the sort of purificatory procession just described; the most important *lustrum* was the censors' purification of the Roman *populus*, marshaled in the Campus Martius, at the end of the census, nominally every 5 years.

[42] Cf. Pliny *Natural History* 8.183.

four choice bulls of surpassing beauty,

where he showed that they're set apart from the herd by saying "choice" and that they're selected for sacrifice by saying "of surpassing beauty."

7. 'A "round-the-fields" [*ambarvalis*] victim, as Pompeius Festus says (Paul. Fest. p. 5.1–2), is one that people who make an offering for the crops lead around the fields preparatory to sacrifice.[40] Virgil mentions this sacrifice in his *Bucolics*, when he talks about Daphnis' apotheosis (5.74–75†):

These rites will always be yours, both when we pay our solemn
vows to the nymphs and when we purify our fields,

where "purify" [*lustrare*] denotes the act of "going around" [*circumire*] the fields:[41] that, of course, is the source of the term for the victim, from going around the fields, but note also in Book 1 of the *Georgics* (345*):

And three times let the auspicious victim circle the new crops.

8. 'It was a regular practice of people offering sacrifice that if the victim put up an exceptional fuss when being led to the altar and showed that it was being brought there unwillingly, it was taken away, because they thought that the god was unwilling to receive it as an offering. But when a victim stood still when it was brought forward, they reckoned that the god was willing to receive it.[42] So our poet says (*G.* 2.395*†):

et ductus cornu stabit sacer hircus ad aras,[25]

et alibi:

et statuam ante aras aurata fronte iuvencum.

9. 'Adeo autem omnem pietatem in sacrificiis quae dis exhibenda sunt ponit, ut propter contrariam causam Mezentium vocaverit contemptorem deorum. neque enim, ut Aspro videtur, ideo contemptor divum dictus est, quod sine respectu deorum in homines impius fuerit, alioquin multo magis hoc de Busiride dixisset, quem longe crudeliorem inlaudatum vocasse contentus est. 10. sed veram huius contumacissimi nominis causam in primo libro originum Catonis diligens lector inveniet: ait enim Mezentium Rutulis imperasse ut sibi offerrent quas dis primitias offerebant, et Latinos omnes similis imperii metu ita vovisse: "Iuppiter, si tibi magis cordi est nos ea tibi dare potius quam Mezentio, uti nos victores facias." 11. ergo quod divinos honores sibi exegerat, merito dictus a Vergilio contemptor deorum. hinc pia illa insultatio sacerdotis:

. . . haec sunt spolia et de rege superbo
primitiae,

25 aras] aram *Verg.*

---

43 Cf. Serv. on *A.* 7.647, 8.7.

44 Cf. *G.* 3.5; Busiris, an Egyptian king, sacrificed foreigners to Zeus until he was killed by Hercules. Virgil's use of "unpraised" to describe him is criticized and defended at 6.7.5ff.

45 Cf. Fest. p. 322.4–20, Dion. Hal. 1.65.1–5, Ov. *F.* 4.877–900, Pliny *Natural History* 14.88, Plut. *Mor.* 275E, Anon. *Origin of the Roman Nation* 15.1–3. When the prayer was answered, the

. . . and led by the horn, the goat meant for the god will stand by the altars,

and elsewhere (*A.* 9.627*):

. . . and I will bring a bullock with gilded horns to stand before the altars.

9. 'Moreover, so perfectly does he represent the requirements of cult that he called Mezentius "despiser of the gods" (*A.* 7.648) for doing the opposite. Nor did he use that phrase, as Asper thinks (p. 137), because Mezentius behaved immorally toward human beings out of lack of respect for the gods[43]—if that were the case, he would have much more reason to use the phrase of Busiris, whom he was content to describe as "unpraised," though he was far crueler.[44] 10. But the attentive reader will find the true origin of this phrase, which denotes the worst sort of defiance, in Book 1 of Cato's *Origins* (fr. 1.12): Mezentius had commanded the Rutulians to offer to him the first fruits that they usually offered to the gods, and the people of Latium, fearing a similar command, made the following vow: "Jupiter, if you prefer that we make that offering to you rather than Mezentius, we pray that you make us victorious."[45] 11. Because he demanded divine honors for himself, then, he earned Virgil's description as "despiser of the gods": hence the priest's[46] pious abuse (*A.* 11.15–16),

. . . these are the spoils and first fruits taken
from the arrogant king . . . ,

vow was paid by the establishment of the Vinalia in Jupiter's honor (cf. *FCRR* 107). [46] I.e., Aeneas, speaking of the trophy set up from Mezentius' arms and dedicated to Mars.

ut nomine contumaciae cui poenas luit raptas de eo notaret exuvias.

6 'Mirandum est huius poetae et circa nostra et circa externa sacra doctrinam. neque enim de nihilo est quod, cum Delon venit Aeneas, nulla ab eo caesa est hostia nisi cum proficisceretur Apollini et Neptuno res facta divina est. 2. constat enim, sicut Cloatius Verus ordinatorum libro secundo docet, esse Deli aram apud quam hostia non caeditur, sed tantum sollenni deum prece venerantur. verba Cloatii haec sunt: "Deli ara est Apollinis Γενέτορος in qua nullum animal sacrificatur, quam Pythagoram velut inviolatam adoravisse produnt." 3. hanc ergo esse quae adoratur ab Aenea Γενέτορος aram poeta demonstrat, si quidem templum ingressus pontifex nullo acto sacrificio statim inchoat precem, et ut Γενέτορα expressius nominaret,

da pater augurium.

4. at vero cum tauro mox immolat Apollini et Neptuno, apud aliam utique aram factum intellegimus, et bene supra tantum modo patrem, quod ibi proprium est, et infra, quod commune est, Apollinem nominat. 5. meminit huius arae et Cato[26] de liberis educandis in haec verba: "nutrix

[26] Cato] Varro Cato *Meurs, edd.* (= *logist. fr. 11 Bolisani*)

---

[47] With the lore gathered in §§1–4 cf. DServ. on *A.* 3.85.

[48] I follow Funaioli (*GRF* 1:470) in understanding the title *Ordinata* (lit. "things set in order") to refer to the use of alphabetization apparent in M.'s subsequent quotations (esp. 3.19.2, 6, 3.20.1).

[49] I.e., by blood sacrifice: Pythagoras practiced vegetarianism.

signifying that the spoils were taken from him because of the defiance for which he paid the penalty.

'We can only marvel at the poet's learning, where both 6
our rites are concerned and those of foreign peoples.[47] For there's a good reason why Aeneas slaughters no victim on reaching Delos but offers sacrifice to Apollo and Neptune on his departure: 2. it's generally agreed, as Cloatius Verus tells us in Book 2 of his *Things Arranged in Alphabetical Order*,[48] that there is an altar on Delos where no victim is slaughtered but they worship the god only with a customary prayer. Here's what Cloatius says (fr. 6 *GRF* 1:470): "On Delos there is the altar of Apollo the Begetter [*Genetôr*], where no animal is sacrificed; they say that Pythagoras regarded it as unpolluted[49] and worshipped at it." 3. The poet shows that the altar where Aeneas prays is the altar of Apollo the Begetter, since the pontiff enters the temple and, without offering sacrifice, immediately begins to pray, saying (*A.* 3.89)

Father, give a sign . . . ,

to identify Apollo the Father more explicitly. 4. But shortly thereafter, when Aeneas sacrifices a bull to Apollo and Neptune, we necessarily understand that he did it at a different altar, the poet taking care to call the god only "father" in the first case, a title specific to that cult, and then in the second case to call him Apollo, the name in general use. 5. Cato also mentions this altar in his *On Raising Children*, saying: "The nurse used to perform all these

haec omnia faciebat in verbenis ac tubis sine hostia ut Deli ad Apollinis Genetivi aram."

6. 'Eodem versu non omittendum puto cur saxo vetusto dixerit extructum templum. Velius Longus, "immutatio est," inquit, "epitheti: vult enim dicere vetustatem templi." hunc multi alii commentatores secuti sunt, sed frigidum est aedificii aetatem notare. 7. Epaphus autem, vir plurimae lectionis, libro septimo decimo ait Delphis quodam tempore evenisse ut templum religiosum antea et intactum spoliatum incensumque sit et adicit multas circa Corinthum urbes insulasque proximas terrae motu haustas, Delon neque antea neque postea hoc incommodo vexatam sed semper eodem manere saxo. 8. Thucydides etiam Historiarum libro tertio idem docet. non mirum ergo si praesidio religionis tutam insulam semper ostendens, ad reverentiam sibi locorum accessisse dicit continuam saxi eiusdem, id est insulae, firmitatem.

9. 'Vt servavit Apollinis Genitoris proprietatem patrem vocando, idem curavit Herculem vocando victorem:

"haec," inquit, "limina victor
Alcides subiit."

---

[50] Varro *Logist*. fr. 11. Meurs' supplement, accepted by M.'s modern editors, assumes that he meant to cite Varro's *Catus on Raising Children* (*Cato* = ablative); it is, however, at least as likely that M. thought Cato had written on that subject (*Cato* = nominative).

[51] §§6–8 are based on the same source as DServ. on A. 3.84, with which it shares much of the wording and the ref. to the prolific but otherwise unknown Epaphus (perhaps a corruption in the common source: Ephorus?).

[52] Thuc. 2.8.3 (differently Pliny *Natural History* 4.66): the reference to book 3 in the text reflects either an error on M.'s part

rites with aromatic branches, to the sound of trumpets and without a victim, just as at the altar of Apollo the Begetter on Delos."[50]

6. 'I think we shouldn't neglect to ask why, in the same verse, he said that the temple was built "of ancient stone."[51] Velius Longus says, "It's a transferred epithet, for he means to speak of the antiquity of the temple": many other commentators have followed him in this, though it's a feeble touch to draw attention to the age of a building. 7. But Epaphus, a man who had read a very great deal, says in his seventeenth book that once upon a time in Delphi a temple that religious sentiment had previously preserved untouched was sacked and burned, adding that many cities around Corinth and the islands nearest the mainland were devastated by an earthquake, and that never before and never since was Delos troubled, but its stones remained ever undisturbed. 8. In Book 3 of his *Histories* Thucydides too tells us the same story.[52] It's not surprising, then, that in showing how the island was always protected by the bulwark of piety the poet says that the undisturbed solidity of the rock—which is to say, of the island—added to the reverence with which he regarded the place.

9. 'Just as he observed the proprieties in the case of Apollo the Begetter, calling him "father," he took the same care in the case of Hercules, calling him "victor"(*A.* 8.362–63†):

> "Over this threshold," he says, "the victor
> Hercules passed. . . ."

(or his source's) or a different system of dividing Thucydides' text (Diod. Sic. 12.37.2 and 13.42.5 refer to a 9-book version, Marcellinus *Life of Thucydides* 58 to a 13-book version).

10. Varro Divinarum libro quarto victorem Herculem putat dictum quod omne genus animalium vicerit. Romae autem Victoris Herculis aedes duae sunt, una ad portam Trigeminam, altera in foro Boario. 11. huius cognomenti[27] causam Masurius[28] Sabinus[29] memorialium[30] libro secundo aliter exponit, "Marcus," inquit,

> Octavius Herrenus, prima adulescentia tibicen, postquam arti suae diffisus est, instituit mercaturam, et bene re gesta decimam Herculi profanavit. postea cum navigans hoc idem ageret, a praedonibus circumventus fortissime repugnavit et victor recessit. hunc in somnis Hercules docuit sua opera servatum. cui Octavius impetrato a magistratibus loco aedem sacravit et signum Victoremque incisis litteris appellavit.

dedit ergo epitheton deo quo et argumentum veterum victoriarum Herculis et commemoratio novae historiae, quae recenti Romano sacro causam dedit, contineretur.

12. 'Nec frustra in eodem loco dixit,

27 cognomenti *Salmasius*: commenti ω

28 Masurius E: massurius ω

29 Sabinus *ed. Lugd. 1538 in marg.*: albinus ω

30 memorialium (memoralium NP2 *in ras*, meralium G, *cf. Gell. 4.20.1, 5.6.13, 7.7.8*)] memorabilium β

---

53 The temple of Hercules Victor (also known as Hercules Invictus, "Invincible") in the Forum Boarium, between the Tiber and the Circus Maximus, was the site of the Supreme Altar (*ara maxima*: see below in text); the other temple stood just to the

10. In Book 4 of the *Divine Antiquities* Varro judges (fr. 61) that Hercules was called "victor" because he defeated every sort of animal. At Rome, however, there are two temples of Hercules Victor, one by the porta Trigemina, the other in the forum Boarium.[53] 11. Masurius Sabinus explains the origin of this surname differently in Book 2 of his *Memoranda*, saying (fr. 2 *IAH* 2.1:368f. = fr. 15 *IAR*[6] = fr. 3 *GRF* 2:360),[54]

> After Marcus Octavius Herrenus, who was a piper in his early youth, despaired of his craft, he became a merchant and, having enjoyed success, made an offering of one tenth his wealth to Hercules. On a later trading voyage he was beset by pirates but fought back very bravely and came away the victor. Hercules revealed in a dream that he had been saved by the god's efforts: Octavius then asked for and received a plot of land from the magistrates and dedicated a temple and statue to Hercules, calling him "Victor" in the carved inscription.

Thus he gave the god a title that both represented Hercules' former victories and commemorated a new story that served as the origin of a fresh Roman cult.

12. 'He also had a specific point in mind when he said in the same passage (A. 8.270†),[55]

south near the porta Trigemina in the Servian wall, between the Tiber and the northern foot of the Aventine (*LTUR* 3: 22–23, with ibid. 15–17 on the Supreme Altar).

54 Cf. also DServ. in A. 8.363.

55 Cf. also (D)Serv. on A. 8.269.

. . . et domus Herculei custos Pinaria sacri.

quidam enim aram maximam, cum vicino conflagraret incendio, liberatam a Pinariis ferunt et ideo sacri custodem domum Pinariam dixisse Vergilium. 13. Asper "κατὰ διαστολὴν," inquit, "Potitiorum, qui ab Appio Claudio praemio corrupti sacra servis publicis prodiderunt." 14. sed Veranius[31] pontificalium[32] eo libro quem fecit de supplicationibus ita ait: Pinariis, qui novissimi comeso prandio venissent cum iam manus pransores lavarent, praecepisse Herculem, ne quid postea ipsi aut progenies ipsorum ex decima gustarent sacranda sibi, sed ministrandi tantum modo causa, non ad epulas convenirent; quasi ministros ergo sacri custodes vocari. 15. ut ipse Vergilius alibi:

at Triviae custos iam dudum in montibus Opis,

id est ministra; nisi forte custodem dixit eam quae se prohibuerit et continuerit a sacris, ut ipse alibi:

et custos furum atque avium cum falce saligna
Hellespontiaci servet tutela Priapi.

hic utique custodem prohibitorem avium furumque significat.

31 Veranius E: veratius ω
32 pontificalium *Merkel*: -calis in ω

---

56 Thus Fest. p. 270.8–14, Livy 1.7.14, DServ. on A. 8.269: as a result Applius Claudius was struck blind and all the Potitii perished.

57 Cf. Fest. p. 270.14–16, Livy. 1.7.13.

> . . . and the house of Pinarius guards the rites of Hercules.

For some people say that the Pinarii rescued the Supreme Altar when it was burning from a fire in the neighborhood, and that is why Virgil said the house of Pinarius guarded the rites. 13. Asper says (p. 137) that Virgil's remark "aims to draw a distinction with the Potitii, who were bribed by Appius Claudius to hand over the rites to the public slaves."[56] 14. But in his book *Practices of the Pontiffs*, on offerings of supplication, Veranius says (fr. 4 *IAH* 2.1:7 = fr. 12 *IAR*[6]) that after the Pinarii were the last to arrive at the midday meal, when the diners were already washing their hands, Hercules forbade them or their descendants to taste from the tithe that was to be offered to him:[57] they should come only to serve as his ministers, not to share the meal, and thus it was as minsters that they were said to "guard the rites." 15. Virgil himself uses the term in this way elsewhere (*A.* 11.836*†):

> But long since did Opis, guard of Trivia, in the mountains . . . ,

that is, Diana's minister—unless perchance he used the term "guard" to mean that she restrained herself and kept apart from the rites, as he says elsewhere (*G.* 4.110–11†),

> And to guard against thieves and birds with his willow scythe,
> the protective power of Hellespontine Priapus, keeps watch.

Here plainly he means by "guard" one who keeps birds and thieves away.

16. Haec ubi dicta, dapes iubet et sublata reponi
pocula gramineoque viros locat ipse sedili.

'Non vacat quod dixit "sedili." nam propria observatio est in Herculis sacris epulari sedentes: et Cornelius Balbus Ἐξηγητικῶν libro octavo decimo ait[33] apud aram maximam observatum ne lectisternium fiat. 17. custoditur in eodem loco ut omnes aperto capite sacra faciant. hoc fit ne quis in aede dei habitum eius imitetur, nam ipse ibi operto capite est. Varro ait Graecum hunc esse morem, quia sive ipse sive qui ab eo relicti aram maximam statuerunt Graeco ritu sacrificaverunt. hoc amplius addit Gavius[34] Bassus: idcirco enim hoc fieri dicit, quia ara maxima ante adventum Aeneae in Italia constituta est, qui hunc ritum velandi capitis invenit.

7 'Ea quoque quae incuriose transmittuntur a legentium plebe non carent profunditate. nam cum loqueretur de filio Pollionis, id quod ad principem suum spectaret adiecit:

ipse sed in pratis aries iam suave rubenti
murice, iam croceo mutabit vellera luto.

33 ait *ed. Paris. 1585*, ita ait C: id $\alpha$, ita $\beta$
34 Gavius MB$^2\beta_2$ (gaius R$^1$): gravius $\alpha\beta_1$ (*n. l.* O)

---

58 On the ritual in question, the *lectisternium*, see 1.6.13n.
59 Cf. 1.17.28n.
60 Cf. (D)Serv. on *A*. 3.407, DServ. on *A*. 8.288, Livy 1.7.3–15.
61 *E*. 4 does not name the child whose birth will be the harbinger of a new golden age; with (e.g.) (D)Serv., M. follows the tradition that identifies the new golden age as the reign of Augustus and the child as Asinius Gallus, the son of Asinius Pollio, in whose consulship (40 BCE) it is said the child will be born (*E*. 4.11–12).

16. After these words, the food and drink that had been removed he bids
be set in place and himself invites the heroes to a seat on the grass. (*A*. 8.175–76*)

'It's not without significance that he said "seat," because in the rites of Hercules proper form calls for the meal to be taken seated, and in Book 18 of his *Interpretations* Cornelius Balbus says (fr. 1 *GRF* 1:541) that at the Supreme Altar it is not the practice to hold a feast for the gods at which they recline on couches.[58] 17. At the Supreme Altar, too, everyone observes the custom of offering sacrifice with uncovered head, so that no one will mimic the god's appearance in his shrine, where he himself has his head covered. Varro says (cf. *Ant. div*. lib. 5 p. 48) that this is the Greek manner,[59] because Hercules himself, or those he left behind who established the Supreme Altar, followed Greek practice in offering sacrifice. Gavius Bassus adds that this happens because the Supreme Altar was established in Italy before the arrival of Aeneas, who originated the ritual practice of covering the head.[60]

'There are also things that ordinary readers carelessly 7
pass by, though their meaning is profound. For when he says of Pollio's son[61] (a remark added with reference to Augustus) (*E*. 4.43–44†),

But the very ram in the field will change the color of his fleece,
now to the creamy blush of purple, now to the rich yellow of saffron,

2. traditur autem in libris[35] Etruscorum, si hoc animal insolito colore fuerit inductum, portendi imperatori rerum omnium felicitatem. est super hoc liber Tarquitii transcriptus ex ostentario Tusco. ibi reperitur: "purpureo aureove colore ovis ariesve si aspergetur, principi ordinis et generis summa cum felicitate largitatem auget, genus progeniem propagat in claritate laetioremque efficit." huius modi igitur statum imperatori in transitu vaticinatur.

3. 'Verbis etiam singulis de sacro ritu quam ex alto petita significet vel hinc licebit advertere:

iniecere manum Parcae telisque sacrarunt
Euandri.

nam quicquid destinatum est dis sacrum vocatur, pervenire autem ad deos non potest nisi libera ab onere corporis fuerit anima, quod nisi morte fieri non potest. ita ergo opportune sacratum Halesum facit quia erat oppetiturus. 4. et hic proprietatem et humani et divini iuris secutus est. nam ex manus iniectione paene mancipium designavit, et sacrationis vocabulo observantiam divini iuris implevit.

5. 'Hoc loco non alienum videtur de condicione eorum hominum referre quos leges sacros esse certis dis iubent, quia non ignoro quibusdam mirum videri quod cum cetera

[35] libris *Eyss. ex DServ. ad loc*: libro *ω*

2. the books of the Etruscans report the traditional belief that a ram's taking on an unusual color means that a commander will succeed in all his undertakings. There is a book by Tarquitius on this topic, translated from an Etruscan book of portents (fr. 5), in which we find the following: "If a ewe or ram is marked with purple or gold, it portends abundance crowned with supreme happiness for the leader of the order or the lineage, and the lineage leads forth its posterity in glory and makes it more prosperous." This is the state of affairs, then, that he prophesies in passing for his emperor.

3. 'We can see from this example, too, how he uses individual words to communicate recondite details of sacred ritual (*A.* 10.419–20†):

> The Fates laid their hands upon [Halaesus] and consecrated him
> to Evander's weapons. . . .

For anything marked out for the gods is said to be "consecrated," while a soul cannot join the gods unless it has been freed from the body's burden, and that can happen only by death: so, then, he represents Halaesus as "consecrated" at just the right moment, when he is about to die. 4. In this case he also observed the niceties of both human and divine law: by the phrase "laid their hands [*manus*] upon" he all but indicated that he was their chattel [*mancipium*], while by speaking of his "consecration" he satisfied the demands of divine law.

5. 'Here it seems appropriate to comment on the condition of those people whom the laws consecrate to specific gods, because I know some people think it strange that a consecrated person may be killed legally when it is against

sacra violari nefas sit, hominem sacrum ius fuerit occidi. 6. cuius rei causa haec est. veteres nullum animal sacrum in finibus suis esse patiebantur sed abigebant ad fines deorum quibus sacrum esset, animas vero sacratorum hominum, quos †zanas†[36] Graeci vocant, dis debitas aestimabant. 7. quem ad modum igitur quod sacrum ad deos ipsos mitti non poterat, a se tamen dimittere non dubitabant, sic animas, quas sacras in caelum mitti posse arbitrati sunt, viduatas corpore quam primum illo ire voluerunt. 8. disputat de hoc more etiam Trebatius religionum libro nono, cuius exemplum, ne sim prolixus, omisi. cui cordi est legere, satis habeat et auctorem et voluminis ordinem esse monstratum.

8 'Non nullorum quae scientissime prolata sunt male enuntiando corrumpimus dignitatem, ut quidam legunt:

> discedo[37] ac ducente dea flammam inter et hostes
> expedior,

cum ille doctissime dixerit "ducente deo," non "dea." 2. nam et apud Calvum Haterianus[38] adfirmat legendum,

> pollentemque deum Venerem,

[36] zanas ω (*ζώανας ed. Ven. 1472*, *ζόανας Rhodigin*, *ζωγάνας Liebrecht, voces nihili*)

[37] discedo] descendo *Verg.*

[38] Haterianus *Marinone*[2] (Aterianus *Jan*): aetherianus ω

---

[62] The archetype's reading is meaningless, and no satisfactory Greek term has been suggested as a correction.

[63] We would say that the textual error in question—*dea* in place of *deo*—is scribal, resulting from a fault in copying; but the word M. uses (*enuntiando*) shows that he thinks of reading as in the first instance an oral/aural process.

the law for all other consecrated things to be treated violently. 6. Here is the reason: because the ancients wanted to have no consecrated animal in their own territory, they used to drive them off to the territory of the gods to whom they were consecrated, whereas they thought that the souls of consecrated persons, whom the Greeks call . . ., [62] are owed to the gods. 7. Therefore, just as they did not hesitate to drive away any consecrated animal that could not be conveyed directly to the gods, so they wanted consecrated souls, which they judged could be conveyed directly to heaven, to be separated from the body and make the journey at the first possible moment. 8. Trebatius, too, discusses this custom in Book 9 of his *Religious Scruples* (fr. 8 *IAH* 1:406 = fr. 6 *IAR*[6]), though I've omitted his evidence, so I wouldn't go on too long. If anyone wants to read it, let him be content with my citation of the author and book number.

'We spoil some of the most exquisite effects of Virgil's 8
learning by faults of pronunciation,[63] as when some read the text as (*A.* 2.632*†-33),

> I depart and with the goddess as my guide find a
> clear way
> between the fire and the enemy,[64]

though his phrase, backed by great learning, was "with the god [*deo*] as my guide," not "the goddess" [*dea*]. 2. For Haterianus confirms that the poet Calvus wrote (fr. 7 *FPL*[3]),

> and the powerful god Venus

[64] Aeneas is describing how his mother Venus led him to safety during the sack of Troy.

non "deam." signum etiam eius est Cypri barbatum, corpore et[39] veste muliebri, cum sceptro ac natura[40] virili et putant eandem marem ac feminam esse. 3. Aristophanes eam Ἀφρόδιτον appellat. Laevius[41] etiam sic ait,

Venerem igitur almum adorans,
sive[42] femina sive mas est,
ita uti alma Noctiluca est.

Philochorus quoque in Atthide eandem adfirmat esse lunam et ei sacrificium facere viros cum veste muliebri, mulieres cum virili, quod eadem et mas aestimatur et femina.

4. 'Hoc quoque de prudentia religionis a Vergilio dictum est:

decidit exanimis vitamque reliquit in astris
aeriis.[43]

Hyginus enim de proprietatibus deorum, cum de astris ac de stellis loqueretur, ait oportere his volucres immolari. docte ergo Vergilius dixit apud ea numina animam volucris remansisse quibus ad litandum data est.

39 et *Timpanaro* (*ita et DServ. ad* A. 2.632): sed ω

40 natura U *DServ. ibid.* (*recte, cf. Courtney FLP*² *p. 139*): statura ω

41 Laevius *Scaliger*: Laevinus ω

42 sive (*contra metrum*)] si *Baehrens*, seu femina isve *Haupt*

43 aeriis *vel* aereis ω (*codd. plerique Verg., Tib.*): aetheriis *codd. aliquot Verg., edd.*

not "goddess." There's also a statue of Venus on Cyprus that's bearded, shaped and dressed like a woman, with a scepter and male genitals, and they conceive her as both male and female.[65] 3. Aristophanes called her *Aphroditos* (fr. 325 *PCG* 3,2:180), and Laevius says (fr. 26 *FPL*[3]):

> Worshipping, then, the nurturing god [*almus*] Venus,
> whether she is female or male,
> just as the Night-shiner [= moon] is a nurturing
> goddess.

In his *Atthis* Philochorus, too, states (no. 328 fr. 184 *FGrH*) that she is also the moon and that men sacrifice to her in women's dress, women in men's, because she is held to be both male and female.

4. 'Virgil's shrewdness in matters of religious practice is the source of this passage too (*A*. 5.517–18*):

> It fell dead and left its life among the sky-high
> stars. . . .

Speaking about the stars and planets in his *On the Gods' Attributes*, Hyginus says (fr. 1 p. 42 Bunte) that birds are properly sacrificed to them: hence Virgil's erudite statement that the bird's life-spirit remained with the divinities to which it was given as an acceptable offering.

[65] Hesych. A.8773 (= no. 757 fr. 1 *FGrH*) refers to an account, by Paion of Amathus in Cyprus, of the goddess represented in the form of a man (cf. Plut. *Thes*. 20.3–7, also relying on Paion); note also John Lydus *On the Months* 4.64, on a bearded Aphrodite worshipped in Pamphylia. These are not to be confused with the androgyne Hermaphroditus, offspring of Hermes and Aphrodite, who is never represented bearded (*LIMC* 5,2:190–98).

5. 'Nec nomen apud se, quod fortuitum esse poterat, vacare permittit:

. . . matrisque vocavit
nomine Casmillae mutata parte Camillam.

6. nam Statius Tullianus de vocabulis rerum libro primo ait dixisse Callimachum Tuscos Camillum appellare Mercurium, quo vocabulo significant praeministrum deorum. unde Vergilius ait Metabum "Camillam" appellasse filiam, Dianae scilicet praeministram. 7. nam et Pacuvius cum de Medea loqueretur:

caelitum camilla, expectata advenis: salve hospita.

Romani quoque pueros et puellas nobiles et investes camillos et camillas appellant flaminicarum et flaminum praeministros.

8. 'Hanc quoque observationem eius non convenit praeterire: "mos erat," inquit,

Hesperio in Latio, quem protinus urbes
Albanae coluere sacrum, nunc maxima rerum
Roma colit.

9. Varro De moribus morem dicit esse in iudicio animi, quem sequi debeat consuetudo. Iulius[44] Festus de verbo-

[44] Iulius (*lapsu nostri*)] *obelis notavit Jan*, sextus *Marinone*[2]

---

[66] Cf. also Varro *Latin Language* 7.34 (also quoting Pacuvius and referring to Callimachus), Paul. Fest. p. 82.16–18, Serv. on *A.* 11.558, *LALE* 99–100. [67] Cf. 1.10.15n. (*flamines*), 1.16.30 (sacrificial obligation of the *flamen Dialis'* wife).

[68] Cf. also Serv. on *A.* 1.7.

5. 'Nor does he allow a proper name, which could be used at random, to be empty of meaning (*A*. 11.542–43†):[66]

> . . . he called her Camilla,
> after her mother, Casmilla, changing a part of the name.

6. For Statius Tullianus, in Book 1 of *On the Names of Things*, cites Callimachus' statement that the Etruscans called Mercury Camillus (fr. 723 Pf.), indicating by that name an attendant of the gods. That's why Virgil says Metabus called his daughter "Camilla," as an attendant of Diana. 7. Pacuvius too, in speaking about Medea, says (fr. 231 *SRPF*[3] 1:121),

> attendant of the gods, your coming has been awaited: greetings, our guest.

The Romans also used the term "camillus" and "camilla" for the noble boys and girls under the age of puberty who serve as attendants of the flamens and their wives.[67]

8. 'It's not appropriate to pass over this careful remark, either: "it was the custom," he says (*A*. 7.601–3*),[68]

> in Hesperian Latium, one that the towns of Alba Longa
> thereafter kept sacred, one that Rome, greatest city in the world,
> now tends.

9. In his *On Customs* Varro says (*Logist*. fr. 74) that a custom depends on the mind's judging it to be something that common practice ought to follow. In Book 13 of his *On the*

rum significationibus libro tertio decimo, "mos est," inquit, "institutum patrium pertinens ad religiones caerimoniasqae maiorum." 10. ergo Vergilius utrumque auctorem secutus et primo quidem Varronem, quoniam ille dixerat morem praecedere, sequi consuetudinem, postquam dixit "mos erat," subiunxit "quem protinus urbes Albanae coluere," et "nunc maxima rerum Roma colit," quo perseverantiam consuetudinis monstrat. 11. et quoniam Festus pertinere ad caerimonias ait, hoc idem docuit Maro adiciendo "sacrum": "quem protinus urbes Albanae coluere sacrum." 12. mos ergo praecessit et cultus moris secutus est, quod est consuetudo: et hic definitionem Varronis implevit. adiciendo deinde "sacrum" ostendit morem caerimoniis dicatum, quod Festus asseruit. 13. idem observavit et in duodecimo libro cum ait:

morem ritusque sacrorum
adiciam,

in quo ostendit aperte morem esse ritus sacrorum. 14. sed historiae quoque fidem in his versibus secutus est,

mos erat Hesperio in Latio

et reliqua. servavit enim regnorum successionem, quippe primi regnaverunt Latini, inde Albani et inde Romani. ideo "mos erat," primum dixit, "Hesperio in Latio," et

---

69 This is of course Pompeius Festus (cf. 3.3.10, 3.5.7): M. himself was probably responsible for the slip that replaced "Pompeius" with the name of Pompey's great enemy.

70 The remarks printed by Thilo as DServ. on *A.* 12.836 also bear on the relation between "custom" and "common practice," though the text is corrupt.

*Meanings of Words*, Julius[69] Festus says (p. 146.3–5), "A custom is a practice established by our forefathers pertaining to the religious beliefs and rituals of our ancestors." 10. Virgil, then, followed both authorities: to start with, since Varro had said that the custom comes first and is followed by common practice, Virgil added, to "it was the custom," both "one that the towns of Alba Longa from there on kept" and "Rome, greatest city in the world, now tends," pointing to the enduring usage. 11. And since Festus says that it pertains to religious rituals, Maro taught the same lesson by adding the word "sacred": "one that the towns of Alba Longa from there on kept sacred." 12. Thus the custom came first, the maintenance of the custom—that is, common practice—second, thereby satisfying Varro's definition. Then by adding "sacred," he showed that the custom was devoted to a religious ritual, as Festus claimed. 13. He had the same definition in mind in Book 12, too, when he says (*A.* 12.836–37):[70]

. . . I shall add the customary observances
of sacred rites, . . .

where he makes plain that a custom is the observance of sacred rites. 14. He also sought historical accuracy in these lines (*A.* 7.601),

it was a custom in Hesperian Latium

and the rest. For he maintained the sequence of the kingdoms, the Latins ruling first, then the people of Alba Longa, then the Romans. That's why he first said "it was the custom in Hesperian Latium," followed by "one that the

postea, "quem protinus urbes Albanae coluere sacrum,"[45] deinde subiecit, "nunc maxima rerum Roma colit."

9 Excessere omnes adytis arisque relictis
di, quibus imperium hoc steterat.

'Et de vetustissimo Romanorum more et de occultissimis sacris vox ista prolata est. 2. constat enim omnes urbes in alicuius dei esse tutela moremque Romanorum arcanum et multis ignotum fuisse ut cum obsiderent urbem hostium eamque iam capi posse confiderent, certo carmine evocarent tutelares deos, quod aut aliter urbem capi posse non crederent aut etiam si posset, nefas aestimarent deos habere captivos. 3. nam propterea ipsi Romani et deum in cuius tutela urbs Roma est et ipsius urbis Latinum nomen ignotum esse voluerunt. 4. sed dei quidem nomen non nullis antiquorum, licet inter se dissidentium, libris insitum et ideo vetusta persequentibus quicquid de hoc putatur innotuit. alii enim Iovem crediderunt, alii Luam,[46] sunt qui Angeronam, quae digito ad os admoto silentium denuntiat, alii autem, quorum fides mihi videtur firmior, Opem

[45] urbes Albanae coluere sacrum S *ex §§8, 10–11*: una Albani coluere viri ω (*cf. A. 5.600* Albani docuere suos)
[46] Luam *Wilamowitz*: lunam ω

---

[71] With the lore in §§2–16 cf. DServ. on A. 2.244, Livy 5.21, Dion. Hal. 13.3, Pliny *Natural History* 28.18 (citing Verrius Flaccus), Plut. *Mor.* 278F-279A. [72] Contrast 5.22.7, where the same lines are said to be Greek in inspiration.

[73] On the secret name of Rome and the punishment of one Valerius Soranus for revealing it, see Pliny *Natural History* 3.65

towns of Alba Longa from there on kept sacred," finally adding "and Rome, greatest city in the world, now tends."

They all departed, abandoning their shrines and altars, 9
the gods who had made this realm stand fast. . . .
4(*A.* 2.351–52*†)[71]

'This statement concerns both the Romans' most ancient custom and their most secret rites.[72] 2. For it is commonly understood that all cities are protected by some god, and that it was secret custom of the Romans (one unknown to many) that when they were laying siege to an enemy city and were confident it could be taken, they used a specific spell to call out the gods that protected it, because they either believed the city could otherwise not be taken or—even if it could be taken—thought it against divine law to hold gods captive. 3. That's why the Romans themselves wanted both the god responsible for protecting Rome and the Latin name of the city itself to remain unknown.[73] 4. Yet the god's name was included in some of the ancients' books—though they disagree among themselves—and for that reason the range of opinion on the matter is familiar to those who delve into ancient beliefs and practices. For some believed the god was Jupiter, others Lua, some Angerona, who calls for silence by putting her finger to her lips, still others—whom I'm more inclined to trust—

(~ Solin. 1.5), 28.18, Plut. ibid., (D)Serv. on *A.* 1.277; acc. to John Lydus *On the Months* 4.73, the secret name was *Erôs*, i.e., *Amor*, the palindrome of *Roma*.

Consiviam esse dixerunt. 5. ipsius vero urbis nomen etiam doctissimis ignoratum est, caventibus Romanis ne quod saepe adversus urbes hostium fecisse se noverant, idem ipsi quoque hostili evocatione paterentur, si tutelae suae nomen divulgaretur.

6. 'Sed videndum ne quod non nulli male aestimaverunt nos quoque confundat, opinantes uno carmine et evocari ex urbe aliqua deos et ipsam devotam fieri civitatem. nam repperi in libro quinto rerum reconditarum Sammonici Sereni[47] utrumque carmen, quod ille se in cuiusdam Furii vetustissimo libro repperisse professus est. 7. est autem carmen huius modi quo di evocantur cum oppugnatione civitas cingitur:

> si deus, si dea est, cui populus civitasque Carthaginiensis est in tutela, teque maxime, ille qui urbis huius populique tutelam recepisti, precor venerorque veniamquea vobis peto ut vos populum civitatemque Carthaginiensem deseratis, loca templa sacra urbemque eorum relinquatis, absque his abeatis 8. eique populo civitatique[48] metum formidi-

[47] Sereni R[2]C: serini *ω*
[48] civitatique *DServ. ad* A. *2.244*: civitati *ω*

---

[74] The Italic goddess Lua Mater (Wilamowitz' conjecture is preferable to the archetype's trivializing *Luna*) twice receives offerings of enemies' burnt weapons in Livy (Livy 8.1.6, 45.33.2, in the latter instance in the company of Mars and Minerva; cf. also Serv. on *A.* 3.139, reading Preller's *Luae* for the MSS' *Lunae*). Angeron(i)a: cf. 1.10.7–9. Ops ("Bounty") was the consort of Saturn (cf. 1.10.18–21): Ops Consiv(i)a (= "Bounty who plants": Varro *Latin Language* 6.21) had her festival on 25 August (*FCRR*

said that she is Ops Consivia.[74] 5. But even the most learned men have not learned the name of the city itself, since the Romans were wary of suffering themselves what they knew they had often inflicted on enemy cities, should the name of their protector-god become known and allow their enemy to summon it forth.

6. 'We should see to it, however, that the mistake some have fallen into not confuse us too—I mean the belief that a single spell both summons the gods from a city and devotes the city to destruction. For I have found both spells in Book 5 of Serenus Sammonicus' *Secret History*, and he says that he found them in the very ancient book of a certain Furius (*IAH* 1:29f. = fr. 1 *IAR*[6]).[75] 7. The following is the spell used to call the gods forth when a city is surrounded and under siege:

> I call upon the one in whose protection are the people and community of Carthage, whether it be a god or a goddess,[76] and upon you above all, who have undertaken to protect this city and people, and ask you all for your favor: may you all desert the people and community of Carthage, leave their sacred places, temples, and city, and depart from them, 8. and upon this people and community heap fear,

181); the epithet (< *consero*) is cognate with the verb (*sero*) from which Saturn's name was commonly derived (1.10.20n., cf. 1.9.16n. on Ianus Consivius).

[75] Generally assumed to be L. Furius Philus (cos. 136 BCE), friend of Scipio Aemilianus, the conqueror of Carthage (146 BCE).

[76] The chief god of the Carthaginians was Baal Hammon (cf. 1.17.66–67n.); his consort was the lunar goddess Tanit.

nem oblivionem iniciatis, propitiique[49] Romam ad me meosque veniatis, nostraque vobis loca templa sacra urbs acceptior probatiorque sit, mihique populoque Romano militibusque meis propitii[50] sitis. si ‹haec› ita feceritis ut sciamus intellegamusque,[51] voveo vobis templa ludosque facturum.

9. 'In eadem verba hostias fieri oportet auctoritatemque videri extorum, ut ea promittant futura. urbes vero exercitusque sic devoventur iam numinibus evocatis, sed dictatores imperatoresque soli possunt devovere his verbis:

10. Dis pater Veiovis Manes, sive vos quo alio nomine fas est nominare, ut omnes illam urbem Carthaginem exercitumque quem ego me sentio dicere fuga formidine terrore compleatis quique adversum legiones exercitumque nostrum arma telaque ferent, uti vos eum exercitum eos hostes eosque homines urbes agrosque eorum et qui in his locis regionibusque agris urbibusque[52] habitant abducatis, lumine supero privetis exercitumque hostium urbes

49 propitiique *Huschke*: proditique *ω*

50 propitii *Huschke*: praepositi *ω*

51 si ‹haec› ita feceritis ut sciamus intellegamusque *Fraenkel* (*Horace 23, coll. §11*): ut sciamus intellegamusque si ita feceritis *ω*

52 -que R: -ve *ω*

---

77 The ritual here concerned is not to be confused with the stories of P. Decius Mus and his homonymous son, who as commanders against the Latins and Gauls, respectively (340 BCE, 295 BCE), "devoted" themselves and the opposing armies to the gods

dread, forgetfulness, and come to Rome, to me and my people, with kindly spirit, and may our sacred places, temples, city be more acceptable and approved in your sight, and may you be well disposed to me and the Roman people and my army. If you all should do these things so that we know and understand them, I vow that I will make temples and games for you.

9. 'The same words should be used in offering a sacrificial victim and inspecting the meaning of entrails, so that they give a guarantee of the future. On the other hand, once the divinities have been called forth, cities and armies are devoted to destruction with the following words, which only dictators and generals are able to use for the purpose:[77]

10. Father Dis, Veiovis, Manes,[78] or by whatever other name it is right to call you: may you all fill that city of Carthage, and that army of which it is my intention to speak, and those who will bear arms and missiles against our legions and army, with the urge to flee, with dread, with panic; and may you lead away that army, that enemy, those people who dwell in these places and regions, fields and cities, deprive them of heaven's light; and the enemy's army and

of the underworld, i.e., sacrificed themselves to secure their armies' safety and victory.

78 Ve(d)iovis was a chthonian reflex of Jupiter, with two temples in Rome (*LTUR* 5: 99–101) and festivals on 1 Jan., 7 March, and 21 May (*FCRR* 56–58). On Dis, see 1.7.30; on the Manes, see 1.10.15n.

agrosque eorum quos me sentio dicere, uti vos eas urbes agrosque capita aetatesque eorum devotas consecratasque habeatis ollis legibus quibus quandoque sunt maxime hostes devoti. 11. eosque ego vicarios pro me ‹meaque›[53] fide magistratuque meo pro populo Romano exercitibus legionibusque nostris do devoveo, ut me meamque fidem imperiumque legiones exercitumque nostrum qui in his rebus gerundis sunt bene salvos siritis esse. si haec ita faxitis ut ego sciam sentiam intellegamque, tunc quisquis votum hoc faxit ubiubi faxit recte factum esto ovibus atris tribus. te Tellus[54] mater teque Iuppiter obtestor.

12. cum Tellurem dicit, manibus terram tangit; cum Iovem dicit, manus ad caelum tollit; cum votum recipere dicit, manibus pectus tangit.

13. 'In antiquitatibus autem haec oppida inveni devota: †Stonios†,[55] Fregellas, Gabios,[56] Veios, Fidenas; haec intra Italiam, praeterea Carthaginem et Corinthum, sed et multos exercitus oppidaque hostium Gallorum Hispanorum Afrorum Maurorum aliarumque gentium quas prisci lo-

[53] meaque *add. Holford-Strevens*
[54] te Tellus *Huschke*: Tellus ω
[55] Thurios *Huschke in app. crit.*
[56] Gabios *ed. Ven. 1472*: cavios ω

---

[79] The color appropriate to victims offered to gods of the Underworld.

[80] Fregellae (94 km SE of Rome) was conquered in 125 BCE, Veii (16 km N of Rome) in 396 BCE, Fidenae (8 km SW of Rome) in 498; Rome's destruction of Gabii, 19 km to the east, is not otherwise recorded, though it was a byword for desolation in the early

the cities and fields of those people of whom it is my intention to speak, may you consider those cities and fields and the people's lives and lifetimes cursed and execrated according to those laws under which enemies have at any time been cursed. 11. In place of myself, my duty, and my office, I dedicate and curse them in place of the Roman people, our armies and legions, that you might vouchsafe the wellbeing of myself, my duty and command, our legions and our army on this campaign. If you do these things so that I know and understand them, then whoever has made this vow, wherever he has made it, may the appropriate action be performed with three black[79] sheep. I call on you, mother Earth, and you, Jupiter, as witnesses.

12. When he mentions Earth, he touches the ground with his hands; when he mentions Jupiter, he raises his hands to heaven; when he mentions taking on the vow, he touches his chest with his hands.

13. 'In the accounts of antiquity I have found these towns devoted to destruction: . . . Fregellae, Gabii, Veii, Fidenae;[80] besides the towns just named in Italy, Carthage and Corinth [146 BCE], and also many armies and towns of our enemies the Gauls, the Spaniards, the Africans, the Moors,[81] and other nations that the old-time annals men-

empire (e.g., Hor. *Epistles* 1.11.7, Prop. 4.1.34, Lucan 7.392–94). Huschke's *Thurios* (= Thurii, mod. Sibari), for the archetype's meaningless *Stonios*, is plausible: a colony was established on the site, 411 km SE of Rome, in 193 BCE, after the city had sided with Hannibal in the Second Punic War.

[81] These other instances are unattested.

quuntur annales. 14. hinc est ergo quod propter huius modi evocationem numinum discessionemque ait Vergilius,

> excessere omnes adytis arisque relictis
> di;

et ut tutelares designaret, adiecit:

> quibus imperium hoc steterat.

15. utque praeter evocationem etiam vim devotionis ostenderet, in qua praecipue Iuppiter ut diximus invocatur, ait:

> . . . ferus omnia Iuppiter Argos
> transtulit.

16. videturne vobis probatum sine divini et humani iuris scientia non posse profunditatem Maronis intellegi?'

10 Hic cum omnes concordi testimonio doctrinam et poetae et enarrantis aequarent, exclamat Evangelus diu se succubuisse patientiae, nec ultra dissimulandum quin in medium detegat inscientiae Vergilianae vulnera. 2. 'et nos,' inquit, 'manum ferulae aliquando subduximus, et nos cepimus pontificii iuris auditum: et ex his quae nobis nota sunt Maronem huius disciplinam iuris nescisse constabit. 3. quando enim diceret:

> caelicolum regi mactabam in litore taurum,

---

[82] The first clause alludes to the corporal punishment commonly used to encourage attentiveness in schools of grammar (cf. Juvenal 1.15, with Mayor's note ad loc., Otto 135); on the significance of the second clause, see Introd. §1 ad fin.

tion. 14. That, then, is why Virgil refers to the mustering out of the gods and their departure in these terms (*A.* 2.351–52),

> They all departed, abandoning their shrines and
> altars,
> the gods;

and to show that they are the tutelary gods, he added (*A.* 2.352),

> who had made this realm stand fast.

15. And beyond the summoning of the gods, he makes plain the power of the curse, in which (as I said) Jupiter is especially invoked, by saying (*A.* 2.326–27):

> . . . fierce Jupiter put all in the hands
> of the Argives.

16. Have I convinced you that the depths of Maro's poetry cannot be appreciated without a knowledge of divine and human law?'

At this point, as all were agreeing that the poet and the 10
speaker were equally learned, Evangelus cried out that he'd suffered patiently long enough and could no longer dissimulate: he intended to lay bare the wounds that Virgil's ignorance had left on his poetic corpus. 2. 'I too,' he said, 'once snatched my hand out from under the teacher's rod, I too have heard lectures on pontifical law:[82] what I learned then will show that Maro knew nothing of divine and human law. 3. For when would he ever say (*A.* 3.21*),

> on the shore I was slaughtering a bull to the king of
> the heaven-dwellers,

si sciret tauro immolari huic deo vetitum aut si didicisset quod Ateius Capito comprehendit? cuius verba ex libro primo de iure sacrificiorum haec sunt: "itaque Iovi tauro verre ariete immolari non licet." 4. Labeo vero sexagesimo et octavo libro intulit, nisi Neptuno Apollini et Marti, taurum non immolari. ecce pontifex tuus quid apud quas aras mactetur ignorat, cum vel aedituis haec nota sint et veterum non tacuerit industria.'

5. Ad haec Praetextatus renidens: 'quibus deorum tauro immoletur si vis cum Vergilio communicare, ipse te docebit:

> . . . taurum Neptuno, taurum tibi, pulcher Apollo.

6. vides in opere poetae verba Labeonis? igitur ut hoc docte, ita illud argute. nam ostendit deo[57] non litatum: ideo secutum,

> horrendum dictu et visu[58] mirabile monstrum.

7. ergo respiciens ad futura hostiam contrariam fecit. sed et noverat hunc errorem non esse inexpiabilem. Ateius enim Capito, quem in acie contra Maronem locasti, adiecit haec verba: "si quis forte tauro Iovi fecerit, piaculum dato." committitur ergo res non quidem impianda, insolita

[57] deo *ed. Bipont. 1788*: ideo *ω*
[58] dictu et visu] et dictu video *Verg.*

---

[83] Cf. DServ. on *A.* 2.202, Serv. on *A.* 12.120.

if he knew that it is forbidden to sacrifice a bull to this god, or if he'd learned what's in Ateius Capito? Here's what he says in Book 1 of his *On the Law of Sacrifices* (fr. 1 *IAH* 2.1:279 = fr. 14 *IAR*[6]): "thus it is forbidden for a bull, boar, or ram to be sacrificed to Jupiter." 4. Indeed, in Book 68 Labeo added (fr. 20 *IAH* 2.1:80 = fr. 6 *IAR*[6]) that a bull is sacrificed only to Neptune, Apollo, and Mars. So there you have it: your pontiff doesn't know what what's sacrificed on which altars, though even temple-wardens knows such things, nor did the ancients' efforts leave them unmentioned.'

5. With a smile, Praetextatus replied, 'If you want to consult Virgil on which of the gods receives a bull as an offering, he'll teach you (*A.* 3.119):

> . . . a bull to Neptune, a bull to you, fair Apollo.

6. Do you recognize Labeo's words in the poet's text? As this was the product of his learning, then, the other example is the product of his cleverness. For he shows that the offering was not acceptable to the god: that's why there follows (*A.* 3.26),

> a portent, dreadful to describe and extraordinary to see.

7. He had his eye on the sequel when he made the victim unfavorable.[83] But he also knew that expiation could be made for this mistake: for Ateius Capito, whom you've set up as Maro's adversary, went on to say (fr. 2 *IAH* 2.1:279), "If anyone should happen to offer a bull to Jupiter, let him make an offering in expiation." The mistake that's made, then, is certainly not irremediable, though it's unusual, and

tamen; et committitur non ignorantia, sed ut locum monstro faceret secuturo.'

11 Subiecit Evangelus: 'si eventu excusantur inlicita, dic quaeso, quod erat monstrum secuturum et cum Cereri libari vino iuberet,

. . . cui tu lacte favos et miti dilue Baccho,

quod omnibus sacris vetatur? 2. vinum autem Cereri non libari debuit illum vel Plautus docere, qui in Aulularia ait,

Cererin,' Strobile, hi[59] sunt facturi nuptias?
. . . quia[60] temeti nihil allatum video.[61]

3. at hic vester flamen et pontifex et omnia—tam quid immoletur quam quid libetur—ignorat et (ne non ubique in libando pari errore sit devius) in octavo ait,

in mensam laeti libant divosque precantur;

cum non in mensam sed in aram secundum morem libare debuerint.'

4. 'Vt prius tibi,' Praetextatus inquit, 'de posteriore quaestione respondeam, fateor te non immerito de usurpata in mensam libatione quaesisse; ampliusque speciem difficultatis auxeras si magis Didonem in mensam similiter libantem notasses:

dixit et in mensam laticum libavit honorem.

59 hi] has *Plaut.*
60 quia] qui? quia *ed. Ven. 1513 ex Plauto*
61 video] intellego *Plaut.*

---

84 A pleonasm, since the *flamines* were a subset of the college of *pontifices*, cf. 1.10.15n.

the poet introduces it not out of ignorance, but to provide an opportunity for the portent to follow.'

Evangelus interposed, 'If forbidden actions find an excuse in their outcome, tell me, please, what portent was going to follow when he also orders wine to be poured out for Ceres (*G.* 1.344*), 11

> . . . and for her bathe honeycomb in milk and mellow Bacchus,

something that's forbidden at all sacrifices? 2. But even Plautus ought to have taught him that wine is not a drink-offering for Ceres, when he says in his *Aulularia* (354–55):

> Do these people mean to celebrate the marriage of Ceres, Strobilus?
> . . . For I see no strong drink's been provided.

3. But this flamen and pontiff[84] of yours is not only globally ignorant—about sacrifices and libations alike—but he also says in Book 8—just to be absolutely consistent in his mistakes about libations—(279†)

> they joyfully pour their libations on the table and pray to the gods,

though customary usage demanded that they make their libations on an altar, not the table.'

4. 'To answer your second point first,' said Praetextatus, 'I grant that you were right to query the practice of pouring a libation on the table—in fact you would have made the matter seem more difficult still if you had rather remarked Dido's similar libation (*A.* 1.736*†):

> she spoke and poured the liquid on the table to honor the gods.

5. nam et Titius[62] cum de ritu sacrorum multa dissereret ait sibi hunc locum in quaestionem venire, nec tamen haesitationem suam requisita ratione dissolvit. ego autem quod mihi magistra lectione compertum est publicabo. in Papiriano enim iure evidenter relatum est arae vicem praestare posse mensam dicatam. 6. "ut in templo," inquit, "Iunonis Populoniae augusta mensa est." namque in fanis alia vasorum sunt et sacrae supellectilis, alia ornamentorum. quae vasorum sunt instrumenti instar habent, quibus semper sacrificia conficiuntur, quarum rerum principem locum obtinet mensa in qua epulae libationesque et stipes reponuntur. ornamenta vero sunt clipei, coronae et cuiusce modi donaria. neque enim dedicantur eo tempore quo delubra sacrantur, at vero mensa arulaeque eodem die quo aedes ipsa dedicari solent, unde mensa hoc ritu dedicata in templo arae usum et religionem obtinet pulvinaris. 7. ergo apud Euandrum quidem fit iusta libatio, quippe apud eam mensam quae cum ara Maxima more utique religionis fuerat dedicata et in luco sacrato et inter ipsa sacra in quibus epulabantur; in convivio vero Didonis, quod tantum regium constat, non etiam sacrum fuisse, apud huma-

[62] Titius *Hertz* (*cf. IAH* 1:131): Tertius ω (terentius $V^2$)

---

[85] Prob. derived ultimately from Granius Flaccus (thus fr. 1 *IAH* 1:261), who wrote on the *ius Papirianum* (next n.) and whom M. cites at 1.18.4 (via Cornelius Labeo).

[86] The "Papirian code" was a collection of existing statutes made by Sex. (or C.) Papirius, supreme pontiff at the start of the Republic, and so a precursor of the Twelve Tables (Dion. Hal. 3.36.4–5, *Dig.* 1.2.2.2). Juno Populonia was the protector of the

5. In his long discussion of sacrificial ritual Titius too says that it occurred to him to query this passage, and though he looked for the explanation he couldn't set aside his hesitation. But I will share with you what I've been taught by my reading.[85] The Papirian code plainly states that a consecrated table can serve as an altar: 6. "as in the temple of Juno Populonia," it says, "there is a sanctified table."[86] In sacred precincts some things count as the equipment and sacred furnishings, other things as ornaments: the things that count as equipment, which are always used in performing sacrifices, are the equivalent of implements, and pride of place among these goes to the table where meals and libations and money-offering are placed. The ornaments, by contrast, are shields, garlands, and offerings of that sort: they are not dedicated to the god at the same day that the shrines are sanctified, whereas the table and small altars are usually dedicated on the same day as the temple, so that a table dedicated in this rite is used in the temple as an altar and has the same religious scruple attaching to it as the god's couch.[87] 7. Certainly in the case of Evander, then, the libation was of the proper sort, seeing that it was made at the table that had been dedicated along with the Supreme Altar in absolute accord with religious custom, in a grove that had been sanctified and in the midst of the very rites that accompanied the feast. By contrast, at Dido's banquet, which we can agree was merely a royal occasion, not a sacred one, the poet had only Dido pour the liba-

Roman citizen body (*populus*), Mart. Cap. 2.149, cf. Arnob. 3.30.2, Aug. *City of God* 6.10.3.

[87] The god's image was placed on the couch (*pulvinar*) for the ritual of the *lectisternium*, cf. 1.6.13n.

nam mensam in triclinio, non in templo, quia non erat religiosa sed usurpata libatio, solam fecit libasse reginam, in cuius persona nulla observationis necessitas et multa ad usurpandum in potestate permissio. 8. at vero hic,

> . . . omnes
> in mensam laeti libant divosque precantur,

[quia][63] quod recte fieri noverat ab omnibus simul in templo epulantibus et uni sacratae adsidentibus mensae factum esse memoravit.

9. 'De illo autem versu,

> cui tu lacte favos et miti dilue Baccho,

paucis quod male accusatur absolvam. poeta enim aeque in rebus doctrinae et in verbis sectator elegantiae, sciens Cereri mulso libari, adiecit "miti Baccho favos dilue," scilicet mitescere vinum dicens, cum mulsum coeperit fieri. 10. nam ita hic "mite" vinum dixit ut alibi ait "domitum":

> . . . et durum Bacchi domitura saporem.

notum autem esse non diffitebere, quod a. d. duodecimum Kalendas Ianuarias Herculi et Cereri faciunt sue praegnante panibus mulso.'

[63] quia *delevi*

---

[88] The ritual is otherwise unattested; it fell (if M. is correct) on the same day as the festival of Angerona, cf. 1.10.7n.

tion—on a table made for human use in a dining room, not a temple, in a gesture that was borrowed from a ritual but was not part of one—because Dido's role is not constrained by religious observance, and royal power has much leeway in borrowings of that sort. 8. In this case, by contrast (*A.* 8.278–79),

> . . . they all
> joyfully pour their libations on the table and pray to
> the gods,

because he knew that the act was proper, he said that it was performed by all of them together, dining in a sacred precinct and seated at a consecrated table.

9. 'Now, concerning the verse you first queried (*G.* 1.344),

> and for her bathe honeycomb in milk and mellow
> Bacchus,

I can quickly acquit him of your ill-conceived charge. For the poet—devoted to scholarship where matters of fact are concerned, and to elegance in choosing his words—knew that Ceres receives offerings of honeyed wine and added "bathe honeycomb in mellow Bacchus," obviously indicating that wine grows mellow when that mixture is made. 10. That's why he called wine "mellow" here, as elsewhere he says it's "tamed" (*G.* 4.102):

> . . . and destined to tame the strong flavor of
> Bacchus.

You'll not deny, furthermore, that (as is well known) on the twelfth day before the Kalends of January [21 Dec.] a pregnant sow, bread, and honeyed wine are offered to Hercules and Ceres.'[88]

12 'Opportune mehercle, Praetextate, fecisti Herculis mentionem, in cuius sacra hic vester gemino errore commisit:

tum Salii ad cantus[64] incensa altaria circum
populeis adsunt evincti tempora ramis.

nam et Salios Herculi dedit, quos tantum Marti dicavit antiquitas, et populeas coronas nominat, cum ad aram maximam sola lauro capita et alia fronde non vinciant. 2. videmus et in capite praetoris urbani lauream coronam, cum rem divinam Herculi facit. testatur etiam Terentius Varro in ea satura quae inscribitur Περὶ κεραυνοῦ maiores solitos decimam Herculi vovere nec decem dies intermittere "quin pollucerent ac populum ἀσύμβολον cum corona laurea dimitterent cubitum."

3. 'Hicine est,' Vettius ait, 'error geminus? at ego in neutro dico errasse Vergilium. nam ut primum de frondis genere dicamus, constat quidem nunc lauro sacrificantes apud aram maximam coronari, sed multo post Romam conditam haec consuetudo sumpsit exordium, postquam in Aventino lauretum coepit virere, quam rem docet Varro humanarum libro secundo. 4. e monte ergo proximo decerpta laurus sumebatur operantibus, quam vicina offerebat occasio. unde recte Maro noster ad ea tempora respexit, quibus Euander ante urbem conditam apud aram

[64] cantus *ed. Ven. 1513*: cantum ω

---

[89] "Poet of yours" here indicates, not that the speaker is a Greek (cf. 2.1.14n.), but that he does not wish to align himself with Praetextatus' view of Virgil. [90] On the Salii, see 1.9.14n.

[91] In accord with the "Greek manner" of sacrifice practiced there, cf. 1.17.28n. [92] §§3–4: cf. DServ. on *A.* 8.276.

'By Hercules, Praetextatus, that was a timely mention of Hercules, against whose rites this poet of yours[89] offended with not one but two mistakes (*A.* 8.285–86†): 12

> Then come the Salii to the singing, around the
> blazing altars,
> their temples wreathed with poplar fronds,

where he both gives Salii[90] to Hercules—though the ancients dedicated them only to Mars—and he calls the wreaths "poplar"—though at the Supreme Altar people wear wreaths of laurel only,[91] and no other leaves. 2. We also see a laurel wreath on the urban praetor's head when he sacrifices to Hercules, and Terentius Varro too, in the satire titled *On Thunder*, bears witness (fr. 413 Cèbe) that our ancestors used to promise a tithe to Hercules and not let ten days pass "without making an offering and sending the populace off to bed crowned in laurel, gratis."

3. 'This is your "not one but two mistakes"?,' Vettius asked. 'Well, *I* say that Virgil was mistaken in neither case. To take up the variety of wreath first:[92] there's no question, of course, that people who *now* sacrifice at the Supreme Altar wear laurel wreaths, but this practice began long after Rome's founding, when a stand of laurels began to grow on the Aventine, as Varro tells us in Book 2 of his *Human Antiquities* (fr. 5).[93] 4. The people performing the sacrifice plucked the laurel from the nearest hill and began to use it, since it was right nearby and readily available. Our Maro, therefore, rightly looks back to a time before the city's founding, when Evander was celebrating the rites at the

[93] I.e., the Lauretum (also spelled "Loretum"): Varro *Latin Language* 5.152, Serv. on *A.* 8.276 (also citing Varro), *LTUR* 3: 190–91.

maximam sacra celebrabat et utebatur populo utique "Alcidae gratissima."

5. 'Salios autem Herculi ubertate doctrinae altioris adsignat, quia is deus et apud pontifices idem qui et Mars habetur. 6. et sane ita Menippea Varronis adfirmat quae inscribitur Ἄλλος οὗτος Ἡρακλῆς, in qua cum de Invicto[65] Hercule loqueretur, eundem esse ac Martem probavit. Chaldaei quoque stellam Herculis vocant, quam reliqui omnes Martis appellant. 7. est praeterea Octavii Hersennii liber qui inscribitur de sacris Saliaribus Tiburtium, in quo Salios Herculi institutos operari diebus certis et auspicato docet. 8. item Antonius Gnipho, vir doctus cuius scholam Cicero post laborem fori frequentabat, Salios Herculi datos probat in eo volumine quo disputat quid sit festra, quod est ostium minusculum in sacrario, quo verbo etiam Ennius usus est. 9. idoneis ut credo auctoribus certisque rationibus error qui putabatur uterque defensus est. si qua sunt alia quae nos commovent, in medium proferamus, ut ipsa collatio nostrum, non Maronis, absolvat errorem.'

10. Tunc Evangelus: 'numquamne tibi, Praetextate, venit in mentem toto, ut aiunt, caelo errasse Vergilium cum Dido sua rem divinam pro nuptiis faceret? "Mactat,"[66] enim inquit,

65 invicto *Mommsen*: multo ω
66 mactat (*cf.* 3.5.2)] -tant *Verg.*

---

94 Cf. Serv on *A.* 8.275 and 285 (cf. Varro *Divine Antiquities* p. 40), Σ Apoll. Rhod. 4.1377–79, sim. [Arist.] *On the Universe* 2 392a25–26, Theon *On the Utility of Mathematics* p. 130.23–24.
95 A detail based on Suet. *Gramm.* 7.2.

Supreme Altar and was using the poplar that was, of course, "most pleasing to Hercules" (*E*. 7.61).

5. 'However, it was the abundance and exceptional depth of his learning that caused him to assign Salii to Hercules, because that god is also identified with Mars by the pontiffs. 6. This is plainly also supported by Varro's Menippean satire titled *This One's Another Hercules*, where in speaking about Hercules the Invincible (fr. 20 Cèbe) he affirmed that he is the same as Mars. The Chaldeans, too, give the name "Hercules" to the planet that everyone else calls Mars.[94] 7. Furthermore, there's Octavius Hersennius' book titled *On the Rites of the Salii at Tibur* (*IAH* 1:110), where he tells us that Salii have been appointed for Hercules and perform their rites on specific days after auspices have been taken. 8. Similarly, Antonius Gnipho, a savant whose school Cicero used to frequent after toiling in the forum,[95] affirms (fr. 2 *GRF* 1:99–100) that Salii were given to Hercules, in the book in which he discusses the meaning of "festra" (a very small opening in a shrine), a word that Ennius also used. 9. These suitable authorities, as I take them to be, and their reliable explanation are enough to defend both supposed errors. If any others like them bother us, let's out with them, so that airing them might free us—not Maro—of error.'

10. 'Has it never occurred to you, Praetextatus,' Evangelus said, 'that Virgil was miles off, as they say, when his Dido offers a sacrifice on behalf of her marriage? For he says (*A*. 4.57–58*†),

lectas de more bidentes
legiferae Cereri Phoeboque patrique Lyaeo;

et quasi expergefactus adiecit,

Iunoni ante omnes, cui vincla iugalia curae . . . [67]

13 'Accipite et M. Varronis verba de agri cultura libro tertio, qui cum de pavonibus in villa nutriendis loqueretur, sic ait: "primus hos Q. Hortensius augurali[68] cena posuisse dicitur, quod potius factum tum luxuriose[69] quam severe boni viri laudabant. quem cito secuti multi extulerunt eorum pretia, ut[70] ova eorum denariis veneant quinis, ipsi facile quinquagenis." 2. ecce res non admiranda solum sed etiam pudenda, ut ova pavonum quinis denariis veneant, quae hodie non dicam vilius sed omnino nec veneunt! 3. is Hortensius platanos suas vino inrigare consuevit, adeo ut in quadam actione quam habuit cum Cicerone susceptam precario a Tullio postulasset ut locum dicendi permutaret secum; abire enim in villam necessario se velle ut vinum

67 accipite *statim post* iugalia *scripsit* ω, curae *recte add.* V$\beta_2$
68 augurali] augurali aditiali *Varro*
69 luxuriose] -si *Varro*
70 ut] ita ut *Varro*

---

96 The long note of (D)Serv. on this passage suggests how the discussion lost in the lacuna must have run, by turns elaborating (in Evangelus' character) reasons why it was inappropriate for Dido to sacrifice to Ceres, Apollo, and Bacchus (= Lyaeus < Gk. *lyein*, "release") and (in Praetextatus' character) reasons why it was appropriate (Ceres, too, is associated with marriage; since Ceres, Apollo, and Bacchus are in various ways associated with civic well-being, Dido sacrifices to them first, "because she was

she slaughters the two-year-old sheep chosen
according to custom
to Ceres the Law-giver and Phoebus and father
Lyaeus,

and then added, as though he'd just woke up (*A.* 4.59),

to Juno above all, in whose care are the bonds of
marriage < . . . >[96]

'Listen to the words of Marcus Varro, too, from his third book on agriculture (3.6.6), where he's talking about raising peacocks on a villa:[97] "Quintus Hortensius is said to have been the first to serve them at a banquet of the college of augurs, which right-thinking people at the time cited as an extravagant act rather than praising it as an austere one. And many soon followed his example, raising the price of peacocks so that their eggs were selling for five denarii each, the birds themselves for 500." 2. There you have it, a situation as astounding as it is shameful, where peacocks eggs go for five denarii each, whereas today—I won't say they're cheaper, there's no market for them at all! 3. The same Hortensius used to irrigate his plane-trees with wine and was so keen on it that in a certain court case he had undertaken with Cicero he begged the latter to do him the favor of changing places with him in the speakers' order: he was dying to leave for his villa so that he himself 13

marrying for the sake of common good," and then to Juno as the goddess of marriage specifically).

97 When the text resumes, it is the afternoon of the second day, 18 December: Caecina Albinus is finishing a discourse on the luxury of the ancient Romans, in response to Horus' (lost) critique of contemporary morals (cf. 3.13.16, 3.14.4).

platano, quam in Tusculano posuerat, ipse suffunderet. 4. sed forte ad notam saeculi sui non sufficit Hortensius, vir alioquin ex professo mollis et in praecinctu ponens omnem decorem. fuit enim vestitu ad munditiem curioso et ut bene amictus iret, faciem in speculo quaerebat, ubi se intuens togam corpori sic adplicabat, ut rugas non forte sed industria locatas artifex nodus astringeret et sinus ex composito defluens modum lateris[71] ambiret. 5. is quondam cum incederet elaboratus ad speciem, collegae de iniuriis diem dixit, quod sibi in angustiis obvius offensu fortuito structuram togae destruxerat, et capital putavit quod in umero suo locum ruga mutasset.

6. 'Ergo hoc praetermisso ad viros venio triumphales, quos victores gentium luxuria vicit: et ut taceam Gurgitem a devorato patrimonio cognominatum, quia insignibus virtutis secutae vitia prioris compensavit aetatis, Metellus Pius in quam foveam luxus et superbiae successuum continuatione pervenit? et ne multis morer, ipsa de eo Sallustii verba subieci:

7. ac[72] Metellus in ulteriorem Hispaniam post an-

[71] modum lateris] nodum lateris P2, nodum latius *Salmasius*
[72] ac] at P, *Non. 222.19.*

---

[98] Cf. Pliny *Natural History* 12.8 (not specifying Hortensius).

[99] Q. Fabius Maximus Gurges ("the whirlpool": the term is commonly applied to other voracious wastrels) celebrated triumphs from victories over Rome's enemies as consul in 292, 276, and 265 BCE.

[100] The anecdote is set in 74 BCE (cf. *MRR* 2:104), when Q. Caecilius Metellus Pius (cos. 80) was directing the war as pro-

could pour the wine out for a plane-tree he had planted on his Tusculan estate.[98] 4. But perhaps more than a Hortensius is needed to stigmatize a whole generation, seeing that he was otherwise overtly effeminate and thought that a fine appearance began and ended with the drape of his toga. He took great pains over the elegance of his clothes, and to make sure he was leaving the house well turned out, he searched his appearance in a mirror, wrapping his toga around his body while he watched and using a skillful knot to keep the pleats in place—no random pleats, but carefully arranged!—and to make sure that the fold of the garment as it fell followed the contours of his upper body. 5. Once, when he was striding along dressed to the nines, he brought a suit against a colleague for a tort—because the man chanced to brush against him when they met in narrow alley-way and mussed the arrangement of his toga—regarding it as a capital offense that a pleat had been dislodged on his shoulder.

6. 'I set him aside, then, and come to men who had celebrated triumphs—men who had vanquished whole nations, but vanquished themselves by luxury. And to say nothing of Gurges, who got his name from gobbling up his inheritance—for he made up for his immoral youth by the signal acts of valor that followed[99]—consider Metellus Pius: what sink of luxury and arrogance did his unbroken string of successes bring him to? To make a long story short, I've subjoined what Sallust has to say about him (*Hist.* fr. 2.70):[100]

7. And after a year Metellus returned to Farther

consul against the Roman rebel Sertorius. The verb "subjoined" (*subieci*) alludes to Postumianus' written version (1.2.13n.).

> num regressus magna gloria, concurrentibus[73] undique virile et muliebre secus, per vias et tecta omnium visebatur. eum quaestor C. Vrbinus aliique cognita voluntate cum ad cenam invitaverant, ultra Romanum ac mortalium etiam morem curabant, exornatis aedibus per aulaea et insignia scaenisque ad ostentationem histrionum fabricatis. 8. simul croco sparsa humus et alia in modum templi celeberrimi. praeterea tum sedenti [in][74] transenna demissum Victoriae simulacrum cum machinato strepitu tonitruum coronam ei[75] imponebat,[76] tum venienti ture quasi deo supplicabatur. 9. toga picta plerumque amiculo erat accumbenti, epulae vero quaesitissimae neque per omnem modo provinciam sed trans maria ex Mauritania volucrum et ferarum incognita antea plura genera. quis rebus aliquantam partem gloriae dempserat maximeque apud veteres et sanctos viros superba illa, gravia, indigna Romano imperio aestimantes.

haec Sallustius, gravissimus alienae luxuriae obiurgator et censor.

10. 'Accipite inter gravissimas personas non defuisse luxuriam. refero enim pontificis vetustissimam cenam

[73] concurrentibus] -tium *Non.*

[74] in *seclusi* (*cf. Non. 180.15*)

[75] ei] capiti *Non. 286.16*, in caput *Serv. ad A. 5.488.*

[76] imponebat] -bant P¹A, *Non.*, (corona . . . ) imponebatur *Serv.*

> Spain in triumph, with people running from all sides to see him, of the male and female sex alike, through the streets and over all the roofs. When his quaestor Gaius Urbinius and others who knew what he liked invited him to a banquet, they looked after him like no ordinary Roman—indeed, like no ordinary mortal—as the building was hung with tapestries and insignia and a stage was built for actors to put on a show. 8. At the same time, the ground was strewn with saffron, and there were other touches of the sort found in a very festive temple. Not just that: while he was seated an image of Victory was lowered from an opening and—to the blare of automated trumpets—placed a crown on his head, and as he moved along incense was burned in supplication, as to a god. 9. His outer garment, as he reclined, was a toga nearly covered with embroidery; the feast was exquisite, with many varieties of birds and animals previously unheard of, brought not just from the whole province but from Mauretania across the sea. The whole affair detracted somewhat from his glory, especially among men of old-fashioned moral views, who judged such things arrogant, grievous, and unworthy of Rome's dominion.

So Sallust, a very stern scold and censor of other men's luxury.[101]

10. 'Understand that luxury was rife even among people of the most serious sort. Here I bring to your attention

[101] "Other men's" is pointed, since one tradition had it that Sallust was expelled from the senate for immorality.

quae scripta est in indice quarto Metelli illius pontificis maximi in haec verba:

11. Ante diem nonum Kalendas Septembres, quo die Lentulus flamen Martialis inauguratus est, domus ornata fuit, triclinia lectis eburneis strata fuerunt, duobus tricliniis pontifices cubuerunt, Q. Catulus, M<am>.[77] Aemilius Lepidus, D. Silanus, C. Caesar,[78] . . . rex sacrorum, P. Scaevola sextus, Q. Cornelius, P. Volumnius, P. Albinovanus et L. Iulius Caesar augur qui eum inauguravit, in tertio triclinio Popillia[79] Perpennia Licinia Arruntia virgines Vestales et ipsius uxor Publicia flaminica et Sempronia socrus eius. 12. cena haec fuit: ante cenam echinos, ostreas crudas quantum vellent, peloridas, sphondylos, turdum asparagos subtus, gallinam altilem, patinam[80] ostrearum peloridum, balanos nigros, balanos albos: iterum sphondylos, glycymaridas,[81] urticas, ficedulas, lumbos capruginos[82] aprugnos,

77 M<am>. *Taylor* (*AJP 63* [*1942*]: *392–93*): m̄ ω (m RA)
78 *post* Caesar *lacunam statuit Eyss*.
79 Popillia] Popilia E[2]S, poplia ω
80 patinam *ed. Ven. 1513*: patina ex ω
81 glycymerides *Guther coll. Plin. NH 32.147*: glyco- ω
82 capruginos *Salmasius*: capragines ω

102 This is Metellus Pius again, *pontifex maximus* from 81 to 64 BCE; given that this excerpt is from his "fourth digest" (= the record of his fourth year of service as *pont. max.* in the capital) and that Pius was away from Rome in the years 78–71, we know that this banquet dates to 22 Aug. 70 BCE (cf. Rüpke 2008, 938 n. 2). The account as quoted omits the choice wines for which priestly banquets were also known (Hor. *Odes* 2.14.25–28).

a very early pontiff's dinner, described in the following terms in the fourth digest of the Metellus who was supreme pontiff:[102]

> 11. On the ninth day before the Kalends of September, on which day Lentulus was inaugurated as flamen of Mars,[103] the house was decked out, the dining rooms laid with ivory couches; the pontiffs reclined in two dining rooms[104]—Quintus Catulus, Mamercus Aemilius Lepidus, Decimus Silanus, Gaius Caesar, . . . the priest in charge of sacrifices,[105] Publius Scaevola sixth, Quintus Cornelius, Publius Volumnius, Publius Albinovanus, and Lucius Julius Caesar, the augur who inaugurated him—in a third dining room there were the Vestal Virgins Popillia, Perpennia, Licinia, and Arruntia,[106] Publicia the wife of the flamen Lentulus, and his mother-in-law, Sempronia. 12. This was the dinner: as a prelude, sea-urchins, raw oysters (as many as they wanted), cockles and mussels, thrush over asparagus, fattened hen, a dish of baked oysters and cockles, white and black acorn-mollusks; mussels again, clams, jellyfish, fig-peckers, loin of roe-deer, loin of

[103] Cf. 1.10.15n. [104] There were 13 other *pontifices* besides Metellus and the new *flamen*: though the list includes only 6, plus 3 minor *pontifices* (Cornelius, Volumnius, and Albinovanus), it is prob. not seriously lacunose (*pace* Marinone 1970).

[105] I.e., the *rex sacrorum*, cf. 1.15.9n.; it is generally assumed that the priest's name has fallen out (hence the lacuna marked in the text), but the assumption is not strictly necessary.

[106] I.e., 4 of the 6 Vestals; the other two were prob. left to tend the sacred flame.

altilia ex farina involuta, ficedulas, murices et purpuras. in cena sumina, sinciput aprugnum, patinam piscium, patinam suminis, anates, querquedulas elixas, lepores, altilia assa, amulum, panes Picentes.

13. ubi iam luxuria tunc accusaretur quando tot rebus farta fuit cena pontificum? ipsa vero edulium genera quam dictu turpia? nam Titius in suasione legis Fanniae obicit saeculo suo quod porcum Troianum mensis inferant, quem illi ideo sic vocabant, quasi aliis inclusis animalibus gravidum, ut ille Troianus equus gravidus armatis fuit.

14. 'Exigebat hoc quoque illa gulae intemperantia, ut et lepores saginarentur teste Varrone, qui de agri cultura libro tertio cum de leporibus loqueretur sic ait: "hoc[83] quoque nuper institutum ut saginarentur,[84] cum exceptos e leporario condant[85] in caveis et loco clauso faciant[86] pingues." 15. si cui hoc mirum videtur quod ait Varro lepores aetate illa solitos saginari, accipiat aliud quod maiore admiratione sit dignum, cochleas saginatas, quod idem Varro in eodem libro refert. verba ipsa qui volet legere, ubi quaerere debeat indicavi. 16. neque ego nunc antiquitati nos

[83] hoc] hos *Varro*

[84] saginarentur] -ent *Varro, deinde* pleraque (*codd.*) *vel* plerumque (*Keil*)

[85] condant *ed. Paris. 1585*: condam ω (quon- β)

[86] faciant P²C: faciam ω

---

[107] On the *lex Fannia* of 161 BCE, see 3.17.3–8. M.'s phrasing (*in suasione legis Fanniae*, sim. 3.16.14) implies that the orator Titius spoke in support of the law at the time of its passage, which would square with his being "a contemporary of Lucilius" (3.16.14), who was born ca. 180 BCE, and with his providing the

boar, fattened fowl wrapped in dough, fig-peckers, murex and purple-shell; for the main courses, sow's udders, boar's cheek, a dish of baked fish, a dish of baked sow's udder, ducks, boiled water-fowl, hares, fattened fowl roasted, gruel, and bread of Picenum.

13. Where could there have been greater scope for denouncing luxury when a pontiffs' meal was stuffed with such things! How disgusting just to list the sorts of food! Indeed, Titius, in his speech supporting the law of Fannius (fr. 3 *ORF*$^2$),[107] reproaches his contemporaries for serving Trojan pig, so-called because it is "pregnant" with other animals enclosed within, just as the famous Trojan horse was "pregnant with armed men."[108]

14. 'That sort of unrestrained gluttony also drove them to force-feed even hares, as Varro reports when he speaks about hares in his third book on agriculture (3.12.5): "The practice of force-feeding, too, has recently been established: they take the hares from the hutch, shut them up in cages, and make them fat in the confined space." 15. If anyone's surprised at Varro's report that they used to force-feed hares in those days, let him take in something that merits even greater surprise: *snails* were force-fed, as Varro also reports in the same book (3.14.5).[109] I've provided the reference, should anyone want to read Varro's own words. 16. Not that I'm saying we should be thought

comic poet Afranius (fl. 150–125 BCE) with a model of Latinity (Cic. *Brutus* 167), but not with Cicero's apparent inclusion of him in a group of orators born in the 130s and 120s (on the problem see Douglas 1966, 128).

[108] For the phrasing cf. the fragment from Ennius' *Alexander* cited at 6.2.25. [109] Cf. Pliny *Natural History* 9.174.

praeferendos vel comparandos dico, sed respondi obiurganti Horo, adserens uti res habet, maiorem illis saeculis deliciarum curam fuisse quam nostro.'

14 Subiecit Rufius Albinus, antiquitatis non minus quam Caecina peritus: 'miror te,' inquit, 'Albine, non rettulisse quanta illis affluentia marinarum procurari solita fuerit copiarum, cuius relatu maximam conviviorum nostrorum sobrietatem doceres.' et Caecina, 'profer,' inquit, 'in medium quae de hac quoque parte lectu comperisti. ultra omnes enim polles memoria vetustatis.'

2. Et Rufius sic ingressus est: 'vetustas quidem nobis semper, si sapimus, adoranda est. illa quippe saecula sunt quae hoc imperium vel sanguine vel sudore pepererunt, quod non nisi virtutum faceret ubertas. sed, quod fatendum est, in illa virtutum abundantia vitiis quoque aetas illa non caruit, e quibus non nulla nostro saeculo morum sobrietate correcta sunt. 3. et de luxu quidem illius temporis circa marinas copias dicere institueram, sed quia in adsertionem nostrae emendationis alia ex aliis proferenda se suggerunt, de piscibus non omitto, sed differo dum de alia lascivia qua nunc caremus admoneo. 4. dic enim, Hore, qui antiquitatem nobis obicis, ante cuius triclinium modo saltatricem vel saltatorem te vidisse meministi? at inter illos saltatio certatim vel ab honestis adpetebatur. ecce enim, ut ab illo ordiar tempore quod fuit optimis moribus, inter duo bella Punica ingenui, quid dicam ingenui, filii se-

---

110 Lost in the lacuna after 3.12.

111 Cf. 3.15 below.

112 M. says "between two Punic Wars," but it become apparent shortly which two he means.

superior to the ancients or should be compared with them, but I've responded to Horus' scolding[110] by just stating the facts: people were keener on luxuries in those days than they are now.'

Rufius Albinus, as expert in antiquity as Caecina, interposed: 'I'm surprised, Albinus,' he said, 'that you haven't told us how extravagant a variety of seafood people used to take pains to acquire: by discussing that you could have made the point about the singular restraint of our festivities.' 'Please,' replied Caecina, 'tell us what your reading has supplied on this topic: there's no one with a better-stocked memory of times long ago.' 14

2. Rufius then began as follows: 'To be sure, we must always revere the days gone by, if we have any sense: those were the generations that produced this dominion of ours with their blood or sweat, and only an abundance of virtues could have made that possible. But it must be conceded that amid that abundance of virtues the age didn't want for vices, some of which the sober standards of our own age have set right. 3. I had in fact thought to speak about the luxury of that age when it came to varieties of seafood, but since one topic after another comes to mind as worth mentioning, to demonstrate the moral improvement of our era, I'll postpone my intended topic[111] and bring to your attention another vice that we've rid ourselves of. 4. Now tell me, Horus—since you're the one using the good old days to reproach us—do you recall seeing a dancer, male or female, in anyone's dining hall nowadays? But in those days even respectable people tried to outdo one another in dancing. For just consider—to start from the period when people's behavior was at its best—that between the Second and Third Punic Wars[112] freeborn boys—what am I

natorum in ludum saltatorium commeabant et illic crotala gestantes saltare discebant! 5. taceo quod matronae etiam saltationem non inhonestam putabant, sed inter probas quoque earum erat saltandi cura dum modo non curiosa usque ad artis perfectionem. quid enim ait Sallustius: "psallere saltare elegantius quam necesse est probae"? adeo et ipse Semproniam reprehendit non quod saltare, sed quod optime scierit. 6. nobilium vero filios et, quod dictu nefas est, filias quoque virgines inter studiosa numerasse saltandi meditationem testis est Scipio Africanus Aemilianus, qui in oratione contra legem iudiciariam Tib. Gracchi sic ait:

> 7. docentur praestigias inhonestas, cum cinaedulis et sambuca psalterioque eunt in ludum histrionum, discunt cantare, quae maiores nostri ingenuis probro ducier voluerunt. eunt, inquam, in ludum saltatorium inter cinaedos virgines puerique ingenui! haec cum mihi quisquam narrabat, non poteram animum inducere ea liberos suos homines nobiles docere: sed cum ductus sum in ludum saltatorium, plus medius fidius in eo ludo vidi pueris virginibusque quinquaginta,[87] in his unum—quod me rei publicae maxime miseritum est—puerum bullatum, petitoris filium non minorem annis duodecim,

[87] quinquaginta F: quingent- ω

---

[113] The only "judicial law" otherwise ascribed to Tiberius Gracchus concerns an attempt to add equestrian members to the senatorial juries (Plut. *Ti. and C. Gracch.* 16.1, Cassius Dio fr. 83.7, cf. Ampel. 26.1). [114] Cf. 1.6.8ff.

saying? *senators' sons*—used to go to dancing school and there learned to dance with castanets! 5. I'll say nothing of the fact that married women used to think that dancing was not disreputable, but even the respectable among them were keen on dancing, albeit not to the point of perfecting the art. What was it Sallust said (*Catiline's War* 25.2)—"playing the lyre, dancing more attractively than a respectable woman should"? So he himself criticizes Sempronia, not for knowing how to dance, but for knowing how to dance exceptionally well. 6. But the younger Scipio Africanus provides evidence that nobles' sons and—disgraceful to say—unmarried daughters counted learning to dance a worthwhile pursuit, speaking as follows in his speech against the judicial law[113] of Tiberius Gracchus (133 BCE, fr. 30 *ORF*[2]):

> 7. "They're taught disreputable tricks, they go to acting school with little pansies toting this and that kind of harp, they learn to sing—things our ancestors wished to be considered disgraceful for free-born children. They go to dancing school, I say, free-born maidens and boys, in a crowd of pansies! When someone told me this, I could not believe that noble men were teaching their own children these things; but when I was taken to a dancing school, 'pon my word, I saw more than fifty boys and maidens there, and among these—this above all made me grieve for our commonwealth—one of them a boy wearing the amulet of the well-born,[114] the son of an office-seeker, not less than twelve years old,

cum crotalis saltare quam saltationem impudicus servulus honeste saltare non posset.

8. vides quem ad modum ingemuerit Africanus quod vidisset cum crotalis saltantem filium petitoris, id est candidati, quem ne tum quidem spes et ratio adipiscendi magistratus, quo tempore se suosque ab omni probro debuit vindicare, potuerit coercere quo minus faceret quod scilicet turpe non habebatur.

'Ceterum superius pleramque nobilitatem haec propudia celebrare conquestus est. 9. sic nimirum M. Cato senatorem non ignobilem Caelium[88] "spatiatorem" et "Fescenninum"[89] vocat eumque staticulos dare his verbis ait: "descendit de cantherio, inde staticulos dare, ridicularia fundere." et alibi in eundem: "praeterea cantat ubi collibuit, interdum Graecos versus agit, iocos dicit, voces demutat, staticulos dat." 10. haec Cato, cui, ut videtis, etiam cantare non serii hominis videtur, quod apud alios adeo non inter turpia numeratum est, ut L. Sulla, vir tanti nominis, optime cantasse dicatur. 11. ceterum histriones non inter turpes habitos Cicero testimonio est, quem nullus ignorat Roscio et Aesopo histrionibus tam familiariter usum ut

[88] Caelium *Eyss.* (*post* M. Caelium *Meurs*): caecilium ω (*an menda iam in fonte nostri inventa*?)

[89] Fescenninum PG: -cennium ω

---

[115] The sentence's logic collapses under the pressure of M.'s eagerness to make two moralizing points simultaneously, about the lapse of one father and about the low standards of the age more generally. [116] Sc. the elder.

[117] For a more complete text of the frag. see Fest. p. 466.19–21, cf. Gell. 1.15.9.

doing a dance with castanets that it would disgrace a shameless little slave to dance.

8. You see how it grieved Africanus to have seen the son of an office-seeker dancing with castanets—a candidate for election, that is, whose hopes and plans for winning a magistracy could not restrain him from doing something that evidently was not considered disgraceful, even at a time when he was obliged to keep himself and his family clear of reproach.[115]

'Yet there's complaint still earlier that most of the nobility were behaving in these shameful ways. 9. Thus Marcus Cato[116] calls the noble senator Caelius an "idler"[117] and "bawdy" (fr. 113 *ORF*²), and says he's a poseur (fr. 114 *ORF*²): "He dismounts from his nag, strikes poses, spouts jokes." He elsewhere attacks the same man in these terms (fr. 115 *ORF*²): "Furthermore, he sings when it strikes his fancy, now and then declaims Greek poetry, tells jokes, talks in different voices, strikes poses." 10. So says Cato, who (as you see) thought even singing was not the mark of a serious person, though others were so far from judging it disgraceful that Lucius Sulla, a man of very great reputation, is said to have been an excellent singer.[118] 11. Cicero, however, gives evidence that actors were not categorized as people of ill-repute,[119] for everyone knows that he was on such friendly terms with Roscius and Aesopus that

118 Cf. Val. Max. 6.9.6, Plut. *Sulla* 2.2–3.

119 Cicero's relations with some individuals notwithstanding, the acting profession overall was viewed as disgraceful, its members treated as *infames* (persons of no reputable standing) subject to legal liabilities; cf. 2.3.10n., on Laberius.

res rationesque eorum sua sollertia tueretur, quod cum aliis multis tum ex epistulis quoque eius declaratur. 12. nam illam orationem quis est qui non legerit, in qua populum Romanum obiurgat quod Roscio gestum agente tumultuarit? et certe satis constat contendere eum cum ipso histrione solitum, utrum ille saepius eandem sententiam variis gestibus efficeret an ipse per eloquentiae copiam sermone diverso pronuntiaret. quae res ad hanc artis suae fiduciam Roscium abstraxit, ut librum conscriberet quo eloquentiam cum histrionia compararet. 13. is est Roscius qui etiam L. Sullae carissimus fuit et anulo aureo ab eodem dictatore donatus est. tanta autem fuit gratia et gloria, ut mercedem diurnam de publico mille denarios sine gregalibus solus acceperit. 14. Aesopum vero ex pari arte ducenties sestertium reliquisse filio constat. Sed quid loquor de histrionibus cum Appius Claudius, vir triumphalis, qui Salius ad usque senectutem fuit, pro gloria obtinuerit, quod inter collegas optime saltitabat?

15. 'Ac priusquam a saltatione discedo, illud adiciam, uno eodemque tempore tribus nobilissimis civibus non

---

[120] Beyond various expressions of admiration for their skill (*Speech on behalf of Archias* 17, *Speech on behalf of Publius Sestius* 120–23, *On the Orator* 1.251, 2.233, 3.102, *On Divination* 1.79–80, cf. Plut. *Cic.* 5.3), Cicero defended Roscius' interests in a matter of private law (*Speech on behalf of Quintus Roscius*) and assisted Aesopus when one of his slaves ran away to Asia, where Cicero's brother was governor (*Letters to Brother Quintus* 1.2.14).

[121] M. confuses the actor with L. Roscius Otho, who as tribune in 67 BCE passed a measure unpopular with the common people, reserving for the knights the first fourteen rows in theatrical pro-

he used his great skill to protect their property and interests, as any number of tokens make plain, even including his correspondence.[120] 12. Indeed, who has not read the speech in which he berates the Roman people for rioting while Roscius was acting?[121] And there's no doubt that he used to compete with the actor himself to see whether the latter could mime a given thought with a variety of gestures in more different ways than he himself could state it with a variety of expressions drawn from his abundant eloquence. This made Roscius so confident of his skill that he wrote a book in which he compared oratorical eloquence with the actor's craft. 13. The same Roscius was a great favorite of Lucius Sulla, who gave him a gold ring, and he achieved such popularity and renown that all by himself, apart from the ordinary members of his troupe, he received 1,000 denarii a day from public funds.[122] 14. As for Aesopus, who was equally skilled, it's well known that he left his son 20,000,000 sesterces. But why am I talking about actors, when Appius Claudius, who had celebrated a triumph [143 BCE] and was one of the Salii up until his old age, had it as a point of pride that he was the best dancer in the brotherhood?[123]

15. 'Before I leave the topic of dancing, let me add one thing: in one and the same period three of the most nota-

ductions (cf. 2.3.10, *MRR* 2:145); the disturbance mentioned here occurred in 63 BCE, when Cicero was consul (Plut. *Cic.* 13.2–4).

[122] Cf. Plut. *Sulla* 36.1 (Sulla's intimacy with Roscius), Pliny *Natural History* 7.125 (Roscius earned HS 500,000 per year, which would be sufficient for the equestrian status that the gold ring would normally signify: cf. 2.3.10n.).

[123] On the Salii see 3.12.1n.

modo studium saltandi, sed etiam, si dis placet, peritiam qua gloriarentur fuisse, Gabinio[90] consulari, Ciceronis inimico, quod ei etiam Cicero non dissimulanter obiecit, et M. Caelio, nato[91] in turbas viro, quem idem Cicero defendit, et Licinio Crasso, Crassi eius qui apud Parthos extinctus est filio.

15 'Sed de saltatione veterum ad praedae marinae transire luxum Liciniorum me nomen admonuit, quos Murenas cognominatos, quod hoc pisce effusissime delectati sint satis constat. 2. huic opinioni M. Varro consentit, adserens eodem modo Licinios appellatos Murenas quo Sergius Orata cognominatus est, quod ei pisces qui auratae vocantur carissimi fuerint. 3. hic est Sergius Orata qui primus balneas pensiles habuit, primus ostrearia in Baiano locavit, primus optimum saporem ostreis Lucrinis adiudicavit. fuit autem aetate L. Crassi illius diserti, qui quam gravis et serius habitus sit etiam Cicero docet. 4. is tamen Crassus, vir censorius—nam cum Cn. Domitio censor fuit—cum supra ceteros disertus haberetur essetque inter clarissimos cives princeps, tamen murenam in piscina domus suae mortuam atratus, tamquam filiam luxit. 5. neque id obscurum fuit;

90 Gabinio OJ²: gavinio *ω*
91 nato *Jan*: noto *ω*

---

124 Cf. *Speech to the Senate on his Return* 13, *Against Piso* 18, 22, *Speech on behalf of Plancius* 87.

125 In the extant *Speech on behalf of Caelius* (April 56 BCE).

126 The young Crassus was killed in the same battle (53 BCE).

127 Cf. Varro *On Agriculture* 3.3.10, Col. 8.16.5 (Orata's nickname is explained differently at Fest. 196.28–31).

128 Cf. Val. Max. 9.1.1, Pliny *Natural History* 9.168–69.

ble citizens not only had a serious interest in dancing but even—if the gods be pleased!—achieved an expertise in which they took great pride: I mean Gabinius, a man of consular rank and an enemy of Cicero, who also openly reproached him for it;[125] Marcus Caelius, a natural born trouble-maker, whom Cicero defended;[126] and Licinius Crassus, son of the Crassus who was annihilated by the Parthians.[126]

'But mention of the Licinii prompts me to move from 15
the ancients' dancing to their extravagant indulgence in the sea's bounty—specifically, the Licinii with the surname Murena ["moray"], earned (it's quite well known) from the exorbitant delight they took in that fish. 2. Marcus Varro agrees, saying that the Licinii gained the surname Murena the way that Sergius Orata got his, from his great fondness for the fish called "gilt-heads" [*auratae*].[127] 3. This is the Sergius Orata who was the first to have heated baths, the first to install his own oyster-beds at his estate in Baiae, the first to decide that oysters from the Lucrine Lake have the best taste.[128] He was a contemporary of the famous orator Lucius Crassus,[129] whose serious and stern character Cicero also describes for us.[130] 4. Although Crassus, a former censor—he was the colleague of Gnaius Domitius [92 BCE]—was considered the most eloquent of all and had pride of place among the men of greatest distinction, he nonetheless put on mourning when a moray of his died in a fishpond at his home and grieved for it like a daughter. 5. It

129 Cf. Cic. *On Appropriate Actions* 3.67 (Orata defended by Crassus).

130 M. refers to the idealized portrait of Crassus in *On the Orator*.

quippe collega Domitius in senatu hoc ei quasi deforme crimen obiecit. neque id confiteri Crassus erubuit sed ultro etiam, si dis placet, gloriatus est censor, piam affectiosamque rem fecisse se iactitans. 6. piscinas autem quam refertas habuerint pretiosissimis piscibus Romani illi nobilissimi principes, Lucullus,[92] Philippus et Hortensius, quos Cicero piscinarios appellat, etiam illud indicium est, quod M. Varro in libro de agri cultura refert M. Catonem qui post Vticae periit, cum heres testamento Luculli esset relictus, pisces de piscina eius quadraginta milibus vendidisse.[93] 7. accersebantur autem murenae ad piscinas nostrae urbis ab usque freto Siculo quod Rhegium a Messana dispescit.[94] illic enim optimae a prodigis esse creduntur tam, Hercules,[95] quam anguillae, et utraeque ex illo loco Graece πλωταί vocantur, Latine flutae, quod in summo supernantes sole torrefactae curvare se posse et in aquam mergere desinunt atque ita faciles captu fiunt. 8. et si enumerare velim quam multi magnique auctores murenas e freto Siculo nobilitarint, longum fiat; sed dicam quid M. Varro in libro qui inscribitur Gallus de admirandis dixerit his verbis: "in Sicilia quoque," inquit "Papirius manu capi murenas flutas, quod eae in summa aqua prae pinguitudine flutentur."

9. 'Haec Varro. sed quis neget indomitam apud illos et, ut ait Caecilius, vallatam gulam fuisse, qui ex tam longin-

[92] Lucullus . . . Luculli J[2]S: lucilius . . . lucilii ω

[93] vendidisse F[2]J[2]: -set ω [94] dispescit *Schrijver* (dispiscit R[1]): dispicit ω [95] Hercules K: -lis ω

---

[131] Acc. to Varro, Cato was not Lucullus' heir but the guardian of his underage son.

was no secret: indeed, his colleague Domitius upbraided him for it in the senate, as though it were an ugly crime. Nor was Crassus ashamed to admit it—far from it, the censor actually boasted of it—if the gods be pleased!—and took credit for acting with affectionate devotion. 6. As for the fishponds of the most noble leading men—I mean Lucullus, Philippus, and Hortensius, the ones Cicero calls "fishpond-fanciers" (*Letters to Atticus* 1.19.6, 1.20.3)—how stuffed they were with the most expensive fish is suggested by the fact that, as Marcus Varro reports in his third book on agriculture (3.2.17), when Marcus Cato (the one who later died at Utica) was left as Lucullus' heir by his will, he sold the fish from the pond for 40,000 sesterces.[131] 7. Furthermore, morays were fetched for our city's fishponds all the way from the strait that separates Rhegium from Messana in Sicily. The wastrels think the ones there are the best, by god, and the anguillas too: both sorts from that area are called "floaters" (*plôtai* in Greek, *flutae* in Latin) because as they swim along the surface they get warmed by the sun and lose the capacity to flex and dive, and so they become an easy catch. 8. It would be a long job, should I want to list all the great authorities that have made the morays from the strait of Sicily famous—but let me just tell what Marcus Varro said in his book titled *Gallus on Marvels* (*Logist*. fr. 55): "In Sicily too," he says, "Papirius [reports] that the floater morays are caught by hand, because their girth makes them float on the surface."

9. 'So Varro. But who would deny that these people displayed the most untamed and, as Caecilius puts it (283 *SRPF*[3] 2:92), "well-fortified gluttony," seeing that they ac-

quo mari instrumenta luxuriae compararent? 10. nec rarus hic Romae piscis, ut peregre accitus, erat. auctor est Plinius C. Caesarem dictatorem cum triumphales cenas populo daret, sex milia murenarum a Gaio[96] Hirrio ad pondus accepisse. huius Hirrii villam, quamvis non amplam aut latam, constat propter vivaria quae habuit quadragies sestertio[97] venum datam.

16 'Nec acipenser, quem maria prodigis nutriunt, illius saeculi delicias evasit; et ut liqueat secundo Punico bello celebre nomen huius piscis fuisse, accipite ut meminerit eius Plautus in fabula quae inscribitur Baccaria ex persona parasiti:

> 2. quis est mortalis tanta fortuna affectus umquam
> qua ego nunc sum, cuius haec ventri portatur pompa?
> vel nunc, qui mihi in mari acipenser latuit antehac,
> cuius ego latus in latebras reddam[98] meis dentibus et
> manibus.[99]

3. et ne vilior sit testis poeta, accipite assertore Cicerone in quo honore fuerit hic piscis apud P. Scipionem Africanum illum et Numantinum. haec sunt in dialogo de fato verba Ciceronis:

> 4. nam cum esset apud se ad Lavernium Scipio unaque Pontius, adlatus est forte Scipioni acipenser, qui admodum raro capitur, sed est piscis, ut ferunt,

[96] Gaio S[1], *Plin.*: Gavio ω [97] sestertio *ed. Lugd. Bat. 1670*: -tium ω [98] in latebras eius reddam latus *Ritschl* [99] manibus] malibus *Ritschl*

[132] Cf. Varro *On Agriculture* 3.17.3.

quired the devices of their luxury from such a distant sea? 10. Nor was that fish uncommon at Rome, so that it had to be fetched from foreign parts: we have it on the authority of Pliny (*Natural History* 9.171) that as dictator Gaius Caesar gave a dinner for the people to celebrate his triumph and bought 6,000 pounds of moray from Gaius Hirrius. It's a well known fact that this Hirrius' villa, though neither splendid nor large, was sold for 4,000,000 sesterces because of its fishponds.[132]

'Nor did the sturgeon, which the seas raise for wast- 16
rels, escape the extravagance of that era. So you can see clearly that the fish's name was well known at the time of the Second Punic War, here's how Plautus speaks of it, in the character of a parasite, in his play titled *Baccaria* (17–20):

> 2. What mortal was ever graced with good fortune as great
> as mine is now, when this procession is brought forth for my belly?
> Now the sturgeon that hid from me in the sea before this—
> my teeth and hands will see that its flesh is hidden away for good.

3. Is the poet's testimony not weighty enough? Then hear Cicero testify to the honor this fish enjoyed in the eyes of Publius Scipio, the great hero of Africa and Numantia. These are Cicero's words in his dialogue *On Fate* (fr. 4):

> 4. For when Scipio was at home with Pontius in his property at Lavernium a sturgeon happened to be brought to him—quite a rare catch, but a fish, they

> in primis nobilis. cum autem Scipio unum et alterum ex his qui eum salutatum venerant invitavisset pluresque etiam invitaturus videretur, in aurem Pontius, "Scipio," inquit, "vide quid agas, acipenser iste paucorum hominum est."

5. nec infitias eo temporibus Traiani hunc piscem in magno pretio non fuisse, teste Plinio Secundo, qui in Naturali historia cum de hoc pisce loqueretur sic ait: "nullo nunc in honore est, quod equidem miror, cum sit rarus[100] inventu." 6. sed non diu stetit haec parsimonia. nam temporibus Severi principis, qui ostentabat duritiam morum, Sammonicus Serenus, vir saeculo suo doctus, cum ad principem suum scriberet faceretque de hoc pisce sermonem, verba Plinii quae superius posui praemisit et ita ipse subiecit:

> 7. Plinius, ut scitis, ad usque Traiani imperatoris venit aetatem. nec dubium est quod ait nullo honore nunc piscem temporibus suis fuisse, verum ab eo dici. apud antiquos autem in pretio fuisse ego testimoniis palam facio, vel eo magis quod gratiam eius video ad epulas quasi postliminio redisse; quippe qui dignatione vestra cum intersum convivio sacro, animadvertam hunc piscem a coronatis ministris cum tibicine introferri. sed quod ait Plinius de acipenseris squamis, id verum esse maximus rerum naturalium indagator Nigidius Figulus ostendit, in

[100] rarus *Marinone e Plin. 9.60*: parvus ω (perrarus J[2] *Jan e coniect.*)

say, that's *la crème de la crème*. But when he had invited to dinner a couple of those who had come to greet him, and it looked as though he was going to invite still more, Pontius said in his ear, "Be careful, Scipio: that sturgeon of yours doesn't like a crowd."

5. I grant that this fish didn't command a high price in Trajan's reign, as Pliny attests when he makes the following remark about the fish in his *Natural History* (9.60):[133] "The fish is not highly prized now, something I myself find surprising, since it's rarely found." 6. But this spirit of thrift didn't last long: when Serenus Sammonicus, a scholar of the day, wrote to the emperor Severus, who made a show of his austere habits, and discoursed on this fish, he started with the words of Pliny that I quoted just above and then added:

7. As you know, Pliny lived all the way to the time of Trajan, and he's no doubt telling the truth when he says, 'The fish is not highly prized now.' But I mean to show that it was prized by the ancients, a point I make particularly because I see that it has returned to favor at our banquets, like an exile with its civic rights restored: for when you deign to include me as a guest at your sacred banquet, I notice that this fish is served by garlanded servants to the sound of a flute. As for Pliny's report about the sturgeon's scales (ibid.), that supreme scholar of the natural order, Nigidius Figulus, shows that it's true: in Book 4

133 The passage reflects the belief, common until the work of Giovanni de Matociis in the 14th century, that the elder Pliny (d. 79 CE) and the younger Pliny (d. ca. 112 CE) were a single person.

cuius libro de animalibus quarto ita positum est: "cur alii pisces squama secunda, acipenser adversa sit."

8. haec Sammonicus, qui turpitudinem convivii principis sui laudando notat, prodens venerationem qua piscis habebatur, ut a coronatis inferretur cum tibicinis cantu, quasi quaedam non deliciarum sed numinis pompa. 9. sed ut minus miremur acipenserem gravi pretio taxari solitum, Asinius Celer, vir consularis, ut idem Sammonicus refert, mullum unum septem[101] milibus nummum mercatus est. in qua re luxuriam illius saeculi eo magis licet aestimare quod Plinius Seeundus temporibus suis negat facile mullum repertum qui duas pondo libras excederet. at nunc et maioris ponderis passim videmus et pretia haec insana nescimus.

10. 'Nec contenta illa ingluvies fuit maris sui copiis. nam Optatus[102] praefectus classis sciens scarum adeo Italicis litoribus ignotum ut nec nomen Latinum eius piscis habeamus, incredibilem scarorum multitudinem vivariis navibus huc advectam inter Ostiam et Campaniae litus in mare sparsit miroque ac novo exemplo pisces in mari tamquam in terra fruges aliquas seminavit idemque tamquam

[101] septem] VIII *Plin.*
[102] Optatus *Gelenius ex Plin. 9. 62*: -mus *α*, -nus *β*

[134] The sturgeon has ganoid scales, which are thick, non-overlapping, and composed of bone overlaid with an enamel-like substance called ganoin, very different in structure and appearance from the ctenoid scales (jagged-edged: e.g., bass) and cycloid scales (smooth-edged: e.g., salmon) of most bony fish.

of his *On animals* we find the topic (fr. 113), "Why the scales of other fish are aligned with the current, the sturgeon's against."[134]

8. So Sammonicus, who by praising the grossness of his prince's banquet stigmatizes it, revealing that the fish used to be held in such reverence that it was served by garlanded servants to the song of a flute, as if it were the procession, not of a delicacy, but of a god. 9. Not that it should come as a surprise that the sturgeon used to carry a hefty price-tag: as Sammonicus also tells us,[135] Asinius Celer, a former consul, bought a single red mullet for 7,000 sesterces. The luxury of the age in this area can be the more easily gauged because Pliny says (*Natural History* 9.64) that in his day it was hard to find a red mullet that weighed more than two pounds—though now we commonly see specimens that weigh more, but we never hear of these crazy prices.

10. 'Nor was the gluttony of those times content with the abundant yield of its own waters.[136] Aware that the parrot-wrasse was so foreign to Italian shores that we do not even have a Latin name for it, Optatus, a prefect of the fleet, imported a vast cargo of the fish in ships rigged as aquaria and scattered them in the sea between Ostia and the Campanian coast, setting a strange, new precedent by "seeding" the sea with fish, just like the fruits of the earth. What's more, he took pains over the next five years—as

[135] Cf. Pliny *Natural History* 9.67, where the price is HS 8,000, Tert. *On the Cloak* 5.6 (HS 6,000); sim. Juv. 4.15–17, on the mullet bought by Crispinus for HS 6,000.

[136] Cf. Pliny *Natural History* 9.62.

summa in hoc utilitatis publicae verteretur, quinquennio dedit operam ut si quis inter alios pisces scarum forte cepisset, incolumem confestim et inviolatum mari redderet.

11. 'Quid stupemus captivam illius saeculi gulam servisse mari, cum in magno vel dicam maximo apud prodigos honore fuerit etiam Tiberinus lupus et omnino omnes ex hoc amni pisces? 12. quod equidem cur ita illis visum sit ignoro; fuisse autem etiam M. Varro ostendit, qui enumerans quae in quibus Italiae partibus optima ad victum gignantur, pisci Tiberino palmam tribuit his verbis in libro rerum humanarum undecimo: "ad victum optima fert ager Campanus frumentum, Falernus vinum, Casinas oleum, Tusculanus ficum, mel Tarentinus, piscem Tiberis." 13. haec Varro de omnibus scilicet huius fluminis piscibus sed inter eos, ut supra dixi, praecipuum locum lupus tenuit, et quidem is qui inter duos pontes captus esset. 14. id ostendunt cum multi alii tum etiam C. Titius, vir aetatis Lucilianae, in oratione qua legem Fanniam suasit. cuius verba ideo pono quia non solum de lupo inter duos pontes capto erunt testimonio, sed etiam mores quibus plerique tunc vivebant facile publicabunt. describens enim homines prodigos in forum ad iudicandum ebrios commeantes quaeque soleant inter se sermocinari sic ait:

> 15. ludunt alea studiose, delibuti unguentis, scortis stipati. ubi horae decem sunt, iubent puerum vocari

---

[137] At the bend in the Tiber between the Aemilian bridge and the Fabrician on the Tiber island (*LTUR* 3: 106–7, 109–10): the Cloaca Maxima emptied out there, providing a spot suited to the fish's habits noted in §17; cf. also Hor. *Satires* 2.2.31, Pliny *Natural History* 9.169.

[138] On the law of Fannius cf. 3.17.13n.

though the public interest turned critically on this venture—to make sure if anyone chanced to catch a parrot-wrasse in a haul of other fish, he returned it immediately to the sea, safe and unharmed.

11. 'Why should we be amazed that the gluttony of that era was slavishly dependent on the sea, when wastrels even paid great—or I should say, greatest—honor to the wolf-fish of the Tiber, and indeed all the fish from this river? 12. I certainly don't know why they were so inclined, but that they were is also made clear by Marcus Varro, who in Book 11 of his *Human Antiquities* (fr. 1) lists the areas of Italy that produce the best foods and awards the palm to the fish of the Tiber, saying, "Campanian land bears the best grain for our use, Falernian the best wine, Casinum the best oil, Tusculum the best figs, Tarentum the best honey, and the Tiber the best fish." 13. That's what Varro says about this river's fish in general, of course, but among them, as I said before, the wolf-fish had pride of place, and in particular those caught between the two bridges.[137] 14. Among the many witnesses to that fact I single out the speech that Gaius Titius, a contemporary of Lucilius, delivered in support of the law of Fannius.[138] I'm quoting what he says not just because it will provide evidence about the wolf-fish caught between the two bridges but also because it will vividly reveal the general character of the people alive at the time. He describes wastrels wandering drunk into the forum to serve as judges and reports the sorts of conversation they held, saying (fr. 2 *ORF*[2]):

> 15. They play dice enthusiastically, smeared with scented oils, cheek-by-jowl with their whores. Come four o'clock, they order that a slave be sum-

ut comitium eat percontatum quid in foro gestum sit, qui suaserint, qui dissuaserint, quot tribus iusserint, quot vetuerint. inde ad comitium vadunt ne litem suam faciant. dum eunt, nulla est in angiporto amphora quam non impleant, quippe qui vesicam plenam vini habeant. 16. veniunt in comitium, tristes iubent dicere. quorum negotium est narrant, iudex testes poscit, ipsus it minctum. ubi redit, ait se omnia audivisse, tabulas poscit, litteras inspicit: vix prae vino sustinet palpebras. eunt[103] in consilium. ibi haec oratio: "quid mihi negotii est cum istis nugatoribus. quin potius[104] potamus mulsum mixtum vino Graeco, edimus turdum pinguem bonumque piscem, lupum germanum qui inter duos pontes captus fuit?"

17. haec Titius. sed et Lucilius, acer et violentus poeta, ostendit scire se hunc piscem egregii saporis qui inter duos pontes captus esset, eumque quasi ligurritorem catillonem appellat, scilicet qui proxime ripas stercus insectaretur. proprie autem catillones dicebantur qui ad polluc-

[103] eunt B2: eunti ω

[104] quin potius *Madvig*: potius quam ω

---

[139] The Comitium was the main assembly place of the Roman people under the Republic, at the foot of the Capitoline between the senate house (*curia Hostilia*) and the forum (*LTUR* 1: 309–14): on the occasion described a tribal assembly was being held to consider a piece of legislation, followed by a judicial hearing.

[140] The idiom Titius uses, *litem suam facere* (lit. "to produce/cause one's own action at law"), refers to the liability a judge incurred through malfeasance.

moned to go to the comitium[139] and ask what business was conducted in the forum, who spoke in favor, who against, how many tribes were pro, how many con. Then they make their way to the comitium to avoid being held liable for dereliction:[140] on their way there's not a single pot in an alleyway that they don't fill, their bladders are so full of wine. 16. They come to the comitium, grumpy, and call for the arguments to be made: the two sides state their cases, the judge asks for the witnesses to be called, while he himself goes to pee. When he comes back, he says he's heard everything, calls for the accounts, peers at the writing—scarcely able to keep his eyelids open for the wine he's drunk. They withdraw for a conference, where the discussion runs like this: "What have I to do with those fools? Why don't we go drink some mead mixed with Greek wine, eat a nice fat thrush and a good piece of fish, the real article, a wolf-fish caught between the two bridges?"

17. So Titius. But Lucilius, too, a sharp and forceful poet, shows that he knows that the sort caught between the two bridges is exceptionally tasty, and calls it a "lapper," from its habit of licking up whatever it found, since it would go after the sewage close by the riverbank. (Strictly speaking, "lappers" [*catillones*] is the term that used to be applied to people who licked the bowls [*catilli*] clean when they

tum Herculis ultimi cum venirent[105] catillos ligurribant. 18. Lucilii versus hi sunt:

fingere praeterea, adferri quod quisque volebat.
illum sumina ducebant atque altilium lanx,
hunc pontes Tiberinus[106] duo inter captus catillo.

17 'Longum fiat si enumerare velim quot instrumenta gulae inter illos vel ingenio excogitata sint vel studio confecta. et hae nimirum causae fuerunt propter quas tot numero leges de cenis et sumptibus ad populum ferebantur, et imperari coepit ut patentibus ianuis pransitaretur et cenitaretur, sic oculis civium testibus factis luxuriae modus fieret. 2. prima autem omnium de cenis lex ad populum Orchia pervenit, quam tulit C. Orchius tribunus plebi de senatus sententia tertio anno quam Cato censor fuerat. cuius verba quia sunt prolixa praetereo, summa autem eius praescribebat numerum convivarum. 3. et haec est lex Orchia de qua Cato mox orationibus suis vociferabatur, quod plures quam praescripto eius cavebatur ad cenam vocarentur.

'Cumque auctoritatem novae legis aucta necessitas imploraret, post annum vicesimum secundum legis Orchiae Fannia lex data est, anno post Romam conditam secundum

105 cum venirent B²ςK²: convenirent ω
106 -nus MK: -nos ω

---

141 This looks to the Pinarii again: see 3.6.14.

142 "Third year," i.e., according to the Roman method of inclusive reckoning (cf. 1.3.9n.): Cato was censor in 184 BCE, Orchius tribune in 182.

were the last to arrive at the sacrificial meal in Hercules' honor.)[141] 18. Here are Lucilius' lines (1193–95):

> . . . to produce, besides, what each one wanted to be served:
> one was drawn to sow's udders and a platter of fattened fowl,
> another, to a lapper from the Tiber, caught between the two bridges.

'It would be a long job, should I wish to catalog all the 17
implements of gluttony that those people applied their wits to dreaming up or their zeal to devising. Of course, that's why so many laws were brought before the people concerning dinners and expenditures, and why it began to be the rule that people had to eat lunch and dinner with their doors wide open, so that the scrutiny of their fellow citizens would set a limit on their luxury. 2. The first of all the laws on dining to come before the people was the law that Gaius Orchius, tribune of the plebs, carried in accordance with a decree of the senate in the third year after Cato's censorship.[142] I won't quote it, because the text is quite long, but in a nutshell it specified the allowable number of guests. 3. This is the law of Orchius about which Cato was soon thundering in his speeches, because people were inviting more guests than the law prescribed (fr. 142 *ORF*[2]).

'When increased luxury showed there was a crying need for another round of strong legislation, the law of Fannius was passed twenty-two years after the law of Orchius,

Gellii opinionem quingentesimo octogesimo octavo. 4. de hac lege Sammonicus Serenus ita refert:

> lex Fannia, sanctissimi Augusti, ingenti omnium ordinum consensu pervenit ad populum, neque eam praetores aut tribuni ut plerasque alias, sed ex omnium bonorum consilio et sententia ipsi consules pertulerunt, cum res publica ex luxuria conviviorum maiora quam credi potest detrimenta pateretur, si quidem eo res redierat, ut gula inlecti plerique ingenui pueri pudicitiam et libertatem suam venditarent, plerique ex plebe Romana vino madidi in comitium venirent et ebrii de rei publicae salute consulerent.

5. haec Sammonicus. Fanniae autem legis severitas in eo superabat Orchiam legem quod in superiore numerus tantum modo cenantium cohibebatur licebatque secundum eam uni cuique bona sua inter paucos consumere, Fannia autem etiam sumptibus modum fecit assibus centum, unde a Lucilio poeta festivitatis suae more "centussis" vocatur.

---

143 "Twenty-two years after the law of Orchius," reckoned inclusively, correctly places the *lex Fannia* in 161 BCE, the year of Fannius' consulship (cf. *MRR* 1:443; contrast Pliny *Natural History* 10.139, "eleven years before the third Punic war [149–46 BCE]"). That, however, was the 593rd year (reckoned inclusively) from the city's founding on the Varronian dating (753 BCE) or the 592nd year on the reckoning of the *fasti Capitolini* (752 BCE: on the issue see 1.11.3n.): either the number in the MSS is corrupt or the historian Gnaius Gellius cited here (fr. 28) was inconsistent in the dating scheme(s) he followed (cf. 1.16.21n.).

144 Plural because Sammonicus was probably addressing both

in the 588th year (on Gellius' reckoning) after the city's founding.[143] 4. About this law Serenus Sammonicus says,

> The law of Fannius, my most holy eminences,[144] came before the people backed by the huge consensus of all the citizen ranks, and it was not the praetors or tribunes who brought it, as they do most other laws, but the consuls themselves, in accordance with the considered judgment of all good men, since extravagant banqueting was inflicting incredible damage on the commonwealth and matters had reached the point that very many freeborn boys, caught in luxury's snare, were peddling their chastity and freedom and many of the plebs were coming to the comitium completely soused and reaching decisions touching the commonwealth's safety while drunk.

5. So Sammonicus. Fannius' law was stricter than Orchius' in that the earlier law limited only the number of banqueters and so permitted every individual to gobble up his estate with a few companions, whereas Fannius' law also limited expenditures to 100 asses, leading the poet Lucilius to call it (1192), with his customary wit, the "100-*as*" law.[145]

Septimius Severus and his son Caracalla, who held the rank of Augustus from 198 CE. [145] Gellius (2.24.3–6) quotes Lucilius' whole phrase, *Fanni centussis misellus* ("Fannius' wretched little hundred *asses*"); the *as* was a small unit of bronze coinage (in 161 BCE, 100 *asses* = 10 sesterces = 1 silver denarius). In §§5–13 M.'s account closely resembles Gell. 2.24 but certainly does not draw exclusively (§6n., §13n.), and prob. not directly (§9n., §13n.), upon it.

6. 'Fanniam legem post annos decem et octo lex Didia consecuta est. eius ferundae duplex fuit causa, prima et potissima ut universa Italia, non sola urbs, lege sumptuaria teneretur, Italicis existimantibus Fanniam legem non in se sed in solos urbanos cives esse conscriptam; deinde ut non soli qui prandia cenasve maiore sumptu fecissent, sed etiam qui ad eas vocitati essent atque omnino interfuissent, poenis legis tenerentur.

7. 'Post Didiam Licinia lex lata est a P. Licinio Crasso Divite, cuius ferundae probandaeque tantum studium ab optimatibus impensum est, ut consulto senatus iuberetur ut ea tantum modo promulgata, priusquam trinundino confirmaretur, ita ab omnibus observaretur quasi iam populi sententia comprobata. 8. lex vero haec paucis mutatis in plerisque cum Fannia congruit. in ea enim ferenda quaesita est novae legis auctoritas, exolescente metu legis antiquioris, ita, Hercules, ut de ipsis duodecim tabulis factum est, quarum ubi contemni antiquitas coepit, eadem illa quae illis[107] legibus cavebantur in alia latorum nomina transierunt. 9. sed legis Liciniae summa ut Kalendis Nonis nundinis Romanis cuique in dies singulos triginta dumtaxat asses edundi causa consumere liceret, ceteris vero

107 illis E: illius ω

146 Only if reckoned non-inclusively: T. Didius passed this measure as tribune of the plebs in 143 BCE (*MRR* 1:472). The account in Gell. 2.24 omits this law.

147 The only known Crassus Dives who fits the chronology is P. Licinius Crassus Dives Mucianus, consul 131, though the measure is not otherwise associated with him. This might be the sumptuary law that the censors of 97 BCE expelled M. Duronius from

6. 'After eighteen years[146] the law of Didius followed Fannius' and was carried for two reasons: first, and more important, so that all of Italy, not just Rome, would be bound by a sumptuary law, since the inhabitants of Italy beyond Rome though that the Fannian law, as it was drafted, concerned only city-dwellers, not themselves; second, so that the law's penalties would affect not only those who gave overly expensive luncheons or dinners but also those who had been invited to them and were present in any capacity.

7. 'After the Didian law Publius Licinius Crassus Dives brought a law[147] whose passage occasioned such enthusiasm among the conservative aristocracy that a decree of the senate directed that as soon as it was promulgated, before it was brought to a vote after the customary three market days had passed,[148] all citizens were to keep its provisions as though it had been ratified by the people. 8. With but a few changes, however, this law agreed in most particulars with Fannius'. The goal of passing it was to gain the authority of a new law when people were no longer cowed by the older law—just as happened, by god, in the case of the XII Tables themselves: when they began to be despised for their antiquity, the same sanctions that they imposed were transferred to new measures under the names of different legislators. 9. The nub of the Licinian law provided that on the Kalends, Nones, and market days each person was permitted to spend thirty asses on comestibles, whereas on other days, for which an exception was not

the senate for abrogating as tribune (Val. Max. 2.9.5); if so, it might have been passed by the P. Licinius Crassus who was consul that year (cf. *MRR* 2:7). 148 Cf. 1.16.35n.

diebus, qui excepti non essent, ne amplius daretur apponeretur quam carnis aridae pondo tria et salsamentorum pondo libra et quod ex terra vite arboreve sit natum. 10. video quid remordeat. ergo indicium sobrii saeculi est ubi tali praescripto legum coercetur expensa cenarum? non ita est. nam leges sumptuariae a singulis ferebantur quae civitatis totius vitia corrigerent; ac nisi pessimis effusissimisque moribus viveretur, profecto opus ferundis legibus non fuisset. vetus verbum est: leges [inquit][108] bonae ex malis moribus procreantur.

11. 'Has sequitur lex Cornelia et ipsa sumptuaria, quam tulit Cornelius Sulla dictator, in qua non conviviorum magnificentia prohibita est nec gulae modus factus, verum minora pretia rebus imposita: et quibus rebus, di boni, quamque exquisitis et paene incognitis generibus deliciarum! quos illic pisces quasque offulas nominat, et tamen pretia illis minora constituit! ausim dicere ut vilitas edulium animos hominum ad parandas obsoniorum copias incitaret et gulae servire etiam qui parvis essent facultatibus possent. 12. dicam plane quod sentio. adprime luxuriosus mihi videtur et prodigus cui haec tanta in epulis vel gratuita ponantur. itaque tanto hoc saeculum ad omnem continentiam promptius ut pleraque harum rerum quae Sullana lege ut vulgo nota comprehenduntur, nemo nostrum vel fando compererit.

13. 'Sulla mortuo Lepidus consul legem tulit et ipse ci-

[108] inquit *del. Willis*, est *del. Eyss.*

made, they were permitted to serve no more than three pounds of dried meat and a pound of salted fish plus whatever grew from earth, vine, or tree.[149] 10. I know the rejoinder to expect: is it the sign of an austere age when the cost of dinners is prescribed by such law? No, it isn't: sumptuary laws were passed by individuals to set the vices of an entire community straight, and if the worst and most extravagant habits were not shaping people's lives, there obviously would be no need to pass laws. There's an old saying: bad habits produce good laws.

11. 'After these came the Cornelian law, itself also a sumptuary measure, which Cornelius Sulla moved as dictator:[150] it did not outlaw extravagant banquets nor set a limit on gluttony but set lower prices on goods—and what goods, my god, what far-fetched and all but unheard of kinds of luxury-items! The fish it names, and the cuts of meat—and yet it sets lower prices for them! It aimed, I venture to say, at bargain prices' encouraging people to amass an abundance of delicacies and become slaves to gluttony even when they have little means. 12. To be frank, I would call someone a wanton and a wastrel even if he served such feasts at no cost. So much more inclined is our age to every sort of self-restraint that no one of our contemporaries would even have heard tell of most of the items covered by Sulla's law as things familiar to everyone.

13. 'After Sulla's death Lepidus moved a law as con-

149 Cf. Gell. 2.24.7, where it is said that spending 100 *asses* was permitted on certain exceptional days, 200 on weddings, 30 on all other days (the allowance of meat and fish is not specified).

150 Prob. in 81, when most of his legislative program was put through (*MRR* 2:75). Cf. Gell. 2.24.11.

bariam (Cato enim sumptuarias leges "cibarias" appellat). Dein paucis interiectis annis alia lex pervenit ad populum ferente Antio Restione. quam legem quamvis esset optima, obstinatio tamen luxuriae et vitiorum firma concordia nullo abrogante irritam fecit. illud tamen memorabile de Restione latore ipsius legis fertur, eum quoad vixit foris postea non cenasse[109] ne testis fieret contemptae legis quam ipse bono publico pertulisset.

14. 'His legibus adnumerarem edictum de sumptibus ab Antonio propositum, qui postea triumvir fuit, ni indignum crederem inter cohibentes sumptum Antonio locum facere, cuius expensae in cenam solitae conferri sola unionis a Cleopatra uxore consumpti aestimatione superatae sunt. 15. nam cum Antonius quicquid mari aut terra aut etiam caelo gigneretur ad satiandam ingluviem suam natum existimans faucibus ac dentibus suis subderet eaque re captus de Romano imperio facere vellet Aegyptium regnum, Cleopatra uxor, quae vinci a Romanis nec

[109] cenasse P: recen- ω

---

[151] Cf. Gell. 2.24.12. M. Aemilius Lepidus (cos. 78 BCE) or Mamercus Aemilius Lepidus Livianus (cos. 77 BCE) has been proposed as the author, though it scarcely suits at least the former's activities. Note, too, that Gellius' account is expressly chronological down to §11, whereas his way of citing this law—'Besides these laws we also find a *lex Aemilia*'—suggests that he did not know how it fit chronologically; "after Sulla's death" might be a mere inference on M.'s part or his source's (Sammonicus?). Pliny *Natural History* 8.223 cites a sumptuary law passed by M. Aemilius Scaurus as consul in 115 BCE (identified with the law cited by Gell. at *MRR* 1:531). [152] 68 BCE, if Antius Restio = the C. Antius who was tribune that year (*MRR* 2:139; the name

sul,[151] calling it a "rations" law (Cato, in fact, gives that name to sumptuary laws [fr. 143 *ORF*²]). Then after a few years Antius Restio brought another law before the people[152]—an excellent law, yet rendered null and void, not because it was formally repealed, but because luxury was firmly planted and the vices were united in an unshakable alliance. Still, one memorable thing is recalled about Restio, the law's mover: afterwards, and for as long as he lived, he never dined out, lest he witness the disdain heaped on the law that he himself had carried for the common good.

14. 'I would put these laws in the same category as the edict on expenditures issued by the Antony who was later a triumvir,[153] if I thought it fit to make room for Antony among those who tried to limit expenditures, when the sums he used to spend on dinner were exceeded only by the value of the pearl downed by his wife Cleopatra. 15. For Antony used to make all the produce of land, sea, and air subject to his teeth and gullet, in the belief that satisfying his gluttony was its natural purpose, and as gluttony's captive he wanted to transform Rome's dominion into the kingdom of Egypt.[154] His wife Cleopatra, who dis-

appears as *C. Anti* . . . in *CIL* 1².2.744); cf. also 1.11.19n., on the Antius Restio proscribed by the triumvirs in 43 BCE. Gell. records the *lex Antia* (2.24.13), but without the detail given here, and a *lex Iulia* of Augustus (2.24.14, cf. Suet. *Aug.* 34.1) that M. omits.

153 Antony could have issued such an edict only as consul in 44, but it is otherwise unattested.

154 §§15–18 are based, directly or indirectly, on Pliny *Natural History* 9.119–21; Pliny omits the invidious touch of calling Cleopatra Antony's "wife" (*uxor*), calling her a "whore" (*meretrix*) instead.

luxuria dignaretur, sponsione provocavit insumere se posse in unam cenam sestertium centies. 16. id mirum Antonio visum, nec moratus sponsione contendit, dignus sculna Munatio Planco, qui tam honesti certaminis arbiter electus est. altera die Cleopatra pertemptans Antonium pollucibilem sane cenam paravit, sed quam non miraretur Antonius quippe qui omnia quae apponebantur ex cotidianis opibus agnosceret. 17. tunc regina adridens fialam poposcit, cui aceti non nihil acris infudit, atque illuc unionem demptum ex aure altera festinabunda demisit eumque mature dissolutum, uti natura est eius lapidis, absorbuit. et quamvis eo facto sponsione vicisset, quippe cum ipsa margarita centies sestertium sine contentione evaluisset, manum tamen et ad alterius unionem auris[110] similiter admovit, nisi Munatius Plancus iudex severissimus superatum Antonium mature pronuntiasset. 18. ipse autem unio cuius fuerit magnitudinis inde colligi poterit, quod qui superfuit postea victa regina et capta Aegypto Romam delatus dissectusque est et factae ex una margarita duae impositaeque simulacro Veneris ut monstruosae magnitudinis in templo quod Pantheum dicitur.'

18 Adhuc dicente Rufio secundae mensae inlata bellaria novo sermoni principium dederunt. Symmachus enim attrectans manu nuces, 'vellem,' inquit 'ex te audire, Servi, tanta nucibus nomina quae causa vel origo variaverit aut unde, tot mala cum hac una appellatione vocitentur, fiunt

[110] unionem auris *Jan post Ioannem Saresberiensem* (auris unionem *ed. Lugd. Bat. 1670*): -nis -rem *ω*

---

[155] Built by Agrippa between 27 and 25 BCE, a few years after Antony and Cleopatra's defeat, the Pantheon had a sanctuary

dained being second to the Romans even in luxury, wagered that she could spend 10,000,000 sesterces on a single dinner. 16. Astounded, Antony immediately accepted the wager, finding a worthy arbitrator in Munatius Plancus, who was selected to judge this oh-so-honorable contest. The next day Cleopatra, teasing Antony, prepared a dinner that was quite sumptuous, though not such as to boggle him, since he recognized that all the dishes served were merely daily fare. 17. Then, with a smile, the queen called for a shallow dish, into which she poured some strong vinegar and, quickly snatching a pearl from one ear, dropped it in the dish: when the pearl rapidly dissolved, as it is the gem's nature to do, she drank it down. And though she had thereby won the wager, seeing that the pearl by itself was indisputably worth 10,000,000 sesterces, she reached for the pearl on the other ear—but Munatius Plancus, a very exact judge, quickly declared Antony defeated. 18. As for the pearl, its great size can be gauged from the fact that after the queen was defeated and Egypt captured, the surviving twin was brought to Rome and cut in two, with the halves then set in the colossal statue of Venus in the temple called the Pantheon.'[155]

While Rufius was still speaking dessert was served,[156] 18
prompting a new topic of conversation. Running his hand over the nuts, Symmachus said, 'Servius, I would have liked to hear you explain what cause or source gave such a wide variety of names to nuts, or why it is that fleshy fruits are covered by the single label *malum* yet have so

containing statues of Mars, Venus, and the deified Julius Caesar (*LTUR* 5: 280–85, Coarelli 2007, 286–89).

156 Evening of the second day, 18 December.

tamen seorsum diversa tam vocabulo quam sapore. ac prius de nucibus absolvas volo quae tibi memoria crebrae lectionis occurrunt.' 2. et Servius: 'nux ista iuglans secundum non nullorum opinionem a iuvando et a glande dicta existimatur. Gavius[111] vero Bassus in libro de significatione verborum hoc refert:

> 3. iuglans arbor proinde dicta est ac "Iovis glans." nam quia id arboris genus nuces habet quae sunt suaviore sapore quam glans est, hunc fructum antiqui illi, qui egregium glandique similem ipsamque arborem deo dignam existimabant, "Iovis glandem" appellaverunt, quae nunc litteris interlisis iuglans nominatur.

4. Cloatius autem Verus in libro a Graecis tractorum ita memorat:

> iuglans—d praetermissum est—quasi "diuglans" id est Διὸς βάλανος, sicut Theophrastus ait: "ἴδια δὲ τῶν ὀρεινῶν[112] ἃ ἐν τοῖς πεδίοις οὐ φύεται, . . . τερέβινθος πρῖνος φιλύρη[113] ἀφάρκη καρύα, ἣ καὶ[114] Διὸς βάλανος." hanc Graeci etiam "basilicam" vocant.

5. 'Nux haec Abellana seu Praenestina, quae est eadem, ex arbore est quae dicitur "corylus," de qua Vergilius dicit "corylum sere." est autem natio hominum iuxta agrum

[111] Gavius *ed. Paris. 1585*: gabius ω

[112] ὀρεινῶν (ΟΡΙΝΩΝ ω)] τὰ τοιάδε ὀρεινῶν *Theoph.*

[113] τερέβινθος πρῖνος φιλύρη] τέρμινθος ἐρινεὸς φιλύκη *Theoph.* (πρῖνος *post* διοσβάλανος)

[114] ἣ καὶ *om. Theoph.*

many different flavors and specific names. And if you'd be so kind, treat the nuts first, drawing on what you recall from your constant study.' 2. 'That walnut [*iuglans*] you've got there,' Servius replied, 'derives its name from two words, "to help" [*iuvare*] and "acorn" [*glans*], according to some people. But Gavius Bassus, in his book *On the Meaning of Words* says (fr. 5 *GRF* 1:489),

> 3. The walnut tree is so called from "Jupiter's acorn" [*Iovis glans*]: because that species of tree has nuts that taste less bitter than the acorn, the ancients named it "Jupiter's acorn," judging the nut to be similar to an acorn and yet exceptional, and judging the tree itself worthy of the god. It's now called *iuglans* because the middle letters have been squeezed out.[157]

4. However, Cloatius Verus, in his book *Words Borrowed from Greek*, say the following (fr. 5 *GRF* 1:469):

> The walnut [*iuglans*] had an initial *d*, *diuglans*, that is to say, *Dios balanos* ["Zeus' acorn"], as Theophrastus says (*Hist. pl.* 3.3.1): "The terebinth, holm oak, lime, hybrid arbutus, and walnut—also known as Zeus' acorn—are peculiar to the mountains and do not grow on the plains." The Greeks also call this the "royal" nut.

5. 'This nut here, the Abellan—or Praenestine, it's the same thing—comes from the tree called the "hazel"; compare Virgil's phrase, "Plant hazel" (*G.* 2.299). There is,

[157] Cf. Varro *Latin Language* 5.102, Pliny *Natural History* 15.91, Serv. on E. 8.29.

Praenestinum qui Carsitani vocantur *ἀπὸ τῶν καρύων*, cuius rei meminit Varro in logistorico qui inscribitur Marius de fortuna: inde scilicet Praenestinae nuces. 6. est et illud apud Naevium in fabula Hariolo:

—quis heri apud te?—Praenestini et Lanuvini
hospites.
—suopte utrosque decuit acceptos cibo,
alteris inanem vulvam madidam[115] dari,
alteris nuces in proclivi profundier.[116]

hanc autem nucem Graeci "Ponticam" vocant, dum una quaeque natio indit huic nuci nomen ex loco in quo nascitur copiosior.

7. 'Nux castanea, de qua Vergilius "castaneasque nuces," vocatur et "Heracleotica." nam vir doctus Oppius in libro quem fecit de silvestribus arboribus sic ait:

Heracleotica haec nux, quam quidam "castaneam" nominant, itemque Pontica nux atque etiam quae dicuntur "basilicae iuglandes," germina atque flores agunt similiter isdem temporibus quibus Graecae nuces.

8. 'Nunc dicendum est quae sit Graeca nux.' ac simul hoc dicens amygdalam de lance tulit et ostendit. 'nux Graeca haec est quae et "amygdale" dicitur: sed et "Tha-

[115] vulvam (bulbam *codd.*) madidam] b. madidantem *Salmasius*, v. madidatam *Schrijver*, volvulam (bulbulam *iam Geppert*) madidam *Ribbeck*

[116] profundier *Schrijver*: profundere *ω*

moreover, a tribe of people near the territory of Praeneste called the Carsitani, from the Greek *karua* ["hazel"], mentioned by Varro in his *Marius on Fortune* (*Logist*. fr. 44): that, of course, is how they come to be known as Praenestine nuts. 6. Note also the following from Naevius' play *The Soothsayer* (21–24 *SRPF*³ 2:10):

—Who visited you yesterday?—Guests from
    Praeneste and Lanuvinum.
—'Twas fitting to entertain them with their native
    food,
  the one set given empty sow's womb, boiled,
  the other, nuts poured out down a hill.[158]

The Greeks call this the "Pontic" nut, and each race gives it a name from the region where it grows with exceptional abundance.[159]

7. 'The chestnut—compare Virgil's phrase (*E*. 2.52) "and chestnuts"—is also called the "nut of Heraclea": the scholar Oppius, in his book *On Woodland Trees*, says (fr. 1 *SRRR* 1:70–71),

> This nut of Heraclea, which some call the "chestnut," and similarly the "Pontic nut," and those called the "royal walnut," bud and blossom alike, at the same time as the Greek nuts.

8. 'Now I should talk about the Greek nut,' he said, at the same time taking an almond from the tray and showing it around. 'The Greek nut is the one also called the "al-

[158] The great temple of Fortune at Praeneste sat atop a large hill. [159] Cf. Pliny *Natural History* 15.88.

sia" eadem nux vocatur. testis est Cloatius in ordinatorum Graecorum libro quarto, cum sic ait: "nux Graeca amygdale." Atta vero in Supplicatione, "nucem Thasiam,"[117] inquit,

favumque[118] adde quantum libet.

9. 'Nucem molluscam licet hiemis nobis tempus invideat, tamen quia de nucibus loquimur, indictam non relinquemus. Plautus in Calceolo sic eius meminit:

molluscam nucem
super eius dixit impendere tegulas.

10. ecce Plautus nominat quidem sed quae sit nux mollusca non exprimit. est autem "Persicum" quod vulgo vocatur et mollusca nux dicitur scilicet quod ceteris omnibus nucibus mollior sit. 11. huius rei idoneus adsertor est Sueius, vir longe doctissimus, in idyllio quod inscribitur Moretum. nam cum loquitur de hortulano faciente moretum, inter cetera quae eo mittit et hoc pomum mitti ait his verbis:

12. admiscet †vaca basilicis†[119] haec nunc partim
partim Persica, quod nomen sic denique fertur
propterea quod qui quondam cum rege potenti,
nomine Alexandro Magno, fera proelia bello
in Persas tetulere, suo post inde reventu
hoc genus arboris in praelatis finibus Grais

117 Thasiam *Ribbeck*: Graecam ω
118 favumque E: fabumque ω
119 admisce tuaca basilicis (*vel* tua caba silicis)] admiscet bacam, basilica *Buechner, alii alia*

160 Cf. Pliny *Natural History* 15.89, Serv. on *E.* 2.52, *G.* 1.187.

mond"; but it's called the "nut of Thasos" too. Cloatius provides evidence in Book 4 of his *Things Greek Arranged in Alphabetical Order*, when he says (fr. 8 *GRF* 1:471), "The Greek nut is the almond";[160] moreover, in his play *Entreaty* Atta says (15–16 *SRPF*[3] 2:191),

> add as much Thasian nut and honeycomb as you'd
> like.

9. 'Though the winter begrudges our enjoying the
*mollusca*, still—since we're talking about nuts—we'll not
let it go without comment. In his play *The Slipper* Plautus 9
mentions it (fr. 47 Goetz):

> He said the *mollusca*
> hangs over his roof tiles.

10. Here, you see, Plautus mentions it but doesn't give a clear idea what a *mollusca* is. It is, however, the sort of nut commonly called "Persian," the name *mollusca* plainly coming from the fact that its shell is softer [*mollior*] than that of all other nuts. 11. Sueius, far and away the most learned sort of fellow, provides suitable support for this view in his pastoral poem titled *Herbed Cheese Spread*, where he describes the gardener making this dish, saying that he adds in this fruit along with the other ingredients (fr. 1 *FPL*[3]):

> 12. Now he mixes in . . . in part,
> in part Persian, so called because
> the soldiers who once fought fierce battles
> with the mighty king named Alexander the Great
> during his war with Persia planted this sort of tree
> in the exalted land of the Greeks after their return,

disseruere, novos fructus mortalibus dantes.
mollusca haec nux est, ne quis forte inscius erret.

13. 'Nux terentina dicitur quae ita mollis est ut vix attrectata frangatur. de qua in libro Favorini sic reperitur: "item quod quidam Tarentinas oves vel nuces dicunt, quae sunt terentinae a 'tereno,'[120] quod est Sabinorum lingua molle, unde Terentios quoque dictos putat Varro ad Libonem primo." quam in culpam etiam Horatius potest videri incidere, qui ait et "molle Tarentum."

14. 'Nux pinea hos nobis qui adpositi sunt nucleos dedit. Plautus in Cistellaria:

qui e nuce nuculeos[121] esse vult frangit nucem.

19 'Et quia mala videmus admixta bellariis, post nuces de malorum generibus disserendum est. sunt de agri cultura scriptores qui nuces et mala sic dividunt, ut nuces dicant omne pomum quod foris duro tegatur et intus habeat quod esui est, malum vero quod foris habeat quod est esui et durum intus includat. secundum hanc definitionem Persicum, quod Sueius poeta superius inter nuces numerat, magis erit inter mala numerandum.

2. 'His praemissis malorum enumeranda sunt genera,

120 tereno $\beta_2$: tenero ω

121 nuculeos αςF (nuculeus M, nuculeum *Plaut.*): nucleos Gπδ (*deest* A)

---

161 *Satires* 2.4.34, where the phrase refers to the effeminacy of Tarentum's inhabitants.

162 A slip: the line cited is from the *Curculio* (55).

163 An apparent slip, confusing the *nux Persica* = *mollusca* mentioned by Sueius with the *malum Persicum* = peach.

giving mortal men new sources of enjoyment.
To leave no one in the dark: this nut is the *mollusca*.

13. 'The nut that's so soft it breaks when you've scarcely touched it is called "terentine." About this nut one finds the following in a book by Favorinus (test. 48): "Similarly, there's the fact that some people call sheep and nuts 'Tarentine' when they are properly 'terentine,' from *terenus*, the Sabine term for 'soft'; Varro, in his first book *To Libo*, expresses the view (fr. 231 *GRF* 1:263) that the Terentii are so called from the same term." Horace could seem to fall into the mistake noted by Favorinus when he speaks of "soft Tarentum," too.[161]

14. 'The pine-cone provided the pine-nuts that have been served to us: thus Plautus in his *Cistellaria*,[162]

the person who wants kernels from the cone starts
by breaking the cone.

'And since we see fleshy fruits [*mala*] intermingled with 19
the sweets, we should talk about their varieties, leaving nuts behind. There are agricultural writers who distinguish nuts and fleshy fruits by calling "nuts" any fruit [*pomum*] that's covered by something hard on the outside and has the edible part inside, whereas a fleshy fruit has the edible part outside and the hard part inside. According to this definition, what the poet Sueius counts among the nuts just above should rather be counted among the fleshy fruits.[163]

2. 'With that as prelude we should catalog the varieties of fleshy fruits, as Cloatius does carefully in Book 4 of his

quae Cloatius in ordinatorum Graecorum libro quarto ita diligenter enumerat:

> sunt autem genera malorum: Amerinum cotonium citreum coccymelum conditivum ἐπιμηλίς musteum Mattianum orbiculatum †ogratianum† praecox pannuceum Punicum Persicum Quiri‹ni›anum[122] prosivum rubrum Scaudianum silvestre struthium Scantianum tubur[123] Verianum.

3. vides Persicum a Cloatio inter mala numeratum, quod nomen originis suae tenuit, licet iam dudum nostri soli germen sit. quod autem ait idem Cloatius citreum, et ipsum Persicum malum est secundum Vergilium:

> . . . felicis mali, quo non praestantius[124] ullum,

et reliqua. 4. et ut nemo dubitet haec de citreo dixisse Vergilium, accipite quae Oppius in libro de silvestribus arboribus dicat: "citrea item[125] malus et Persica, altera generatur in Italia et in Media altera." et paulo post de citreo loquens ait:

> est autem odoratissimum, ex quo interiectum vesti tineas necat. fertur etiam venenis contrarium, quod tritum cum vino purgatione virium suarum bibentes servat. generantur autem in Perside omni tempore

122 Quirinianum (*cf. Caton. De agr. 7.3, Varr. RR 1.59.1*)] quirianum ω

123 tubur *dubitanter Jan* (*cf. Plin. NH 15.47, Martial. 13.42.1*): tibur ω

124 praestantius] praesentius *Verg.*

125 item *ed. Ven. 1513*: idem ω

*Things Greek Aranged in Alphabetical Order* (fr. 7 *GRF* 1:470):

> There are, moreover, the following varieties of fleshy fruits: Amerian, quince, citron, plum, the sort for preserves, pear, juicy quince, Mattian apple, round apple, . . . early-ripening, shriveled, pomegranate, peach, Quirinian, prosivum, red apple, Scaudian, woodland apple, sparrow-apple, Scantian, tubur, Verian.[164]

3. Notice that among the fleshy fruits Cloatius counts the "Persian fruit" [= peach], which has kept its original name, though it has long since been naturalized on our soil. But what Cloatius calls the citron is itself the "Persian fruit" according to Virgil (*G.* 2.127*):

> . . . of the auspicious fruit, which none surpasses,

and so forth. 4. Lest anyone doubt that Virgil was referring to the citron, here's what Oppius says in his book *On Woodland Trees* (fr. 2–3 *SRRR* 1:71–72): "Similarly, the citron tree is also the tree of the Persian fruit, the former being grown in Italy, the latter in the land of the Medes." And soon after, when he's talking about the citron, he says:

> Moreover, it has a very strong scent, which kills moth larvae if you place it among your garments. It is also said to be an antidote to poisons, saving those who drink it as a purgative ground up in wine. Citrons are grown in Persia in every season: while some

164 Cf. Cato *On Agriculture* 7.3, Col. 5.10.19–20, Pliny *Natural History* 15.37–52.

mala citrea. alia enim praecarpuntur, alia interim maturescunt.

5. vides hic et citreum nominari et omnia signa poni quae de eo Vergilius dixit, licet nomen citrei ille non dixerit. nam et Homerus qui citreum "*θύον*" appellat, ostendit esse odoratum pomum:

> *θύον δ' ἀπὸ καλὸν*[126] *ὀδώδει.*

et quod ait Oppius inter vestem poni citreum, idem significat et Homerus cum dicit,

> *εἵματα δ'*[127] *ἀμφιέσασα θυώδεα σιγαλόεντα.*[128]

hinc et Naevius poeta in bello Punico ait "citrosam vestem."

6. 'Pira haec quae videmus varietas nominum numerosa discernit. nam idem Cloatius sic eorum vocabula describit:

> Anicianum, cucurbitivum, cirritum, cervisca, calculosum, Crustuminum, decimanum, Graeculum, Lollianum, Lanuvinum, laureum, Lateresianum, myrapium, Milesium murteum,[129] Naevianum, orbiculatum, Praecianum, rubile, Signinum, Tullianum, Titianum, thymosum, Turranianum praecox, volaemum, mespilum serum, sementivum serum, Sextilianum serum, Tarentinum serum, Valerianum serum.

[126] *δ' ἀπὸ καλὸν*] *τ' ἀνὰ νῆσον Hom.*
[127] *δ'*] *τ' Hom.*
[128] *σιγαλόεντα* (*cf. Il.* 22.154, *Od.* 6.26)] *καὶ λούσασα Hom.*
[129] musteum *ed. Lugd. Bat. 1597 coll. Plin. NH 15.56*

are picked first, the others are meanwhile allowed to ripen.

5. Here you see the fruit being called a citron and all the distinctive markers that Virgil mentioned in connection with it are included, thought Virgil did not use the name "citron." Homer too, who called the citron a *thyon*, shows that it is a scented fruit (*Od.* 5.60):

> it gives off the fair scent of citron.[165]

And the same point that Oppius makes about putting a citron in your garments is made by Homer, too, when he says (*Od.* 5.264),

> . . . put on the glossy, citron-scented garments.

Hence, too, the poet Naevius uses the phrase "citron-scented garment" in his *Punic War* (fr. 19 *FPL*$^3$).

6. 'Many different names are used to distinguish the kinds of pears that we find. Cloatius again catalogs their names (fr. 10 *GRF* 1:471):

> Anician, gourd-pear, bearded, cerviscan, pebbled, Crustumine, outsized, little Greek, Lollian, Lanuvian, laurel, Lateresian, scented, Milesian, myrtle, Naevian, round, Praecian, rubile, Signian, Tullian, Titian, thyme-scented, early Turranian, volaemum, late medlar, late seed-time, late Sextilian, late Tarentine, late Valerian.[166]

[165] Gk. *thyon* denotes the wood, not the fruit, of the citron.
[166] Cf. Cato *On Agriculture* 7.4, Col. 5.10.18, Pliny *Natural History* 15.53–58.

20 'Admonent nos et fici aridae ut enumeremus genera ficorum, eodem Cloatio nos de his ut de aliis instruente. sic enim diversas ficos diligentiae suae more dinumerat:

> Africa albula harundinea asinastra, atra, palusca, Augusta, bifera, Carica, Chal<ci>dica[130] alba nigra, Chia alba nigra, Calpurniana alba nigra, cucurbitiva, duricoria, Herculanea, Liviana, Lydia, leptolydia,[131] Marsica, Numidica pulla, Pompeiana praecox, Tellana atra.

2. sciendum quod ficus alba ex felicibus sit arboribus, contra nigra ex infelicibus. docent nos utrumque pontifices. ait enim Veranius de verbis pontificalibus: "felices arbores putantur esse quercus, aesculus, ilex, suberies,[132] fagus, corylus, sorbus, ficus alba, pirus, malus, vitis, prunus, cornus, lotus." 3. Tarquitius[133] autem Priscus in ostentario arborario sic ait:

> arbores quae inferum deorum avertentiumque in tutela sunt, eas infelices nominant: alaternum,[134] <virgam> sanguine<a>m,[135] filicem, ficum atram quaeque bacam nigram nigrosque fructus ferunt, itemque aquifolium,[136] pirum silvaticum, rus-

[130] Chalcidica *Salmasius Exercit. Plin. p. 658*: caldica ω

[131] Lydia, leptolydia *Meurs, ed. Lugd. Bat. 1597*: ludia leptoludia ω

[132] suberies *Jan*: suberius α, superus β

[133] Tarquitius *ed. Lugd. Bat. 1597*: Tarquinius ω

[134] alaternum *Salamsius Exercit. Plin. p. 430* (*cf. iam Turneb. Advers.18.4*): alternum ω

[135] virgam sanguineam *conieci* (*cf. Plin. 24.43*): sanguinem ω

[136] aquifolium *Salmasius Exercit. Plin. p. 191* (*cf. iam Turneb. loc. cit.*): acri- ω

'The dried figs before us remind me to list the kinds of figs, too, relying on Cloatius here as in the other cases. Here's his characteristically careful catalog of different sorts of figs (fr. 9 ibid.): 20

> African, white, reed-fig, asinastra, black, marsh, Augustan, twice-yielding, Carian, white and black Chalcidic, white and black Calpurnian, gourd-fig, tough-skinned, Herculanean, Livian, Lydian, slender Lydian, Marsian, dark Numidian, early Pompeian, black Tellan.[167]

2. You should realize that white figs are produced by trees of good omen, black figs, by contrast, by ill-omened trees. The two types are distinguished for us by the pontiffs: thus Veranius says, concerning the words of the pontiffs (fr. 3 *GRF* 1:431 = fr. 1 *IAH* 2.1:6 = fr. 5 *IAR*[6]), "Among trees of good omen are reckoned the oak, durmast, holm oak, cork oak, beech, hazel, service tree, white fig, pear, apple, vine, plum, cornel, and nettle." 3. Tarquitius Priscus, however, in his *Portents Derived from Trees*, says (fr. 6),

> They call "ill-omened" the trees that are under the protection of the gods of the underworld and apotropaic powers: buckthorn, red cornel, fern, black fig, those that bear a black berry and black fruit, similarly holly, woodland pear, butcher's-

[167] Cf. Cato *On Agriculture* 8, Col. 5.10.10, Pliny *Natural History* 15.68–71.

cum,[137] rubum sentesque quibus portenta prodigiaque mala comburi iubere oportet.

4. quid quod ficum tamquam non pomum secerni a pomis apud idoneos reperimus? Afranius in Sella:[138]

pomum holus ficum uvam.

sed et Cicero oeconomicon libro tertio: "neque serit vitem neque quae[139] sata est diligenter colit: oleum ficos poma non habet." 5. nec hoc ignorandum est, ficum solam ex omnibus arboribus non florere. [lacti proprie ficorum dicitur.][140] "grossi" appellantur fici quae non maturescunt. hos Graeci dicunt ὀλύνθους. Mattius:

in milibus tot [ficorum][141] non videbitis grossum,

et paulo post ait:

sumas ab alio lacte diffluos grossos.

et Postumius Albinus annali primo de Bruto: "ea causa sese stultum brutumque faciebat, grosullos ex melle edebat."

6. 'Olearum genera haec enumerantur: Africana, albiceris,[142] Aquilia, Alexandrina, Aegyptia Culminea, conditi-

137 ruscum *ed. Paris. 1585, Salamasius ibid.*: pruscum ω

138 Sella *ed. Paris. 1585*: selia ω

139 quae E²: quaeque ω

140 lacti . . . dicitur *seclusi*

141 ficorum *secl. Bothe*

142 albiceris *dubitanter Jan, coll. Caton. Agr. 6.1, Varr. R.R. 1.24.1*: albigerus ω

> broom, briar, and the brambles with which one should order evil portents and prodigies to be burnt.

4. What are we to make of the fact that we find suitable authors distinguishing the fig from fruit [*pomum*], as though it were not one of them? Thus Afranius in his *Sella* (300 *SRPF*$^3$ 2:241):

> fruit, vegetable, fig, grape.

But Cicero too, in Book 3 of his *On Household Management*, says (fr. 18), "He neither plants a vine nor carefully tends the one that has been planted: he has no olive oil, figs, fruit." 5. One should also be aware that the fig is the only tree that does not bloom. Figs that do not ripen are called *grossi*; the Greeks call them *olynthoi*. Mattius says (fr. 14–15 *FPL*$^3$):

> in so many thousands you'll not see not one unripe [*grossus*],

and a little later,

> you could get from another unripe figs [*grossi*] dripping with milky juice.

Postumius Albinus, too, in Book 1 of his *Annals*, says of Brutus (no. 812 fr. 3 *FGrH* = fr. 4 Ch.), "that is why he took on the character of a doltish fool and was eating little unripe figs [*grossuli*] with honey."

6. 'Here's a catalog of olive varieties:[168] African, yellow, Aquilian, Alexandrian, Egyptian, Culminian, the sort for

[168] Cf. Cato *On Agriculture* 6.1–2, Varro *On Agriculture* 1.24, 60, Col. 5.8.3–4, Pliny *Natural History* 15.13–47.

va, Liciniana, orchas, oleaster, pausia, phaulia, radius, Sallentina, Sergiana, termitea,[143] 7. sicut uvarum ista sunt genera: Aminea—scilicet a regione, nam Aminei fuerunt ubi nunc Falernum est—asinusca atrusca, albuelis,[144] abena,[145] apiana, Apicia, bumamma—aut ut Graeci dicunt *βούμασθος*—duracina, labrusca, melampsithia, Maronia Mareotis, Nomentana,[146] precia, pramnia, psithia, pilleolata, Rhodia, stephanitis, venucula, variola lagea.' 8. inter haec Praetextatus: 'velim Servium nostrum diutius audire, sed hora nos quietis admonet ut exorto iubare eloquio Symmachi domi suae fruamur.' atque ita facta discessio est.[147]

143 termitea (*cf. Gratt. 447, Col.* 7.8.6)] termutia *ω*

144 albuelis *dubitanter Jan, coll. Col. 3.2.24, Plin. NH 14.31*: albiverus *ω*

145 albena *ed. Ven.1513*

146 Nomentana *Meurs*: numentana *ω*

147 *post* est *nihil subscriptum in* NGO (*spat. 1 lin. relict. in* N, *desinit* O), EXPLICIT LIBER II SATVRNALIORVM INCIPIT TERTIVS IN LAVDE VIRGILII P, MACROBII THEODOSII (THEOSII L) VIRI CONVIVIORVM SECVNDI EXPLICIT ML, EXPLICIT V, EXPLICIT LIBER E, MACROBII THEODOSII VIR INLVSTRIS CONVIVIORVM SECVNDI DIEI EXPLICIT $\beta_2$ (*deest* A)

preserving, Licinian, testicle-shaped, wild, pausia, coarse, ray, Sallentine, Sergian, termitea. 7. Similarly, one of grape varieties:[169] Aminean—named, of course, from the region where the Aminei lived, now the Falernian territory—asinusca, atrusca, albuelis, abena,[170] apiana, Apician, udder-shaped (or as the Greeks say, *boumasthos*), hard-berry, wild, black-raisin, Maronian, Mareotic, Nomentan, precia, pramnia, psithia, pilleolata, Rhodian, wreath-vine, venucula, variola, hare-grape.' 8. As Servius spoke Praetextatus said, 'I'd like to listen longer to our friend Servius, but the hour puts us in mind of sleep, so that "with the first light risen" (cf. *A.* 4.130) we may enjoy Symmachus' holding forth at his own house.' And with that they departed.

169 Cf. Cato *On Agriculture* 6.4–7.2, Varro *On Agriculture* 1.25, 59, Col. 3.2, Pliny *Natural History* 14.15–75.

170 The name of this variety—whether the archetype's *abena* or the *albena* of the Venetian edition of 1513—is not otherwise attested.

# <LIBER QVARTVS>[1]

1 . . . :

. . . <nec magis incepto vultum>[2] sermone movetur,
quam si dura silex aut stet Marpesia cautes.
tandem corripuit sese atque inimica refugit.

item pathos est et in hoc versu:

obstupui steteruntque comae et vox faucibus haesit.

2. 'Sed et tota Daretis fatigatio habitu depingitur:

[1] *add. edd., inscript. caret* ω
[2] *haec dumtaxat Macrob. profecto inclusit.*

---

[1] Morning of the third day, 19 December, in the house of Symmachus, whose discourse on Virgil the rhetorician has been lost: the speaker, not expressly identified in the surviving portion of Book 4, is probably Eusebius, expounding on Virgil the orator (cf. Introd. §4 and 4.6.24n.).

[2] The poor remnant of the discussion preserved here is wholly concerned with the rhetorical means used to represent or stir the emotions (Gk. *pathê*, Lat. *adfectus*), which received much attention in the rhetorical tradition: see esp. Arist. *Rhet.* 2.2–11 1378a30–1388b30, Cic. *On Invention* 1.98–109, *On the Orator* 2.185–211, Quint. 6.1–2. After surveying the use of demeanor

# <BOOK FOUR>[1]

< . . . > (*A.* 6.470–72): 1

> . . . her look no more changed by what he had begun to say
> than if a hard flint stone should stand there, or a crag on Mt. Marpessos.
> At last she tore herself away and fled, now his enemy.

Similarly, there is emotion[2] expressed in this verse too (*A.* 2.774):

> I gaped, my hair stood on end, my voice caught in my throat.

2. 'Furthermore, Dares' demeanor also puts his utter exhaustion before our eyes (*A.* 5. 468–70):

(*habitus*) and "tenor of speech" to represent various emotions (4.1 and 4.2, respectively), M. shifts to resources for stirring emotions, esp. pity and indignation: these include personal condition (4.3, *habitus* again: age, infirmity, fortune, etc.); the ethically inflected causes of actions or states of affairs (4.4.1–11); manner and means (4.4.12–18); or some combination of these (4.4.19–22). A different but complementary set of categories is used starting at 4.5.1(n.); cf. also 4.2.6n.

ast illum fidi aequales genua aegra trahentem
quassantemque[3] utroque caput crassumque cruorem
ore eiectantem . . . .

sociorum quoque eius trepidationem breviter ostendit:

. . . galeamque ensemque vocati
accipiunt,

quasi non sponte accepturi munus quod erat damnum verecundiae. ex eodem genere est illud:

. . . totoque loquentis[4] ab ore
scintillae absistunt, oculis micat acribus ignis.

3. 'Est et in descriptione languoris habitus, ut est tota descriptio pestilentiae apud Thucydiden et:

labitur infelix studiorum atque immemor herbae
victor equus,

et:

. . . demissae aures, incertus ibidem
sudor et ille quidem morituris frigidus . . .

4. 'Est inter pathe et pudor ut circa Deiphobum,

[3] quassantemque (*cf. A. 7.292, 12.894*)] iactantemque *Verg.*
[4] loquentis (*cf. A. 7.118, Tib.*)] ardentis *Verg.*

---

[3] So far from being a "consolation," as intended (*A.* 5.367), the helmet and sword would only remind Dares of his defeat and loss of face: cf. Deiphobus' shame at his mutilation (§4 below), which entailed a loss of face in both the literal and the figurative senses of the phrase.

[4] Cf. esp. Thuc. 2.51.4–6.

But his loyal comrades [take him away], his knees
weak, trailing on the ground,
as his head wobbles from side to side and he spits up
thick gore . . . .

The poet also economically portrays his comrades' concern (*A.* 5.471–72*):

. . . when summoned they take his helmet
and his sword,

as though they would not on their own take a gift that detracted from his honor.[3] The same sort of thing is found in the following (*A.* 12.101–2†):

. . . his whole countenance gave off sparks
as he spoke, fire gleamed in his sharp glance.

3. 'Demeanor is also crucial in describing enfeeblement, as we find in Thucydides' whole description of the plague[4] and also (*G.* 3.498–99)

Once a winner, the luckless horse collapses, without
thought of his training
and his pasturage

and (*G.* 3.500–1)

. . . his ears drooped, a fitful sweat at once
follows,
cold and clammy indeed when a presage of death. . . .

4. 'The emotions also include shame, as in the case of Deiphobus (*A.* 6.498–99*),

. . . pavitantem et[5] dira tegentem
supplicia . . .

et luctus habitu proditur ut in Euryali matre:

expulsi[6] manibus radii revolutaque pensa;
evolat infelix,

et Latinus, quia miratur,

. . . defixa . . .
obtutu tenet ora,

et Venus quia rogatura est,

tristior et lacrimis oculos suffusa nitentes . . . ,

et Sibylla quia insanit,

. . . subito non vultus, non color unus,
non comptae mansere comae.

2 'Nunc videamus pathos quo tenore orationis exprimitur. ac primum quaeramus quid de tali oratione rhetorica arte praecipitur. oportet enim ut oratio pathetica aut ad indignationem aut ad misericordiam dirigatur, quae a Graecis *οἶκτος καὶ δείνωσις* appellantur. horum alterum accusatori necessarium est, alterum reo.

5 et (*codd. plerique Verg., Tib., Serv. ad Aen. 1.356*)] ac *codd.* MP *Verg., edd. nonnull.*
6 expulsi] excussi *Verg.*

---

5 The line that specifies the punishment, including loss of ears and nose (*A.* 6.497), is quoted at 4.2.8 below.

> . . . trembling and covering his loathsome
> punishment. . . .[5]

Demeanor also betrays grief, as in the case of Euryalus' mother (*A.* 9.476–77):

> the shuttle shot from her hands, the wool tumbled to
> the ground;
> unhappy, she hastens off . . . ,

and Latinus, in wonder (*A.* 7.249–50),

> holds his features
> fixed in a steady gaze . . . ,

and Venus, on the verge of making a request (*A.* 1.228),

> quite subdued, her gleaming eyes brimming with
> tears . . . ,

and Sibyl, out of her mind (*A.* 6.47–48),

> . . . all at once her expression and complexion
> change,
> her artfully arranged hair comes undone.

'Now let's see how the tenor of one's speech makes one's emotions clear, starting with the textbook line on such speech: emotional speech must be aimed at producing either indignation or pity (in Greek, *deinôsis* and *oiktos*, respectively),[6] the former relied on by the prosecution, the latter by the defendant. 2

[6] On the rousing of indignation (*indignatio/amplificatio*) and pity (*conquestio/(com)miseratio*) cf. Lausberg §§438–39.

2. 'Et necesse est initium abruptum habeat, quoniam satis indignantibus leniter incipere non convenit. ideo apud Vergilium Iuno sic incipit:

> . . . quid me alta silentia cogis
> rumpere?

et alibi:

> . . . mene incepto desistere victam?

et alibi:

> heu stirpem invisam et fatis contraria nostris
> fata Phrygum . . .

et Dido:

> "moriemur inultae,
> sed moriamur," ait . . .

et eadem:

> "pro Iuppiter! ibit
> hic . . . ?," ait,

et Priamus:

> "at tibi pro scelere," exclamat, "pro talibus ausis . . . "

3. nec initium solum tale esse debet, sed omnis si fieri potest oratio videri pathetica et brevibus sententiis et crebris figurarum mutationibus debet velut inter aestus ira-

2. 'Indignation must begin to be expressed without preamble, since a slow and gradual start is not appropriate for those experiencing the emotion fully. That is why Virgil's Juno begins as follows (*A.* 10.63–64):

> . . . why do you force me to shatter my deep
> silence?

and elsewhere (*A.* 1.37),

> . . . am *I* to stand down from what I've begun,
> beaten?

and elsewhere (*A.* 7.293–94),

> Ah, that hated race, and the Phrygians' fates
> dead set against my own. . . .

and Dido (*A.* 4.659–60),

> "I will die unavenged,"
> she said, "but let me die. . . ."

and again (*A.* 4.590–91*),

> "By god!," she said,
> will he just leave . . . ?,"

and Priam (*A.* 2.535),

> "But for you," he cries out, "in return for your crime
> and brazen deeds. . . ."

3. Not only should the speech start that way, but the whole of it should (if possible) appear the product of strong emotion, with the thought expressed in a clipped fashion with frequent shifts in the figures used, as though tossed by

cundiae fluctuare. 4. una ergo nobis Vergiliana oratio pro exemplo sit:

Heu stirpem invisam . . .

initium ab ecphonesi, deinde sequuntur breves interrogatiunculae:

. . . num Sigeis occumbere campis
num capti potuere capi? num incensa cremavit
Troia viros?

deinde sequitur hyperbole:

. . . medias acies mediosque per ignes
invenere viam . . .

deinde ironia:

. . . at credo mea numina tandem
fessa iacent, odiis aut exsaturata quievi.

5. deinde ausus suos inefficaces queritur:

. . . per undas
ausa sequi et profugis toto me opponere ponto.

secunda post haec hyperbole:

absumptae in Teucros vires caelique marisque.

---

[7] The analysis, which extends through §8 and concentrates esp. on figures of thought (e.g., irony, hyperbole: cf. 4.6.10ff.), is a relatively uncommon example of ancient Virgilian criticism, in that it is not focused on the isolated word or line, in the manner of the Servian commentaries, but considers a substantial block of verse as a whole; cf. Tiberius Claudius Donatus' rhetorical paraphrase of the same passage, 2:47–51.

seething waves of anger. 4. Let's take, then, a single speech of Virgil's as an example (*A.* 7.293):[7]

> Ah, that hated race . . . ,

starting with an exclamation, then two short questions follow (*A.* 7.294–96),

> . . . Couldn't they fall on the fields of Sigeum,
> couldn't they stay captive once captured? Couldn't Troy in flames
> have consumed her heroes?

Then an overstatement follows (*A.* 7.296–97),

> . . . through the midst of battle and the midst of the flames
> they found a way. . . .,

then irony (*A.* 7.297–98),

> . . . No doubt my godhead at last lies prostrate,
> exhausted, no doubt I've found peace, my hatred slaked.

5. Then she complains that her own bold moves were foiled (*A.* 7.299–300):

> . . . over the waves I dared pursue them
> and put myself in the refugees' way all across the sea.

After this, another overstatement (*A.* 7.301),

> The resources of sky and sea spent against the Trojans,

inde dispersae querelae:

> quid Syrtes aut Scylla mihi, quid vasta Charybdis
> profuit?

6. iungitur deinde argumentum a minore ut pathos augeatur:

> . . . Mars perdere gentem
> immanem Lapithum valuit,

minor scilicet persona: ideo illud sequitur:

> ast ego, magna Iovis coniunx, . . .

deinde cum causas quoque contulisset, quanto impetu dea dixit,

> infelix quae memet in omnia verti!

nec dixit, "non possum perdere Aeneam," sed

> vincor ab Aenea . . .

7. deinde confirmat se ad nocendum et, quod proprium est irascentis, etsi desperat perfici posse, tamen impedire contenta est:

> flectere si nequeo superos, Acheronta movebo.
> non dabitur regnis, esto, prohibere Latinis . . .

---

[8] From this point through 4.4 analysis proceeds primarily by identifying the *loci* ("places" or "topics") where the means of persuasion could be found; the key concepts and texts are surveyed at Lausberg §§373–99. On the particular *locus* referred to here, involving comparison of persons or things of different status or value, cf. Lausberg §§395–97.

then fragmented complaints (*A.* 7.302–3),

> What good for me did Syrtes or Scylla do, what good
> awful Charybdis?

6. To this is next joined an 'argument from the lesser' [sc. person or circumstance],[8] to raise the emotional level (*A.* 7.304–5),

> . . . Mars was able to destroy
> the Lapiths' monstrous race,

Mars of course being the lesser character; that's why she follows with (*A.* 7.308),

> But *I*, Jupiter's great consort, . . .

and when she has compared the two cases, look at the force with which the goddess says (*A.* 7.309),

> Unhappy I am, who have tried every tack, in vain!

And she did not just say, "I cannot destroy Aeneas," but rather (*A.* 7.310),

> I am defeated by Aeneas. . . .

7. Then she girds herself to do him harm, and though she despairs of succeeding, she is nonetheless content—as an angry person actually would be—just to create an obstruction (*A.* 7.312–13, 315–16):

> If I cannot move the gods above, I'll stir up Hell
> below.
> Keeping them from the Latins' realm will not be
> granted. Fine . . .

at trahere atque moras tantis licet addere rebus,
at licet amborum populos excindere regum.

8. post haec in novissimo, quod irati libenter faciunt, maledicit:

sanguine Troiano et Rutulo dotabere, virgo,

et protinus argumentum a simili conveniens ex praecedentibus:

. . . nec face tantum
Cisseis praegnans ignes enixa iugales.

9. vides quam saepe orationem mutaverit ac frequentibus figuris variaverit, quia ira, quae brevis furor est, non potest unum continuare sensum in loquendo.

10. 'Nec desunt apud eundem orationes misericordiam commoventes. Turnus ad Iuturnam:

an miseri fratris[7] letum ut crudele videres?

et idem cum auget invidiam occisorum pro se amicorum:

vidi oculos ante ipse meos me voce vocantem
Murranum.

11. et idem cum miserabilem fortunam suam faceret, ut victo sibi parceretur:

7 miseri fratris] fratris miseri *Verg.*

---

9 Sc. person or circumstance: cf. Lausberg §394.

10 A commonplace: cf. Sen. *On Anger* 1.1.2, *Moral Epistles* 114.3, Otto 177.

> Still, dragging things out, heaping delay on history *is* allowed,
> cutting both kings' followers to pieces *is* allowed.

8. After this, at the very end of her speech, she utters a curse, something angry people are much inclined to do (*A.* 7.318),

> Your dowry, maiden, will be Trojan and Rutulian blood,

followed immediately by an "argument from the comparable"[9] that nicely meshes past with present (*A.* 7.319–20):

> . . . not Cisseus' daughter alone,
> a torch in her womb, brought forth flames from the marriage-bed.

9. You see how often he changed the tenor of the speech and used figures frequently to give it variety, because anger—a kind of brief madness[10]—is not capable of maintaining a single line of thought when it speaks.

10. 'And there are also plenty of speeches in Virgil that stir pity. Turnus to Juturna (*A.* 12.636):

> . . . or was it to see your wretched brother's cruel death?

Turnus again, playing up the ill-will felt by friends slain on his behalf (*A.* 12.638–39):

> Before my very eyes I myself saw Murranus calling upon me.

11. And Turnus again, making his lot seem pitiable, so he might be spared in defeat (*A.* 12.936–37):

vicisti et victum tendere palmas
Ausonii videre,

id est quos minime vellem. et aliorum preces orantium vitam:

per te, per qui te talem genuere parentes,

et similia.

3 'Nunc dicamus ex[8] habitu pathos, quod est vel in aetate vel in debilitate et ceteris quae sequuntur. eleganter hoc servavit ut ex omni aetate pathos misericordiae moveret: 2. ab infantia,

infantumque animae flentes in limine primo;

3. a pueritia,

infelix puer atque impar congressus Achilli,

et

parvumque patri tendebat Iulum,

ut non minus miserabile sit periculum in parvo quam in filio, et

. . . superet coniuxne Creusa
Ascaniusque puer?

et alibi,

. . . et parvi casus Iuli;

[8] ex *Willis*: et ω, de J²S *ed. Ven. 1472*

[11] Cf. Lausberg §376, on the different forms of the argument *a persona*.

> You have prevailed, and the Ausonians have seen the vanquished
> hold out his hands in supplication,

that is, the people I'd least want to be witnesses. There are also entreaties of other characters begging for their life (*A.* 10.597):

> I call on you, I call on your parents who brought you forth as the man you are,

and the like.

'Now let's talk about emotion based on a person's condition,[11] which is a function of age or weakness or any other qualities that follow from them. He hit this off so neatly that he could wring compassion from every stage of life: 3
2. infancy (*A.* 6.427),

> . . . and souls of infants weeping at the very threshold of life;

3. childhood (*A.* 1.475),

> . . . unhappy boy, no equal opponent for Achilles,

and (*A.* 2.674)

> he was holding little Iulus out to his father—

making the peril equally pitiable because he was small and because he was his son—and (*A.* 2.597–98)

> . . . whether your wife, Creusa, still lives,
> and the boy Ascanius?

and elsewhere (*A.* 2.563)

> . . . and the lot of little Iulus;

4. a iuventa vero,

> impositique[9] rogis iuvenes ante ora parentum,

<et>[10]

> pubentesque genae et iuvenali in corpore pallor;

5. a senecta,

> . . . Dauni miserere senectae,

et

> ducitur infelix aevo confectus Aletes,[11]

et

> canitiem multo deformat pulvere . . .

6. 'Movit et a fortuna modo misericordiam, modo indignationem: misericordiam,[12]

> . . . tot quondam populis terrisque superbum
> regnatorem Asiae . . .

et Sinon:

> et nos aliquod nomenque decusque
> gessimus,

et:

> . . . Ausoniisque olim ditissimus arvis;

7. indignationem vero ex verbis Didonis,

[9] -tique CJ²S: -tisque ω [10] et *add. ed. Lugd. Bat. 1670, om.* ω [11] Aletes] Acoetes *Verg.*
[12] misericordiam CS, *om.* ω

4. youth (*A.* 6.308 = *G.* 4.477),

> young men placed on the funeral pyre before their parents' eyes,

and (*A.* 12.221)

> his downy cheeks and pale young body;

5. old age (*A.* 12.934),

> . . . take pity on Daunus' old age,

and (*A.* 11.85*)

> Aletes is led along, undone by long time's passage,

and (*A.* 10.844)

> he fouls his gray head with heaps of dust. . . .

6. 'He also used a person's fortune now to stir pity, now resentment: pity (*A.* 2.556–57),

> . . . proud ruler, once, over so many nations
> and lands of Asia . . . .,

and Sinon (*A.* 2.89–90),

> We too have enjoyed some reputation and
> honor,

and (*A.* 7.537)

> . . . once the richest owner of Ausonian fields;

7. resentment, from the words of Dido (*A.* 4.591),

. . . et nostris illuserit advena regnis?—

eleganter enim ex contemptu Aeneae auget iniuriam suam—et Amata:

exulibusne datur ducenda Lavinia Teucris?

et Numanus:

bis capti Phryges . . .

8. 'Movit pathos misericordiae et ex debilitate:

. . . ex quo me divum pater atque hominum rex
fulminis adflavit ventis et contigit igne,[13]

et alibi

. . . et truncas inhonesto vulnere nares,

et de Mezentio,

. . . attollit in aegrum
se femur,

et

huc caput atque illuc umero ex utroque pependit,

et

te decisa suum, Laride, dextera quaerit,

et

. . . aterque cruento
pulvere perque pedes traiectus lora tumentes.

[13] igne] igni *Verg.*

. . . and shall that newcomer mock my realm?—

subtly using Aeneas' disdain to make the insult appear greater—and Amata (*A*. 7.359),

Is Lavinia being given to exiled Trojans to wed?,

and Numanus (*A*. 9.599),

twice-captive Phrygians. . . .

8. 'He also stirred the emotion of pity based on weakness (*A*. 2.648–49):

. . . ever since the father of gods and the king of men
blasted me with the thunderbolt and touched me with his fire,

and elsewhere (*A*. 6.497),

. . . and his nose cut off with a disfiguring blow,

and on Mezentius (*A*. 10.856–57),

. . . he raised himself onto his enfeebled leg,

and (*A*. 9.755),

[split,] the head hung to right and left on his shoulders,

and (*A*. 10.395),

your right hand, sliced off, looks for you, its master, Larides,

and (*A*. 2.272–73),

. . . black with bloody
dust, his swollen feet pierced by the leather thong.

9. 'Movit pathos misericordiae frequenter et a loco:

> cum vitam in silvis inter deserta ferarum
> lustra domosque traho,

et

> Libyae deserta peragro,

et

> at nos hinc alii sitientes ibimus Afros,
> pars Scythiam et rapidum cretae veniemus Oaxem.[14]

10. et illud egregie et breviter

> ter circum Iliacos raptaverat Hectora muros—

"Iliacos," id est patriae muros, quos ipse defenderat, pro quibus efficaciter per decem annorum spatia pugnaverat—11. et illud

> nos patriam fugimus,

et

> litora cum patriae lacrimans portusque relinquo,

et

> dulces moriens reminiscitur Argos,

et

> ignarum Laurens habet ora Mimanta,

14 Oaxem] -en *Verg.*

---

12 Cf. Lausberg §§382–84.

9. 'He also frequently stirred the emotion of pity based on geographical location (*A.* 3.646–47†):[12]

> while I drag out my life in the woods, amid the wild beasts' desolate
> haunts and lairs,

and (*A.* 1.384),

> I wander through the deserts of Libya,

and (*E.* 1.64–65),

> But some of us will go hence to the thirsty Africans,
> some will come to Scythia and the Oaxes, carrying chalk in its swift stream,

10. and this marvelously concise phrase (*A.* 1.483),

> thrice he had swiftly dragged Hector around Ilium's walls—

"Illium's," that is, his ancestral walls, which he himself had defended and on behalf of which he had fought effectively over the course of ten years—11. and this (*E.* 1.4)

> we flee from our homeland,

and (*A.* 3.10)

> as I leave my homeland's shores and ports in tears,

and (*A.* 10.782)

> he recalls sweet Argos as he dies,

and (*A.* 10.706)

> the Laurentian shore hold Mimas, though he knows it not,

<et>[15]

> Lyrnesi domus alta, solo Laurente sepulchrum.

12. et ut Agamemnonem indigne ostenderet occisum, adsumpsit locum:

> prima inter limina dextra
> oppetiit,

et illud:

> moenibus in patriis atque inter tuta domorum.

13. 'Sacer vero locus praecipue pathos movet. occisum inducit Orphea, et miserabiliorem interitum eius a loco facit:

> inter sacra deum nocturnique orgia Bacchi.

et in eversione Troiae:

> . . . perque domos et religiosa deorum
> limina.

14. Cassandrae quoque raptum vel deminutionem quam miserabilem fecit sacer locus:

> ecce trahebatur . . .
> a templo . . . adytisque Minervae!

[15] et *add. Jan, om.* ω

---

[13] The line concerns not Agamemnon, but the Latin troops in retreat at the end of Book 11; it seems to have been brought to mind by the phrase "at the very threshold" (*limine in ipso*: cf. A. 11.267 just above) that immediately precedes the words quoted.

and (*A.* 12.547)

> his lofty home in Lyrnesus, his tomb on Laurentian soil;

12. and to show that Agamemnon's murder was an unworthy deed, he made an issue of its location (*A.* 11.267–68)

> just within the threshold [of his palace] he died by [his wife's] right hand,

and (*A.* 11.882)

> within the walls of their ancestors' city, in the sanctuary of their homes.[13]

13. 'But a sacred place is especially effective in stirring emotion. Virgil introduces the slain Orpheus and makes his death the more pitiable by reason of its setting (*G.* 4.521):

> amid the rites of the gods and the mysteries of Bacchus, god of the night.

And when Troy is overthrown (*A.* 2.365–66),

> . . . throughout the gods' abodes and across their holy thresholds.

14. See how pitiable the holy location rendered Cassandra's kidnapping and enslavement (*A.* 2.403–4):

> Look, there she was, being dragged . . .
> from the temple . . . and inner sanctuary of Minerva!

et alibi:

. . . divae armipotentis ad aram
procubuit.[16]

15. et Andromache cum de Pyrrhi nece diceret, ut invidiam occidentis exprimeret:

excipit incautum patriasque obtruncat ad aras.

et Venus quod Aeneas in mari vexatur ira Iunonis quam invidiose de loco queritur Neptuno:

in regnis hoc ausa tuis?

16. 'Fecit sibi pathos saepe et ex tempore:

. . . priusquam
pabula gustassent Troiae Xanthumque bibissent.

et Orpheus miserabilis ex longo dolore;

septem illum totos perhibent ex ordine menses,

et Palinurus:

. . . vix lumine quarto
prospexi Italiam,

et Achemenides:

tertia iam lunae se cornua lumine complent,

[16] procubuit (*Charis. 117.11 B.*)] -cumbit *Verg.*

---

[14] Cf. Lausberg §§385–89.

and elsewhere (*A.* 2.425–26),

> . . . [Coroebus] fell at the altar of the goddess
> who is mighty in battle.

15. And when Andromache is describing the killing of Pyrrhus, she conveys the resentment attaching to the killer by saying (*A.* 3.332),

> . . . catches him off guard and butchers him at the ancestral altar.

And when Aeneas is harried at sea by Juno's anger, note how indignantly Venus specifies the location in making her complaint to Neptune (*A.* 5.792):

> she dared this in your realm?

16. 'He also often used the timing of an action to produce an emotional response (*A.* 1.472–73):[14]

> . . . before
> they had tasted Troy's fodder and drunk of the Xanthus;

and Orpheus, made pitiable by his long mourning (*G.* 4.507):

> for seven whole months in a row, they say, . . .

and Palinurus (*A.* 6.356–57),

> . . . I just made out Italy
> in the distance on the fourth dawn,

and Achaemenides (*A.* 3.645†),

> already now the moon's crescent is filling out a third time,

et:

septima post Troiae excidium iam vertitur aestas.

4 'Frequens apud illum pathos a causa: re vera enim plerumque efficit causa ut res aut atrox aut miserabilis videatur, ut Cicero in Verrem, qui ob sepulturam in carcere necatorum a parentibus rogabatur. hic enim non tam rogari aut pecuniam exigere quam ob hanc causam indignum erat. 2. et Demosthenes cum queritur quendam a Midia circumventum, ex causa auget invidiam: "circumvenit," inquit, "arbitrum qui inter me atque se integre iudicaverat." 3. ergo et Vergilius egregie saepe ex hoc loco traxit affectum. "occiditur," inquit, "in acie Galesus": hoc per se non est dignum misericordia belli tempore, sed admovit causam:

dum paci medium se offert.

4. idem alio loco:

sternitur infelix, . . .

deinde subicit causam miserabilem

. . . alieno vulnere,

id est, cum ad alium telum esset emissum. 5. et cum Palameden indigne occisum vellet:

---

[15] Cf. Lausberg §§378–81.

and (*A.* 5.626),

> now the seventh summer is coming 'round since
> Troy's destruction.

'In Virgil emotion often depends on an action's cause:[15] in fact, it's the cause that for the most part makes a state of affairs appear either cruel or pitiable, as in Cicero's attack on Verres (2.5.119), from whom the parents of those he had killed in prison asked leave to bury the dead: the source of resentment wasn't so much his being asked or his attempt to extort money but the reason underlying their request and his attempt. 2. Demosthenes, too, in complaining that Midias had cheated a certain person, uses the reason for his cheating to increase people's indignation at the deed (21.83ff.): "He cheated a judge," he says, "who had honestly decided a case involving the two of us." 3. Virgil too, then, often derived emotion from this source in a first-rate fashion. "Galaesus" he says, "is killed in battle"—not an event worthy of pity per se in a time of war, but then he added the cause (*A.* 7.536): 4

> while coming between the two sides in the interest of
> peace.

4. So too elsewhere (*A.* 10.781):

> He is laid low, unhappy man, . . .

then he adds the pitiable reason

> . . . by a wound meant for another,

that is, since the spear had had another man as its target. 5. And when he wants to convey that Palamedes was slain unworthily (*A.* 2.83–85*†):

. . . quem falsa sub proditione Pelasgi
insontem infando indicio, quia bella vetabat
demisere neci.

6. et Aeneas ut ostenderet magnitudinem timoris sui bene causam posuit:

et pariter comitique onerique timentem.

7. quid? Iapyx ut contemptis ceteris artificiis "inglorius," quem ad modum poeta ait, viveret, qualis causa proponitur?

ille ut depositi proferret fata parentis.

8. ex eodem genere est:

fallit te incautum pietas tua.

haec enim causa illum hostibus etiam miserabilem fecit. 9. sed Aeneas cum hortatur ut sepeliantur occisi, quam causam proponit?

. . . qui[17] sanguine nobis
hanc patriam peperere suo.

10. 'Nec non et indignatio demonstratur a causa ut illic:

multa gemens ignominiam plagasque superbi
victoris, tum quos amisit inultus amores.

[17] qui] quae (*sc.* animae) *Verg.*

---

[16] A Trojan beloved by Apollo, Iapyx rejected the skills the god offered—prophecy, music, archery—and chose to follow his father's calling as a physician (*A.* 12.391ff.).

. . . treacherously betrayed, innocent, the victim
of an unspeakable informer, he was sent down to death by the Pelasgi
because he urged against the war.

6. Aeneas, too, did well to state the reason for his fear in giving a sense of its magnitude (*A.* 2.729):

and fearing alike for my companion [sc. Ascanius] and my burden [sc. Anchises].

7. Consider Iapyx:[16] what reason is given for his rejecting all other skills and living "without glory" (*A.* 12.397), as the poet says? (*A.* 12.395)

. . . that he might carry on the destiny of his father, now laid to rest.

8. This is the same sort of thing (*A.* 10.812):

Led astray by filial devotion, you've dropped your guard,

and that was the reason even his enemies found Lausus worthy of pity. 9. But when Aeneas urges that the dead be buried, what reason does he give? (*A.* 11.24–25†)

. . . with their own blood
they have created this homeland for us.

10. 'Just resentment, too, is sometimes conveyed by reference to its cause, as in this case (*G.* 3.226–27):

groaning deeply at the disgrace, at the blows the haughty
victor dealt, and at the lovers he has lost, unavenged.

11. 'Et illud a causa est ex affectu indignantis:

. . . an[18] solos tangit Atridas
iste dolor, solisque licet capere arma Mycenis?

et illud:

. . . at tu dictis, Albane, maneres.

et illa omnia:

vendidit hic auro patriam, . . .
quique ob adulterium caesi, . . .
. . . nec partem posuere suis.

12. 'Ad pathos movendum nec duos illos praetermisit locos quos rhetores appellant a modo et a materia. modus est cum dico: occidit manifeste vel occulte. 13. materia est cum dico ferro an veneno. Demosthenes de modo invidiam Midiae facit, se pulsatum cothurno; Cicero Verri cum nudum quendam dicit ab eo statuae impositum. 14. Vergilius non minus evidenter:

. . . altaria ad ipsa trementem
traxit et in multo lapsantem sanguine nati,

18 an (*cf. Hom. Il. 9.340* ἦ μοῦνοι . . . )] nec *Verg.* (*et Macrob.* 5.9.2)

---

17 Cf. Lausberg §§390–91.

18 Cf. Demosth. 21.71ff.: if M. wrote *cothurno* (= a kind of elevated boot worn by tragic actors), he appears to have mistranslated *kondylois* ("punches") in Demosthenes' text (§72), though it is at least as likely that that he wrote κονδύλῳ (in Greek), which was then corrupted to *cothurno*. In any case, the "punches" Demosthenes refers to were not inflicted on him by Midias.

11. 'In this case the reason is given from the perspective of the person feeling the resentment (*A*. 9.138–39):

> . . . or does anguish of that sort touch
> only Atreus' sons, is Mycenae alone allowed to go to war?

and in this case (*A*. 8.643):

> . . . But you, Alban, would have done well to keep your word;

and in all these cases (*A*. 6.621, 612, 611):

> This one sold his homeland for gold . . . ,
> and those killed as adulterers . . . ,
> . . . and [those who] set aside nothing for their kin.

12. 'Nor did he omit the two sources for stirring emotion that the rhetoricians call "according to manner" and "according to means."[17] "Manner" is involved when I say, "He committed murder openly or stealthily." 13. "Means" is involved when I say ". . . with a word or poison." Demosthenes uses manner to stir up resentment against Midias by saying that he was struck by a tragic buskin;[18] Cicero does the same against Verres when he says that he caused a certain man to be placed naked upon a statue (2.4.86–87). 14. Virgil's practice is no less clear (*A*. 2.550–51):

> . . . he dragged him to the very altar,
> trembling and sliding in all the blood his son had shed,

et:

> . . . capulo tenus abdidit ensem.

15. et illa omnia a modo sunt:

> . . . rostroque immanis vultur adunco[19]
> immortale iecur tondens, . . .

et reliqua, et:

> quos super atra silex iam iam lapsura cadentique
> imminet adsimilis.

16. 'Sed et misericordiam a modo saepe commovet ut de Orpheo,

> latos iuvenem sparsere per agros,

et illud,

> obruit Auster aqua involvens navemque virosque,

et,

> saxum ingens volvunt alii, . . .

et,

> mortua quin etiam iungebat corpora vivis, . . .

et in Georgicis,

> nec via mortis erat simplex, . . .

et cetera in descriptione morbi. 17. sed et materia apud

[19] adunco (*codd.* Pγ *Verg.*)] obunco *codd. plerique Verg., Tib.* (*et Macrob.* 5.7.14)

and (*A*. 2.553),

> . . . he buried the sword to the hilt.

15. All these instances, too, are based on manner (*A*. 6.597–98):

> . . . a loathsome vulture crops his imperishable liver
> with its hooked beak,

and so on, and (*A*. 6.602–3),

> above whom looms a black flint stone, ever tottering
> and appearing to fall.

16. 'But manner often stirs pity, too, as when he says about Orpheus (*G*. 4.522),

> they scattered the youth over the broad fields,

and in this case (*A*. 6.336),

> the South Wind buries ship and crew, rolling them
> over in the sea,

and (*A*. 6.616),

> others roll a huge stone . . . ,

and (*A*. 8.485)

> nay, he even used to bind corpses and living men
> together . . . ,

and in the *Georgics* (3.482),

> nor was there one straight path to death, . . .

and everything else found in the description of the plague. 17. But rhetoricians recognize means, too, as a way of stir-

rhetoras pathos movet, ut dum queritur Cicero flammam ex lignis viridibus factam atque ibi inclusum fumo necatum. hoc enim a materia est, quoniam hic usus est fumo materia ad occidendum—ut alius gladio, alius veneno—et ideo acerrimum pathos ex hoc motum est. idem facit et cum flagellis caesum queritur civem Romanum. 18. invenies idem apud Vergilium:

> at pater omnipotens densa inter nubila telum
> contorsit: non ille faces nec fumea taedis
> <lumina>[20] . . .

et reliqua. eleganter autem illius quidem materiam elusit, ex huius autem vera et vehementi materia expressit iracundiam.

19. 'Et singula quidem enumeravimus, ex quibus apud rhetoras pathos nascitur, quibus ostendimus usum Maronem. sed non numquam Vergilius in una re ad augendum pathos duobus aut pluribus locis coniunctis utitur, 20. ut in Turno ab aetate:

> . . . miserere parentis
> longaevi . . . ,

a loco:

> . . . quem nunc maestum patria Ardea longe
> dividit,

[20] lumina *addidi, om.* ω

---

[19] Referring to the punishment of Salmoneus, who hurled torches in place of lightning bolts in his attempt to imitate Jupiter and claim divine honor.

ring emotion, as when Cicero laments the fire made with damp wood used to kill the person who was confined with it (*Verr.* 2.1.45). This instance is based on means, since Verres used smoke as the means to commit the murder—as one man might use a sword, another poison—and on that account aroused a very strong emotional reaction. Cicero does the same thing, too, when he complains that a Roman citizen was flogged (*Verr.* 2.5.140–42). 18. You'll find the same sort of thing in Virgil (*A.* 6.592–93):

> But the almighty father hurled his missile among the dense
> clouds—no firebrand for him, nor smoky glow
> of a pine torch,[19]

and so on: he subtly mocked the devices used by the one while conveying the anger of the other by reference to his real and forceful device.

19. 'I've now cataloged the individual sources of emotion, according to rhetorical doctrine, and I've shown how Maro used them. But Virgil sometimes uses a combination of two or more sources in a single instance, to increase the emotional response: 20. so in the case of Turnus he relies both on age (*A.* 12.43–44),

> . . . take pity on your aged
> father . . . ,

and on location (*A.* 12.44–45),

> . . . whom now the city of your ancestors, Ardea,
> keeps far off, sunk in sadness;

21. et circa Cassandram ex modo:

ecce trahebatur. . . .

ex habitu corporis:

. . . passis Priameia virgo
crinibus,

ex loco:

. . . a templo . . . adytisque Minervae.

22. et circa Agamemnonem a patria:

ipse Mycenaeus . . .

a fortuna:

. . . magnorum ductor Achivum, . . .

a necessitudine:

. . . coniugis, . . .

a loco:

. . . prima inter limina,

a causa:

. . . possedit[21] adulter.

23. 'Tacite quoque et quasi per definitionem pathos movere solet, cum res quae miserationem movet non dilucide dicitur sed datur intellegi, ut cum dicit Mezentius,

[21] possedit (*codd. aliquot Verg., Tib.*)] subsedit *codd. plerique Verg., Serv.*

21. and in the case of Cassandra, he relies on manner (*A.* 2.403),

> there, look, she was being dragged . . .

and on her physical state (*A.* 2.403–4),

> . . . Priam's maiden daughter, her hair
> fanned out behind her,

and on location (*A.* 2.404),

> . . . from the temple and inner sanctuary of Minerva;

22. and in the case of Agamemnon, he relies on his homeland (*A.* 11.266),

> The very master of Mycenae . . .

and on his lot in life (ibid.),

> . . . leader of the great Achaeans, . . .

and on his relationship (*A.* 11.267),

> . . . of his wife, . . .

and on the location (ibid.),

> . . . just within the threshold,

and on the cause (*A.* 11.268*),

> . . . an adulterer held sway.

23. 'He often stirs emotion by implication, too, and by speaking in a way that in a sense captures the situation's essence, when the cause of pity is not expressly denoted as such but is left to be understood, as when Mezentius says (*A.* 10.850),

. . . nunc alte vulnus adactum:

quid enim aliud ex hoc intellegendum est quam hoc altum vulnus esse amittere filium? 24. et rursus idem,

. . . haec via sola fuit qua perdere posses.

sed et hic scilicet accipiendum est perire esse amittere filium. 25. et Iuturna cum queritur quod adiuvare fratrem prohibeatur,

immortalis ego? . . .

quid enim sequitur? non est immortalitas in luctu vivere. 26. haec, ut dixi, vim definitionis habent et a poeta eleganter introducta sunt.

5 'Sunt in arte rhetorica ad pathos movendum etiam hi loci qui dicuntur circa rem, et movendis affectibus peropportuni sunt. ex quibus primus est a simili. huius species sunt tres: exemplum, parabola, imago; Graece *παράδειγμα, παραβολή, εἰκών*. 2. ab exemplo Vergilius:

si potuit Manes accersere[22] coniugis Orpheus,
Threicia fretus cithara fidibusque canoris,

[22] accersere (*codd.* MPRacγ *Verg., gramm aliquot*)] arcessere *codd. plerique Verg. medii aevi, Serv., gramm. plerique*

---

[20] The categories of analysis used in the rest of the book, involving various forms of argument (4.5.1–4.6.9) or figures of thought (4.6.10–24), complement and overlap categories previously used: so, e.g., Mars' destruction of the Lapiths, cited in 4.5.6, was mentioned already under the "argument from the lesser" (4.2.6) and was used in the latter case to represent indignation, whereas the "argument from the lesser" adduced below

. . . now the wound is driven deep:

what could one infer from this save that losing his son is a deep wound? 24. And Mezentius again (*A.* 10.879),

. . . this was the one path by which you could destroy [me]:

here too one must obviously understand that to lose a son is to be destroyed. 25. And when Juturna complains that she's barred from helping her brother (*A.* 12.882†),

*I* am immortal? . . . ,

what follows from this? That it is not true immortality to live in grief. 26. The poet quite delicately inserted these expressions, which (as I remarked) get their power from their precision.

'For stirring emotion rhetoric also has the sources that 5
are called "sources related to the matter at hand," and they are very handy for that purpose.[20] Foremost of these is argument from likeness,[21] which has three specific forms: the precedent, the comparison, and the image (in Greek, *paradeigma, parabolê, eikôn*). 2. Virgil uses the argument from precedent (*A.* 6.119–23*):

If Orpheus could summon his wife's dead spirit,
relying on his Thracian lyre's tuneful strings,

(4.6.1–4) aims at pity; cf. 4.6.2, where "location" and "manner," discussed at 4.3.9–15 and 4.4.14–16, are shown to be effective in the "argument from the lesser."

[21] Cf. Lausberg §§422–25.

si fratrem Pollux alterna morte redemit
<itque reditque viam totiens>[23]—quid Thesea, magnum
quid memorem Alciden? <et mi genus ab Iove summo>.[24]
[Antenor potuit mediis elapsus Achivis.][25]

haec enim omnia misericordiam movent, quoniam indignum videtur negari sibi quod aliis indultum ait. 3. deinde vide unde auget invidiam:

si potuit Manes accersere coniugis Orpheus . . .

habes causam disparem: Manes illic coniugis, hic patria; illic accersere, hic videre.

Threicia fretus cithara . . .

hic materiam eius irrisit.

4. si fratrem Pollux alterna morte redemit
itque reditque viam totiens . . .

hoc iam a modo, plus est enim saepe ire quam semel.

. . . quid Thesea, magnum
quid memorem Alciden?

hic propter egregias personas non habuit quod minueret vel augeret: verum quod in illis elucebat hoc sibi iactat cum his esse commune:

[23] itque . . . totiens *add.* W, *Willis* (*coll.* §*4 infra*), *om.* ω

[24] et mi genus ab Iove summo *add. Marinone*[2] (*coll.* §*4 infra*), *om.* ω

[25] *secl. Jan*

> if Pollux redeems his brother, taking his turn among the dead,
> ‹back and forth along the path, again and again›—why need I speak
> of Theseus, of great Achilles? ‹My line too descends from Jupiter supreme.›

All these precedents arouse pity, since it seems disrespectful that he be denied what he says was granted to others. 3. Furthermore, look at the source he relies on for heightening his resentment:

> If Orpheus could summon his wife's dead spirit. . . .

You have two quite unequal cases: in the one, his wife's dead spirit, in the other, his homeland; in the one case, the relevant act is fetching, in the other, seeing.

> relying on his Thracian lyre . . .

Here Aeneas mocked Orpheus' means.

> 4. If Pollux redeems his brother, taking his turn among the dead,
> back and forth along the path, again and again . . .

Now this argument is based on manner, for making the journey often is more of a concession than making it once.

> . . . why need I speak
> of Theseus, of great Achilles?

Because of the great personages involved he didn't have the grounds to diminish them or puff himself up; but he claims that he shares the trait in which they are distinguished:

et mi genus ab Iove summo.

5. simile est et illud ab indignatione: "quid enim?," ait Iuno,

Pallasne exurere classem
Argivum . . . potuit?[26]

iam hoc plus est, classem victricem quam reliquias fugientium. deinde causam minuit:

unius ob noxam et furias Aiacis Oïlei.

quam minuit ut "noxam" diceret, quod levis culpae nomen est, et "unius," quod facile possit ignosci, et "furentis" ut nec culpa sit. 6. et alibi:

. . . Mars perdere gentem
immanem Lapithum valuit.

vides easdem observationes, "gentem" et "immanem." deinde aliud exemplum:

. . . concessit in iras
ipse deum antiquam genitor Calydona Dianae.

"antiquam," ut plus honoris accederet ex vetustate: deinde in utroque causam minuit:

quod scelus aut Lapithis tantum aut Calydone merente?

7. 'A parabola vero quoniam magis hoc poetae convenit,

[26] potuit *add.* P, *om.* ω

> My line too descends from Jupiter supreme.

5. The argument based on indignation is a similar gambit. "What!," says Juno (*A.* 1.39–40*),

> Pallas Athena could burn the Argive fleet?

In this case destroying the victor's fleet entails more of a concession than destroying the exiled remnant. The next step is to undercut the reason for the concession (*A.* 1.41):

> on account of the mad blunder of a single man, Ajax
> son of Oïleus.

The undercutting consists of calling it a "blunder"—a term used for a venial fault—and "of a single man"—hence something that could easily be overlooked—and "mad"—so that he is not even culpable. 6. And elsewhere (*A.* 7.304–5),

> . . . Mars was able to destroy
> the Lapiths' monstrous race,

you see Juno focusing on the same features, "race" and "monstrous." Then another example (*A.* 7.305–6),

> . . . The father of the gods himself
> yielded over ancient Calydon to Diana's rage:

she used the epithet "ancient" to bestow more honor on the city from its antiquity; then she undercuts the reason for both actions (*A.* 7.307):

> what crime so awful had made Lapiths or Calydon
> deserving?

7. 'But since it better suits a poet, he very often stirs

saepissime pathos movit cum aut miserabilem aut iracundum vellet inducere. miserabilem sic:

qualis populea maerens philomela sub umbra, . . .
. . . qualis commotis excita sacris
Thyas,[27] . . .
qualem virgineo demessum pollice florem . . .

et aliae plurimae patheticae parabolae in quibus miseratus est. 8. quid de ira?

ac veluti pleno lupus insidiatus ovili
cum fremit ad caulas . . .

et:

mugitus veluti[28] fugit cum saucius aram
taurus . . .

et alia plura similia qui quaerit inveniet.

9. 'Et imago, quae est a simili pars tertia, idonea est movendis affectibus. ea fit cum aut forma corporis absentis describitur aut omnino quae nulla est fingitur. utrumque Vergilius eleganter fecit: 10. illud prius circa Ascanium,

o mihi sola mei super Astyanactis imago,
sic oculos, sic ille manus, sic ora ferebat;

11. fingit vero cum dicit,

[27] Thyas F (*codd.* F[1]Mn *Verg.*, thias ω)] Thyias *codd. plerique Verg., edd.*

[28] mugitus veluti] qualis mugitus *Verg.* (*et Macrob. 5.13.10*)

emotion with the argument from comparison, when he wants to bring on a pitiable or wrathful character. Pitiable, as follows (*G.* 4.511, *A.* 4.301–2, 11.68):

like a nightingale moaning in a poplar's shade . . . ,
. . . like a bacchant roused when the sacred implements
have been shaken, . . .
like a flower plucked by a maiden's hand . . . ,

and very many other affecting comparisons that he used to express pity. 8. What about anger? (*A.* 9.59–60)

and just as when a wolf lies in wait at a sheepfold
and growls around the pens . . . ,

and (*A.* 2.223–24),

a bellowing just as when a wounded bull flees
the altar . . . ,

and many similar comparisons that you'll find if you look for them.

9. 'An image too, which is the third kind of argument from likeness, is suitable for stirring the emotions. It is produced either when an absent person's physical form is described or when a non-existent form is imagined. Virgil subtly produced both kinds: 10. the first in the case of Ascanius (*A.* 3.489–90),

o, the only likeness of my Astyanax left to me:
such were his eyes, such his hands, such his face;

11. but he produces an imagined image when he says (*E.* 6.74*–75),

. . . quam fama secuta est
candida succinctam latrantibus inguina monstris.

sed prior forma *οἶκτον* praestat, haec *δείνωσιν*, id est prior misericordiam commovet, horrorem secunda, sicut alibi:

12. et scissa gaudens vadit Discordia palla,
quam cum sanguineo sequitur Bellona flagello,

et omnia illa quae de Fama dixit. sed et illud nimium pathetice:

. . . Furor impius intus
saeva sedens super arma, et centum vinctus aenis
post tergum nodis fremit[29] horridus ore cruento.

6 'Diximus a simili: nunc dicamus a minore pathos a poeta positum. nempe cum aliquid proponitur quod per se magnum sit, deinde minus esse ostenditur quam illud quod volumus augeri, sine dubio infinita miseratio movetur: 2. ut est illud,

o felix una ante alias Priameia virgo,
hostilem ad tumulum Troiae sub moenibus altis
iussa mori . . .

primum quod ait "felix," comparationem sui fecit, deinde posuit a loco, "hostilem ad tumulum," et a modo, quod non

[29] fremit] fremet *Verg.*

---

[22] For this argument and the converse (§5 below) cf. Lausberg §420b.

. . . who (rumor has it)
is girt round her fair groin with baying monsters.

But where the first stirs *oiktos*—that is, pity—the second stirs *deinôsis*—that is, horror—just as elsewhere (*A.* 8.702–3),

12. and Discord, her garment rent, makes her way exulting,
and behind her follows Bellona with her bloody lash,

and the whole description of Rumor (*A.* 4.173–88). But this description, too, has emotional power (*A.* 1.294–96):

. . . within, unholy Furor
sits upon its savage weapons: one hundred knots of bronze bind
its hands behind its back, its bloody mouth bellows dreadfully.

'So much for the argument from likeness: now let's describe the way the poet uses the argument from what is lesser.[22] Obviously, when something is put before us that is great in itself, but it is then shown to be less than the thing we want to make appear greater, it cannot help but stir boundless pity. 2. For example (*A.* 3.321–23†), 6

O Priam's maiden daughter, fortunate before all others,
ordered to die at an enemy's tomb before Troy's
lofty walls . . .

First, by saying "fortunate," Andromache established a comparison with herself; then she used location—"at an enemy's tomb"—and (a touch no less bitter) manner—

minus acerbum est: "iussa mori." sic ergo haec accipienda sunt: quamvis "hostilem ad tumulum," "quamvis iussa mori," felicior tamen quam ego, quia "sortitus non pertulit ullos." 3. simile est et illud:

> . . . o terque quaterque beati!

et quod de Pasiphaë dicit:

> Proetides implerunt falsis mugitibus agros,

deinde ut minus hoc esse monstraret:

> at non tam turpes pecudum tamen ulla secuta est[30]
> concubitus . . .

4. quid, illud non vehementer patheticum est a minore?

> nec vates Helenus, cum multa horrenda moneret,
> hos mihi praedixit luctus, non dira Celaeno.

quid hic intellegimus, nisi omnia quae passus erat minora illi visa quam patris mortem?

5. 'A maiore negaverunt quidam augeri rem posse; sed eleganter hoc circa Didonem Vergilius induxit:

> . . . non aliter quam si immissis ruat hostibus omnis
> Carthago aut antiqua Tyros . . .

[30] secuta est (*codd. plerique Verg.*)] secuta *codd.* MP *Verg.*, *edd.*

---

[23] Cf. DServ. on *E.* 6.47.

"ordered to die"—as sources of emotion. We are to understand her words this way: though she was "ordered to die at an enemy's tomb," she is still more fortunate than I, because "she did not endure being shared out as booty" (*A.* 3.323). 3. This case is similar (*A.* 1.94):

> . . . o thrice and four times blessed!;

and when he remarks, apropos of Pasiphaë (*E.* 6.48),[23]

> Proetus' daughters made the fields resound with
> counterfeit lowing,

he shows that that was a less miserable by adding (*E.* 6.49–50),

> but none of them ever sought intercourse—
> disgusting!—
> with cattle. . . .

4. Is the following argument from the lesser not terribly moving? (*A.* 3.712–13*)

> Neither Helenus the seer—though he warned of
> many horrors—
> nor dreadful Celaeno predicted that I would feel
> such grief.

Here we can only conclude that he judged all his past suffering less grievous than his father's death.

5. 'Some have said that the argument from what is greater cannot be used in the same way, but Virgil introduced it subtly in treating Dido (*A.* 4.669–70):

> . . . just as if the enemy had been let in and all
> Carthage were to fall, or ancient Tyre. . . .

dixit enim non minorem luctum fuisse ex unius morte quam si tota urbs, quod sine dubio esset maius, ruisset. et Homerus idem fecit:

> . . . ὡς εἰ ἅπασα
> Ἴλιος ὀφρυόεσσα πυρὶ σμήχοιτο[31] κατ᾽ ἄκρης.

6. 'Est apud oratores et ille locus idoneus ad pathos movendum qui dicitur praeter spem. hunc Vergilius frequenter exercuit:

> nos tua progenies, caeli quibus adnuis arcem

et cetera. et Dido:

> hunc ego si potui tantum sperare dolorem,
> et perferre, soror, potero.

7. Aeneas de Euandro,

> et nunc ille quidem spe multum captus inani
> fors et vota facit,

et illud:

> . . . advena nostri,
> quod numquam veriti sumus, ut possessor agelli
> diceret: haec mea sunt, veteres migrate coloni.

8. 'Invenio tamen posse aliquem et ex eo quod iam speraverit movere pathos, ut Euander:

31 σμήχοιτο *α (om. $\beta_2$), codd. duo Hom., fort. Didymo notum:* σμύχοιτο *codd. Hom.*

By this he meant that the death of a single person produced as much grief as the destruction of an entire city, something unquestionably greater. Homer, too, did the same thing (*Il.* 22.410–11):

> . . . as if all
> of looming Ilium, from its citadel down, were wiped
> out by fire.

6. 'Orators also use the source of emotion that is called "contrary to expectation." Virgil often put it to work (*A.* 1.250):

> We, your offspring, to whom you grant heaven's
> citadel . . .

and the rest. And Dido (*A.* 4.419–20):

> If I was able to anticipate this great grief,
> I will be able to endure it, too, my sister.

7. Aeneas, speaking of Evander (*A.* 11.49–50),

> And now perhaps, very much a captive of empty
> hope,
> he is even making vows,

and this (*E.* 9.2–4*):

> . . . that a newcomer—
> a thing I never feared—should say, as the new tenant
> of my small plot: this is mine, you old dwellers clear
> out.

8. 'I see, however, that one can also stir emotion by referring to something that he did already expect, as Evander (*A.* 11.154):

haud ignarus eram quantum nova gloria in armis
et praedulce decus.

9. 'Oratores homoeopathian vocant quotiens de similitudine passionis pathos nascitur, ut apud Vergilium,

. . . fuit et tibi talis
Anchises genitor,

et,

. . . <animum>[32] patriae strinxit pietatis imago

et,

. . . subiit cari genitoris imago

et Dido,

me quoque per multos similes fortuna labores . . . .

10. 'Est et ille locus ad permovendum pathos, in quo sermo dirigitur vel ad inanimalia vel ad muta, quo loco oratores frequenter utuntur. utrumque Vergilius bene pathetice tractavit, vel cum ait Dido:

. . . dulces exuviae, dum fata deusque sinebant,[33]

vel cum Turnus:

[32] animum *addidi, om.* ω [33] sinebant (*codd. plerique Verg., CIL 11.7476*)] -bat *codd.* MPbn *Verg., Serv., Tib.*

---

[24] This is "compassion" in the etymological sense, a shared sentiment arising out of common experience: though the examples cluster around "compassion" in the common sense, as a species of pity, a "passion" such as indignation could in principle be generated in the same way.

I was not unaware how very sweet the first taste
of glory is, and honor in battle.

9. 'Orators call it "homoeopathy"[24] when one emotion emerges from another emotion very like it, as in Virgil (*A.* 12.933–34),

. . . in Anchises you too had
such a one as your father,

and (*A.* 9.294*),

. . . there stole upon his mind an image of a son's
devotion to his father

and (*A.* 2.560),

. . . the image of his dear father came to him

and Dido (*A.* 1.628),

me too, over the course of many similar toils,
fortune. . . .

10. 'There is also a resource for stirring emotion, much used by orators, whereby one addresses oneself to things either inanimate or mute.[25] Virgil used both to good emotional effect, when Dido says (*A.* 4.651),

. . . sweet these mementos, while fate and the god
allowed,

or when Turnus says (*A.*12.777–78),

[25] Cf. Serv. on *A.* 4.659. As the examples show, focus on the character of the addressee allows the category to range from virtual self-address (the first and last examples) to actual prayer (the second).

. . . tuque optima, ferrum,
Terra, tene,

et idem alibi:

. . . nunc o numquam frustrata vocatus
hasta meos,

et:

Rhaebe, diu, res siqua diu mortalibus ulla est,
viximus.

11. 'Facit apud oratores pathos etiam addubitatio quam Graeci "ἀπόρησιν" vocant. est enim vel dolentis vel irascentis dubitare quid agas:

en quid ago? rursusne procos inrisa priores
experiar?,

12. et illud de Orpheo,

quid faceret? quo se rapta bis coniuge ferret?

et de Niso,

quid faciat? qua vi iuvenem, quibus audeat armis
eripere?,

et Anna permoventer,

. . . and you, most excellent Earth,
hold that weapon fast,

and again elsewhere (*A.* 12.95–96*),

. . . o my spear, that has never disappointed
my summons,

and (*A.* 10.861–62),

Rhaebus, we've had a long life, if mortals enjoy
anything
long.

11. 'Orators also use uncertainty (the Greeks call it *aporêsis*) to produce emotion,[26] for it's characteristic of one experiencing grief or anger to be uncertain of what to do next (*A.* 4.534–55):

Look at me, what am I doing? Shall I try again my
former suitors
now I've been mocked?;

12. and this, about Orpheus (*G.* 4.504),

What was he to do? Where was he to go, with his
wife snatched away a second time?;

and about Nisus (*A.* 9.399–400),

What could he do? What strength had he, what
weapons, to boldly rescue
the young man?;

and Anna, very emotionally (*A.* 4.677–78),

[26] Cf. Lausberg §§776–78.

quid primum deserta querar? comitemne sororem
<sprevisti moriens?>[34]

13. 'Et attestatio rei visae apud rhetoras pathos movet. hoc Vergilius sic exequitur:

ipse caput nivei fultum Pallantis et ora
ut vidit levique patens in pectore vulnus,

14. et illud,

implevitque sinum sanguis,

et,

moriensque suo se in sanguine[35] versat

et,

crudelis nati monstrantem vulnera cernit,

et,

ora virum tristi pendebant pallida tabo,

et,

volvitur Euryalus . . . pulchrosque per artus
it cruor,

[34] sprevisti moriens *addidi*
[35] sanguine PA$^{m}$FC$^{m}$ (s. RA$^{1}$, *om.* NG, *n. l.* C): vulnere *Verg.*

What should I lament first in my desolation? Did you spurn your sister
as a companion in your dying?

13. 'Teachers of rhetoric hold that causing the audience to witness a scene also stirs the emotions.[27] Virgil achieves that goal in this passage (*A.* 11.39–40):

When he himself saw Pallas' head propped up, his face
deathly pale, and the gaping wound in his smooth chest,

14. and this (*A.* 10.819),

and blood filled the fold of his tunic,

and (*A.* 11.669),

and he writhes in his own blood as he dies,

and (*A.* 6.446),

he sees her pointing to the wound her son had cruelly dealt,

and (*A.* 8.197),

men's heads were hanging there, pale and grimly rotting,

and (*A.* 9.433–34),

Euryalus spins and falls . . . and the gore runs
over his fair limbs,

[27] On the use of "vividness" (Gk. *enargeia*, Lat. *evidentia*) cf. Lausberg §§810–19.

et,

> vidi egomet duo de numero . . . corpora nostro . . .

15. 'Facit hyberbole, id est nimietas, pathos, per quam exprimitur vel ira vel misericordia: ira, ut cum forte dicimus "milies ille perire debuerat," quod est apud Vergilium,

> omnes per mortes animam sontem ipse dedissem,

miseratio, cum dicit,

> Daphni, tuum Poenos etiam ingemuisse leones
> interitum . . . .

16. nascitur praeter haec de nimietate vel amatorium vel alterius generis pathos,

> si mihi non haec lux toto iam longior anno est . . . ,

et illud seorsum,

> . . . maria ante exurere Turno
> quam sacras dabitur pinus,

et,

> . . . non si tellurem effundat in undas.

17. 'Exclamatio, quae apud Graecos "ἐκφώνησις" dicitur, movet pathos. haec fit interdum ex persona poetae,

---

28 Cf. Lausberg §§909–10.
29 Cf. Lausberg §809.

and (*A*. 3.623),

I myself saw two of our company, their bodies . . .

15. 'Hyperbole—that is, overstatement[28]—produces an emotional response in giving expression to anger or pity: anger, as when we say, perhaps, "He should have died a thousand times," a thought found in Virgil (*A*. 10.854),

would that I myself had given up my guilty life in any and every kind of death!;

pity, when he says (*E*. 5.27–28*),

Daphnis, even lions of Carthage lamented your passing. . . .

16. In addition, overstatement produces an emotional response typical of a lover or someone of the opposite sort (*E*. 7.43),

If this day now doesn't seem to me longer than a whole year . . . ,

and quite differently (*A*. 9.115–16),

. . . Turnus will sooner be allowed to burn up the seas than my sacred pines,

and (*A*. 12.204),

. . . not if it should send the earth tumbling into the sea.

17. 'An exclamation (in Greek, *ekphônêsis*)[29] arouses emotion, sometimes when it's spoken in the poet's own

non numquam ex ipsius quem inducit loquentem. 18. ex poetae quidem persona est:

> Mantua vae miserae nimium vicina Cremonae!
> infelix, utcumque ferent ea facta nepotes![36]
> . . . crimen amor vestrum!

et alia similia. 19. ex persona vero alterius,

> . . . di capiti ipsius generique reservent!,

et,

> di, talia Grais
> instaurate, pio si poenas ore reposco!,

et,

> di talem terris avertite pestem!

20. 'Contraria huic figurae ἀποσιώπησις, quod est taciturnitas. nam ut illic aliqua exclamando adicimus,[37] ita hic aliqua tacendo subducimus, quae tamen intellegere possit auditor. 21. hoc autem praecipue irascentibus convenit, ut Neptunus,

> "quos ego—sed motos praestat componere fluctus,"

[36] nepotes] minores *Verg.*
[37] adicimus *Willis in app.*: dicimus ω

character, sometimes when the poet introduces a speaking character. 18. From the poet's persona there is

> Mantua, alas, too near unhappy Cremona! (*E*. 9.28)
> . . . unhappy, however his posterity will speak of those deeds! (*A*. 6.822)
> . . . your crime, Love! (*A*. 10.188)

and other passages like these. 19. From another's persona (*A*. 8.484),

> . . . may the gods hold [such evil] in store for himself and his kin!,

and (*A*. 6.529–30),

> Gods, bring such things afresh
> upon the Greeks, if I call for vengeance with pious lips!

and (*A*. 3.620),

> Gods, avert such a plague from my lands!

20. 'The opposite of this figure is *aposiôpêsis*, that is, falling silent:[30] for as in the previous case we insert something further by shouting it out, in this case we subtract something by keeping quiet—though the listener can still infer what it is. 21. This figure, however, is chiefly suited to angry people, like Neptune (*A*. 1.135*†),

> whom I'll—but better now to settle the troubled seas,

30 Cf. Lausberg §§887–89.

et Mnestheus,

> . . . nec[38] vincere certo,
> quamquam o—sed superent, quibus hoc, Neptune, dedisti,

et Turnus,

> quamquam o si solitae quicquam virtutis adesset!

et in Bucolicis,

> novimus et qui te transversa tuentibus hircis,
> et quo—sed faciles Nymphae risere—sacello.

22. sed et miseratio ex hac figura mota est a Sinone:

> . . . donec Calchante ministro—
> sed quid ego haec autem nequiquam ingrata revolvo?

23. 'Nascitur pathos et de repetitione, quam Graeci "ἐπαναφορὰν" vocant, cum sententiae ab isdem nominibus incipiunt. hinc Vergilius:

> . . . Eurydicen vox ipsa et frigida lingua,
> a! miseram Eurydicen anima fugiente vocabat.
> Eurydicen toto referebant flumine ripae,

et illud,

[38] nec] neque *Verg.*

---

[31] Despite the exclamatory *o* (cf. Serv. on this passage) this is not a case of *aposiôpêsis* like the preceding.

[32] Again, not quite *aposiôpêsis*: "understand 'corrupted,' which he omitted from a sense of delicacy" (Serv.).

[33] Cf. Lausberg §§629–30.

and Mnestheus (*A*. 5.194–95),

> . . . nor do I strive to win,
> yet o—but let those prevail, Neptune, whom you've favored,

and Turnus (*A*. 11.415),

> yet o!, if any of our usual valor were with us![31]

and in the *Bucolics* (*E*. 3.8–9),

> I know both who . . . you[32] while the goats looked askance,
> and in which little shrine—but the Nymphs are quick to laugh.

22. But Sinon uses this figure to stir pity, too (*A*. 2.100–1*†):

> . . . until with Calchas' help—
> but why pointlessly call back these unpleasant memories?

23. 'Repetition (the Greeks call it *epanaphora*)[33] also produces emotion, when successive thoughts begin with the same name or pronoun. Hence Virgil (*G*. 4.525–27):

> . . . "Eurydice!" his very voice and chill tongue called,
> "a! poor Eurydice" he called, as his soul departed.
> "Eurydice!" the banks echoed down all the river's course,

and this (*G*. 4.465–66),

te dulcis coniunx, te solo in litore secum,
te veniente die, te decedente canebat,

et illud,

te nemus Angitiae, vitrea te Fucinus unda,
te liquidi flevere lacus.

24. 'ἐπιτίμησις, quae est obiurgatio, habet et ipsa pathos, id est cum obiecta isdem verbis refutamus:

"Aeneas ignarus abest": ignarus et absit.[39]

[39] *post* absit *nihil subscriptum sed reliqua pars lineae vacat in* α, DE STILO VIRGILII *add.* $\beta_2$; *lacunam ab Arnaldo Vesaliensi constitutam recte negavit Marinone*[2]. *Liber quintus sine titulo sequitur.*

Of you your dear husband sang, of you by himself on the lonely shore,
of you he sang as day began, of you as it departed,

and this (*A.* 7.759–60),

For you the grove of Angitia wept, for you Fucinus' glassy wave,
for you the limpid pools.

24. 'Reproach—in Greek, *epitimêsis*[34]—also entails strong feeling, particularly when we squelch remarks made against us by casting the same words back at the speaker (*A.* 10.85*):

"Aeneas is away and unaware"—and let him stay away and unaware.'[35]

[34] Cf. Lausberg §785.

[35] The rhetoric of the emotions was commonly treated with ref. to the speech's conclusion (*peroratio*), where rousing the audience's pity or indignation (etc.) was thought especially apt, and the subject therefore typically occupied the final position in analyses of a standard speech's parts: thus it stands at the end of Book 1 in Cicero's *On Invention* and at the end of Book 2 in the anonymous treatise *Rhetoric for Herennius*. That it is the only topic treated in the surviving part of Book 4 might suggest that that part is in fact the last part of the speaker's treatment of his subject: this would confirm Marinone's argument (1977, 72) that there is no lacuna between Books 4 and 5 (*pace* Arnoldus Vesaliensis [ed. Colon. 1521], followed by Jan, Eyssenhardt, and Willis) and that the speaker must be Eusebius (cf. 5.1.1).

# ‹LIBER QVINTVS›[1]

1 Post haec cum paulisper Eusebius quievisset, omnes inter se consono murmure Vergilium non minus oratorem quam poetam habendum pronuntiabant, in quo et tanta orandi disciplina et tam diligens observatio rhetoricae artis ostenderetur. 2. et Avienus, 'dicas mihi,' inquit, 'volo, doctorum optime, si concedimus, sicuti necesse est, oratorem fuisse Vergilium, si quis nunc velit orandi artem consequi, utrum magis ex Vergilio an ex Cicerone proficiat?' 3. 'video quid agas,' inquit Eusebius, 'quid intendas, quo me trahere coneris, eo scilicet quo minime volo, ad comparationem Maronis et Tullii. verecunde enim interrogasti uter eorum praestantior, quando quidem necessario is plurimum collaturus sit qui ipse plurimum praestat. 4. sed istam mihi necessitatem altam et profundam remittas volo: quia "non nostrum" inter illos "tantas componere lites," nec ausim in utramvis partem talis sententiae auctor videri. hoc solum audebo dixisse, quia facundia Mantuani multiplex et multiformis est et dicendi genus omne complectitur. ecce enim in Cicerone vestro unus eloquentiae tenor est, ille

[1] *add. edd.*

---

[1] I.e., the question that Avienus asked—which of the two would better repay study by a would-be orator?—implied another, potentially awkward question—which of them is supe-

# ‹BOOK FIVE›

After these remarks, when Eusebius had had a brief re- 1
spite, all declared, with no murmur of dissent, that Virgil had to be considered no less an orator than a poet, seeing that he was shown to be so skilled in the ways or oratory and so keen a student of rhetoric. 2. And Avienus said, 'Please tell me this, best of teachers: if we grant (as we must) that Virgil was an orator, would someone now aiming to become a skilled orator gain more from reading Virgil or Cicero?' 3. 'I see what you're up to,' Eusebius said, 'I see where you're headed and where you're trying to drag me—to a place I don't at all want to go, a comparison of Maro and Tully. You put circumspectly the question you really want answered—which of them is superior—since he will inevitably provide the greatest benefit who is himself the greatest.[1] 4. But please release me from the need to answer so lofty and profound a question: "it rests not with me to settle that great dispute" (*E*. 3.108) between them, nor would I dare appear to support either side in the matter. I will be so bold as to say only this: the Mantuan's eloquence is many-sided and diverse, embracing every style. Just look: your Cicero keeps to a single manner,

rior?—but Avienus showed proper respect and circumspection (*verecundia*: cf. Introd. §3) by proceeding indirectly rather than baldy asking the latter question.

abundans et torrens et copiosus. 5. oratorum autem non simplex nec una natura est, sed hic fluit et redundat, contra ille breviter et circumcise dicere adfectat; tenuis quidam et siccus et sobrius amat quandam dicendi frugalitatem, alius pingui et luculenta et florida oratione lascivit. in qua tanta omnium dissimilitudine unus omnino Vergilius invenitur qui eloquentiam ex omni genere conflaverit.' 6. respondit Avienus: 'apertius vellem me has diversitates sub personarum exemplis doceres.'

7. 'Quattuor sunt,' inquit Eusebius, 'genera dicendi: copiosum in quo Cicero dominatur, breve quo Sallustius regnat, siccum quod Frontoni adscribitur, pingue et floridum in quo Plinius Secundus quondam et nunc nullo veterum minor noster Symmachus luxuriatur. sed apud unum Maronem haec quattuor genera reperies. 8. vis audire illum tanta brevitate dicentem, ut artari magis et contrahi brevitas ipsa non possit?

et campos ubi Troia fuit . . .

---

[2] Cicero himself, who insisted that the truly eloquent orator must master all styles (e.g., *Orator* 20, 69), would certainly have rejected this characterization.

[3] Standard rhetorical theory held that there were, broadly speaking, three styles (*genera dicendi*: refs. in Lausberg §1078–82): the "grand" ("robust," "forceful"), the "precise" ("fine," "slender"), and the "middle" ("gentle," "blossoming"); but note that Demetrius *On Style* 36 admits four ("plain," "elevated," "elegant," and "forceful"). Though the traits assigned the stylists here are in some cases elsewhere so ascribed—e.g., Caesar called Cicero "virtually the prince of abundant inventiveness" (*copia: On Analogy* fr. 1 *GRF* 1:146), Quintilian speaks of "Sallustian brevity"

being substantial and marvelously fluent and inventive.[2] 5. But the nature of orators is not a single, simple thing: this one is fluent and overflowing while that one aims to speak briefly and concisely, the spare, dry, and sober sort likes a certain austerity of speech, another frolics with a rich, flashy, and flowery style. Amid the great variety that they all display, Virgil alone is found to have achieved an eloquence that is melded together from every style.' 6. Avienus replied, 'I'd like you to explain this variety in greater detail, with examples from specific speakers.'

7. 'There are,' Eusebius said, 'four different speaking styles:[3] the abundantly inventive, which is Cicero's domain; the brief, where Sallust holds sway; the dry, which is regarded as Fronto's; and the rich and blossoming, in which Pliny once reveled, as now our friend Symmachus does, second to none of the ancients.[4] But in Maro alone will you find all four styles. 8. Would you like to hear him speaking with such brevity that brevity itself could not be confined within a narrower compass? (*A.* 3.11)

And the plains where Troy was . . .:

(4.2.45, cf. 8.3.32)—they are not clearly or simply used to characterize any of the traditional styles: "blossoming" (*floridum* = Gk. *anthêron*) is used of both the "middle" (Quint. 12.10.58) and the "grand" (Fortunat. 3.9, *RLM* p. 126.4); "dry" is otherwise used to describe a fault of the "precise" style (Fortunat. ibid p. 126.6–7); "rich" (*pingue*) is rare and uncomplimentary (Cic. *Speech on behalf of Archias* 26, cf. Quint. 1.7.27, *TLL* 10,1:2174.6–15).

[4] Symmachus is twice cited as an authoritative source, alongside Cicero, Sallust, Terence, and Virgil, in a grammatical compilation (*Exemplary Expressions*) by the contemporary rhetorician Arusianus Messius.

ecce paucissimis verbis maximam civitatem hausit, absorbsit, non reliquit illi nec ruinam. 9. vis hoc ipsum copiosissime dicat?

venit summa dies et ineluctabile tempus
Dardaniae: fuimus Troes, fuit Ilium et ingens
gloria Teucrorum. ferus omnia Iuppiter Argos
transtulit: incensa Danai dominantur in urbe.

10. O patria, o divum domus Ilium, et inclita bello
moenia Dardanidum! . . .

Quis cladem illius noctis, quis funera fando
explicet aut possit lacrimis[2] aequare dolorem?[3]
urbs antiqua ruit multos dominata per annos.

quis fons, quis torrens, quod mare tot fluctibus quot hic verbis inundavit! 11. cedo nunc siccum illud genus elocutionis:

Turnus, ut ante volans tardum praecesserat agmen,
viginti lectis equitum comitatus et urbi
improvisus adest: maculis quem Thracius albis
portat equus cristaque tegit galea aurea rubra.

[2] possit lacrimis *Verg.*: lacrimis possit ω (*nisi credendum Macrob.* -sit *longum in thesi putasse)*

[3] dolorem (dolores *Orosius 2.18.4*)] labores *Verg.*

there, you see, in the smallest number of words he drained the largest city, swallowed it down, and left it not even a remnant. 9. Would you like him to convey the same idea with the greatest elaboration?

> It has come, the final day, the time that Dardania
> cannot avoid: we Trojans , Ilium, and the Teucrians' great name
> were but are no more. To Argos has savage Jupiter shifted
> all that was ours: the Greeks are masters in a city reduced to ash. (*A.* 2.324–27)

> 10. O my homeland, o Ilium, home of the gods, the Dardanians' walls
> famed in war! . . . " (*A.* 2.241–42)

> Who could unfurl in speech that night's catastrophe,
> who the deaths? Who could take grief's measure in tears?
> The ancient city falls after many years as master. (*A.* 2.361–63)

What spring, what torrent, what sea has ever overflowed with as many waves as he did with words! 11. Now, here you have the well-known dry style (*A.* 9.47–50):

> When Turnus, speeding ahead, had gone before the slow troop-column,
> he arrives at the city with a company of twenty chosen men
> unexpectedly: a Thracian horse dappled white
> carries him, a golden helmet, red-crested, covers his head.

12. hoc idem quo cultu, quam florida oratione, cum libuerit, profertur!

forte sacer Cybelae[4] Choreus[5] olimque sacerdos
insignis longe Phrygiis fulgebat in armis,
spumantemque agitabat equum, quem pellis aenis
in plumam squamis[6] auro conserta tegebat.
ipse peregrina ferrugine clarus et ostro
spicula torquebat Lycio Gortynia cornu . . .
pictus acu tunicas et barbara tegmina crurum.

13. 'Sed haec quidem inter se separata sunt. vis autem videre quem ad modum haec quattuor genera dicendi Vergilius ipse permisceat et faciat unum quoddam ex omni diversitate pulcherrimum temperamentum?

14. saepe etiam steriles incendere profuit agros
atque levem stipulam crepitantibus urere flammis:
sive inde occultas vires et pabula terrae
pinguia concipiunt, sive illis omne per ignem
excoquitur vitium atque exsudat inutilis umor,
seu plures calor ille vias et caeca relaxat
spiramenta, novas veniat qua sucus in herbas,
seu durat magis et venas adstringit hiantes,

4 Cybelae (-le *cod.* γ *Verg.*)] -lo *Verg.*
5 Choreus (*cod.* M *Verg.*)] Chlor- *Verg.* (*cf. 5.15.12*)
6 in plumam squamis C, *om.* ω

---

5 "Outlandish" and "barbarous" because the man in question is a foreigner from the point of view of the Italian warrior Camilla who is tracking him in this passage.

12. Yet how richly, how colorfully he produces the same idea when it pleases him! (*A.* 11.768–73, 777)

> Choreus, by chance, a devotee of Cybele and once her priest
> was conspicuous from afar in his gleaming Phrygian arms,
> riding a foaming horse that was covered in mail of bronze
> scales fastened with gold in a feather pattern.
> He himself, a brilliant sight of outlandish red and purple,
> was shooting Cretan arrows from a Lycian bow . . .
> his tunic and barbarous[5] leggings were embroidered.

13. 'But the examples I've given are distinct in their styles: would you like to see how Virgil himself mingles the four styles and makes a kind of beautifully balanced mixture from their whole diverse range? (*G.* 1.84–93)

> 14. Often, too, it has helped to burn infertile fields
> and scorch the light stubble with crackling flames:
> whether because the lands take from that an invisible strength
> and rich sustenance, or because the fire bakes out
> all flaws and sweats out unhelpful dampness,
> or because the heat opens more paths and
> unseen passages, to let the juice reach new-grown grass,
> or rather because it toughens and constricts the gaping channels,

ne tenues pluviae rapidive potentia solis
acrior aut Boreae penetrabile frigus adurat.

15. ecce dicendi genus quod nusquam alibi deprehendes, in quo nec praeceps brevitas nec infrunita copia nec ieiuna siccitas nec laetitia pinguis.

16. 'Sunt praeterea stili dicendi duo dispari moralitate diversi. unus est maturus et gravis, qualis Crasso assignatur. hoc Vergilius utitur cum Latinus praecipit Turno:

o praestans animi iuvenis, quantum ipse feroci
virtute exsuperas, tanto me impensius aequum est
consulere . . .

et reliqua. 17. alter huic contrarius ardens et erectus et infensus, quali est usus Antonius. nec hunc apud Vergilium frustra desideraveris:

. . . haud talia dudum
dicta dabas. morere et fratrem ne desere frater.

18. 'Videsne eloquentiam omnium varietate distinctam? quam quidem mihi videtur Vergilius non sine quodam praesagio, quo se omnium profectibus praeparabat, de industria permiscuisse idque non mortali sed divino ingenio praevidisse: atque adeo non alium secutus ducem quam ipsam rerum omnium matrem naturam, hanc per-

---

6 For the *gravitas* of Crassus, cf. Cic. *Brutus* 143; for the vigor of Antonius, *On the Orator* 3.32.

lest the fine rains or the ravenous sun's power, when it's
too fierce, or the North wind's piercing cold do damage.

15. There you have a style that you'll find nowhere else, with a brevity that's not abrupt, an abundance that's not mindless, a dryness that's not barren, a luxuriance that's not cloying.

16. 'There are, furthermore, two styles that provide an ethical contrast.[6] One is the mature and serious sort associated with Crassus, which Virgil uses when Latinus advises Turnus (*A.* 12.19–21):

O young man of surpassing spirit, the more you exult
in your fierce valor, the more earnestly should I
take counsel. . . .

and so on. 17. The other style is the opposite: it's the fiery, confident, and aggressive sort that Antonius used—nor would you look for it in vain in Virgil (*A.* 10.599–600):

. . . That's not the sort of thing you were saying
just now. Die and—a good brother—go keep your brother company.

18. 'Do you perceive how Virgil's eloquence is distinguished by combining all the different styles? I think, in fact, that Virgil took pains to achieve this blend because he sensed that he was preparing himself to serve as a universal resource, and I further believe that this foresight of his was the product of a divine, not merely mortal, intelligence: he followed no guide but nature, the very mother of all things, and he wove her into the fabric of his verse, like the har-

texuit velut in musica concordiam dissonorum. 19. quippe si mundum ipsum diligenter inspicias, magnam similitudinem divini illius et huius poetici operis invenies. nam qualiter eloquentia Maronis ad omnium mores integra est, nunc brevis, nunc copiosa, nunc sicca, nunc florida, nunc simul omnia, interdum lenis aut torrens: sic terra ipsa hic laeta segetibus et pratis, ibi silvis et rupibus hispida, hic sicca harenis, hic irrigua fontibus, pars vasto aperitur mari. 20. ignoscite nec nimium me vocetis, qui naturae rerum Vergilium comparavi. intra ipsum enim mihi visum est, si dicerem decem rhetorum qui apud Athenas Atticas floruerunt stilos inter se diversos hunc unum permiscuisse.'[7]

2 Tunc Evangelus irridenti similis, 'bene,' inquit 'opifici deo a rure Mantuano poetam comparas quem Graecos rhetoras, quorum fecisti mentionem, nec omnino legisse adseveraverim! unde enim Veneto rusticis parentibus nato, inter silvas et frutices educto, vel levis Graecarum notitia litterarum?' 2. et Eustathius, 'cave,' inquit, 'Euangele, Graecorum quemquam vel de summis auctoribus tantam Graecae doctrinae hausisse copiam credas, quantam sollertia Maronis vel adsecuta est vel in suo opere di-

[7] *post* permiscuisse *add.* DE R(H)ET(H)ORICIS OBSERVATIONIBVS VIRGILII (VER- N) FINIT ω, *om.* P

---

[7] Though Homer was often regarded as a philosopher, theologian, or allegorist, and his poetry was often read allegorically (see esp. Lamberton 1986, Lamberton and Keaney 1992), I know of no parallel to this comparison of the poet himself, or his eloquence, to the whole natural world (cf. Coulter 1976 on the work of literature as analogous to the cosmos). [8] The notion of "god the craftsman" (*deus opifex*) descends from Plato's "Demiurge" (< Gk. *dêmiourgos*, "artisan"), the all-good shaper of the sensible world

mony produced by different tones in music. 19. Indeed, if you carefully examine the world itself, you will see a great similarity between that divine creation and this poetic one: just as Maro's eloquence is a complete whole that responds to the characters of all people—now brief, now abundant, now dry, now colorful, now all at once, sometimes gentle, sometimes turbulent—so the earth itself has fertile fields and meadows in one place, shaggy woods and rugged crags in another, dry desert sands here, places soaked by springs there, and part opened up to the desolate expanse of the sea. 20. Forgive me, then, and don't say that I exaggerate in comparing Virgil to the natural world:[7] for I thought it would fall short of his true measure, were I to say that he combined, all by himself, the divergent styles of the ten orators who flourished in the Athens of Attica.'

Then Evangelus said, with a mocking expression, 2
'Bravo! You compare to god the craftsman[8] a poet from the hinterland of Mantua who—I'm quite certain—never even read the Greek orators you've mentioned! How could a native of the Veneto born to peasant parents and raised amid the woods and thickets acquire even a smattering of Greek literature?'[9] 2. 'Don't suppose, Evangelus,' Eustathius replied, 'that any of the Greeks—even among the greatest authors—drank as deeply of Greek learning as the skillful Maro, or incorporated as much in his work.

in the *Timaeus* (28A6 and *passim*), influential in later philosophy (cf. *Comm.* 1.6.2, 23–24, 30, 47). [9] The remark assumes the modest background described in the biographical tradition attached to Virgil, though his father there is usually said to have been a potter (*figulus*), not a peasant (but cf. Phocas *Life of Virgil* 30–31 "the tiller of a little plot,/as others report").

gessit. nam praeter philosophiae et astronomiae amplam illam copiam de qua supra disseruimus, non parva sunt alia quae traxit a Graecis et carmini suo tamquam illic nata conseruit.' 3. et Praetextatus, 'oratus sis,' inquit, 'Eustathi, ut haec quoque communicata nobiscum velis, quantum memoria repente incitata suffecerit.' omnes Praetextatum secuti ad disserendum Eustathium provocaverunt. ille sic incipit:[8]

4. 'Dicturumne me putatis ea quae vulgo nota sunt, quod Theocritum sibi fecerit pastoralis operis auctorem, ruralis Hesiodum, et quod in ipsis Georgicis tempestatis serenitatisque signa de Arati phaenomenis traxerit, vel quod eversionem Troiae cum Sinone suo et equo ligneo ceterisque omnibus quae librum secundum faciunt a Pisandro ad verbum paene transcripserit, 5. qui inter Graecos poetas eminet opere quod a nuptiis Iovis et Iunonis incipiens universas historias, quae mediis omnibus saeculis usque ad aetatem ipsius Pisandri contigerunt, in unam seriem coactas redegerit et unum ex diversis hiatibus temporum corpus effecerit, in quo opere inter historias ceteras interitus quoque Troiae in hunc modum relatus est, quae Maro fideliter interpretando fabricatus sibi est

[8] *post* incipit *add.* QVAE VIRGILIVS TRAXIT A GRAECIS *ω*, *om.* P[1], *add.* P[m]

---

[10] The subjects treated by Eustathius in the lacuna between the end of Book 2 and beginning of Book 3 as they now survive. The remark here ("beyond the abundant knowledge . . . no small amount of *other* material from the Greeks") shows that Eustathius cast his earlier discussion as a survey of Virgil's borrowings from

For beyond the abundant knowledge of philosophy and astronomy that we discussed before,[10] he derived no small amount of other material from the Greeks and implanted it in his poetry as though it were native growth.' 3. And Praetextatus said, 'Please let us prevail upon you, Eustathius, to share with us as much along these lines as your memory, roused of a sudden into action, will provide.' When everyone followed Praextatus in calling on Eustathius to hold forth, he began as follows:

4. 'Do you think I'm going to go over the well-known ground—that Virgil made Theocritus his model for his pastoral poetry, Hesiod for the agricultural, and that in those *Georgics* he derived the signs for storms and clear weather from Aratus' *Phaenomena*,[11] or that he copied the sack of Troy, with Sinon, the wooden horse, and all the rest that make up the *Aeneid*'s second book nearly word for word from Pisander, 5. who holds a distinguished place among Greek poets for producing a single long narrative history of the whole world—beginning with the wedding of Jupiter and Juno and covering the whole intervening period down to Pisander's own day—and for creating from a series of separate epochs a single unified chronology in which among all the other stories Troy's destruction was retold, too, an account that Virgil accurately translated in

Greek culture: if that discussion was thus a counterpart to the survey that will occupy the rest of Book 5, was it also, perhaps, as long?

[11] Cf. Serv. on *G.* 1.175, 354 and preface to *E.* and *G.*

Iliacae urbis ruinam? 6. sed et haec et talia pueris decantata praetereo.

'Iam vero Aeneis ipsa, nonne ab Homero sibi mutuata est errorem primum ex Odyssea, deinde ex Iliade pugnas? quia operis ordinem necessario rerum ordo mutavit, cum apud Homerum prius Iliacum bellum gestum sit, deinde revertenti de Troia error contigerit Vlixi, apud Maronem vero Aeneae navigatio bella quae postea in Italia sunt gesta praecesserit. 7. rursus Homerus in primo, cum vellet iniquum Graecis Apollinem facere, causam struxit de sacerdotis iniuria: hic ut Troianis Iunonem faceret infestam, causarum sibi congeriem comparavit. 8. nec illud cum magna cura relaturus sum, licet ut aestimo non omnibus observatum, quod cum primo versu promisisset producturum se de Troiae litoribus Aenean

. . . Troiae qui primus ab oris
Italiam fato profugus Lavinaque venit
litora,

ubi ad ianuam narrandi venit, Aeneae classem non de Troia, sed de Sicilia producit:

vix e conspectu Siculae telluris in altum
vela dabant laeti,

---

12 The poet described must be Pisander of Laranda, author of *Heroic Marriages of the Gods* (Heitsch 1961–64, 2:44–47), an epic poem of world history in 60 books; active under Alexander Severus, he was obviously more likely influenced by Virgil than vice versa. M. (or his source) evidently confused him with another man with that common name, either the poet of Rhodes (7th/6th cent. BCE) who wrote a genealogical poem on Hêraklês or the Hellenistic mythographer (no. 16 *FGrH*).

fashioning his own sack of Troy?[12] 6. No, I'm passing these items by, and others like them that comprise the schoolboy's catechism.

'As for the *Aeneid* itself, didn't it borrow from Homer, taking first the wanderings from the *Odyssey* and then the battles from the *Iliad*? Yes, because the order of events necessarily changed the order of the narrative: whereas in Homer the war was fought at Troy first, with Ulysses become a wanderer on his return from Troy, in Maro Aeneas' voyage preceded the wars that were subsequently fought in Italy. 7. Or again, when Homer wanted to represent Apollo as hostile to the Greeks in *Iliad* 1, he based the reason on a wrong done to the god's priest; when Virgil represented Juno as hostile to the Trojans, he gathered together a heap of reasons. 8. Nor will I take great pains to recount—though I judge not everyone has noticed—that while he promised in the *Aeneid*'s first line that he would bring Aeneas forth from the coast of Troy (*A*. 1.1–3)

> . . . who first from the coast of Troy,
> made a refugee by fate, came to Italy and the
> Lavinian
> shores,

when he reaches the threshold of the actual narrative he brings Aeneas forth not from Troy but from Sicily (*A*. 1.34–35†),

> Scarcely out of sight of Sicily they were joyfully
> setting sail
> into the deep,

quod totum Homericis filis texuit. 9. ille enim vitans in poemate historicorum similitudinem, quibus lex est incipere ab initio rerum et continuam narrationem ad finem usque perducere, ipse poetica disciplina a rerum medio coepit et ad initium post reversus est. 10. ergo Vlixis errorem non incipit a Troiano litore describere, sed facit eum primo navigantem de insula Calypsonis, et ex persona sua perducit ad Phaeacas. illic in convivio Alcinoi regis narrat ipse quem ad modum de Troia ad Calypsonem usque pervenerit. post Phaeacas rursus Vlixis navigationem usque ad Ithacam ex persona propria poeta describit. 11. quem secutus Maro Aenean de Sicilia producit, cuius navigationem describendo perducit ad Libyam. illic in convivio Didonis ipse narrat Aeneas usque ad Siciliam de Troia navigationem et addit uno versu quod iam copiose poeta descripserat:

hinc me digressum vestris deus appulit oris.

12. post Africam quoque rursus poeta ex persona sua iter classis usque ad ipsam descripsit Italiam:

interea medium Aeneas iam classe tenebat
certus iter . . .

13. 'quid quod et omne opus Vergilianum velut de quodam Homerici operis speculo formatum est? nam et tempestas mira imitatione descripta est—versus utriusque qui

---

[13] Cf. Serv.'s preface to *A.* (citing Hor. *Ars Poetica* 43–44), DServ. on *A.* 1.34; the canonical statement is Horace *Ars Poetica* 148–49 (cf. Brink's comm. ad loc.).

all of which he wove together with Homeric thread. 9. For in his poetry Homer avoided copying the historians, whose rule it is to begin at the beginning of their story and to draw an unbroken narrative line to the end: instead, as poetry demands, he began in the middle of the story and then later returned to the beginning.[13] 10. That's why he doesn't begin to recount Ulysses' wandering from the shore of Troy but has him first sail from Calypso's island, taking the narrative as far as the Phaeacians in his own voice. There, at king Alcinous' banquet, Ulysses himself relates how he came from Troy all the way to Calypso. After the Phaeacians the poet again narrates Ulysses' voyage all the way back to Ithaca in his own voice. 11. Maro followed Homer in bringing Aeneas forth from Sicily, and in recounting the voyage he takes him to Libya. There, in Dido's banquet, Aeneas describes his voyage from Troy all the way to Sicily and adds in a single verse what the poet had already elaborately described (*A.* 3.715):

> When I had left there, the god drove me to your
> shores.

12. After Africa, too, the poet again described the fleet's journey in his own voice, all the way to Italy itself (*A.* 5.1):

> Meanwhile, Aeneas was already reaching the
> journey's midpoint with his fleet,
> his mind resolved. . . .

13. 'What of the fact that the whole of Virgil's poem is shaped as a kind of mirror-image of Homer's? For the description of the storm is a wonderful imitation of Homer—if anyone wants to compare the verses of each, let him do

volet conferat—et[9] Venus in locum Nausicaae[10] Alcinoi filiae successit, ipsa autem Dido refert speciem regis Alcinoi convivium celebrantis. 14. Scylla quoque et Charybdis et Circe decenter attingitur et pro Solis armentis Strophades insulae finguntur. at pro consultatione inferorum descensus ad eos cum comitatu sacerdotis inducitur: 15. ibi Palinurus Elpenori, sed et infesto Aiaci infesta Dido et Tiresiae consiliis Anchisae monita respondent. iam proelia Iliadis et vulnerum non sine disciplinae perfectione descriptio et enumeratio auxiliorum duplex et fabricatio armorum et ludicri certaminis varietas, ictumque inter reges et ruptum foedus et speculatio nocturna et legatio reportans a Diomede repulsam[11] Achillis exemplo, et super Pallante ut Patroclo lamentatio, et altercatio ut Achillis et

[9] et *Timpanaro*: ut ω

[10] in locum Nausicaae] in locum nausiace C, in nausiacae locum R (in Nausicaae locum *ed. Flor. 1515*), innausia caelo cum ω (cum *om.* P[1])

[11] repulsam GFC: -sa NPRA

---

[14] The verb M. chooses, *finguntur*, might suggest that he thought the incident one of Virgil's "fictions"—an episode without a model in the literary tradition (cf. 5.17.1, Serv. on *A.* 3.46, 9.82)—though Serv. on *A.* 3.209 shows that knowledge of Virgil's imitation of Ap. Rhod. 2.223ff. was part of the scholastic tradition.

[15] Contrast Serv. (on *A.* 6.107), for whom Elpenor corresponds to Misenus. [16] Cf. Serv. on *A.* 6.468.

[17] Double catalogue: *Il.* 2.485–760 (Greeks), 816–77 (Trojans) ~ *A.* 7.641–817 (Italians), 10.163–214 (Etruscan).

[18] The relevant passages in the *Iliad*, 3.276–92 and 4.104ff., could be taken to correspond both to the initial agreement between the Trojans and Latinus, subsequently made void by the

so (*Od.* 5.291ff. ~ *A.* 1.81–156)—and Venus took the place of Nausicaa, Alcinous' daughter (*Od.* 6.139ff ~ *A.* 1.314–24), while Dido herself is the very image of king Alcinous convening his banquet (*Od.* 8.57ff. ~ *A.* 1.697–700). 14. Scylla, too, and Charybdis and Circe are mentioned briefly but tastefully (*Od.* 12.235–59 ~ *A.* 3.420–28, *Od.* 10.135ff. ~ *A.* 7.10–20), and the Strophades are conjured up[14] in place of the cattle of the Sun (*Od.* 12.262ff. ~ *A.* 3.209–13). But instead of Ulysses' consultation of the spirits of the dead Aeneas is represented as going down to them with the priestess as his companion (*Od.* 11.23ff. ~ *A.* 6.236–73): 15. there Palinurus corresponds to Elpenor,[15] as does the hostile Dido to the hostile Ajax[16] and the warnings of Anchises to the advice of Tiresias (*Od.* 11.51–89, 543–65, 90ff. ~ *A.* 6.337–83, 450–75, 679ff.). Soon, there are the *Iliad*'s battles and woundings, rendered with consummate skill, the double catalogue of allies,[17] the forging of the arms (*Il.* 18.369–477 ~ *A.* 8.370–453), the range of contests in the games (*Il.* 23.257–897 ~ *A.* 5.104ff.), the treaty between the kings struck and then broken,[18] the nocturnal scouting mission (*Il.* 10.272–579 ~ *A.* 9.176–445),[19] the embassy that reports Diomedes' rebuff, after the example of Achilles (*Il.* 9.182–694 ~ *A.* 11.225ff.), the lamentation over Pallas, like that over Patroclus (*Il.* 18.22–51 ~ *A.* 11.36–58), the bitter exchange of Drances and Turnus, like that of Achilles and Agamemnon—in each

outbreak of war (*A.* 7.259–73, 341–622), and especially to the agreement before the duel between Aeneas and Turnus, subsequently violated by the Italians under Juturna's influence (*A.* 12.161–215, 216–86).

19 Cf. Serv. on *A.* 9.1.

Agamemnonis, ita Drancis et Turni—utrobique enim alter suum, alter publicum commodum cogitabat—pugna singularis Aeneae atque Turni ut Achillis et Hectoris, et captivi inferiis destinati, ut illic Patrocli, hic Pallantis:

> . . . Sulmone creatos
> quattuor hic iuvenes,[12] totidem quos educat Vfens,
> viventes rapit, inferias quos immolet umbris.

16. quid quod pro Lycaone Homerico, qui inter fugientes deprehensus non mirum si ad preces confugerat, nec tamen Achilles propter occisi Patrocli dolorem pepercit, simili condicione Magus in medio tumultu subornatus est?

> inde Mago procul infestam[13] contenderat hastam,

et cum ille genua amplectens supplex vitam petisset, respondit,

> . . . belli commercia Turnus
> sustulit ista prior iam tum Pallante perempto.

17. sed et insultatio Achillis in ipsum Lycaonem iam peremptum in Tarquitium[14] a Marone transfertur. ille ait,

> ἐνταυθοῖ νῦν[15] κεῖσο

[12] iuvenes GP²: -nis ω
[13] infestam (*codd.* PRγ *Verg.*)] infensam *cett. codd. Verg., Tib.*
[14] Tarquitium] Tarquitus *Verg.*
[15] νῦν *ed. Ven. 1472*: NΥ ω (NI N)

case one party thinking about his own interest, the other the common interest (*Il.* 1.121ff. ~ *A.* 11.336–444)—the single combat of Aeneas and Turnus, like that of Achilles and Hector (*Il.* 22.21ff. ~ *A.* 12.697–952), the captives marked out for the shades of Patroclus, on the one hand (*Il.* 21.26–32), and of Pallas, on the other (*A.* 10.517–19):

> . . . four youths,
> Sulmo's offspring, and as many again that Ufens raised,
> he captures alive, to slaughter as offerings to the dead.

16. Then there's Homer's Lycaon, caught amid the rout and reduced (no surprise) to begging, though Achilles did not spare him in his grief for the slain Patroclus (*Il.* 21.34–135). He's replaced by Magus, who finds himself in similar circumstances in the midst of the fray (*A.* 10.521):

> thereafter he had aimed from afar his hostile spear at Magus,

and when he grasped Aeneas' knees and begged for his life as a suppliant, Aeneas replied (*A.* 10.532–33),

> . . . Turnus did away with that sort
> of barter in war, back then when he killed Pallas.

17. But where Achilles also mocks Lycaon when he's already dead, Maro transfers this to the death of Tarquitius. The former says (*Il.* 21.122),

> Lie there now

et cetera, at hic vester:

istic nunc, metuende, iace,

et reliqua.

3 'Et si vultis me et ipsos proferre versus ad verbum paene translatos, licet omnes praesens memoria non suggerat, tamen qui se dederint obvios adnotabo.

2. *νευρὴν μὲν*[16] *μαζῷ πέλασεν, τόξῳ δὲ σίδηρον.*[17]

totam rem quanto compendio lingua ditior explicavit? vester licet periodo usus idem tamen dixit:

adduxit[18] longe, donec curvata coirent
inter se capita et manibus iam tangeret aequis,
laeva aciem ferri, dextra nervoque papillam.

3. ille ait:

. . . *οὐδέ τις ἄλλη*
*φαίνετο γαιάων, ἀλλ' οὐρανὸς ἠδὲ θάλασσα.*

. . . nec iam amplius ulla
apparet tellus,[19] caelum undique et undique pontus.

[16] *νευρὴν μὲν ed. Ven. 1472*: ΝΥΡΗΝ α, ΝΕΥΡΕΗΝ $\beta_2$

[17] ΔΗΡΟΝ ω (-ΡΩ F); *hinc usque ad finem libri Graecae litterae fere desunt in* G$\beta_2$, *spat. relict. in* GR (*nota* "GR" *ad omissa indicanda saepe utuntur* AC). *deferre mendas quae codices* NP *passim deformant supervacuum habeo.*

[18] adduxit] et duxit *Verg.*

[19] ulla apparet tellus (*hic et 5.6.1, cf.* A. *5.8–9* ulla/occurrit tellus)] ullae apparent terrae *Verg.*

and so on, but your poet says (*A.* 10.557),

> Lie there now, you terror,

and so on.

'And if you'd like me to put before you the actual verses that Virgil took over almost word for word, I'll remark on those that occur to me, though I can't remember them all right now. 3

2. He brought the bowstring to his breast, the iron tip to the bow (*Il.* 4.123).

See how concisely the Greek—a richer language[20]—set the whole scene out? Though your poet used a complex sentence, he still conveyed the same idea (*A.* 11.860–62*):

> She drew back a long time, until the bow-tips bent
> and came together, her hands dead level, the left now
> touching the iron tip, the right, with the bowstring, her breast.

3. Homer says (*Od.* 12.403–4):

> . . . nor was any other
> land in view, but only the sky and the sea.

> . . . no more now is any
> land in view, but the sky on all sides and on all sides the sea. (*A.* 3.192–93)

[20] Cf. 1.2.16n.

4. *πορφύρεον δ' ἄρα κῦμα παρίστατο,*[20] *οὔρει ἶσον,*
*κυρτωθέν*

curvata in molis[21] faciem circumstetit unda.

5. et de Tartaro ille ait:

*τόσσον ἔνερθ' Ἀΐδεω ὅσον οὐρανός ἐστ' ἀπὸ γαιής,*
bis patet in praeceps tantum tenditque sub umbras
quantus ad aetherium caeli suspectus Olympum.

6. *αὐτὰρ ἐπεὶ πόσιος καὶ ἐδητύος ἐξ ἔρον ἕντο.*

postquam exempta fames et amor compressus edendi.

7. *τῷ δ' ἕτερον μὲν δῶκε θεός,*[22] *ἕτερον δ' ἀνένευσε.*

audiit et votis[23] Phoebus succedere partem
mente dedit, partem volucres dispersit in auras.

8. *νῦν δὲ δὴ Αἰνείαο βίη Τρώεσσιν ἀνάσσει*[24]
*καὶ παίδων παῖδες, τοί κεν μετόπισθε γένωνται.*

[20] *παρίστατο Jan* (ΠΑΠΙΣΤΑΤΟ *a*): *περιστάθη ed.Ven. 1528 ex Hom.*

[21] molis] montis *Verg.*

[22] *δῶκε θεός* (*e.g. Il.* 7. 288)] *ἔδωκε πατήρ Hom., ed. Ven. 1472*

[23] votis (*Tib.*)] voti *Verg.*

[24] *ἀνάσσει*] *ἀνάξει Hom.*

4. Then a surging wave was right at hand, mountain high,
overhanging (*Od.* 11.243–44),

Arched and massive, the wave rose all around. (*G.* 4.361)

5. About Tartarus Homer says,

As far beneath Hades as heaven is from earth (*Il.* 8.16),
It opens out into the abyss and stretches beneath the shades twice
as far as the view of heaven reaches up to lofty Olympus. (*A.* 6.578–79)

6. But when they put aside the desire for drink and food . . . (*Il.* 1.469)

After hunger was banished and the desire for eating was checked . . . (*A.* 8.184)

7. To him the god granted the one but refused the other. (*Il.* 16.250)

Phoebus heard and in his mind granted to his vows
that part succeed, but part he scattered to the winged breezes. (*A.* 11.794–95)

8. Now indeed the might of Aeneas lords it over the Trojans,
and so his children's children, and any born thereafter. (*Il.* 20.307–8)

hic domus Aeneae cunctis dominabitur oris
et nati natorum et qui nascentur ab illis.

9. *καὶ τότ' Ὀδυσσῆος λύτο γούνατα καὶ φίλον ἦτορ,*

et alibi:

*Αἴας δ' ἐρρίγησε*[25] *κασιγνήτοιο πεσόντος.*·

hic de duobus unum fabricatus est,

extemplo Aeneae solvuntur frigore membra.

10. *πότνι' Ἀθηναίη, ἐρυσίπτολι, δῖα θεάων,*
*ἆξον δὴ ἔγχος Διομήδεος, ἠδὲ καὶ αὐτὸν*
*πρηνέα δὸς πεσέειν Σκαιῶν προπάροιθε πυλάων.*

armipotens, praesens belli, Tritonia virgo,
frange manu telum Phrygii praedonis et ipsum
pronum sterne solo portisque effunde sub ipsis.[26]

11. *οὐρανῷ ἐστήριξε κάρη καὶ ἐπὶ χθονὶ βαίνει.*

ingrediturque solo et caput inter nubila condit.

12. ille de somno ait:

*νήδυμος*[27] *ἥδιστος, θανάτῳ ἄγχιστα ἐοικώς.*

[25] ἐρρίγησε (*cf. Il. 15.436*)] οὐκ ἀμέλησε *Hom.*
[26] ipsis (*cf. A. 9.330, 11.499*)] altis *Verg.*
[27] νήδυμος (*ex priore versu*)] νήγρετος *Hom.*

Here the house of Aeneas will be master over all shores,
and so his sons' sons, and those who will be born from them. (*A.* 3.97–98*)

9. And then Ulysses' knees gave way and his own dear heart (*Od.* 5.297),

and elsewhere,

Ajax shuddered when his brother fell (*Il.* 8.330):

From these two verses Virgil crafted one (*A.* 1.92†),

At once Aeneas' limbs grow chill and limp.

10. Lady Athena, the city's bulwark, fairest of goddesses,
shatter the lance of Diomedes and make the man himself
fall outstretched before the Skaian gates. (*Il.* 6.305–7)

Mighty in arms, a ready aid in war, Tritonian maiden,
break the Phrygian bandit's lance with your hand and himself
lay low with his face in the dirt, sprawled before the very walls. (*A.* 11.483–85*)

11. Her head is set fast in heaven as she walks upon the earth. (*Il.* 4.443)

. . . and she strides upon the earth, her head hidden among the clouds. (*A.* 4.177 = 10.767)

12. About sleep Homer says (*Od.* 13.80),

Pleasant, very sweet, most like in appearance to death.

hic posuit:

dulcis et alta quies placidaeque simillima morti.

13. *ναὶ μὰ τόδε σκῆπτρον, τὸ μὲν οὔποτε φύλλα καὶ ὄζους*
*φύσει, ἐπεὶ δὴ πρῶτα τομὴν ἐν ὄρεσσι λέλοιπεν,*
*οὐδ' ἀναθηλήσει, περὶ γάρ ῥά ἑ χαλκὸς ἔλεψεν*
*φύλλα τε καὶ φλοιόν· νῦν αὖτέ μιν υἷες Ἀχαιῶν*
*ἐν παλάμαις φορέουσι δικασπόλοι οἵ τε θέμιστας*
*πρὸς Διὸς εἰρύαται.*

14. "ut sceptrum hoc"—dextra sceptrum nam forte gerebat—
"numquam fronde levi fundet virgulta neque umbram,[28]
cum semel in silvis imo de stirpe recisum
matre caret posuitque comas et brachia ferro,
olim arbos, nunc artificis manus aere decoro
inclusit[29] patribusque dedit gestare Latinis."

15. 'sed iam, si videtur, a collatione versuum translatorum facesso, ut nec uniformis narratio pariat ex satietate fastidium, et sermo ad alia non minus praesenti causae apta vertatur.'

16. 'perge quaeso,' inquit Avienus, 'omnia quae Homero subtraxit investigare. quid enim suavius quam duos praecipuos vates audire idem loquentes? quia cum tria

[28] umbram *ed. Ven. 1472 ex Verg.*: umbra *ω*
[29] inclusit C: -sis *ω* (-si R[2])

Virgil wrote (*A.* 6.522):

> Rest sweet and deep, most like untroubled death.

> 13. Aye, by this scepter, which never will grow leaves
> and shoots, after it first left its stump in the mountains,
> nor sprout again, no, for the bronze stripped away all around
> its leaves and bark: now the sons of the Akhaians
> bear it in their hands, those who give judgments and uphold
> ordinances from Zeus. (*Il.* 1.234–39)

> 14. "As this scepter"—for he chanced to hold the scepter in his right hand—
> "will never send forth shady growth with delicate foliage,
> when once it has been cut from its base in the woods,
> motherless, and has lost its crown and limbs to the blade,
> a tree once, now a craftsman's hand has encased it
> in comely bronze and given it to the fathers of Latium to wield." (*A.* 12.206*–11)

15. 'But now, if you're amenable, I'll stop comparing the verses Virgil took over—lest the tale's monotony leave you feeling you've had much more than enough—and let my discourse take another direction no less suited to our current concerns.'

16. 'Please do go on,' Avienus said, 'and track down everything he took from Homer: what could be more pleasant than hearing the two foremost poets treating the same subjects? These three things are all reckoned equally

haec ex aequo impossibilia putentur, vel Iovi fulmen vel Herculi clavam vel versum Homero subtrahere, quod etsi fieri possent, alium tamen nullum deceret vel fulmen praeter Iovem iacere, vel certare praeter Herculem robore, vel canere quod cecinit Homerus: hic opportune in opus suum quae prior vates dixerat transferendo fecit ut sua esse credantur. ergo pro voto omnium feceris si cum hoc coetu communicata velis quaecumque vestro noster poeta mutuatus est.'

17. 'cedo igitur,' Eustathius ait, 'Vergilianum volumen, quia locos singulos eius inspiciens Homericorum versuum promptius admonebor.' cumque Symmachi iussu famulus de bibliotheca petitum librum detulisset, temere volvit Eustathius ut versus quos fors obtulisset inspiceret et, 18. 'videte,' inquit, 'portum ad civitatem Didonis ex Ithaca migrantem:

> est in secessu longo locus: insula portum
> efficit obiectu laterum, quibus omnis ab alto
> frangitur inque sinus scindit sese unda reductos.
> hinc atque hinc vastae rupes geminique minantur
> in caelum scopuli, quorum sub vertice late
> aequora tuta silent; tum silvis scaena coruscis
> desuper horrentique atrum nemus imminet umbra.

---

[21] The theft of Hercules' club figures in a response to his critics attributed to Virgil by one of his defenders, Asconius Pedianus (late 1st cent. CE: Donatus *Life of Virgil* 46).

[22] Eustathius says *volumen* (> Engl. "volume"), which should strictly denote a papyrus scroll; but we are evidently to suppose that the text contains the entire *Aeneid*, which implies the codex-format that had become the norm by M.'s day (cf. also *folia* = "leaves" of a book in 5.4.1).

impossible: taking a thunderbolt from Jupiter, his club from Hercules, or a line from Homer.[21] And even if it could be managed, still no one could fittingly hurl a thunderbolt save Jupiter, or wield a club in combat save Hercules, or sing what Homer sang: yet by choosing just the right spot in his own work to take over the earlier bard's words he caused them to be thought his own. So you'll satisfy us all if you'll kindly share with the present company all that our poet borrowed from yours.'

17. 'Very well then,' Eustathius said, 'let me have a text[22] of Virgil, because I'll more readily be reminded of Homer's lines by looking at individual passages of Virgil.' When at Symmachus' bidding a slave had brought the book he requested from the library, Eustathius turned it over at random, to see what lines turned up by chance, and said, 18. 'Look there: the port that migrated from Ithaca to Dido's city (*A.* 1.159–69 ~ *Od.* 13.96–104):

> There is a spot far at the head of a bay: an island makes it
> a safe haven by offering its flanks as a barrier against which
> every wave from the open sea smashes and disperses into deep coves.
> On this side and that are massive crags, twinned cliffs that rise
> menacingly to heaven: beneath their peaks, far and wide,
> the sea's surface is silent and safe; atop them rustling woods
> form a backdrop, a looming dark grove that casts a trembling shade.

fronte sub adversa scopulis pendentibus antrum:
intus aquae dulces vivoque sedilia saxo,
nympharum domus. hic fessas non vincula naves
ulla tenent, unco non alligat anchora morsu.

19. Φόρκυνος δέ τίς ἐστι λιμήν, ἁλίοιο γέροντος,
ἐν δήμῳ Ἰθάκης· δύο δὲ προβλῆτες ἐν αὐτῷ
ἀκταὶ ἀπορρῶγες λιμένος ποτιπεπτηυῖαι·
αἵ τ᾿ ἀνέμων σκεπόωσι δυσαήων μέγα κῦμα
ἔκτοθεν· ἔντοθεν δέ τ᾿ ἄνευ δεσμοῖο μένουσιν
νῆες ἐύσσελμοι, ὅτ᾿ ἂν ὅρμου μέτρον ἵκωνται.
αὐτὰρ ἐπὶ κρατὸς λιμένος τανύφυλλος ἐλαίη·
ἀγχόθι δ᾿ αὐτῆς ἄντρον ἐπήρατον ἠεροειδές
ἱρὸν νυμφάων αἳ νηϊάδες καλέονται.᾿

4 Et cum rogasset Avienus ut non sparsim sed ab initio per ordinem adnotaret, ille manu retractis in calcem foliis sic exorsus est:

2. Aeole—namque tibi divum pater atque hominum rex
et mulcere dedit fluctus et tollere vento—. . .

κεῖνον γὰρ ταμίην ἀνέμων ποίησε Κρονίων,
ἠμὲν παυέμεναι ἠδ᾿ ὀρνύμεν ὅν κ᾿ ἐθέλῃσιν.

---

[23] Literally, "with the leaves drawn back (*retractis*) to the end (*calcem*)": if the text is a codex (5.3.17n.), we are evidently to suppose that the partly opened page-block was turned over to the right (i.e., in the direction of the end), so that the book rested on its back cover and the first leaf was at the top.

[24] Before this point in the poem (D)Serv. note Virgil's following "after Homer" at A. 1.4, 17, 30, 34, and 35.

In the cliff-face, a cave with overhanging boulders:
within, fresh water and benches formed from the living rock,
the home of nymphs. Here no lines keep the wearied ships
in place, no anchor binds them with its hooked purchase.

19. There is a certain port named for Phorkys, an old god of the sea,
in a district of Ithaka. There two headlands jut out,
sheer cliffs that are a bulwark for the port:
they ward off the great swells from the stormy winds
outside; within, the well-benched ships ride
without mooring whenever the reach safe haven's goal.
But at the head of the port is an olive tree with tapering leaves:
near to it is a cave, lovely and dark, a place
sacred to the nymphs who are called Naiads.'

And when Avienus had asked him to make his observa- 4
tions, not higgledy-piggledy, but in sequence right from
the start, he turned the leaves back to the beginning[23] and
set out as follows:

2. Aeolus—for the father of gods and king of men
made it yours to soothe the waves and raise them with the wind—. . . (*A.* 1.65–66)[24]

For the son of Kronos made him the steward of the winds,
both to make them cease and to rouse them up as he wishes. (*Od.* 10.21–22)

3. sunt mihi bis septem praestanti corpore nymphae,
quarum quae forma pulcherrima Deïopea
conubio iungam stabili propriamque dicabo.

ἀλλ' ἴθ', ἐγὼ δέ κέ τοι Χαρίτων μίαν ὁπλοτεράων
δώσω ὀπυιέμεναι καὶ σὴν κεκλῆσθαι ἄκοιτιν.

4. tempestas Aeneae Aeolo concitante cum allocutione ducis res suas conclamantis de Vlixis tempestate et allocutione descripta est, in qua Aeoli locum Neptunus obtinuit. versus, quoniam utrobique multi sunt, non inserui: qui volet legere ex hoc versu habebit exordium:

haec ubi dicta, cavum conversa cuspide montem . . .

et apud Homerum de primo[30] Odysseae:

ὣς εἰπὼν σύναγεν νεφέλας, ἐτάραξε δὲ πόντον.

5. ut primum lux alma data est, exire locosque
explorare novos, quas vento accesserit oras,
qui teneant—nam inculta videt—hominesne feraene
quaerere constituit sociisque exacta referre.

ἀλλ' ὅτε δὴ τρίτον ἦμαρ ἐϋπλόκαμος τέλεσ' Ἠώς

[30] primo] quinto *ed. Ven. 1472, edd.*

---

[25] A slip on M.'s part, after quoting a line from Book 1 of the *Aeneid*.

> 3. I have seven nymphs of surpassing beauty:
> the fairest of these in form, Deïopea,
> I shall join with you in lasting union and make her your own. (*A*. 1.71–73)

> But come, I shall give you one among the younger
> Graces, to marry and be called your wife. (*Il*. 14.267–68)

4. The storm that Aeolus stirred up for Aeneas, with the leader's address to his men lamenting his plight, is copied from the storm of Ulysses and his address, where Neptune took the part played by Aeolus. I haven't quoted all the verses, which run to quite a number in both texts; if anyone wants to read them, he can take this verse as a starting point (*A*. 1.81):

> When these things had been said, he turned his spear and the hollow mountain . . . ,

and in Homer, from Book 1[25] of the *Odyssey* (5.291):

> He spoke thus, then gathered the clouds and stirred the sea.

> 5. As soon as comforting daylight returned, he decided to go out
> and scout the new setting, find out what shores he'd been blown to,
> whether the inhabitants were people or beasts—for he sees
> no signs of cultivation—and report his findings to his companions. (*A*. 1.306–9)

> But when fair-haired Dawn brought the third day,

καὶ τότ' ἐγὼν ἐμὸν ἔγχος ἑλὼν καὶ φάσγανον ὀξὺ
καρπαλίμως παρὰ νηὸς ἀνήϊον ἐς περιωπήν,
εἴ πως ἔργα ἴδοιμι βροτῶν ἐνοπήν τε πυθοίμην.

6. nulla tuarum audita mihi neque visa sororum,
o—quam te memorem, virgo? namque haud tibi vultus
mortalis nec vox hominem sonat, o dea certe
(an Phoebi soror an nympharum sanguinis una?) . . .

γουνοῦμαι σε, ἄνασσα· θεός νύ τις ἦ βροτός ἐσσι;
εἰ μέν τις θεός ἐσσι, τοὶ οὐρανὸν εὐρὺν ἔχουσιν,
Ἀρτέμιδί σε ἐγώ γε, Διὸς κούρῃ μεγάλοιο,
εἶδός τε μέγεθός τε φυήν τ' ἄγχιστα ἐΐσκω.

7. o dea, si prima repetens ab origine pergam
et vacet annales nostrorum audire laborum,
ante diem clauso componet Vesper Olympo.

τίς κεν ἐκεῖνα
πάντα γε μυθήσαιτο καταθνητῶν ἀνθρώπων;
οὐδ' εἰ πεντάετές γε καὶ ἑξάετες παραμίμνων
ἐξερέοις, ὅσα κεῖθι πάθον κακὰ δῖοι Ἀχαιοί.

then I took my spear and sharp sword
swiftly from the ship and mounted a vantage point,
if I might see the work of men and hear their speech.
(*Od.* 10.144–47)

6. I have heard none of your sisters, nor have I seen them,
o—how am I to address you, maiden? For your face is scarce
a mortal's nor does your voice sound human, o goddess surely
(Phoebus sister? or one of the race of nymphs?) . . .
(*A.* 1.326–29)

I beseech you, my lady: are you a god or a mortal?
If you are some god, of those who hold broad heaven,
I liken you most nearly to Artemis, great Zeus' daughter,
in appearance and size and bearing. (*Od.* 6.149–52)

7. O goddess, should I start at the beginning and go on from there,
and had you time to hear our labors' chronicles, the evening star
would sooner put the day to rest, the doors of Olympus close. (*A.* 1.372–74)

Who among mortals
could speak of all those things? Not even
should you abide five years, yes, and six,
could you tell all the woes the brilliant Achaians suffered there. (*Od.* 3.113–16)

8. at Venus obscuro gradientis aëre saepsit
et multo nebulae circum dea fudit amictu,
cernere ne quis eos neu quis contingere posset
molirive moram aut veniendi poscere causas.

*καὶ τότ' Ὀδυσσεὺς ὦρτο πόλινδ' ἴμεν· ἀμφὶ δ' Ἀθήνη*
*πολλὴν ἠέρα χεῦε φίλα φρονέουσ' Ὀδυσῆϊ,*
*μή τις Φαιήκων μεγαθύμων ἀντιβολήσας*
*κερτομέοι τ' ἐπέεσσι καὶ ἐξερέοιθ' ὅτις εἴη.*

9. qualis in Eurotae ripis aut per iuga Cynthi
exercet Diana choros, quam mille secutae
hinc atque hinc glomerantur Oreades: illa pharetram
fert umero gradiensque deas supereminet omnis,
Latonae tacitum pertemptant gaudia pectus:
talis erat Dido, talem se laeta ferebat.

10. *οἵη δ' Ἄρτεμις εἶσι κατ' οὔρεος*[31] *ἰοχέαιρα*
*ἢ κατὰ Τηΰγετον περιμήκετον ἢ Ἐρύμανθον*

[31] *οὔρεος* (*codd. plerique Hom.*)] *-ρεα codd. cett. Hom.*, Σ, *edd.*

8. But as they went Venus walled them about with a covering mist
and around them the goddess shed a generous cloak of cloud,
so that no one might see them or be in contact with them
or devise a delay or demand their reasons for coming. (*A*. 1.411–14)

And then Odysseus started for the town: around him Athena
poured a great mist, taking friendly thought for Odysseus,
lest some great-spirited one among the Phaiakians fall in with him
and taunt him with words or ask who he is. (*Od*. 7.14–17)

9. Like Diana, when she sets her choruses in motion on the Eurotas' banks
or the ridges of Mount Cynthus: her followers, a thousand mountain nymphs,
are massed around her on every side; she bears her quiver
on her shoulder, and as she strides along, taller than all the other goddesses,
joy touches the inmost depths of Latona's quiet heart:
such was Dido, such her joyous bearing as she went. (*A*. 1.498–503)

10. Such is Artemis, the arrow-shooter, as she goes down from the mountain,
whether along lofty Taygetos or Erymanthos,

τερπομένη κάπροισι καὶ ὠκείῃσ' ἐλάφοισι·
τῇ δέ θ' ἅμα νύμφαι, κοῦραι Διὸς αἰγιόχοιο,
ἀγρονόμοι παίζουσι· γέγηθε δέ τε φρένα Λητώ·
πασάων δ' ὑπὲρ ἥ γε κάρη ἔχει ἠδὲ μέτωπα,
ῥεῖα δ' ἀριγνώτη πέλεται, καλαὶ δέ τε πᾶσαι·
ὣς ἥ γ' ἀμφιπόλοισι μετέπρεπε παρθένος ἁγνή.[32]

11. restitit Aeneas claraque in luce refulsit
os umerosque deo similis. namque ipsa decoram
caesariem nato genetrix lumenque iuventae
purpureum et laetos oculis adflarat honores:
quale manus addunt ebori decus aut ubi flavo
argentum Pariusve lapis circumdatur auro.

12. αὐτὰρ Ὀδυσσῆα μεγαλήτορα ᾧ ἐνὶ οἴκῳ
Εὐρυνόμη ταμίη λοῦσεν καὶ χρῖσεν ἐλαίῳ·
ἀμφὶ δέ μιν φᾶρος καλὸν βάλεν ἠδὲ χιτῶνα·
αὐτὰρ κὰκ κεφαλῆς χεῦεν πολὺ κάλλος Ἀθήνη,
μείζονά τ' εἰσιδέειν[33] καὶ πάσσονα· κὰδ δὲ κάρητος
οὔλας ἧκε κόμας, ὑακινθίνῳ ἄνθει ὁμοίας.
ὡς δ' ὅτε τις χρυσὸν περιχεύεται ἀργύρῳ ἀνὴρ
ἴδρις, ὃν Ἥφαιστος δέδαεν καὶ Παλλὰς[34] Ἀθήνη
τέχνην παντοίην, χαρίεντα δὲ ἔργα τελείει,

32 ἁγνή (*codd. aliquot Hom., cf. Od.* 5.123, 18.202, 20.71)] ἀδμής *codd. cett. Hom., edd.*

33 εἰσιδέειν] εσ- *Hom.*

34 Παλλὰς *ed. Ven. 1472 ex Hom.*: ΠΑΣΣΟΝΑΚΑΔΔΕΣ *a* (*ex Od.* 23.157 *supra*)

rejoicing in the boars and swift deer;
with her the nymphs, daughters of Zeus who holds the aegis,
range over the country in their play; and Leto feels great gladness in her mind.
Above them all she holds her head,
easily recognized as she goes, and they are all lovely:
so the pure maiden is conspicuous among her attendants. (*Od.* 6.102–9)

11. Aeneas was left standing there, brilliant in the bright light,
his face and torso like a god's. For his mother herself
had breathed upon her son the grace
of fair hair, the rosy glow of youth,
a look of joy and dignity in his eyes:
like the beauty skilled hands add to ivory, or
when tawny gold is set in silver or Parian marble. (*A.* 1.588–93)

12. Then the maid Eurynome bathed Odysseus
in his house and anointed him with oil,
and about him set a handsome mantle and tunic.
Then from the crown of his head Athena caused
much beauty to flow, made him taller and sturdier to look upon,
and from his head sent forth his hair in curls, like the hyacinth.
As when someone surrounds silver with liquid gold,
a skilled man whom Hephaistos and Pallas Athena have taught
craft of every sort, who makes works of alluring delicacy:

ὣς ἄρα[35] τῷ περίχευε χάριν κεφαλῇ τε καὶ
 ὤμοις.[36]

13. . . . coram, quem quaeritis, adsum,
Troïus Aeneas, Libycis ereptus ab undis.

ἔνδον μὲν δὴ ὅδ᾽ αὐτὸς ἐγὼ, κακὰ πολλὰ
 μογήσας,
ἤλυθον εἰκοστῷ ἔτεϊ ἐς πατρίδα γαῖαν.

Conticuere omnes intentique ora tenebant.

ὣς ἔφαθ᾽, οἱ δ᾽ ἄρα πάντες ἀκὴν ἐγένοντο σιωπῇ.

2. infandum, regina, iubes renovare dolorem,
Troianas ut opes et lamentabile regnum
eruerint Danai.

ἀργαλέον, βασίλεια, διηνεκέως ἀγορεῦσαι
κήδε᾽, ἐπεί μοι πολλὰ δόσαν θεοὶ οὐρανίωνες.

3. pars stupet innuptae donum exitiale Minervae
et molem miratur equi primusque Thymoetes
duci intra muros hortatur et arce locari,
sive dolo seu iam Troiae sic fata ferebant.
at Capys et quorum melior sententia menti
aut pelago Danaum insidias suspectaque dona

[35] *ἄρα (PRyl. 53, s. iii–iv)] μὲν Hom.*
[36] *μείζονά τ᾽ εἰσιδέειν . . . καὶ ὤμοις secl. edd. Hom., cf. Od. 6. 230–35*

so then did she wreathe his head and shoulders with grace. (*Od.* 23.153–62)

13. . . . I am here before you, the one you seek,
Trojan Aeneas, snatched from the Libyan waves. (*A.* 1.595–96)

Here I am, at home, many evil toils behind me,
come now in the twentieth year to my ancestral land. (*Od.* 21.207–8)

All fell silent and kept their gaze intent upon him. (*A.* 2.1)

So he spoke, and they all softly fell silent. (*Il.* 7.92)

2. You bid me, queen, to live again an unspeakable pain,
how the Greeks overthrew the wealth of Troy and
its pitiable dominion. (*A.* 2.3–5)

Painful it is, queen, to tell of my woes start to end,
since the gods of heaven have given me many. (*Od.* 7.241–42)

3. Some stare openmouthed at maiden Minerva's deadly gift
and marvel at the horse's mass. Thymoetes is the first
to press for bringing it inside the walls and mounting it on the citadel,
out of treachery or because Troy's fate already that way tended.
But Capys and all the others with more sense
bid them either cast the Greeks' trap into the sea—send the

praecipitare iubent subiectisque urere flammis,
aut terebrare cavas uteri et temptare latebras.
scinditur incertum studia in contraria vulgus.

4. ὣς ὁ μὲν ἑστήκει, τοὶ δ' ἄκριτα πόλλ' ἀγόρευον,
ἥμενοι ἀμφ' αὐτόν· τρίχα δὲ σφίσιν ἥνδανε βουλή,
ἠὲ διατμῆξαι[37] κοῖλον δόρυ νηλέϊ χαλκῷ,
ἢ κατὰ πετράων βαλέειν ἐρύσαντας ἐπ' ἄκρας,[38]
ἢ ἐαᾶν μέγ' ἄγαλμα θεῶν θελκτήριον εἶναι,
τῇ περ δὴ καὶ ἔπειτα τελευτήσεσθαι ἔμελλεν·
αἶσα γὰρ ἦν ἀπολέσθαι, ἐπὴν πόλις ἀμφικαλύψῃ
δουράτεον μέγαν ἵππον, ὅθ' εἵατο[39] πάντες ἄριστοι
Ἀργείων,[40] Τρώεσσι φόνον καὶ κῆρα φέροντες.

5. vertitur interea caelum et ruit Oceano nox,
involvens umbra magna terramque polumque.

ἐν δ' ἔπεσ' Ὠκεανῷ λαμπρὸν φάος ἠελίοιο,
ἕλκον νύκτα μέλαιναν ἐπὶ ζείδωρον ἄρουραν.

6. ei mihi, qualis erat, quantum mutatus ab illo
Hectore qui redit exuvias indutus Achilli

37 διατμῆξαι (*codd. Hom.*)] διαπλῆξαι *Aristarch., edd.*

38 ἄκρας (*codd. nonnull. Hom., Eustath.*)] ἄκρης *codd. cett. Hom.*

39 εἵατο] ἥατο *Hom.*

40 Ἀργείων (*codd. aliquot Hom.*, ΑΡΓ- *α*)] Ἀργεῖοι *codd. cett. Hom.*

mistrusted gift crashing, put fire to it and burn it—
or else bore into its belly's hollow lair and test it.
The crowd wavers, divided between urgent but opposing aims. (*A*. 2.31–39)

4. Thus it stood, while they spoke at length and to no clear end,
sitting around it. Three different plans were finding favor,
either to cut through the hollow wood with pitiless bronze,
or to haul it up to the citadel and cast it down from the rocks,
or to let it be a great offering to charm the gods' favor—
the very way that was going to be fulfilled thereafter.
For destruction was decreed, once the city embraced
the great wooden horse, where sat all the best
of the Argives, bringing to the Trojans murder and doom. (*Od*. 8.505–13)

5. The heavens, meanwhile, revolve and night rushes on from Ocean,
wrapping earth and sky in deep shadow. (*A*. 2.250–51)

The sun's bright light sank in Ôkean, drawing
black night over the wheat-bearing earth. (*Il*. 8.485–86)

6. Woe, woe, how he looked, how changed from the great
Hector who returned clad in the spoils of Achilles

vel Danaum Phrygios iaculatus puppibus ignes!

ὢ πόποι, ἦ μάλα δὴ μαλακώτερος ἀμφαφάασθαι
Ἕκτωρ ἢ ὅτε νῆας ἐνέπρησεν πυρὶ κηλέῳ.

7. . . . iuvenisque Coroebus
Mygdonides illis ad Troiam forte diebus
venerat insano Cassandrae incensus amore
et gener auxilium Priamo Phrygibusque ferebat.

8. πέφνε γὰρ Ὀθρυονῆα Καβησόθεν ἔνδον ἐόντα,
ὅς ῥα νέον πολέμοιο μετὰ κλέος εἰληλούθει.
ᾔτεε δὲ Πριάμοιο θυγατρῶν εἶδος ἀρίστην,
Κασσάνδρην ἀνάεδνον, ὑπέσχετο δὲ μέγα ἔργον,
ἐκ Τροίης ἀέκοντας ἀπωσέμεν υἷας Ἀχαιῶν.
τῷ δ᾽ ὁ γέρων Πρίαμος ὑπό τ᾽ ἔσχετο καὶ κατένευσε
δωσέμεναι· ὁ δὲ μάρναθ᾽ ὑποσχεσίῃσι πιθήσας.

9. sic animis iuvenum furor additus. inde lupi ceu
raptores atra in nebula, quos improba ventris
exegit caecos rabies catulique relicti
faucibus exspectant siccis, per tela, per hostes

or hurled Phrygian fire at the ships of the Greeks! (*A.* 2.274–76)

My my, much easier to deal with now is Hektor
than when he burned the ships with blazing fire. (*Il.* 22.373–74)

7. . . . and young Coroebus,
Mygdon's son, had chanced to come to Troy in just those
days, on fire with a frenzied love for Cassandra,
bringing a son-in-law's aid to Priam and the Phrygians. (*A.* 2.341–44)

8. For he struck down Othryoneus, who dwelt in Kabesos
but had come to seek fresh glory in war.
He asked to marry the loveliest of Priam's daughters,
Kassandra, promising no bride-price but a great deed instead:
to drive the sons of the Akhaians from Troy willy-nilly.
Aged Priam agreed and promised that he would give
her to him, and so he fought, trusting in those promises. (*Il.* 13.363–69)

9. Thus frenzy stoked our young men's courage: from there, like wolves
hunting in a black cloud—blinded and driven by the belly's relentless
craving, by the whelps left behind waiting to be fed,
their throats parched—we make our way amid the missiles,

vadimus haud dubiam in mortem mediaeque tenemus
urbis iter: nox atra cava circumvolat umbra.

10. βῆ ῥ' ἴμεν ὥς τε λέων ὀρεσίτροφος, ὅστ' ἐπιδευὴς
δηρὸν ἔῃ κρειῶν, κέλεται δέ ἑ θυμὸς ἀγήνωρ
μήλων πειρήσοντα καὶ ἐς πυκινὸν δόμον ἐλθεῖν.
εἴ περ γάρ χ' εὕρῃσι μετ'[41] αὐτόθι βώτορας ἄνδρας
σὺν κυσὶ καὶ δούρεσσι φυλάσσοντας περὶ μῆλα,
οὔ ῥά τ' ἀπείρητος μέμονε σταθμοῖο δίεσθαι.
ἀλλ' ὅ γ' ἄρ' ἤ' ἥρπαξε μεθάλμενος,[42] ἠὲ καὶ αὐτὸς
ἔβλητ' ἐν πρώτοισι θοῆς ἀπὸ χειρὸς ἄκοντι.

11. improvisum aspris veluti qui sentibus anguem
pressit humi nitens, trepidusque repente refugit
attollentem iras et caerula colla tumentem:
haud secus Androgeos visu tremefactus abibat.

ὡς δ' ὅτε τίς τε δράκοντα ἰδὼν παλίνορσος ἀπέστη
οὔρεος ἐν βήσσῃς, ὑπό τε τρόμος ἔλλαβε γυῖα,
ἂψ τ' ἀνεχώρησεν, ὦχρός τέ μιν εἷλε παρειάς,
ὣς αὖτις καθ' ὅμιλον ἔδυ Τρώων ἀγερώχων
δείσας Ἀτρέος υἱὸν Ἀλέξανδρος θεοειδής.

41 μετ'] *παρ' Hom.* (*cf.* 5.10.9)
42 μεθάλμενος] *μετ- Hom.* (*cf.* 5.10.9)

among the enemy, to certain death, heading onward to the city's
center: black night flutters about us with its enveloping shade. (*A.* 2.355–60)

10. He went striding like a lion raised in the mountains, who too long
has been without meat, and his valiant spirit urges him on
to go and make an attempt on a crowded fold of sheep:
if he finds there the men who tend them,
keeping watch on the sheep with dogs and spears,
he has no wish to leave the farmstead untested
but either pounces and makes his kill or himself
is struck at once by a swift hand's spear-cast. (*Il.* 12.299–306)

11. Like one who has stepped on a snake lurking in rough brambles,
pinning him to the ground, then quickly starts back trembling
as the snake raises its dark neck, swollen with anger:
just so did Androgeos start back panic-stricken at the sight. (*A.* 2.379†–82)

As when someone sees a snake and recoils
in mountain glens, and his knees suddenly tremble,
he draws back, away, his cheeks grow pale:
so godlike Alexandros, in terror at the son of Atreus,
plunged into the ranks of lordly Trojans. (*Il.* 3.33–37)

12. qualis ubi in lucem coluber mala gramina pastus,
frigida sub terra tumidum quem bruma tegebat,
nunc, positis novus exuviis nitidusque iuventa,
lubrica convolvit sublato pectore terga
arduus ad solem et linguis micat ore trisulcis.

*ὡς δὲ δράκων ἐπὶ χειῇ ὀρέστερος ἄνδρα μένῃσι*
*βεβρωκὼς κακὰ φάρμακ', ἔδυ δέ τέ μιν χόλος αἰνός,*
*σμερδαλέον δὲ δέδορκεν ἑλισσόμενος περὶ χειῇ·*
*ὣς Ἕκτωρ ἄσβεστον ἔχων μένος οὐχ ὑπεχώρει.*

13. non sic, aggeribus ruptis cum spumeus amnis
exiit oppositasque erupit[43] gurgite moles,
fertur in arva furens cumulo, camposque per omnes
cum stabulis armenta trahit . . .

*ὡς δ' ὁπότε πλήθων ποταμὸς πεδίον δὲ κάτεισι*
*χειμάρρους κατ' ὄρεσφιν ὀπαζόμενος Διὸς ὄμβρῳ,*
*πολλὰς δὲ δρῦς ἀζαλέας, πολλὰς δέ τε πεύκας*
*ἐσφέρεται, πολλὸν δέ τ' ἀφυσγετὸν εἰς ἅλα βάλλει.*

[43] erupit] evicit *Verg.*

12. Like a snake that has fed upon poisonous plants and
lain swollen underground in midwinter's cold,
now it sheds its skin and—renewed and glistening with youth—
uncoils it slippery length into the light, raising its bulk
high up toward the sun, its forked tongue darting from its mouth. (*A.* 2.471–75)

Like a snake in its mountain lair lying in wait for a man,
fed full of evil poisons and possessed by a terrible anger,
it coils round its lair, striking terror with its glance:
so Hector, with unquenchable fury, did not give way. (*Il.* 22.93–96)

13. More violently than a foaming river that bursts its levees, pours out,
and with its torrent breaks through the masses set in its way,
tumbling, boiling into the fields and over all the plain,
carrying off cattle and stables together . . . . (*A.* 2.496–99)

As when a swollen river comes down upon the plain,
driven from the mountains in a wintry flood by the rain of Zeus,
it sweeps along many parched oaks, many pines,
and hurls much debris into the sea. (*Il.* 11.492–95)

14. ter conatus ibi collo dare bracchia circum,
ter frustra comprensa manus effugit imago,
par levibus ventis volucrique simillima fumo.[44]

*τρὶς μὲν ἐφωρμήθην,*[45] *ἑλέειν τέ με θυμὸς ἀνώγει,*
*τρὶς δέ μοι ἐκ χειρῶν σκιῇ εἴκελον ἢ καὶ ὀνείρῳ*
*ἔπτατ᾽· ἐμοὶ δ᾽ ἄχος ὀξὺ γενέσκετο κηρόθι μᾶλλον.*

6 'Alia tempestas Aeneae hic et illic Vlixis, numerosis ambae versibus. sed incipiunt haec ita:

postquam altum tenuere rates nec iam amplius ulla[46]
. . .

ille ait:

*ἀλλ᾽ ὅτε δὴ τὴν νῆσον ἐλείπομεν, οὐδέ τις ἄλλη*
. . .

2. accipe et haec, manuum tibi quae monumenta mearum
sint, puer . . .

[44] fumo] somno *Verg.*
[45] ἐφωρμήθην (*codd. nonnull. Hom.*)] ἐφορ- *codd. cett. Hom.*
[46] ulla (*cf.* 5.3.3)] ullae *Verg.*

---

[26] The same lines describe Aeneas' attempt to embrace his wife Creusa's shade in Book 2 and his father Anchises' shade in Book 6: in the former, Aeneas speaks the lines as first-person narrator, in the latter, the narrator refers to Aeneas in the third person. As the lines are quoted here, the verbal person is, strictly

14. Three times then [I] tried to enfold her in my arms,
three times her image, embraced in vain, fled from my grasp,
light as the winds and very like a winged wisp of smoke. (*A.* 2.792–94 ~ 6.700–702)[26]

Three times I darted forward, my spirit bidding me to hold her,
three times she flew from my grasp like a shadow
or a dream: heartily indeed did I feel sharp grief. (*Od.* 11.206–8)

'Here is another storm for Aeneas, corresponding to 6
one for Ulysses, both of them very long, but they begin as follows (*A.* 3.192):

After our ships had gained the open seas and there was no longer any . . . ;

Homer says (*Od.* 12.403):

But when at last we were leaving the island and no other . . .

2. Take these too, my child, that they might be a reminder
of my hands' work . . . (*A.* 3.486–87)

speaking, ambiguous; but since Eustathius is working through the text seriatim, we are to assume that it is the passage from Book 2 that M. has in mind. Cf. 5.7.8n.

*τῇ νῦν καί σοι τοῦτο, τέκος,*[47] *κειμήλιον ἔστω,*
*μνῆμ' Ἑλένης χειρῶν . . .*

3. tendunt vela Noti: fugimus spumantibus undis,
qua cursum ventusque gubernatorque vocabat.

*ἡμεῖς δ' ὅπλα ἕκαστα πονησάμενοι κατὰ νῆα*
*ἥμεθα· τὴν δ' ἄνεμός τε κυβερνήτης τ' ἴθυνε.*

4. dextrum Scylla latus, laevum implacata Charybdis
obsidet atque imo barathri ter gurgite vastos
sorbet in abruptum fluctus rursusque sub auras
erigit alternos et sidera verberat unda.
at Scyllam caecis cohibet spelunca latebris
ora exertantem et naves in saxa trahentem.
prima hominis facies et pulchro pectore virgo
pube tenus, postrema immani corpore pistris,[48]
delphinum caudas utero commissa luporum.
praestat Trinacrii metas lustrare Pachyni
cessantem, longos et circumflectere cursus,
quam semel informem vasto vidisse sub antro

[47] *τέκος*] *γέρον Hom.*
[48] pistris] pistrix *Verg.*

May this be stored up for you now as a treasure, my child,
a reminder of Helen's hands . . . (*Il.* 23.618 + *Od.* 15.126)

3. The South winds fill the canvas: we hasten away on the foaming waves
where the wind and the pilot were summoning us to sail. (*A.* 3.268–69)

When we had worked hard at all the tackle the length of the ship,
we sat, and the wind and the pilot kept our course true. (*Od.* 11.9–10)

4. Scylla blocks the path to starboard, to port relentless Charybdis,
thrice sucking huge whirlpools straight down to the depths
of the sea, then sending them back up in turn
to the breezes above, striking the stars with the waves.
Scylla a cave contains in her lightless lair
as she sticks her maw out and draws boats onto the rocks.
Human in appearance at first, a fair-breasted maiden
as far as the groin, the rest a monstrous creature of the sea,
wolves at her belly joined to dolphins' tails.
Better to circle the turning point of Sicilian Pachynus
and bear the delay, steering the long way around,
than once to have looked up at horrible Scylla in her vast

Scyllam et caeruleis canibus resonantia saxa.

5. Homerus de Charybdi:

δεινὸν ἀνερροίβδησε[49] θαλάσσης ἁλμυρὸν ὕδωρ.
ἦ τοι ὅτ' ἐξεμέσειε, λέβης ὣς ἐν πυρὶ πολλῷ,
πᾶσ' ἀναμορμύρεσκε κυκωμένη· ὑψόσε δ' ἄχνη
ἄκροισι σκοπέλοισιν ἐπ' ἀμφοτέροισιν ἔπιπτεν.
ἀλλ' ὅτ' ἀναβρόξειε θαλάσσης ἁλμυρὸν ὕδωρ,
πᾶσ' ἔντοσθε φάνεσκε κυκωμένη, ἀμφὶ δὲ πέτρη
δεινὸν βεβρύχει, ὑπένερθε δὲ γαῖα φάνεσκε
ψάμμῳ κυανέῃ· τοὺς δὲ χλωρὸν δέος ᾕρει.

6. Homerus de Scylla:

ἔνθα δ' ἐνὶ Σκύλλη ναίει, δεινὸν λελακυῖα·
τῆς ἦ τοι φωνὴ μὲν ὅση σκύλακος νεογιλῆς
γείνεται,[50] αὐτὴ δ' αὖτε πέλωρ κακόν· οὐδέ κέ τίς
μιν
γηθήσειεν ἰδών, οὐδ' εἰ θεὸς ἀντιάσειεν.[51]
τῆς ἦ τοι πόδες εἰσὶ δυώδεκα πάντες ἄωροι,
ἓξ δέ τέ οἱ δειραὶ περιμήκεες, ἐν δὲ ἑκάστῃ
σμερδαλέη κεφαλή, ἐν δὲ τρίστοιχοι ὀδόντες,
πυκνοὶ καὶ θαμέες, πλεῖοι μέλανος θανάτοιο.
μέσση μέν τε κατὰ σπείους κοίλοιο δέδυκεν,
ἔξω δ' ἐξίσχει κεφαλὰς δεινοῖο βερέθρου·
αὐτοῦ δ' ἰχθυάᾳ σκόπελον περιμαιμώωσα,

49 ἀνερροίβδησε] ἀνερρύβ- *Hom.* (*sic et bis infra*, §8)
50 γείνεται] γίγν- *Hom.*
51 ἀντιάσειεν] –σειε *Hom.*

cave and at the rocks that echo with the baying sea-hounds. (*A*. 3.420*–32)

5. Homer, on Charybdis (*Od*. 12.236–43):

Terribly did she suck down the briny water of the sea;
then when she spewed it out, like a cauldron on a high blaze,
she roared, all seething, and high up the foam fell
upon the tall cliffs on both sides.
But when she gulped down the briny water of the sea,
all was seen to seethe within, the rocks all around
bellowed terribly, and below the sea bed was visible
with its dark sand. And pale fear seized them.

6. Homer, on Scylla (*Od*. 12.85–97):

Within dwells Skylla, eerily puling,
no louder than the sound of a new-born pup,
but she herself is an evil monster: no one would be glad
to look upon her, not even if a god should meet her.
Twelve feet she has, all like tentacles,
six long necks, and on each neck
a gruesome head with three rows of teeth,
close-packed and crowded, full of black death.
She is hidden up to her middle in the hollow cave
but sticks her heads out of the dreadful hole:
there she fishes, scanning eagerly around her rock

δελφῖνάς τε κύνας τε καὶ εἴ ποθι μεῖζον ἕλῃσι
κῆτος, ἃ μυρία βόσκει ἀγάστονος Ἀμφιτρίτη.

7. o mihi sola mei super Astyanactis imago!
sic oculos, sic ille manus, sic ora ferebat.

κείνου γὰρ τοιοίδε πόδες τοιαίδε τε χεῖρες
ὀφθαλμῶν τε βολαὶ κεφαλή τ᾽ ἐφύπερθέ τε χαῖται.

8. ter scopuli clamorem inter cava saxa dedere,
ter spumam elisam et rorantia vidimus astra.

τῷ δ᾽ ὑπὸ δῖα Χάρυβδις ἀναρροιβδεῖ μέλαν ὕδωρ.
τρὶς μὲν γάρ τ᾽ ἀνίησιν ἐπ᾽ ἤματι, τρὶς δ᾽ ἀναροιβδεῖ . . .

9. . . . qualis coniecta cerva sagitta,
quam procul incautam nemora inter Cresia fixit
pastor agens telis, liquitque volatile ferrum
nescius: illa fuga silvas saltusque peragrat
Dictaeos, haeret lateri letalis harundo.

10. . . . ἀμφ᾽ ἔλαφον κεραὸν βεβλημένον, ὅν ρ᾽[52] ἔβαλ᾽ ἀνὴρ

[52] ρ᾽] τ᾽ *Hom.*

for dolphins she might catch, or dogfish or any larger sea-beast
that groaning Amphitritê feeds by the thousands.

7. O, the only likeness of my Astyanax left to me:
such were his eyes, such his hands, such his face. (*A.* 3.489*–90)

For such were his feet and such his hands,
the glance of his eyes, his head, and the hair upon it. (*Od.* 4.149–50)

8. Three times the crags produced a bellow from within the hollowed rocks,
three times we saw the foam sprayed out, the stars drenched. (*A.* 3.566–67)

Beneath it awful Kharybdis sucks down the black water.
Three times a day she sends it forth, three times she sucks it down . . . (*Od.* 12.104–5)

9. . . . like a hind in the groves of Crete
that a shepherd has pierced with an arrow he shot—
far off she was and unaware, as he flushed out game with his weapons—
and he left the flying dart, not knowing it had found its mark:
she flees through the forest and the Dictaean
passes, the deadly shaft clinging fast to her flank. (*A.* 4.69–73)

10. . . . around a horned stag that's been shot: a man struck him

ἰῷ ἀπὸ νευρῆς· τὸν μέν τ' ἤλυξε πόδεσσι
φεύγων, ὄφρ' αἷμα λιαρὸν καὶ γούνατ' ὀρώρῃ·
αὐτὰρ ἐπεὶ δὴ τόν γε δαμάσσεται ὠκὺς ὀϊστός,
ὠμοφάγοι μιν θῶες ἐν οὔρεσι δαρδάπτουσιν . . .

11. dixerat. ille patris magni parere parabat
imperio et primum pedibus talaria nectit
aurea, quae sublimem alis sive aequora iuxta[53]
seu terram rapido pariter cum flamine portant.
tunc virgam capit: hac animas ille evocat Orco
pallentes, alias sub Tartara tristia mittit,
dat somnos adimitque et lumina morte resignat.
illa fretus agit ventos et turbida tranat
nubila.

12. ὣς ἔφατ', οὐδ' ἀπίθησε διάκτορος
Ἀργειφόντης.
αὐτίκ' ἔπειθ' ὑπὸ ποσσὶν ἐδήσατο καλὰ πέδιλα
ἀμβρόσια χρύσεια, τά μιν φέρον ἠμὲν ἐφ' ὑγρὴν
ἠδ' ἐπ' ἀπείρονα γαῖαν ἅμα πνοιῇς ἀνέμοιο·
εἵλετο δὲ ῥάβδον, τῇ τ' ἀνδρῶν ὄμματα θέλγει

[53] iuxta] supra *Verg.*

with an arrow from his bowstring, the stag escaped, nimble
on his feet as long as his blood was warm, his knees driving;
but when at length the swift arrow overcomes him,
the jackals that eat raw flesh feast upon him in the mountains . . . (*Il.* 11.475–79)

11. [Jupiter] had finished speaking, and [Mercury] made ready to obey the great father's
command: first he binds on his feet the golden sandals
that carry him aloft on their wings, swift as the wind,
skimming across the sea or over the earth.
Then he takes up his staff: this he uses to call some souls,
pale as death, from Orcus and to send others under grim Tartarus,
to grant sleep and take it away, to open eyes that have been sealed in death.
With its aid he drives the winds before him and glides across the stormy
clouds. (*A.* 4.238–46)

12. So he spoke, nor was his minister, Argus' slayer, heedless.
At once he bound on his feet his fair sandals
—ambrosial, golden—that carry him over the sea
or over the boundless earth, keeping pace with the wind.
He took up his staff, too, with which he beguiles the sight of men

ὧν ἐθέλει, τοὺς δ' αὖτε καὶ ὑπνώοντας ἐγείρει·
τὴν μετὰ χερσὶν ἔχων πέτετο κρατὺς
Ἀργειφόντης.

13. ac velut annoso validam cum robore quercum
Alpini Boreae nunc hinc, nunc flatibus illinc
eruere inter se certant: it stridor et alte[54]
consternunt terram concusso stipite frondes.
illa[55] haeret scopulis, et quantum vertice ad auras
aethereas,[56] tantum radicem in Tartara tendit.

14. οἷον δὲ τρέφει ἔρνος ἀνὴρ ἐριθηλὲς ἐλαίης
χώρῳ ἐν οἰοπόλῳ, ὅθ' ἅλις ἀναβέβρυχεν[57] ὕδωρ,
καλὸν τηλεθάον, τὸ δέ τε πνοιαὶ δονέουσι
παντοίων ἀνέμων καί τε βρύει ἄνθεϊ λευκῷ·
ἐλθὼν δ' ἐξαπίνης ἄνεμος σὺν λαίλαπι πολλῇ
βόθρου τ' ἐξέστρεψε καὶ ἐξετάνυσσ' ἐπὶ γαίῃ.[58]

15. et iam prima novo spargebat lumine terras
Tithoni croceum linquens Aurora cubile.

Ἠὼς δ' ἐκ λεχέων παρ' ἀγαυοῦ Τιθωνοῖο

[54] alte ((*D*)*Serv.*)] altae *codd. Verg.*
[55] illa] ipsa *Verg.*
[56] aethereas] -ias *Verg.*
[57] ἀναβέβρυχεν *ed. Basil. 1535 in marg., codd. Hom., Aristarch.* (-βροχεν *Zenod.*): -βρυσεν α
[58] γαίῃ *ed. Basil. 1535 in marg.*: πολλῇ α (*ex versu priore, utrum librarii an Macrob. lapsu haud scio*)

---

[27] Cf. also 5.9.11: the verses are treated as indirect imitations of Homer, via Lucretius and Furius, at 6.1.25 and 31.

as he choose, while others he rouses even as they sleep.
Taking it in his hands, the mighty slayer of Argus flew off. (*Il*. 24.339–45)

13. And just as when the North winds in the Alps compete
to uproot a sturdy oak, its trunk rich with years,
blasting now on this side, now on that: they shriek, the trunk
is shaken, the ground is layered deep with leaves.
The great tree clings to the ridge, sending its roots as far down
toward Tartarus as its crown reaches to heaven's breezes. (*A*. 4.441–46)

14. Like a verdant shoot of an olive tree that a man raises
in a lonely plot of ground, when enough water bubbles up,
a fair flourishing thing: gusts of every wind from every quarter
toss it and it teems richly with white flowers.
But then of a sudden a blast comes with a whirlwind's force,
tearing it from its trench and laying it low upon the earth. (*Il*. 17.53–58)

15. And already Aurora was leaving Tithonus' saffron-hued bed
and starting to dapple the lands with a new day's light. (*A*. 4.584–85)[27]

From noble Tithonos' bed Eos rose,

*ὤρνυθ᾽, ἵν᾽ ἀθανάτοισι φόως φέροι ἠδὲ βροτοῖσι*

. . .

*Ἠὼς μὲν κροκόπεπλος ἐκίδνατο πᾶσαν ἐπ᾽ αἶαν.*

7 Ut pelagus tenuere rates, nec iam amplius ulla
occurrit tellus, maria undique et undique caelum:
olli caeruleus supra caput adstitit imber
noctem hiememque ferens et inhorruit unda tenebris.

*ἀλλ᾽ ὅτε δὴ τὴν νῆσον ἐλείπομεν οὐδέ τις ἄλλη*
*φαίνετο γαιάων, ἀλλ᾽ οὐρανὸς ἠδὲ θάλασσα,*
*δὴ τότε κυανέην νεφέλην ἔστησε Κρονίων*
*νηὸς ὕπερ γλαφυρῆς, ἤχλυσε δὲ πόντος ὑπ᾽ αὐτῆς.*

2. vinaque fundebat pateris animamque vocabat
Anchisae magni manesque Acheronte remissos.

*οἶνον ἀφυσσάμενος*[59] *χαμάδις χέε, δεῦε δὲ γαῖαν*
*ψυχὴν κικλήσκων Πατροκλῆος δειλοῖο.*

3. levibus huic hamis consertam auroque trilicem
loricam, quam Demoleo detraxerat ipse
victor apud rapidum Simoënta sub Ilio alto.

[59] -*άμενος* (*codd. plerique Hom.*)] –*όμενος codd. cett. Hom., edd.*

to bring light to immortals and mortals. . . .
Eos of the saffron gown was spread over all the earth. (*Il.* 11.1–2, 8.1)

When the ships had gained the open seas and there was no longer 7
any land to meet them, sea on all sides and on all sides sky,
a dark cloud came to stand above his head, bringing
night and foul weather, and the waves turned rough in the darkness. (*A.* 5.8–11)

When at last we were leaving the island, nor was
any other land to be seen, only sky and sea, just then
did Kronos' son cause a black cloud to stand
over our hollow ship, and the sea darkened beneath it. (*Od.* 12.403–6 = 14.301–4)

2. Pouring wine from a shallow bowl, he was calling on the soul
of great Anchises and the spirits released from Acheron. (*A.* 5.98–99)

Having drawn the wine, he poured it on the ground and wet the earth,
calling on the soul of unhappy Patroklos. (*Il.* 23.220–21)

3. . . . to him a corselet fastened with delicate hooks and triply sewn
with gold, which he himself had stripped from Demoleus
as victor by the swift Simois before lofty Troy. (*A.* 5.259–61)

*δώσω οἱ θώρηκα, τὸν Ἀστεροπαῖον ἀπηύρων*
*χάλκεον, ᾧ πέρι χεῦμα φαεινοῦ κασσιτέροιο*
*ἀμφιδεδίνηται· πολέος δέ οἱ ἄξιον*[60] *ἔσται.*

4. et cursorum certamen utrobique simile. et quia versibus est apud utrumque numerosis, locum loco similem lector inveniet. initia haec sunt:

haec ubi dicta, locum capiunt signoque repente . . .

*στὰν δὲ μεταστοιχεί: σήμαινε*[61] *δὲ τέρματ' Ἀχιλλεύς . . .*

5. pugilum certamen incipit apud hunc:

constitit in digitos extemplo arrectus uterque;

apud illum:

*τὼ δὲ ζωσαμένω βήτην ἐς μέσσον ἀγῶνα,*
*ἄντα δ' ἀνασχομένω χερσὶ στιβαρῇσιν ἄμ' ἄμφω . . .*

6. si velis comparare certantes sagittis, invenies haec utriusque principia:

protinus Aeneas celeri certare sagitta . . .

*αὐτὰρ ὁ τοξευτῆρσι*[62] *τίθει ἰόεντα σίδηρον . . .*

60 *ἄξιον* (*codd. plerique Hom.*)] -*ος codd. cett. Hom., edd.*
61 *σήμαινε* (*codd. duo Hom.*)] *σήμηνε codd. cett. Hom., edd.*
62 *τοξευτῆρσι*] *τοξευτῇσι Hom.*

---

28 Serv. on A. 5.426 adduces Apollonius (2.68ff.) as Virgil's model.

I shall give him the breastplate that I took from Asteropaios,
bronze, and about its rim a stream of gleaming tin
swirls round: it will be a thing he values highly. (*Il.* 23.560–62)

4. The footrace in both poems is similar too: since both versions are very long, the reader will find the one passage that is like the other. They begin as follows:

After these words they take their marks and at the signal, suddenly . . . (*A.* 5.315)

As they stand in a line, Akhilleus marks out the turning post . . . (*Il.* 23.358)

5. The boxing match begins in Virgil this way (*A.* 5.426),[28]

At once both are on their toes and alert,

in Homer, this way (*Il.* 23.685–86):

The two girded themselves, then strode to the middle of the arena,
face to face, their sturdy fists raised, both at once . . .

6. If you want to compare the archery contests, you'll find that the two passages begin thus:

Straightway Aeneas . . . to contend with the swift arrow . . . (*A.* 5.485)

Moreover, he sets out for the bowmen the dark iron . . . (*Il.* 23.850)

7. 'capita locorum, ubi longa narratio est, dixisse sufficiet ut quid unde natum sit lector inveniat.

8. dixerat et tenues fugit ceu fumus in auras.
Aeneas "quo deinde ruis? quo proripis?" inquit,
"quem fugis aut quis te nostris complexibus arcet?"
ter conatus erat[63] collo dare bracchia circum,
ter frustra comprensa manus effugit imago.

*ὣς ἔφατ', αὐτὰρ ἔγω γ' ἔθελον φρεσὶ μερμηρίξας*
*μητρὸς ἐμῆς ψυχὴν ἑλέειν κατατεθνηυίης.*
*τρὶς μὲν ἐφωρμήθην,*[64] *ἑλέειν τέ με θυμὸς ἀνώγει,*
*τρὶς δέ μοι ἐκ χειρῶν σκιῇ εἴκελον ἢ καὶ ὀνείρῳ*
*ἔπτατ'· ἐμοὶ δ' ἄχος ὀξὺ γενέσκετο κηρόθι μᾶλλον.*

9. sepultura Palinuri formata est de Patrocli sepultura. haec incipit:

principio pinguem taedis et robore secto . . .

illa sic:

*οἱ δ' ἴσαν ὑλοτόμους πελέκεας ἐν χερσὶν ἔχοντες* . . .

63 erat] ibi *Verg.*
64 *ἐφωρμήθην* (*codd. aliquot Hom.*)] *ἐφορ-* *codd. cett. Hom., edd.*

---

29 That M. wrote "he had tried" (*conatus erat*) shows that he was thinking of the passage in Book 6 where these lines describe Aeneas' attempt to embrace his father's shade: see 5.5.14n.
30 Rather, Misenus.

7. 'When the passages are long it will be enough to indicate the chief points, so that the reader might discover what emerges from them.

8. [Father Anchises] finished speaking and vanished
like smoke in the light breeze.
"Where are you hurrying now?," Aeneas said, "Where
are you rushing?
Whom are you trying to avoid? Who keeps you from
my embrace?" (*A.* 5.740–42)

Three times he had tried[29] to enfold him in his arms,
three times the image, embraced in vain, fled from
his grasp. (*A.* 6.700–1)

So she spoke, but in my anxiety I wanted
to take in my arms my dead mother's soul.
Three times I darted forward, my spirit bidding me
to hold her,
three times she flew from my grasp like a shadow
or a dream: heartily indeed did I feel sharp grief.
(*Od.* 11.204–8)

9. The burial of Palinurus[30] is modeled on the burial of Patroclus; the former begins (*A.* 6.214),

First, thick with pine and hewn oak . . .

the latter (*Il.* 23.114),

They went, holding axes in their hands to cut the
wood . . .

et alibi:

*ποίησαν δὲ πυρὴν ἑκατόμπεδον ἔνθα καὶ ἔνθα.*

10. ipsa vero utriusque tumuli insignia quam paria?

at pius Aeneas ingenti mole sepulchrum
imponit suaque arma viro remumque tubamque
monte sub aerio, qui nunc Misenus ab illo
dicitur aeternumque tenet per saecula nomen.

*αὐτὰρ ἐπεὶ νεκρός τ᾽ ἐκάη καὶ τεύχεα νεκροῦ,*
*τύμβον χεύαντες καὶ ἐπὶ στήλην ἐρύσαντες*
*πήξαμεν ἀκροτάτῳ τύμβῳ εὐῆρες ἐρετμόν.*

11. tunc[65] consanguineus Leti Sopor . . .

*ἔνθ᾽ ὕπνῳ ξύμβλητο κασιγνήτῳ Θανάτοιο.*

12. quod te per caeli iucundum lumen et auras
per genitorem oro, per spes surgentis Iuli,
eripe me his, invicte, malis, aut tu mihi terram
inice, namque potes, portusque require Velinos.

13. *νῦν δέ σε τῶν ὄπιθεν γουνάζομαι, οὐ παρεόντων,*
*πρός τ᾽ ἀλόχου καὶ πατρός, ὅ σ᾽ ἔτρεφε τυτθὸν ἐόντα,*
*Τηλεμάχου θ᾽, ὃν μοῦνον ἐνὶ μεγάροισιν ἔλειπες·*

[65] tunc] tum *Verg.*

and a bit farther on (*Il.* 23.164),

They made a pyre one hundred feet on every side.

10. Consider, too, how similar the emblems on each tomb are:

But loyal Aeneas sets up a tomb, massive, huge,
and on it puts the hero's own arms, his oar, and his horn,
at the base of the sky-high mountain that now is called Misenus
after him and keeps his name forever through the ages. (*A.* 6.232–35)

But when the dead man was burned, and the dead man's armor,
we heaped up a tomb, dragged up a gravestone,
and planted a well-fitted oar at the top of the tomb. (*Od.* 12.13–15)

11. Then Death's brother, Sleep . . . (*A.* 6.278*)

There she met Sleep, Death's brother. (*Il.* 14.231)

12. By heaven's sweet light and breezes, by your father,
I beg you, by the hope placed in Iulus as he grows,
save me, all-conquering, from these woes, or go back
to the port of Velia (this you can) and cast some earth upon me. (*A.* 6.363–66)

13. Now I beg you, not by those now with you but by those you left behind,
by your wife, by the father who raised you as a boy,
by Têlemakhos, the only son you left in your halls.

οἶδα γὰρ ὡς ἐνθένδε κιὼν δόμου ἐξ Ἀΐδαο
νῆσον ἐς Αἰαίην σχήσεις εὐεργέα νῆα.
ἔνθα σ' ἔπειτα, ἄναξ, κέλομαι μνήσασθαι ἐμεῖο.
μή μ' ἄκλαυτον ἄθαπτον ἰὼν ὄπιθεν καταλείπῃς[66]
νοσφισθείς, μή τοί τι θεῶν μήνιμα γένωμαι,
ἀλλά με κακκῆαι σὺν τεύχεσιν, ὅσσα[67] μοί ἐστι,
σῆμά τέ μοι χεῦαι πολιῆς ἐπὶ θινὶ θαλάσσης,
ἀνδρὸς δυστήνοιο, καὶ ἐσσομένοισι πυθέσθαι·
ταῦτά τέ μοι τελέσαι, πῆξαί τ' ἐπὶ τύμβῳ
ἐρετμόν,
τῷ καὶ ζωὸς ἔρεσσον ἐὼν μετ' ἐμοῖς ἑτάροισιν.

14. nec non et Tityon, Terrae omniparentis alumnum,
cernere erat: per tota novem cui iugera corpus
porrigitur, rostroque immanis vultur obunco
immortale iecur tondens fecundaque poenis
viscera rimaturque epulis habitatque sub alto
pectore, nec fibris requies datur ulla renatis.

15. καὶ Τιτυὸν εἶδον, Γαίης ἐρικυδέος υἱόν,
κείμενον ἐν δαπέδῳ. ὁ δ' ἐπ' ἐννέα κεῖτο πέλεθρα,
γῦπε δέ μιν ἑκάτερθε παρημένω ἧπαρ ἔκειρον,
δέρτρον ἔσω δύνοντες· ὁ δ' οὐκ ἀπαμύνετο
χερσίν.

66 καταλείπῃς (*codd. aliquot Hom.*)] -λείπειν *codd. cett. Hom., edd.*

67 ὅσσα] ἄσσα *Hom.*

For I know that you will go hence from the house of Hades
and steer your well-made ship to the island of Aiaia.
There I ask you, lord, be mindful of me, do not go
and leave me behind, unmourned, unburied, do not
forsake me—lest I bring the wrath of the gods down upon you—
but place me on a pyre with my weapons, such as I have,
and heap up a monument for me, an unlucky man,
on the gray sea's shore, for later men to learn of.
Do these things for me, and fix my oar upon my tomb,
the one I rowed as a living man with my companions.
(*Od.* 11.66–78)

14. Tityos too, whom the Earth, mother of all, had raised,
was there to see: his body is sprawled over nine
acres, a loathsome vulture crops his imperishable liver
with its hooked beak, rummaging for a feast in innards
that give great scope to vengeance. His spacious chest is
the bird's lair, his guts, ever renewed, know no peace.
(*A.* 6.595*–600)

15. I saw Tityos too, the son of glorious Earth,
lying on the ground: over nine acres he lay,
two vultures, one each side, trimmed his liver and
settled in his bowels, his hands no use to keep them off.

*Λητὼ γὰρ εἵλκυσε,*[68] *Διὸς κυδρὴν παράκοιτιν,*
*Πυθώδ' ἐρχομένην διὰ καλλιχόρου Πανοπῆος.*

16. non mihi si linguae centum sint oraque centum,
ferrea vox, omnis scelerum comprendere formas,
omnia poenarum percurrere nomina possem.[69]

*πληθὺν δ' οὐκ ἂν ἐγὼ μυθήσομαι οὐδ' ὀνομήνω,*
*οὐδ' εἴ μοι δέκα μὲν γλῶσσαι, δέκα δὲ στόματ' εἶεν,*
*φωνὴ δ' ἄρρηκτος, χάλκεον δέ μοι ἦτορ ἐνείη.*

8 hinc exaudiri gemitus iraeque leonum
vincla recusantum et sera sub nocte rudentum,
setigerique sues atque in praesepibus ursi
saevire ac formae magnorum ululare luporum,
quos hominum ex facie dea saeva potentibus herbis
induerat Circe in vultus ac terga ferarum.

*εὗρον δ' ἐν βήσσῃσι τετυγμένα δώματα Κίρκης*
*ξεστοῖσιν λάεσσι, περισκέπτῳ ἐνὶ χώρῳ.*
*ἀμφὶ δέ μιν λύκοι ἦσαν ὀρέστεροι ἠδὲ λέοντες,*
*τοὺς αὐτὴ κατέθελξεν, ἐπεὶ κακὰ φάρμακ' ἔδωκεν.*

68 *εἵλκυσε* (*codd. aliquot Hom.*)] ἕλκησε Hom. (ut vid.)
69 possem] possim *Verg.*

---

31 These lines are treated as an indirect imitation of Homer, via Hostius, at 6.3.6.

For he dragged off Leto, Zeus' glorious bedmate,
as she returned to Pytho through Panopeus, city of fine dances. (*Od.* 11.576–81)

16. Not if I should have one hundred tongues, one hundred mouths,
a voice of iron, could I encompass every form of trespass
or list in full the name of every retribution. (*A.* 6.625*–27)[31]

The full throng I could not speak or name,
not if I had ten tongues, ten mouths,
a voice that could not break, a heart of bronze within. (*Il.* 2.488–90)

From there you could hear the angry groans of lions 8
straining at their chains and roaring near the end of night,
bristling boars, too, and bears in their pens
growling, the silhouettes of great wolves howling:
all of them the wild goddess had, with potent charms, changed
from men and dressed in the look and shape of beasts. (*A.* 7.15–20)

In the woods they found the house of Kirke, fitted together
with polished stone, in the middle of a clearing.
All around it were wolves of the mountains and lions,
which she had bewitched after giving them wicked drugs. (*Od.* 10.210–13)

2. quid petitis? quae causa rates aut cuius egentes
litus ad Ausonium tot per vada caerula vexit?
sive errore viae seu tempestatibus acti,
qualia multa mari nautae patiuntur in alto . . .

*ὦ ξεῖνοι, τίνες ἐστέ; πόθεν πλεῖθ' ὑγρὰ κέλευθα;*
*ἤ τι κατὰ πρῆξιν ἦ μαψιδίως ἀλάλησθε*
*οἷά τε ληϊστῆρες ὑπεὶρ ἅλα, τοί τ' ἀλόωνται*
*ψυχὰς παρθέμενοι, κακὸν ἀλλοδαποῖσι φέροντες;*

3. ceu quondam nivei liquida inter nubila cycni[70]
cum sese e pastu referunt et longa canoros
dant per colla modos: sonat amnis et Asia longe
pulsa palus.

*τῶν δ', ὥστ' ὀρνίθων πετεηνῶν ἔθνεα πολλὰ*
*χηνῶν ἢ γεράνων ἢ κύκνων δουλιχοδείρων*
*Ἀσίῳ ἐν λειμῶνι Καϋστρίου ἀμφὶ ῥέεθρα*
*ἔνθα καὶ ἔνθα ποτῶνται ἀγαλλόμεναι[71] πτερύγεσσι*
*κλαγγηδὸν προκαθιζόντων, σμαραγεῖ δέ τε λειμών.*

4. illa vel intactae segetis per summa volaret
gramina nec teneras cursu laesisset aristas

70 ceu . . . cycni P (*om.* liquida, cinthi *pro* cycni): *om.* ω

71 -*μεναι* (*cod. plerique Hom.*)] -*μενα cod. cett. Hom., Aristarch.*

2. What are you after? What reason or need has brought
your ships to the western shore over so many sea-dark shoals?
Whether you've lost your way or been driven by storms,
the sorts of things that sailors often suffer on the deep . . . (*A*. 7.197–200)

Strangers, who are you? Where do you come from, sailing the watery lanes?
Do you come for trade or wander at random
like pirates upon the sea, roving at risk
to their own lives while bringing woe to strangers? (*Od*. 3.71–74)

3. As when at times through the luminous clouds snow-white
swans return from feeding and their long necks issue
tuneful measures: the river resounds and the Asian marsh
re-echoes from afar. (*A*. 7.699–702)

Like the many breeds of winged birds,
of geese or cranes or long-necked swans,
in the meadow of Asia 'round Kastrios' stream
they fly here and there, delighting in their wings,
alighting with a clamor, and the meadow re-echoes. (*Il*. 2.459–63)

4. She could fly over the topmost growth of wheat
still unculled and bruise not one tender ear as she sped,

vel mare per medium fluctu suspensa tumenti
ferret iter, celeris nec tangeret aequore plantas.

*αἳ δ' ὅτε μὲν σκιρτῷεν ἐπὶ ζείδωρον ἄρουραν,*
*ἄκρον ἐπ' ἀνθερίκων καρπὸν θέον οὐδὲ κατέκλων·*
*ἀλλ' ὅτε δὴ σκιρτῷεν ἐπ' εὐρέα νῶτα θαλάσσης,*
*ἄκρον ἐπὶ ῥηγμῖνος ἁλὸς πολιοῖο θέεσκον.*

5. vescitur Aeneas simul et Troiana iuventus
perpetui tergo bovis et lustralibus extis.
postquam exempta fames et amor compressus edendi,
rex Euandrus ait . . .

*νώτοισιν δ' Αἴαντα διηνεκέεσσι γέραιρεν*
*ἥρως Ἀτρεΐδης εὐρὺ κρείων Ἀγαμέμνων.*
*αὐτὰρ ἐπεὶ πόσιος καὶ ἐδητύος ἐξ ἔρον ἕντο,*
*τοῖς ὁ γέρων πάμπρωτος ὑφαίνειν ἤρχετο μῆτιν.*

6. Euandrum ex humili tecto lux suscitat alma
et[72] matutinus[73] volucrum sub culmine cantus.
consurgit senior tunicaque inducitur artus,
et Tyrrhena pedum circumdat vincula plantis.
tum lateri[74] atque umeris Tegeaeum subligat ensem,

[72] et C: atque *ω*
[73] matutinus] -ni *Verg*.
[74] lateri *ed. Ven. 1472 ex Verg*.: latere *ω*

or make her way through the middle of the sea, suspended
above the swollen waves, nor wet the swift soles of her feet. (*A.* 7.808–11)

And when they gamboled over the fruitful earth,
they sped above the tip-top ears of grain without breaking them off;
but when they gamboled over the seas' broad back,
they sped over the gray salt waves' surging surface. (*Il.* 20.226–29)

5. Aeneas feasts and with him the Trojan youth
on the ox's long loin and sacrificial innards.
After hunger was banished and the desire for eating was checked,
king Evander said . . . (*A.* 8.182*–85)

The hero, Atreus' son, wide-ruling Agamemnon
honored Aias with long loins of beef.
But when they put aside the desire for drink and food,
the old man, first, began to weave his advice for them. (*Il.* 7.321–24)

6. The nourishing light rouses Evander from his humble hut,
and with it the morning song of birds beneath the eaves.
The old man rises, puts on his close-fitting tunic,
and binds the Tyrrhenian sandals to the soles of his feet.
Then he girds his shoulders and side with his Tegaean sword,

demissa ab laeva pantherae terga retorquens.
nec non et gemini custodes limine in ipso
praecedunt gressumque canes comitantur erilem.

7. *ὤρνυτ'*[75] *ἄρ' ἐξ εὐνῆφιν Ὀδυσσῆος φίλος υἱός,*
*εἵματα ἑσσάμενος, περὶ δὲ ξίφος ὀξὺ θέτ' ὤμοις,*[76]
*ποσσὶ δ' ὑπὸ λιπαροῖσιν ἐδήσατο καλὰ πέδιλα,*
*βῆ ῥ' ἴμεν εἰς ἀγορήν, παλάμῃ δ' ἔχε χάλκεον ἔγχος,*
*οὐκ οἶος, ἅμα τῷ γε κύνες πόδας*[77] *ἀργοὶ ἕποντο.*

8. o mihi praeteritos referat si Iuppiter annos,
qualis eram, cum primam aciem Praeneste sub ipsa
stravi scutorumque incendi victor acervos
et regem hac Erimum[78] dextra sub Tartara misi,
nascenti cui tris animas Feronia mater
(horrendum dictu) dederat: terna arma movenda,
ter leto sternendus erat, cui tunc tamen omnis
abstulit haec animas dextra et totidem exuit armis.

9. *αἲ γάρ, Ζεῦ τε πάτερ καὶ Ἀθηναίη καὶ Ἄπολλον,*

[75] *ὤρνυτ'* (*codd. plerique Hom.*)] *ὄρνυτ' codd. cett. Hom., edd.*
[76] *ὤμοις*] *ὤμῳ Hom.*
[77] *κύνες πόδας* (*codd. aliquot Hom.*)] *δύω κύνες codd. cett. Hom.*
[78] Erimum] Erylum *Verg.*

sweeping back over his left shoulder a panther's hide.
On his very threshold, too, the hounds, his twin guardians,
lead the way, matching their master stride for stride. (*A.* 8.455–62*)

7. The dear son of Odysseus stirred from the bedding,
donning his garments, making the sharp sword swing from his shoulder,
binding the fair sandals beneath his gleaming feet:
he strode to the market, bronze sword in hand,
not alone, but the nimble hounds followed along. (*Od.* 2.2–4, 10–11)

8. O, if Jupiter should give me back the years that are gone,
such as I was when at the foot of Praeneste itself I laid low
the enemy's first line and made a victor's bonfire of shields in heaps
and sent king Erimus under Tartarus with this right hand.
When he was born his mother Feronia had given him
three souls (I shudder as I say it): three times I had to take up arms,
three times I had to lay him low in death—but still this right hand
three times took his life away and three times stripped him of his arms. (*A.* 8.560–67)

9. If only, father Zeus and Athena and Apollo, I might be

ἡβῷμ᾽ ὡς ὅτ᾽ ἐπ᾽ ὠκυρόῳ Κελάδοντι μάχοντο
ἀγρόμενοι Πύλιοί τε καὶ Ἀρκάδες ἐγχεσίμωροι
Φειᾶς πὰρ τείχεσσιν Ἰαρδάνου ἀμφὶ ῥέεθρα . . .
ἀλλ᾽ ἐμὲ θυμὸς ἀνῆκε πολυτλήμων πολεμίζειν
θάρσεϊ ᾧ· γενεῇ δὲ νεώτατος ἔσκον ἁπάντων·
καὶ μαχόμην οἱ ἐγώ, δῶκεν δέ μοι εὖχος Ἀθήνη.
τὸν δὴ μήκιστον καὶ κάρτιστον κτάνον ἄνδρα·
πολλὸς γάρ τις ἔκειτο παρήορος ἔνθα καὶ ἔνθα.
εἴθ᾽ ὣς ἡβώοιμι, βίη δέ μοι ἔμπεδος εἴη·
τώ κε τάχ᾽ ἀντήσειε μάχης κορυθαίολος Ἕκτωρ.

10. qualis ubi Oceani perfusus Lucifer unda,
quem Venus ante alios astrorum diligit ignes,
extulit os sacrum caelo tenebrasque resolvit.

οἷος δ᾽ ἀστὴρ εἶσι μετ᾽ ἀστράσι νυκτὸς ἀμολγῷ
Ἕσπερος, ὃς κάλλιστος ἐν οὐρανῷ ἵσταται
ἀστήρ.

11. "en perfecta mei promissa coniugis arte
munera, ne mox aut Laurentis, nate, superbos

young, as when by the swift-flowing Keladon the assembled
men of Pylos battled the Arkadians, who fight with the spear,
near Pheia's walls along the streams of the Iardanos. . . .
but my bold spirit drove me on to wage war
with native courage, though I was the youngest of all in age:
I did battle with [Ereuthalion], and Athena gave me grounds for boasting.
The man who was tallest and strongest, I killed him,
stretched out he lay, covering much ground this way and that.
Would that I were in my prime, and the might still in me:
soon would Hektor of the gleaming helmet find himself in a fight. (*Il.* 7.132–35, 152–58)

10. Like the Morning Star drenched by Ocean's wave,
the star that Venus loves beyond all other stars,
when it has raised its holy face to heaven and banished the dark. (*A.* 8.589†–91)

Like the star that goes forth amid stars in the dead of night,
Hesperos, the fairest star that stands in heaven. (*Il.* 22.317–18)

11. "Behold, my husband has completed with his craft this gift
I promised, lest you be slow, my son, to challenge the arrogant

aut acrem dubites in proelia poscere Turnum."
dixit et amplexus nati Cytherea petivit,
arma sub adversa posuit radiantia quercu.
ille deae donis et tanto laetus honore
impleri[79] nequit atque oculos per singula volvit
miraturque interque manus et bracchia versat.

12. *τύνη δ' Ἡφαίστοιο πάρα κλυτὰ τεύχεα δέξο*
*καλὰ μάλ', οἷ' οὔ πώ τις ἀνὴρ ὤμοισι φόρησεν.*
*ὣς ἄρα φωνήσασα θεὰ κατὰ τεύχε' ἔθηκε*
*πρόσθεν Ἀχιλλῆος· τὰ δ' ἀνέβραχε δαίδαλα πάντα . . .*
*τέρπετο δ' ἐν χείρεσσιν ἔχων θεοῦ ἀγλαὰ δῶρα.*

9 Iri, decus caeli, quis te mihi nubibus actam
detulit in terras?

*Ἶρι θεά, τίς γάρ*[80] *σε θεῶν ἐμοὶ ἄγγελον ἧκεν;*

2. . . . nec solos tangit Atridas
iste dolor . . .

*ἦ μοῦνοι φιλέουσ' ἀλόχους μερόπων ἀνθρώπων Ἀτρεΐδαι;*

[79] impleri (*codd.* nγ[1] *Verg.*)] expleri *Verg.*

[80] *γάρ* (*cod. plerique Hom.*)] *τάρ Aristarch. ed. alt.*, *τ' ἄρ codd. aliquot Hom.*

Laurentians to battle, or fierce Turnus."
The goddess of Cythera spoke and sought her son's embrace,
laying the radiant arms before his gaze at the base of an oak.
He could not get his fill, rejoicing in the goddess' gifts and
the honor, but glanced this way and that over every detail,
handling them in wonder and getting their feel. (*A.* 8.612–19)

12. "But you receive these glorious arms from Hephaistos,
handsome indeed: never has a man worn such armor."
But when the goddess had spoken she set the arms down
before Akhilleus, and all the intricately crafted armor clattered. . . .
He rejoiced as he held the god's radiant gifts. (*Il.* 19.10–13, 18)

Iris, heaven's adornment, who sent you down to me on earth 9
like a shot through the clouds? (*A.* 9.18–19)

Iris, goddess, who of the gods sent you to me as a messenger? (*Il.* 18.182)

2. . . . nor does anguish of that sort touch
only Atreus' sons. (*A.* 9.138–39)

Or do only Atreus' sons, among mortal men, love
their wives? (*Il.* 9.340–41)

3. sed vos, o lecti, ferro qui scindere vallum
apparat et mecum invadit trepidantia castra?

*ὄρνυσθ', ἱππόδαμοι Τρῶες, ῥήγνυσθε δὲ τεῖχος*
*Ἀργείων καὶ νηυσὶν ἐνίετε θεσπιδαὲς πῦρ.*

4. "quod superest, laeti bene gestis corpora rebus
procurate, viri, et pugnam sperate parari."

*νῦν δ' ἔρχεσθ' ἐπὶ δεῖπνον, ἵνα ξυνάγωμεν Ἄρηα.*
*εὖ μέν τις δόρυ θηξάσθω, εὖ δ' ἀσπίδα θέσθω.*

5. sic ait illacrimans: umero simul exuit ensem
auratum, mira quem fecerat arte Lycaon
Cnosius atque habilem vagina aptarat eburna.
dat Niso Mnestheus pellem horrentisque leonis
exuvias, galeam fidus permutat Aletes.
6. protinus armati incedunt, quos omnis euntis
primorum manus ad portas iuvenumque senumque
prosequitur votis nec non et pulcher Iulus.

---

[32] Cf. Serv. on A. 9.307.

3. But who among you, my chosen men, is ready to smash the palisade
with his blade and with me assault their quivering camp? (*A.* 9.146–47)

Rise up, Trojans, masters of horses, smash the Argives'
wall and hurl the god-kindled fire onto the ships. (*Il.* 12.440–41)

4. As for the rest, take pleasure in what you've accomplished, see to
your bodies' needs, and look ahead to the battle being readied. (*A.* 9.157–58)

Now come take your meal, so that we can join battle.
Let each one sharpen well his spear and set his shield in order. (*Il.* 2.381–82)

5. So he spoke, in tears, at the same time taking from his shoulder
the gilded sword that the Cretan Lycaon had made with
wondrous skill, fitting it snug to an ivory scabbard.
To Nisus Mnestheus gives the hide and claws of a bristling
lion and loyal Aletes gives him his helmet[32] in exchange.
6. At once they set out under arms, and as they go
the whole throng of youths and elders, all the best, follows
to the gates, offering vows as they go, and with them fair Iulus. (*A.* 9.303–10)

7. Τυδεΐδῃ μὲν δῶκε μενεπτόλεμος Θρασυμήδης
φάσγανον ἄμφηκες (τὸ δ' ἑὸν παρὰ νηῒ λέλειπτο)
καὶ σάκος· ἀμφὶ δέ οἱ κυνέην κεφαλῆφιν ἔθηκε
ταυρείην, ἄφαλόν τε καὶ ἄλλοφον, ἥ τε καταῖτυξ
κέκληται, ῥύεται δὲ κάρη θαλερῶν αἰζηῶν.
Μηριόνης δ' Ὀδυσῆϊ δίδου βιὸν ἠδὲ φαρέτρην
καὶ ξίφος· ἀμφὶ δέ οἱ κυνέην κεφαλῆφιν ἔθηκε
ῥινοῦ ποιητήν· πολέσιν δ' ἔντοσθεν ἱμᾶσιν
ἐντέτατο στερεῶς, ἔκτοσθε δὲ λευκοὶ ὀδόντες
ἀργιόδοντος ὑὸς θαμέες ἔχον ἔνθα καὶ ἔνθα
εὖ καὶ ἐπισταμένως, μέσσῃ δ' ἐνὶ πῖλος ἀρήρει.

8. egressi superant fossas noctisque per umbram
castra inimica petunt, multis tamen ante futuri
exitio: passim somno vinoque per herbam
corpora fusa vident, arrectos litore currus,
inter lora rotasque viros, simul arma iacere,
vina simul. prior Hyrtacides sic ore locutus:
"Euryale, audendum dextra: nunc ipsa vocat res.
hac iter est. tu ne qua manus se attollere nobis
a tergo possit, custodi et consule longe.
haec ego vasta dabo et recto[81] te limite ducam."

81 recto] lato *Verg.*

---

33 Cf. Serv. on *A.* 9.319.

7. To Tydeus' son Thrasymedes, steady in battle, gave
a two-edged sword (his own had been left by the ship)
and shield, but about his head he set a helmet
of bull's-hide, without crest or plume, the kind called
a kataityx, that protects the heads of hardy youths.
Meriones gave Odysseus a bow and quiver and
sword, but about his head he set a helmet
made of hide: it was firmly plaited inside
with many straps, outside the gleaming tusks
of a white-toothed boar were set thick this way and that,
a job done well and with skill; its middle was close-fitted with felt. (*Il.* 10.255–65)

8. Out beyond the trenchworks they pass, through the night's shadows
they make for the enemy camp, yet destined to bring death
to many: here and there they see bodies sprawled on the grass
in sleep and drink, chariots tipped shafts-up on the shore,
men tangled in the tackle and the wheels, their arms lying beside them,
wine too. Hyrtacus' son speaks first,[33] thus:
"Euryalus, now it's time to boldly strike: now the very scene invites it.
This is the way: you keep watch from afar and take care
that no platoon can come at us from behind.
I'll lay waste to all that's here and lead you forward on a straight path." (*A.* 9.314–23)

9. τὼ δὲ βάτην προτέρω διά τ' ἔντεα καὶ μέλαν αἷμα,
αἶψα δ' ἐπὶ Θρῃκῶν ἀνδρῶν τέλος ἷξον ἰόντες.
οἳ δ' εὗδον καμάτῳ ἀδηκότες, ἔντεα δέ σφιν
καλὰ παρ' αὐτοῖσιν χθονὶ κέκλιτο εὖ κατὰ κόσμον
τριστοιχί·[82] παρὰ δέ σφιν ἑκάστῳ δίζυγες ἵπποι.
Ῥῆσος δ' ἐν μέσῳ εὗδε, παρ' αὐτὸν[83] δ' ὠκέες ἵπποι
ἐξ ἐπιδιφριάδος πυμάτης ἱμᾶσι δέδεντο.
τὸν δ' Ὀδυσεὺς προπάροιθεν ἰδὼν Διομήδεϊ δεῖξεν·
οὗτός τοι, Διόμηδες, ἀνήρ, οὗτοι δέ τοι ἵπποι,
οὓς νῶϊν πίφαυσκε Δόλων, ὃν ἐπέφνομεν ἡμεῖς.
ἀλλ' ἄγε δὴ πρόφερε κρατερὸν μένος· οὐδέ τί σε χρὴ
ἑστάμεναι μέλεον σὺν τεύχεσιν· ἀλλὰ λύ' ἵππους·
ἠὲ σύ γ' ἄνδρας ἔναιρε, μελήσουσιν δ' ἐμοὶ ἵπποι.

10. sed non auguriis poterat[84] depellere pestem.

ἀλλ' οὐκ οἰωνοῖσιν ἐρύσατο κῆρα μέλαιναν.

11. et iam prima novo spargebat lumine terras
Tithoni croceum linquens Aurora cubile.

[82] τριστοιχί (*codd. aliquot Hom.*)] -χεί *codd. cett. Hom.*
[83] αὐτὸν] αὐτῷ *Hom.*
[84] auguriis poterat] -io potuit *Verg.*

9. The two walked on through arms and dark blood,
then came suddenly to their goal, a troop of Thracians:
overwhelmed by weariness they slept, their handsome
weapons rested on the ground beside them, well ordered
in three rows, and by each man a yoked pair of horses.
Rhesos slept in the middle, alongside him his swift horses
were tethered by straps to the chariot cart's rim.
Seeing him first, Odysseus pointed him out to Diomedes:
"There's the man, Diomedes, there his horses
that Dolon, the one we killed, made known to us.
But come, bring on your mighty fury: no need for you
to stand idle with your weapons, but release the horses,
or else you slay the men and the horses will be for me to see to." (*Il.* 10.469–81)

10. But he could not use his augur's skill to ward off destruction. (*A.* 9.328*)

But he could not use the birds of omen to ward off black death. (*Il.* 2.859)

11. And already Aurora was leaving Thithonus' saffron-hued bed
and starting to dapple the lands with a new day's light. (*A.* 9.459–60 = 4.584–85)

Ἠὼς δ' ἐκ λεχέων παρ' ἀγαυοῦ Τιθωνοῖο
ὤρνυθ', ἵν' ἀθανάτοισι φόως φέροι ἠδὲ
βροτοῖσιν.

12. 'Mater Euryali ad dirum nuntium, ut excussos de manibus radios et pensa demitteret, ut per muros et virorum agmina ululans et comam scissa decurreret, ut effunderet dolorem in lamentationum querelas, totum de Andromache sumpsit lamentante mortem mariti.

13. o vere Phrygiae, neque enim Phryges . . .

ὦ πέπονες, κακ' ἐλέγχε', Ἀχαιΐδες, οὐκέτ' Ἀχαιοί
. . .

14. quos alios muros, quae iam[85] ultra moenia
habetis?
unus homo et vestris, o cives, undique saeptus
aggeribus tantas strages impune per urbem
ediderit? iuvenum primos tot miserit Orco?
non infelicis patriae veterumque deorum
et magni Aeneae segnes[86] miseretque pudetque?

15. ὦ φίλοι, ἥρωες Δαναοὶ, θεράποντες Ἄρηος,
ἀνέρες ἔστε, φίλοι, μνήσασθε δὲ θούριδος ἀλκῆς.

[85] quae iam *ed. Ven. 1513, codd. plerique Verg., Tib.*: aut quae iam ω, quaeve *codd. aliquot Verg.*

[86] segnes *ed. Ven. 1472, om.* ω

From noble Tithonos' bed Eos rose,
to bring light to immortals and mortals. (*Il.* 11.1–2)

12. 'When Euryalus' mother reacts to the dreadful news by hurling her shuttles and wool from her hands, running with a howl and tearing her hair among the ranks along the walls, pouring out her grief in a torrent of plaintive lamentation, the whole passage is taken from Andromache's lament at her husband's death (*A.* 9.473ff. ~ *Il.* 22.460ff.).

13. O you ladies of Phrygia, for sure, not men . . . (*A.* 9.617)

O you darlings, low cowards, ladies of Achaia, no longer men . . . (*Il.* 2.235)

14. What other walls do you have, what other encampment now?
Will one man, all alone, enclosed on every side by *your* ramparts,
comrades, produce such devastation throughout our settlement
and go off scot free? Will he send so many of our best young men to Hades?
Do you not pity your unhappy homeland, your gods, great
Aeneas, you sluggards, do you not feel shame before them all? (*A.* 9.782–87)

15. O my friends, heroes of the Greeks, Ares' comrades,
be men, my friends, and be mindful of your dashing valor.

*ἠέ τινάς φαμεν εἶναι ἀοσσητῆρας ὀπίσσω,*
*ἦέ τι τεῖχος ἄρειον, ὅ κ' ἀνδράσι λοιγὸν ἀμύνοι;*[87]
*οὐ μέν τις*[88] *σχεδόν ἐστι πόλις πύργοις ἀραρυῖα,*
*ᾗ κ' ἀπαμυναίμεσθ' ἑτεραλκέα δῆμον ἔχοντες·*
*ἀλλ' ἐν γὰρ Τρώων πεδίῳ πύκα θωρηκτάων*
*πόντῳ κεκλιμένοι ἑκὰς ἥμεθα πατρίδος αἴης·*
*τὼ ἐν χερσὶ φόως, οὐ μειλιχίῃ πολέμοιο.*

10 Tela manu iaciunt, quales sub nubibus atris
Strymoniae dant signa grues atque aethera tranant
cum sonitu fugiuntque Notos clamore secundo.

*ἠΰτε περ κλαγγὴ γεράνων πέλει οὐρανόθι πρό·*
*αἵ τ' ἐπεὶ οὖν χειμῶνα φύγον καὶ ἀθέσφατον ὄμβρον*
*κλαγγῇ ταί γε πέτονται ἐπ' Ὠκεανοῖο ῥοάων.*

2. ardet apex capiti cristisque ac[89] vertice flamma
funditur et vastos umbo vomit aureus ignis;
non secus ac liquida si quando nocte cometae
sanguinei lugubre rubent, aut Sirius ardor:
ille sitim morbosque ferens mortalibus aegris
nascitur, et laevo contristat lumine caelum.

[87] *ἀμύνοι*] *ἀμύναι ed. Lugd. 1550 ex Hom.* (*ἀμυύαι* [*sic*] *ed. Basil. 1535*)

[88] *τις* (*codd. plerique Hom.*)] *τι codd. cett. Hom., Aristarch.*

[89] ac (*codd. plerique Verg., DServ.*)] a *codd. aliquot Verg., Tib., Non. 240.28, 313.10, edd.*

Or do we claim that there are some saviors behind us,
some better bulwark that might keep men from destruction?
No, there is no other city well-fitted with towers
to use in our defense, no people able to turn the tide of battle:
we sit far from our ancestral land, our backs to the sea,
on the plain of the Trojans massed in their armor.
The light of life rests with our hands, not with feebleness in battle. (*Il.* 15.733–41)

The spears they threw were like cranes from the Strymon
that call to each other beneath darkening clouds, a noise that glides
across the sky as they flee the south winds with a heartening clamor. (*A.* 10.264–66)

Just as when a clamor of cranes comes forth from the sky,
when they flee a storm's indescribable downpour
and fly with a clamor over Ôkean's streams. (*Il.* 3.3–5)

2. On his head the topmost point blazes, spilling fire from crest
and plume, and his shield's golden boss spews enormous flames:
just as when on a cloudless night blood-red comets
glow with a mournful hue, or the Dog-Star's heat:
it brings thirst and disease to feeble mortals
and makes the heavens baleful with its ill-omened glare. (*A.* 10.270*–76)

3. τὸν δ' ὁ γέρων Πρίαμος πρῶτος ἴδεν ὀφθαλμοῖσι,
παμφαίνονθ' ὥς τ' ἀστέρ' ἐπεσσύμενον πεδίοιο,
ὅς ῥά τ' ὀπώρης εἶσιν, ἀρίζηλοι δέ οἱ αὐγαί
φαίνονται πολλοῖσι μετ' ἀστράσι νυκτὸς ἀμολγῷ,
ὅν τε κύν' Ὠρίωνος ἐπίκλησιν καλέουσι.
λαμπρότατος μὲν ὅδ'[90] ἐστί, κακὸν δέ τε σῆμα τέτυκται,
καί τε φέρει πολλὸν πυρετὸν δειλοῖσι βροτοῖσιν·
ὣς τοῦ χαλκὸς ἔλαμπεν ἐπὶ[91] στήθεσσι θέοντος.

4. stat sua cuique dies, breve et inreparabile tempus
omnibus est vitae . . .
fata vocant metasque dati pervenit ad aevi.

αἰνότατε Κρονίδη, ποῖον τὸν μῦθον ἔειπες.
ἄνδρα θνητὸν ἐόντα, πάλαι πεπρωμένον αἴσῃ,
ἂψ ἐθέλεις θανάτοιο δυσηχέος ἐξαναλῦσαι;
μοῖραν δ' οὔ τινά φημι πεφυγμένον ἔμμεναι ἀνδρῶν,
οὐ κακὸν, οὐδὲ μὲν ἐσθλόν, ἐπὴν τὰ πρῶτα γένηται.

5. "per patrios manes, per spes surgentis Iuli
te precor hanc animam serves natoque patrique.
est domus alta: iacent penitus defossa talenta
caelati argenti, sunt auri pondera facti

90 ὅδ' (*codd. pauci Hom.*)] ὅ γ' *codd. et testt. cett. Hom.*
91 ἔλαμπεν ἐπὶ] ἔλαμπε περὶ *Hom.*

3. Aged Priam was first to see him with his eyes,
moving over the plain like a star for all to see:
it comes in late summer, its brilliant rays
outshining the many stars in the dead of night;
the hound of Orion is the name they give it.
Brightest it is, but it is a baleful sign
and brings great fever to wretched mortals.
So did his bronze armor shine upon his chest as he ran. (*Il*. 22.25–32)

4. Each man's day stands fixed, the time of each man's life is short
and cannot be recalled . . .
The fates beckon: he has reached the end of his allotted time. (*A*. 10.467–68, 472)

Most dread son of Zeus, what's that you've you said!
The man is mortal, long since assigned his due portion:
do you wish to release him from woeful death? (*Il*. 16.440–42)

I declare that no man—not the low, not the noble—
has escaped his allotted portion, after it is first ordained. (*Il*. 6.488–89)

5. "By the your dead father's spirit, by the hope of Iulus as he grows,
I pray that you spare this life of mine for my son and my father.
I have a lofty house, where talents of chased silver lie
deeply hidden, I have weights of gold, in bullion and

infectique mihi. non hic victoria Teucrum
vertitur aut anima una dabit[92] discrimina tanta."
dixerat. Aeneas contra cui talia reddit:
"argenti atque auri memoras quae magna[93] talenta
gnatis parce tuis. belli commercia Turnus
sustulit ista prior iam tum Pallante perempto.
hoc patris Anchisae manes, hoc sentit Iulus."
sic fatus galeam laeva tenet atque reflexa
cervice orantis[94] capulo tenus abdidit[95] ensem.

6. *ζώγρει, Ἀτρέος υἱέ, σὺ δ' ἄξια δέξαι ἄποινα·*
*πολλὰ δ' ἐν Ἀντιμάχοιο δόμοις κειμήλια κεῖται,*
*χαλκός τε χρυσός τε πολύκμητός τε σίδηρος,*
*τῶν κέν τοι χαρίσαιτο πατὴρ ἀπερείσι' ἄποινα,*
*εἰ νῶϊν*[96] *ζωοὺς πεπύθοιτ' ἐπὶ νηυσὶν Ἀχαιῶν.*
*ὣς τώ γε κλαίοντε προσαυδήτην βασιλῆα*
*μειλιχίοις ἐπέεσσιν· ἀμείλικτον δ' ὄπ' ἄκουσαν·*
*εἰ μὲν δὴ Ἀντιμάχοιο δαΐφρονος υἱέες ἐστόν,*
*ὅς ποτ' ἐνὶ Τρώων ἀγορῇ Μενέλαον ἄνωγεν,*
*ἀγγελίην ἐλθόντα σὺν ἀντιθέῳ Ὀδυσῆϊ*
*αὖθι κατακτεῖναι μηδ' ἐξέμεν ἂψ ἐς Ἀχαιούς,*
*νῦν μὲν δὴ τοῦ πατρὸς ἀεικέα τίσετε λώβην.*
*ἦ, καὶ Πείσανδρον μὲν ἀφ' ἵππων ὦσε χαμᾶζε,*

[92] dabit *ed. Ven. 1472, Verg.*: dabat *ω*

[93] magna] multa *Verg.*

[94] orantis (*codd. plerique Verg., Tib.*)] oranti *codd.* P¹b *Verg., edd. nonnull.*

[95] abdidit F (*cf.* A. 2.553): addidit *ω*, applicat *Verg.*

[96] *νῶϊν*] *νῶϊ Hom.*

in ware. The Trojans' victory does not turn on this
encounter, one life will make no very great
difference."
He finished speaking, and Aeneas replied as follows:
"Those great talents of silver and gold that you speak
of—
save them for your sons. Turnus did away with barter
of that sort in war, back then when he killed Pallas.
The spirit of dead Anchises knows this, Iulus knows
this."
With those words he takes the helmet in his left hand
and, twisting
back his neck as he begs, buries his sword to the hilt.
(*A.* 10.524–36)

6. "Take us alive, son of Atreus, and get your due
ransom. Much treasure is stored up in Antimakhos'
house, bronze and gold and well-wrought iron:
from this my father would grant boundless ransom,
should he learn that we two are alive on the
Akhaians' ships."
So the two cried as they addressed the king with
winning
words, but then they heard his unrelenting reply:
"If you are the sons of hot-hearted Antimakhos,
who once in the Trojans' marketplace ordered that
Menelaus,
who had come on an embassy with godlike Odysseus,
be killed on the spot and not return back to the
Akhaians,
pay now for the shameful outrage of your father."
So he spoke, and drove Peisander from his chariot to

δουρὶ βαλὼν πρὸς στῆθος· ὁ δ' ὕπτιος οὔδει ἐρείσθη.
Ἱππόλοχος δ' ἀπόρουσε, τὸν αὖ χαμαὶ ἐξενάριξε,
χεῖρας ἀπὸ ξίφεϊ τμήξας ἀπό τ' αὐχένα κόψας,
ὅλμον δ' ὣς ἔσσευε κυλίνδεσθαι δι' ὁμίλου.

7. impastus stabula alta leo ceu saepe peragrans,[97]
(suadet enim vesana fames), si forte fugacem
conspexit capream aut surgentem in cornua cervum,
gaudet hians immane comasque arrexit et haeret
visceribus super accumbens; lavit improba taeter
ora cruor—
sic ruit in densos alacer Mezentius hostes.

8. ὥς τε λέων ἐχάρη μεγάλῳ ἐπὶ σώματι κύρσας
εὑρὼν ἢ' ἔλαφον κεραὸν ἢ' ἄγριον αἶγα
πεινάων· μάλα γάρ τε κατεσθίει, εἴ περ ἂν αὐτὸν
σεύωνται ταχέες τε κύνες θαλεροί τ' αἰζηοί·
ὣς ἐχάρη Μενέλαος Ἀλέξανδρον θεοειδέα
ὀφθαλμοῖσιν ἰδών· φάτο γὰρ τείσεσθαι[98] ἀλείτην.

97 saepe peragrans R2C: *om.* ω
98 τείσεσθαι] τισ- *codd. et testt. Hom.*

the ground,
striking his chest with a spear and pinning him on his back in the dirt.
Hippolokhos made to flee, but the other slew him on the ground,
slicing his hands from his sword, his head from his neck,
and sent him rolling like a smooth, round stone through the fray. (*Il.* 11.131–47)

7. Like a famished lion that often haunts the lofty pens
(insane hunger drives him on), should he happen to spy
a roe-deer in flight or a stag towering high with his rack,
his monstrous maw gapes gleefully, his mane bristles, and he clings
to the innards as he reclines at his meal: gross gore washes
his relentless jaws—
so Mezentius rushes eagerly upon his foes' dense ranks. (*A.* 10.723–79)

8. Like a lion that rejoices in coming upon a great-bodied prey,
when he has found a horned stag or wild goat
in his hunger: he devours it greedily, should swift
hounds or sturdy youths come rushing down upon him.
So Menelaus rejoiced when he spied with his eyes godlike
Alexandros: he had in mind to punish the sinner. (*Il.* 3.23–28)

9. <βῆ ῥ' ἴμεν ὥς τε λέων ὀρεσίτροφος, ὅς τ' ἐπιδευὴς>[99]
δηρὸν ἔῃ κρειῶν, κέλεται δέ ἑ θυμὸς ἀγήνωρ
μήλων πειρήσοντα καὶ ἐς πυκινὸν δόμον ἐλθεῖν.
εἴ περ γάρ χ' εὕρῃσι παρ' αὐτόθι[100] βώτορας ἄνδρας
σὺν κυσὶ καὶ δούρεσσι φυλάσσοντας περὶ μῆλα,
οὔ ῥά τ' ἀπείρητος μέμονε σταθμοῖο δίεσθαι,
ἀλλ' ὅ γ' ἄρ' ἤ' ἥρπαξε[101] μετάλμενος, ἠὲ καὶ αὐτὸς
ἔβλητ' ἐν πρώτοισι θοῆς ἀπὸ χειρὸς ἄκοντι·
ὥς ῥα τότ' ἀντίθεον Σαρπηδόνα θυμὸς ἐνῆκε[102]
τεῖχος ἐπαΐξαι διά τε τμήξασθαι[103] ἐπάλξεις.

10. spargitur et tellus lacrimis, sparguntur et arma.

δεύοντο ψάμαθοι, δεύοντο δὲ τεύχεα φωτῶν.

11. cingitur ipse furens certatim in proelia Turnus
iamque adeo rutilum thoraca indutus aënis
horrebat squamis surasque incluserat auro,
tempora nudus adhuc, laterique adcinxerat ensem
fulgebatque alta decurrens aureus arce.

12. ὣς φάτο, Πάτροκλος δὲ κορύσσετο νώροπι χαλκῷ.
κνημῖδας μὲν πρῶτα περὶ κνήμῃσιν ἔθηκε

99 βῆ . . . ἐπιδευὴς *suppl. ed. Basil. 1535 in marg., om. α*
100 αὐτόθι (-TOЄI α)] -φι *vulg. Hom.*
101 ἥρπαξε (*cf.* 5.5.10)] -ζε α
102 ἐνῆκε] ἀνῆκε *Hom.*
103 τμήξασθαι] ῥήξ- *Hom.*

9. He went striding like a lion raised in the mountains, who too long
has been without meat, and his valiant spirit urges him on
to go and make an attempt on a crowded fold of sheep:
if he finds there the men who tend them,
keeping watch on the sheep with dogs and spears,
he has no wish to leave the farmstead untested
but either pounces and makes his kill or himself
is struck at once by a swift hand's spear-cast.
So then did his spirit drive godlike Sarpedon on
to dash at the wall and hack a way through the battlements. (*Il.* 12.299–308)

10. Tears are scattered upon the earth, weapons scattered too. (*A.* 11.191)

The sands grow wet, warriors' arms grow wet also. (*Il.* 23.15)

11. In a frenzy, Turnus girds himself hastily for battle,
already dressed now in his cuirass, glowing warmly, bristling
with brazen scales, his calves encased in gold,
head still bare, his sword hitched to his side
as he runs, a golden thunderbolt, down from the lofty citadel. (*A.* 11.486–90)

12. So he spoke, but Patroklos armed himself with the glittering bronze:
first he placed around his shins handsome greaves

*καλάς, ἀργυρέοισιν ἐπισφυρίοις ἀραρυίας·
δεύτερον αὖ θώρηκα περὶ στήθεσσιν ἔδυνε
ποικίλον ἀστερόεντα ποδώκεος Αἰακίδαο.
ἀμφὶ δ' ἄρ' ὤμοισιν βάλετο ξίφος ἀργυρόηλον
χάλκεον· αὐτὰρ ἔπειτα σάκος μέγα τε στιβαρόν
τε·
κρατὶ δ' ἐπ' ἰφθίμῳ κυνέην εὔτυκτον ἔθηκεν
ἵππουριν· δεινὸν δὲ λόφος καθύπερθεν ἔνευεν.
εἵλετο δ' ἄλκιμα δοῦρε, τά οἱ παλάμηφιν ἀρήρει.*

13. purpureus veluti cum flos succisus aratro
languescit moriens, lassove papavera collo
demisere caput, pluvia cum forte gravantur.

*μήκων δ' ὣς ἑτέρωσε κάρη βάλεν, ἥ τ' ἐνὶ κήπῳ
καρπῷ βριθομένη νοτίῃσί τε εἰαρινῇσιν·
ὣς ἑτέρωσ' ἤμυσε κάρη πήληκι βαρυνθέν.*

11 'Et haec quidem iudicio legentium relinquenda sunt, ut ipsi aestiment quid debeant de utriusque collatione sentire. si tamen me consulas, non negabo non numquam Vergilium in transferendo densius excoluisse, ut in hoc loco:

2. qualis apes aestate nova per florea rura
exercet sub sole labor, cum gentis adultos

well-fitted with silver clasps at the ankles;
next on his chest he put the cuirass of Aiakos'
swift grandson, intricate in its work, sparkling;
then around his shoulders he draped the silver-studded sword
made of bronze, after that the shield, large and thick;
and upon his noble head he set the well-made helmet
with its horse-tail plume, the crest nodding terribly from above.
He took up two sturdy spears and fit them to his hands. (*Il.* 16.130–39)

13. Just as when a rosy blossom has been sliced by the plough
and droops as it dies, or when poppies bend, their necks wearied
from supporting a head made heavy by a passing shower. (*A.* 9.435*–37)

As a poppy droops its head to one side, when it is weighed down
in a garden by its blossom and spring showers,
so his head drooped to one side under his helmet's weight. (*Il.* 8.306–8)

'I should leave it to the readers' judgment to decide what they should make of the comparison between the two. Still, if you ask my opinion, I'll not deny that Virgil was occasionally more elaborate in his borrowing, as in this case (*A.* 1.430–36): 11

2. Like the toil that sets the bees in motion across the flowering fields
under the new summer's sun, when they bring out

educunt fetus, aut cum liquentia mella
stipant et dulces[104] distendunt nectare cellas,
aut onera accipiunt venientum aut agmine facto
ignavum fucos pecus a praesepibus arcent:
fervet opus redolentque thymo fraglantia[105] mella.

3. ἠΰτε ἔθνεα εἶσι μελισσάων ἁδινάων
πέτρης ἐκ γλαφυρῆς αἰεὶ νέον ἐρχομενάων,
βοτρυδὸν δὲ πέτονται ἐπ᾽ ἄνθεσιν εἰαρινοῖσιν·
αἳ μέν τ᾽ ἔνθα ἅλις πεποτήαται, αἳ δέ τε ἔνθα·
ὣς τῶν ἔθνεα πολλὰ νεῶν ἄπο καὶ κλισιάων
ἠϊόνος προπάροιθε βαθείης ἐστιχόωντο
ἰλαδὸν εἰς ἀγορήν· μετὰ δέ σφισιν Ὄσσα
δεδήει.

4. vides descriptas apes a Vergilio opifices, ab Homero vagas: alter discursum et solam volatus varietatem, alter exprimit nativae artis officium. 5. in his quoque versibus Maro extitit locupletior interpres:

o socii (neque enim ignari sumus ante malorum),
o passi graviora, dabit deus his quoque finem.
vos et Scyllaeam rabiem penitusque sonantes
accestis scopulos, vos et Cyclopea[106] saxa

104 dulces] dulci *Verg.*

105 fraglantia $\beta_2$, *codd. aliquot Verg.*: flagrantia αε, *codd. cett. Verg.*, fragrantia S, *Serv.*

106 Cyclopea (*codd. nonnull. Verg.*)] -pia *codd. cett. Verg.*

their clan's
young, now grown, or when they pack the dripping honey tight
and make the sweet comb full to bursting with nectar,
or receive the loads of their returning mates or marshal up
to keep the drones—a lazy lot—from their enclosure:
the project's aboil, the glowing honey is perfumed with thyme.

3. As when the clans of swarming bees
pour endlessly from a hollowed rock and
fly over the springtime flowers balled in a mass,
some swarming this way, others that:
so from the ships and tents the many clans
advanced along the wide sea-shore
to assemble in a mass, and Rumor blazed among them. (*Il.* 2.87–93)

4. You can see how Virgil describes the worker bees in specific terms whereas Homer speaks in general terms: the latter conveys only their departure and the different directions of their flight, the former the duties they perform with instinctive skill. 5. In the following verses, too, we find Maro's exposition richer (*A.* 1.198–204):

My companions—indeed, we have known disaster before now—
you who have borne with worse: the god will put an end to these woes too.
You faced Scylla's frenzy, too, and the deep-resounding
cliffs, you passed through the trial of the Cyclops'

experti: revocate animos maestumque timorem
mittite; forsan et haec olim meminisse iuvabit.
per varios casus . . .

et reliqua.

6. ὦ φίλοι, οὐ γάρ πώ τι κακῶν ἀδαήμονές εἰμεν·
οὐ μὲν δὴ τόδε μεῖζον ἔπι κακόν, ἢ' ὅτε Κύκλωψ
εἴλει ἐνὶ σπῆϊ γλαφυρῷ κρατερῆφι βίηφιν·
ἀλλὰ καὶ ἔνθεν ἐμῇ ἀρετῇ βουλῇ τε νόῳ τε
ἐκφύγομεν, καί που τῶνδε μνήσεσθαι ὀΐω.

7. Vlixes ad socios unam commemoravit aerumnam: hic ad sperandam praesentis mali absolutionem gemini casus hortatur eventu. deinde ille obscurius dixit,

. . . καί που τῶνδε μνήσεσθαι ὀΐω.

hic apertius,

. . . forsan et haec olim meminisse iuvabit.

8. 'Sed et hoc quod vester adiecit solacii fortioris est. suos enim non tantum exemplo evadendi, sed et spe fu-

boulders: summon up your courage again, send gloomy
fears away. Perhaps you will one day gladly recall these trials too.
In our varied fortune's course . . .

and so on.

6. My friends—no, to be sure, we are not unacquainted with disaster—
this is certainly not a greater trial than when the Kyklops
seized us, violently, mightily, in his hollow cave,
but there too we escaped, thanks to my courage and planning
and good sense, and I imagine that you will call those events to mind. (*Od.* 12.208–12)

7. Ulysses recalled only one cause of misery to his companions, whereas Aeneas points to the outcome of two disasters in urging his men to look forward to release from the misfortune they were facing. Furthermore, Ulysses was rather elliptical in saying,

. . . and I imagine that you will call those events to mind,

whereas Aeneas more plainly says,

. . . Perhaps you will one day gladly recall these trials too.

8. 'Another point: the thought your poet added provides a more powerful kind of consolation, since he caused his men to think not only of their past escapes but also of their

turae felicitatis animavit, per hos labores non solum sedes quietas sed et regna promittens. 9. hos quoque versus inspicere libet:

ac veluti summis antiquam in montibus ornum
cum ferro accisam crebrisque bipennibus instant
eruere agricolae certatim: illa usque minatur
et tremefacta comam concusso vertice nutat,
vulneribus donec paulatim evicta supremum
congemuit traxitque iugis avulsa ruinam.

ἤριπε δ' ὡς ὅτε τις δρῦς ἤριπεν ἢ' ἀχερωΐς
ἠὲ πίτυς βλωθρή, τήν τ' οὔρεσι τέκτονες ἄνδρες
ἐξέταμον πελέκεσσι νεήκεσι νήϊον εἶναι.

magno cultu vester difficultatem abscidendae arboreae molis expressit, verum nullo negotio Homerica arbor abscidditur.

10. haud segnis strato surgit Palinurus et omnes
explorat ventos atque auribus aëra captat:
sidera cuncta notat tacito labentia caelo,
Arcturum Pliadasque[107] Hyadas geminosque Triones,
armatumque auro circumspicit Oriona.[108]

107 Pliadasque (*codd. aliquot Verg., cf. G. 1.138*)] pluviasque *Verg.*

108 Oriona (*cf. §12, Verg.*)] Orionem *ω*

future happiness, in promising that after their present toils they would enjoy not just a peaceful place to settle but even a kingdom. 9. I would like to consider these verses, too (*A.* 2.626–31):

> And just as when on a mountaintop farmers compete to hew
> an ancient ash with blow after iron blow of their two-headed axes,
> and then to bring it down: all along it looks about to fall
> and tremblingly bows its foliage, shaken to its crown,
> until little by little it is overcome by its wounds and—with a final
> groan—is torn from the ridge, bringing down ruin as it falls.

> He fell as when an oak or white poplar falls
> or a tall pine, which builders in the mountains
> fell with newly sharpened axes to be timber for ships. (*Il.* 13.389–91 = 16.482–84)

Your poet very elaborately conveyed how hard it is to cut down a massive tree, whereas Homer's tree is cut down with no trouble.

> 10. No lazy hand, Palinurus rises from his bed and tests
> all the winds, cocking his ear to catch the air's sound:
> he marks all the constellations as they glide in the silent heavens,
> Arcturus, the Pleiades, the Hyades, the two Bears,
> and looks around for Orion of the golden arms. (*A.* 3.513–17)

αὐτὰρ ὁ πηδαλίῳ ἰθύνετο τεχνηέντως
ἥμενος· οὐδέ οἱ ὕπνος ἐπὶ βλεφάροισιν ἔπιπτεν[109]
Πληϊάδας τ' ἐσορῶντι καὶ ὀψὲ δύοντα Βοώτην
Ἄρκτον θ', ἣν καὶ ἄμαξαν ἐπίκλησιν καλέουσιν,
ἥ τ' αὐτοῦ στρέφεται καί τ' Ὠρίωνα δοκεύει.

11. Gubernator qui explorat caelum crebro reflectere cervicem debet, captando de diversis caeli regionibus securitatem sereni. hoc mire et velut coloribus Maro pinxit. nam quia Arcturus iuxta septemtrionem est, Taurus vero in quo Hyades sunt, sed et Orion, in regione austri sunt, crebram cervicis reflexionem in Palinuro sidera consulente descripsit. 12. "Arcturum" inquit: ecce intuetur partem septemtrionis; deinde "Pliadasque Hyadas": ecce ad austrum flectitur; "geminosque Triones": rursus ad septemtriones vertit aspectum; "armatumque auro circumspicit Oriona": iterum se ad austrum reflectit. sed et verbo "circumspicit" varietatem saepe se vicissim convertentis ostendit. 13. Homerus gubernatorem suum semel inducit intuentem Pliadas, quae in australi regione sunt, semel Booten et Arcton, quae sunt in septemtrionali polo.

14. nec tibi diva parens, generis nec Dardanus auctor,
perfide, sed duris genuit te cautibus horrens
Caucasus Hyrcanaeque admorunt ubera tigres.

109 ἔπιπτεν] -τε *Hom.*

But then he skillfully steers a straight course, seated
at the rudder: no sleep falls upon his lids, as he
looks for the Pleiades and late-setting Boötes
and the Bear, which men also name the Wagon:
it wheels about a single fixed point and looks toward
Orion. (*Od.* 5.270–74)

11. A pilot who scans the heavens cannot help but turn his neck frequently to search out assurance of clear weather in the different quarters of the sky. Maro captured this wonderfully, as though in a painting: because Arcturus is toward the north, while the Bull (where the Hyades are found), and Orion too, are in the south, he captured Palinurus' frequent turning of his neck as he looked out for the constellations. 12. "Arcturus," he says: there, Palinurus looks to the north; then "the Pleiades, the Hyades"—there, he turns to the south; "and the two Bears"—he turns his gaze back to the north; "and looks around for Orion of the golden arms"—once again he turns back to the south. Not just that, the verb "looks around" convey the action of someone repeatedly swiveling this way and that by turns. 13. Homer brings on his pilot looking once to the Pleiades, which are in the south, once to Boötes and the Bear, which are in the northern sky.

14. Nor was a goddess your mother, nor Dardanus
the author of your line,
treacherous liar, but the rugged Caucasus gave you
birth on hard
flint stone, and Hyrcanian tigers gave you their teats.
(*A.* 4.365–67†)

*νηλεές, οὐκ ἄρα σοί γε πατὴρ ἦν ἱππότα Πηλεύς,*
*οὐδὲ Θέτις μήτηρ, γλαυκὴ δέ σε τίκτε θάλασσα.*

15. 'Plene Vergilius non partionem solam, sicut ille quem sequebatur, sed educationem quoque nutricationis tamquam belualem et asperam criminatus est. addidit enim de suo:

. . . Hyrcanaeque admorunt ubera tigres,

quoniam videlicet in moribus inolescendis magnam fere partem nutricis ingenium et natura lactis tenet, quae infusa tenero et mixta parentum semini adhuc recenti, ex hac gemina concretione unam indolem configurat. 16. hinc est quod providentia naturae similitudinem natorum atque gignentium ex ipso quoque nutricatu praeparans, fecit cum ipso partu alimoniae copiam nasci. nam postquam sanguis ille opifex in penetralibus suis omne corpus effinxit atque aluit, adventante iam partus tempore idem ad corporis materni superna conscendens in naturam lactis albescit, ut recens natis idem sit altor qui fuerat fabricator. 17. quam ob rem non frustra creditum est, sicut valeat ad fingendas corporis atque animi similitudines vis et natura seminis, non secus ad eandem rem lactis quoque ingenia et proprietates valere. 18. neque in hominibus id solum sed in pecudibus quoque animadversum. nam si ovium lacte haedi aut caprarum agni forsitan alantur, constat ferme in his lanam duriorem, in illis capillum gigni teneriorem.

---

[34] §§15–19 are based on Gell. 12.1.13–16, 20.

[35] Like milk, semen was thought to be derived from blood.

Pitiless thing, the horseman Peleus, then, was not your father
nor Thetis your mother, but the gray sea gave you birth. (*Il.* 16.33–34)

15. 'Virgil developed the figure fully, not just treating the character's birth, as his model did, but also reproaching his upbringing as harsh and bestial.[34] For he added on his own,

. . . and Hyrcanian tigers gave you their teats,

obviously because in implanting one's character a large role is generally played by the qualities of one's nurse and the nature of the milk received, which enters the tender babe and mingles with the parents' seed when it is still fresh, as the two-fold mixture shapes a single nature. 16. That is why a provident nature caused the capacity for nursing to coincide with the delivery itself, so that the very act of nurturing would make children and parents resemble each other. For after the blood, like a craftsman, has shaped the body's every nook and cranny and fed it, the same blood rises to the upper regions of the mother's body as the delivery approaches and takes on the nature of white milk, so that it might nurture the new-born as it had previously crafted it. 17. That is why it is correctly believed that milk's innate properties have the same capacity as seed's natural force to produce a likeness of body and minds.[35] 18. And this fact has been observed not only in the case of human beings but in the case of domestic animals too: if goats happen to be raised on ewes' milk or lambs on she-goats', it's well known that in the latter case the wool turns out coarser while in the former the hair becomes finer.

19. in arboribus etiam et frugibus ad earum indolem vel detrectandam vel augendam maior plerumque vis et potestas est aquarum atque terrarum quae alunt quam ipsius quod iacitur seminis, ac saepe videas laetam nitentemque arborem, si in locum alterum transferatur, suco terrae deterioris elanguisse. ad criminandos igitur mores defuit Homero quod Vergilius adiecit.

20. non tam praecipites biiugo certamine campum
corripuere ruuntque effusi carcere currus,
nec sic immissis aurigae undantia lora
concussere iugis pronique in verbera pendent.

*οἱ δ',*[110] *ὥς τ' ἐν πεδίῳ τετράοροι ἄρσενες ἵπποι,*
*πάντες ἀφορμηθέντες*[111] *ὑπὸ πληγῇσιν ἱμάσθλης,*
*ὑψόσ' ἀειρόμενοι ῥίμφα πρήσσουσι κέλευθα*[112]
. . .

21. Graius poeta equorum tantum meminit flagro animante currentium, licet dici non possit elegantius quam quod adiecit *ὑψόσ' ἀειρόμενοι*, quo expressit quantum natura dare poterat impetum cursus. 22. verum Maro et currus de carcere ruentes et campos corripiendo praecipites mira celeritate descripsit, et accepto brevi semine de Homerico flagro pinxit aurigas concutientes lora undantia et pronos in verbera pendentes: nec ullam quadrigarum partem intactam reliquit, ut esset illi certaminis plena descriptio.

110 *οἱ δ'*] *ἡ δ' Hom.*
111 *ἀφορμηθέντες*] *ἅμ' ὁρμη- Hom.*
112 *κέλευθα*] *κέλευθον Hom.*

19. For trees and plants, too, the water and earth in which they're raised has more power and influence in improving their quality or making it worse than the very seed from which they're sown: you would often see a productive tree aglow with health be made sickly by the juice of inferior soil if it is transplanted. For the purpose of reproaching bad character, then, Homer lacked what Virgil added.

> 20. With no such reckless abandon have chariots ever snatched up the course
> when they've spilled with a rush from the gate in a race of matched pairs,
> never so freely have drivers given teams their heads, cracking their
> rippling lashes as they lean forward to put more into the blow. (*A.* 5.144–47)

> But like stallions yoked four abreast on the course,
> all rushing on together under lashes from the whip,
> stepping high and swiftly completing their course . . . (*Od.* 13.81–83)

21. The Greek poet merely mentions that the horses are running with the whip's encouragement, though adding "stepping high" is the most delicate possible touch, conveying how much the horse's nature contributes to the race's momentum. 22. But Maro described the chariots rushing from the gate and hurrying over the field with wonderful speed, and by taking over the germ of an idea planted by Homer's whip he painted a verbal picture of the drivers "cracking their rippling lashes" and "leaning forward to put more into the blow": he touched on every aspect of a chariot race to give a complete description of the contest.

23. magno veluti cum flamma sonore
virgea suggeritur costis undantis aëni,
exsultantque aestu latices, furit intus aquai,[113]
fumidus atque alte spumis exuberat amnis.
nec iam se capit unda, volat vapor ater ad auras.

*ὡς δὲ λέβης ζεῖ ἔνδον ἐπειγόμενος πυρὶ πολλῷ
κνίσῃ[114] μελδόμενος ἁπαλοτρεφέος σιάλοιο
πάντοθεν ἀμβολάδην, ὑπὸ δὲ ξύλα κάγκανα κεῖται,
ὣς τοῦ καλὰ ῥέεθρα πυρὶ φλέγετο, ζέε δ' ὕδωρ.*

24. Graeci versus aeni continent mentionem multo igne ebullientis, et totum ipsum locum haec verba ornant, *πάντοθεν ἀμβολάδην*, nam scaturrigines ex omni parte emergentes sic eleganter expressit. 25. in Latinis versibus tota rei pompa descripta est, sonus flammae et pro hoc quod ille dixerat *πάντοθεν ἀμβολάδην*, exultantes aestu latices et amnem fumidum exuberantem spumis atque intus furentem: unius enim verbi non reperiens similem dignitatem compensavit quod deerat copiae varietate descriptionis. adiecit post omnia, "nec iam se capit unda," quo expressit quod semper usu evenit suppositi nimietate caloris. bene ergo se habet poeticae tubae cultus, omnia quae in hac re eveniunt comprehendens.

113 aquai (*v. paraphrasin in §25, ubi noster lectionem* vis *nescire videtur*) *codd. nonnull. Verg.*, (*D*)*Serv.*, *edd.*: aquae vis ω, *codd. cett. Verg.*

114 κνίσῃ (*vel* –η) (*Hom. vulg.*)] κνίσην *Aristarch. et al.*, *codd. aliquot Hom.*, *edd.*

23. As when a roaring fire
of brush is stoked beneath the sides of a seething cauldron,
the liquid leaps as it boils, the water raging violently within,
and a smoking stream bubbles high with foam. No longer
can the water contain itself, but dark vapor flies up to the winds. (*A.* 7.462–66)

As a cauldron seethes within when urged on by a high fire,
rendering the fat of the pampered plump hog,
bubbling all around, and the dry wood lies beneath it:
so [the river Xanthos'] fair streams burned with the flame, his water boiled. (*Il.* 21.362–65)

24. The Greek lines mention a bronze cauldron bubbling over a large fire, and the whole passage gains in adornment from the phrase "bubbling all around," which subtly conveys the bubbles that leap up from every direction. 25. The Latin lines describe the whole sequence of events, the sound of the flame and, in place of Homer's "bubbling all around," there's "the liquid leaping as it boils and "a smoking stream bubbling high with foam" and "raging within": unable to find a single word that had a comparable worth, he made up for the lack with a suite of different descriptions. Then he capped it by saying "no longer can the water contain itself," conveying what always happens in fact when too hot a fire has been built. Poetry in the grand style is nicely elaborated here by inclusion of all the things that happen in this sort of scene.

26. portam, quae ducis imperio commissa, recludunt
freti armis, ultroque invitant moenibus hostem.
ipsi intus dextra ac laeva pro turribus adstant,
armati ferro et cristis capita alta coruscis.[115]
quales aëriae liquentia flumina circum,
sive Padi ripis Athesim seu propter amoenum,
consurgunt geminae quercus intonsaque caelo
attollunt capita et sublimi vertice nutant.

27. *τὼ μὲν ἄρα προπάροιθε πυλάων ὑψηλάων*
*ἕστασαν ὡς ὅτε τε δρύες οὔρεσιν ὑψικάρηνοι,*
*αἵ τ' ἄνεμον μίμνουσι καὶ ὑετὸν ἤματα πάντα,*
*ῥίζῃσιν μεγάλῃσι διηνεκέεσσ' ἀραρυῖαι·*
*ὣς ἄρα τὼ χείρεσσι πεποιθότες ἠδὲ βίηφι*
*μίμνον ἐπερχόμενον μέγαν Ἄσιον, οὐδὲ φέβοντο.*

28. Graeci milites Polypoetes et Leonteus stant pro portis, et immobiles[116] Asium advenientem hostem velut fixae arbores opperiuntur. hactenus est Graeca descriptio. 29. verum Vergiliana Bitian et Pandarum portam ultro recludere facit, oblaturos hosti quod per vota quaerebat, ut compos castrorum fieret, per hoc futuros[117] in hostium potestate: et geminos heroas modo turres vocat, modo describit luce cristarum coruscos nec arborum, ut ille, simili-

[115] coruscis] -ci *Verg.*
[116] et immobiles R²C: etiam mobiles *ω*
[117] futuros *ed. Lugd. 1532*: futurus *ω*

---

[36] At 6.2.32 the episode is said to have been taken from Ennius *Annals* 15.

26. They throw open the gate assigned them by their leader's command,
confident in their arms, and actually invite the enemy to enter.
They themselves stand just within, right and left, like towers,
armed with swords, shimmering crests atop their heads.
Like a pair of oaks that rise sky-high along a clear-flowing
stream, on the banks of the Po, perhaps, or beside
the beguiling Adige: they raise their shaggy heads
to heaven, their lofty crowns swaying in the breeze. (*A.* 9.675–82)[36]

27. Before the lofty gates, then, the two men stood,
like high-crowned oaks in the mountains
that withstand wind and rain for all their days,
firmly planted with their great long roots:
so then the two, putting their trust in might and main,
withstood the charge of great Asios and did not flee. (*Il.* 12.131–36)

28. The Greek soldiers Polypoetes and Leonteus stand before the gates and await the approach of the enemy soldier Asius, as unmoved as planted trees: so far the description in the Greek. 29. But Virgil has Bitias and Pandarus actually open the gate as though to give the enemy what he prayed for—control of the camp—so they would end up in the enemy's power. He first calls the pair of heroes "towers," then describes them as "shimmering" from the gleam of their crests, and he followed Homer in using the simile

tudinem praetermisit, sed uberius eam pulchriusque descripsit. 30. nec hoc negaverim cultius a Marone prolatum:

olli dura quies oculos et ferreus urguet
somnus, in aeternam clauduntur lumina noctem.

ὣς ὃ μὲν ἔνθα[118] πεσὼν κοιμήσατο χάλκεον
ὕπνον.

12 'In aliquibus par paene splendor amborum est, ut in his:

. . . spargit rara[119] ungula rores
sanguineos mixtaque cruor calcatur arena.

. . . αἵματι δ' ἄξων
νέρθεν ἅπας πεπάλακτο καὶ ἄντυγες αἳ περὶ
δίφρον.

2. . . . et luce coruscus aëna.

αὐγῇ χαλκείῃ κορύθων ἄπο λαμπομενάων . . .

3. . . . quaerit pars semina flammae.

σπέρμα πυρὸς σώζων . . .

4. Indum sanguineo veluti violaverit ostro
si quis ebur . . .

ὡς δ' ὅτε τίς τ' ἐλέφαντα γυνὴ φοίνικι μίηνῃ.

5. . . . si tangere portus

118 ἔνθα] αὖθι *Hom.*
119 rara] rapida *Verg.*

of the trees but developed it more richly and beautifully. 30. Nor would I deny that Maro's version here is better developed too:

> Upon his sight a cruel peace presses, a sleep of iron, and his eyes close in a night that will never end. (*A.* 10.745–46)

> So there he tumbled and fell into a sleep of bronze. (*Il.* 11.241)

'In some passages both poets are equally splendid, for example: 12

> . . . here and there a horse's hoof spatters a bloody dew, trampling on the gore that mingles with the sand. (*A.* 12.339–40)

> . . . below, the axle is all stained with blood, and the rim that runs round the cart. (*Il.* 11.534–35)

> 2. . . . and shimmering with a brazen light. (*A.* 2.470)

> a brazen gleam from the shining helmets . . . (*Il.* 13.341)

> 3. . . . some search for the seeds of fire. (*A.* 6.6*)

> . . . keeping safe the seed of fire. (*Od.* 5.490)

> 4. as if one defiled Indian ivory with blood-red dye . . . (*A.* 12.67*–68)

> as when some woman defiles ivory with purple . . . (*Il.* 4.141)

> 5. . . . if that unspeakable person

infandum[120] caput ac terris adnare necesse est
et sic fata Iovis poscunt, hic terminus haeret,
at bello audacis populi vexatus et armis,
finibus extorris, complexu avulsus Iuli
auxilium imploret videatque indigna suorum
funera, nec cum se sub leges pacis iniquae
tradiderit, regno aut optata luce fruatur,
sed cadat ante diem mediaque inhumatus arena.

6. *κλῦθι, Ποσείδαον γαιήοχε κυανοχαῖτα·*
*εἰ ἐτεόν γε σός εἰμι, πατὴρ δ' ἐμὸς εὔχεαι εἶναι,*
*δὸς μὴ 'Οδυσσῆα πτολιπόρθιον οἴκαδ' ἱκέσθαι,*[121]
*ἀλλ' εἰ καί οἱ μοῖρα φίλους τ'*[122] *ἰδέειν καὶ ἱκέσθαι*
*οἶκον ἐς ὑψόροφον*[123] *καὶ ἑὴν ἐς πατρίδα γαῖαν,*
*ὀψὲ κακῶς ἔλθοι, ὀλέσας ἄπο πάντας ἑταίρους,*
*νηὸς ἐπ' ἀλλοτρίης, εὕροι δ' ἐν πήματα οἴκῳ.*

7. proxima Circaeae raduntur litora terrae,
dives inaccessos ubi Solis filia lucos
assiduo resonat cantu tectisque superbis

120 infandum RC: infantum *ω*

121 *Od.* 9. 531 (*υἱὸν Λαέρτεω . . . οἰκί' ἔχοντα*) *om. cum α tum fere omnes Homerici*

122 *εἰ καὶ οἱ μοῖρα φίλους τ'* (*εἰ οἱ καὶ μ. φ. nonnull. Hom.*)] *εἴ οἱ μοῖρ' ἐστὶ φίλους plerique Hom.*

123 *ἐς ὑψόροφον* (*Hom. Venet.* 457, *cf. Od.* 5. 42, 115, 7. 77)]

37 Cf. Serv. on *A.* 4.613.

really must glide in to land and touch safe harbor,[37] if
that's what Jupiter's decrees demand, the goal
unmovable, still:
let him be harried under arms in war with a daring
people,
let him be driven from his territory, torn from Iulus'
embrace,
let him beg for aid and see his people die
undeserving,
and when he has given himself over to the terms of
an unjust
peace, let him not enjoy his realm or the life he's
longed for,
but let him die before his time and lie unburied in
the midst of the sands. (*A.* 4.612–20)

6. Hear me, dark-haired Poseidon, who hold the
earth in your embrace:
if I am truly yours, if you claim to be my father,
grant that Odysseus, the sacker of cities, not reach
home;
but if it is his portion to see his dear ones and reach
his high-roofed house and come to his fathers' land,
may he arrive late and wretched, all his companions
lost,
on a ship not his own, and may he find misery in his
house. (*Od.* 9.528–35)

7. They scrape by the nearest tracts of Circe's land,
where the rich daughter of the Sun makes the
unreachable
groves resound with ceaseless song and in her proud
dwelling

urit odoratam nocturna in lumina cedrum,
arguto tenues percurrens pectine telas.

8. ᾔϊεν, ὄφρα μέγα σπέος ἵκετο, τῷ ἔνι νύμφη
ναῖεν ἐϋπλόκαμος, δεινὴ θεός, αὐδήεσσα.[124]
πῦρ μὲν ἐπ' ἐσχαρόφιν μέγα καίετο, τηλόσε δ' ὀδμὴ
κέδρου τ' εὐκεάτοιο θύου τ' ἀνὰ νῆσον ὀδώδει
δαιομένων· ἡ δ' ἔνδον ἀοιδιάουσ' ὀπὶ καλῇ
ἱστὸν ἐποιχομένη χρυσείῃ κερκίδ' ὕφαινεν.

9. . . . Maeonio regi quem serva Li‹cymnia furtim›[125]
sustulerat vetitisque ad Troiam miserat armis.

Βουκολίων δ' ἦν υἱὸς ἀγαυοῦ Λαομέδοντος
πρεσβύτατος γενεήν,[126] σκότιον δέ ἑ γείνατο μήτηρ.

10. ille autem exspirans: "non me, quicumque es, inulto,
victor, nec longum laetabere: te quoque fata
prospectant paria atque eadem mox arva tenebis."
ad quae[127] subridens mixta Mezentius ira:

*ἐϋκτίμενον Hom.*

124 δεινὴ θεός, αὐδήεσσα (= *Od. 10. 136*)] τὴν δ' ἔνδοθι τέτμεν ἐοῦσαν *Hom.*

125 cinia [*sic*] furtim *suppl. ed. Ven. 1472 ex Verg., om.* ω

126 γενεήν] γενεῇ *Hom.*

127 ad quae C (*codd.* Vd *Verg., cf. Sil. 10.59* ad quae suspirans . . . ): atque ω (*codd.* MP2ω *Verg.*), adque R2A, ad quem *ed. Ven.*

sends the perfumed smoke of cedar rising to the stars,
running her chattering shuttle through the delicate warp. (*A.* 7.10–14)

8. He went until he reached the great grotto where dwelt the nymph,
fair-haired, a terrible divinity who speaks with a human voice.
A fire burned high on the hearth, from afar the scent
of well-split cedar and citron could be savored all through island
as they burnt. Within she sang with her lovely voice
going up and down before the loom, weaving with a golden shuttle. (*Od.* 5.57–62)

9. . . . whom Licymnia, a slave, had borne in secret to Maeonia's
king and had sent to Troy in forbidden arms. (*A.* 9.546–47)

Boukolion was the son of noble Laömedon,
eldest by birth, but his mother bore him in secret. (*Il.* 6.23–24)

10. Breathing his last, he said, "I will be avenged, whoever you are,
and you'll not enjoy your victory for long:[38] a fate like mine
has you in view and soon you will have a grave like mine."
In reply Mezentius smiled an angry smile:

[38] Cf. Serv. on A. 10.740.

"nunc morere, ast de me divum pater atque hominum rex
‹viderit›[128] . . ."

11. ἄλλο δέ τοι ἐρέω, σὺ δ' ἐνὶ φρεσὶ βάλλεο σῇσιν·
οὔ θην οὐδ' αὐτὸς δηρὸν βέῃ, ἀλλά τοι ἤδη
‹ἄγχι παρέστηκεν θάνατος καὶ μοῖρα κραταιή,›[129]
χερσὶ δαμέντ' Ἀχιλῆος ἀμύμονος Αἰακίδαο.

et alibi:

τὸν καὶ τεθνηῶτα προσηύδα δῖος Ἀχιλλεύς·
τέθναθι· κῆρα δ' ἐγὼ τότε δέξομαι ὁππότε κεν δὴ
Ζεὺς ἐθέλῃ τελέσαι ἠδ' ἀθάνατοι θεοὶ ἄλλοι.

12. qualis ubi aut leporem aut candenti corpore cycnum
sustulit alta petens pedibus Iovis armiger uncis,
quaesitum aut matri multis balatibus agnum
Martius a stabulis rapuit lupus: undique clamor
tollitur, invadunt et fossas aggere complent.

13. οἴμησεν δὲ ἀλεὶς ὥς τ' αἰετὸς ὑψιπετήεις,
ὅς τ' εἶσιν πεδίονδε διὰ νεφέων ἐρεβεννῶν

*1472* (*codd.* Refnv *Verg.*, *Tib.*)

[128] viderit *suppl. ed. Ven. 1472 ex Verg.*, *om.* ω

"Die now, and let the father of gods and king of men see
about me . . . " (*A.* 10.739–44)

11. I will speak another word to you, and you store it away in your mind:
you yourself will not live long, surely not, but already death
and a mighty doom stand at your side: you will be
broken by the hands of blameless Akhilleus, grandson of Aiakos. (*Il.* 16.851–54)

and elsewhere:

Brilliant Akhilleus addressed him as he lay dead:
"Die: I shall accept my doom at whatever time
Zeus and the other immortal gods wish to achieve it." (*Il.* 22.364–66)

12. As when Jupiter's squire has caught up a hare with his
hooked talons, or a dazzling white swan, and makes for the heavens,
or when a wolf of Mars has snatched a lamb from out of the fold,
as it bleats again and again for its mother: shouts are raised
on every side as the soldiers charge on and fill the trenches with earth. (*A.* 9.563–67)

13. He gathered himself and swooped, like a high-flying eagle
through black clouds toward the plain,

*ἁρπάξων ἢ ἄρν' ἀμαλὴν ἢ πτῶκα λαγωόν·*
*ὣς Ἕκτωρ οἴμησε τινάσσων φάσγανον ὀξύ.*

13 'Et quia non est erubescendum Vergilio si minorem se Homero vel ipse fateatur, dicam in quibus mihi visus sit gracilior auctore.

2. tunc[130] caput orantis nequiquam et multa parantis
dicere deturbat terrae truncumque reliquit.[131]

hi duo versus de illo translati sunt:

*φθεγγομένου δ' ἄρα τοῦδε[132] κάρη κονίῃσιν ἐμίχθη.*

vide nimiam celeritatem salvo pondere, ad quam non potuit conatus Maronis accedere. 3. in curuli certamine Homerus alterum currum paululum antecedentem et alterum paene coniunctum sequendo qua luce signavit:

*πνοιῇ δ' Εὐμήλοιο μετάφρενον ἠδὲ καὶ ὤμους[133]*
*θέρμετ'· ἐπ' αὐτῷ γὰρ κεφαλὰς καταθέντε πετέσθην.*

at iste:[134]

. . . umescunt spumis flatuque sequentum.

4. mirabilior est celeritas consequentis priorem in cursu pedum apud eundem vatem:

129 *ἄγχι . . . κραταιή suppl. ed. Ven. 1472 ex Hom., om. α*

130 tunc] tum *Verg.* 131 reliquit (*cf. A. 12.382*)] tepentem *Verg.* 132 *τοῦδε*] *τοῦ γε Hom.*

133 *ἠδὲ καὶ ὤμους* (= *Od. 8. 528, cf. et Il. 2.265*)] *εὐρέε τ' ὤμω*

aiming to snatch a tender lamb or timid hare:
so Hektor swooped as he brandished his sharp blade.
(*Il.* 22.308–11)

'And since Virgil himself need not blush to acknowledge Homer as his superior, let me tell you of the passages where he seems to me less robust than his model. 13

2. Then as he begged in vain and made ready to say still more,
Aeneas lopped his head to the ground and left just his trunk upright. (*A.* 10.554–55)

The latter verses were adapted from this one (*Il.* 10.457):

Then his head met the sand as he still spoke.

Observe how, with no loss of weight, he achieves a great speed that Maro's venture could not approach. 3. Look at how brilliantly, in the chariot race, Homer conveyed that one chariot was just slightly in front, with the other one practically linked to it as it followed (*Il.* 23.380–81):

They warmed Eumelos' back and shoulders with their
breath, their heads nodding above him as they flew.

But that poet of yours has (*G.* 3.111):

. . . grow damp from the pursuers' panting spittle.

4. In the foot race, too, the same poet more marvelously conveys the pursuer's speed (*Il.* 23.764):

*ἴχνια ποσσὶν ἔτυπτε*[135] *πάρος κόνιν ἀμφιχυθῆναι.*

est autem huius versus hic sensus: si per solum pulvereum forte curratur, ubi pes fuerit de terra a currente sublatus, vestigium sine dubio signatum videtur, et tamen celerius cogitatione pulvis qui ictu pedis fuerat excussus vestigio superfunditur. 5. ait ergo divinus poeta ita proximum fuisse qui sequebatur ut occuparet antecedentis vestigium antequam pulvis ei superfunderetur. at hic vester idem significare cupiens quid ait?

. . . calcemque terit iam calce Diores.

6. vide et in hoc Homeri cultum:

*κεῖτ' ἀποδοχμώσας πλατὺν αὐχένα.*

iste ait:

cervicem inflexam posuit . . .

7. hos quoque versus si videtur comparemus:

*ἅρματα δ' ἄλλοτε μὲν χθονὶ πίλνατο*
*πουλυβοτείρῃ,*
*ἄλλοτε δ' ἀΐξασκε μετήορα . . .*

iamque humiles[136] iamque elati sublime videntur
aëra per tenerum[137] ferri . . .

*Hom.* [134] at iste PG: *om.* N$\beta_2$
[135] *ποσσὶν ἔτυπτε*] *τύπτε πόδεσσι* *Hom.*
[136] humiles *S*: *-lis* *ω*

> he landed in the other's tracks before the dust settled
> around them.

The meaning of this line is as follows: if a race happens to be run over dusty ground, a runner of course leaves a track when he raises his foot from the earth, and yet quicker than thought the dust raised by a footfall settles back over the track. The godlike poet's point, then, is that the pursuer is so close that he plants his foot in the other's track before the dust settles upon it. But what does your poet say when he wants to convey the same thing? (*A.* 5.324)

> . . . and now Diores treads on the other's heel with
> his own

6. Consider Homer's refinement in this line (*Od.* 9.372):

> he lay with his broad neck bent to one side.

But that poet of yours says (*A.* 3.631):

> he rested his bent neck. . . .

7. Let's compare these lines too, if you're agreeable:

> The chariots now alit on the much-nourishing earth,
> now sprang up in mid-air . . . . (*Il.* 23.368–69)

> Now they seem borne along on the ground, now
> raised up on high
> through the unresisting air . . . . (*G.* 3.108–9)

8. *πασάων δ' ὑπὲρ ἥ γε κάρη ἔχει ἠδὲ μέτωπα*

. . . ingrediensque[138] deas supereminet omnes.

9. *ὑμεῖς γὰρ θεαί ἐστε, πάρεστέ τε ἴστέ τε πάντα.*

et[139] meministis enim, divae, et memorare potestis.

10. clamores simul horrendos ad sidera tollit,
qualis mugitus, fugit cum saucius aram
taurus et incertam excussit cervice securim.

*αὐτὰρ ὃ θυμὸν ἄϊσθε καὶ ἤρυγεν, ὡς ὅτε ταῦρος*
*ἤρυγεν ἑλκόμενος Ἑλικώνιον ἀμφὶ ἄνακτα*
*κούρων ἑλκόντων· γάνυται δέ τε τοῖς Ἐνοσίχθων.*

11. inspecto hic utriusque filo quantam distantiam deprehendes? sed nec hoc minus eleganter quod de tauro ad sacrificium tracto loquens meminit et Apollinis: *Ἑλικώνιον ἀμφὶ ἄνακτα.* sed et Neptuni meminit: *γάνυται δέ τε τοῖς Ἐνοσίχθων.* his autem duobus praecipue rem divinam fieri tauro testis est ipse Vergilius:

taurum Neptuno, taurum tibi, pulcher Apollo . . .

137 tenerum (*cf.* A. 9.699)] vacuum *Verg.*
138 ingrediensque] gradiensque *Verg.* (*et* 5.4.9)

---

39 Mt. Helicon in Boeotia was sacred to the Muses, with whom Apollo was associated from the archaic period of Greek culture onward; but in Homer the "lord of Helikon" is Poseidon (= Neptune), cf. Σ Vet. *Il.* 20.404, *Homeric Hymn to Poseidon* 3.

8. Above them all she holds her head . . . (*Od.* 6.107)

. . . as she strides along, taller than all the other goddesses. (*A.* 1.501)

9. For you are goddesses, you are everywhere and know all things. (*Il.* 2.485)

For you have both the recall, goddesses, and the power to tell us. (*A.* 7.645)

10. At the same time he raises a chilling cry to the stars,
a bellowing just as when a wounded bull flees
the altar and shakes the errant axe from its neck. (*A.* 2.222–24)

Then he breathed out his spirit and roared, as when a bull
roars as it is dragged around the lord of Helikon's shrine
and the Earth-shaker delights in the youths who drag it. (*Il.* 20.403–5)

11. Do you see the difference once you take a good look at what each one's made of? Equally subtle is the fact that in speaking of the bull dragged to the sacrifice he mentions both Apollo[39]—"around the lord of Helikon's shrine"—and Neptune—"the Earth-shaker delights in them." Virgil himself, moreover, attests that a bull is sacrificed to these two gods especially (*A.* 3.119):[40]

A bull to Neptune, a bull to you, fair Apollo. . . .

[40] Cf. 3.10.5.

12. in segetem veluti cum flamma furentibus Austris
incidit aut rapidus montano flumine torrens
sternit agros, sternit sata laeta boumque labores
praecipitesque trahit silvas: stupet inscius alto
accipiens sonitum saxi de vertice pastor.

*ὡς δ' ὅτε πῦρ ἀΐδηλον ἐν ἀξύλῳ ἐμπέσῃ ὕλῃ,*
*πάντῃ τ' εἰλυφόων ἄνεμος φέρει, οἱ δέ τε θάμνοι*
*πρόρριζοι πίπτουσιν ἐπειγόμενοι πυρὸς ὁρμῇ.*

13. *θῦνε γὰρ ἂμ πεδίον ποταμῷ πλήθοντι ἐοικὼς*
*χειμάρρῳ, ὅς τ' ὦκα ῥέων ἐκέδασσε γεφύρας·*
*τὸν δ' οὔτ' ἄρ τε γέφυραι ἐεργμέναι ἰσχανόωσιν,*
*οὔτ' ἄρα ἕρκεα ἴσχει ἀλωάων ἐριθηλέων*
*ἐλθόντ' ἐξαπίνης ὅτ' ἐπιβρίσῃ Διὸς ὄμβρος·*
*πολλὰ δ' ὑπ' αὐτοῦ ἔργα κατήριπε κάλ' αἰζηῶν·*
*ὣς ὑπὸ Τυδεΐδῃ πυκιναὶ κλονέοντο φάλαγγες.*

et duas parabolas temeravit ut unam faceret, trahens hinc ignem, inde torrentem, et dignitatem neutrius implevit.

14. adversi rupto ceu quondam turbine venti

12. Just as when fire falls upon a field of grain as the South wind
rages or the ravening torrent of a mountain stream
lays the fields low, lays low the abundant crops and the oxen's labors,
drags whole forests headlong: hearing the sound on some high rocky
pinnacle, a shepherd is stunned but does not know its cause. (*A.* 2.304–8)

As when a destructive fire fall upon a dense forest
and the whirling wind carries it in every direction, the thickets
perish utterly under the force of the fire's onslaught. (*Il.* 11.155–57)

13. For he charged over the plain like a river in full spate,
storm-fed, swift-flowing, bursting the dikes:
neither the dikes have the strength to restrain it
nor again the hedges of the flourishing orchards, as
it comes of a sudden when Zeus' rain falls heavily down.
Many fine labors of vigorous men fall before it.
So were the close-packed ranks routed by Diomedes. (*Il.* 5.87–93)

He spoiled two comparisons for the sake of producing one, deriving the fire from the first, the torrent from the second, and doing justice to neither.

14. Just as in a cyclone's burst winds from different quarters clash,

confligunt, Zephyrusque Notusque et laetus Eois
Eurus equis: stridunt silvae saevitque tridenti
spumeus atque imo Nereus ciet aequora fundo.

15. ὡς δ' ἄνεμοι δύο πόντον ὀρίνετον ἰχθυόεντα
Βορέης καὶ Ζέφυρος, τώ τε Θρῄκηθεν ἄητον
ἐλθόντ' ἐξαπίνης· ἄμυδις δέ τε κῦμα κελαινὸν
κορθύεται, πολλὸν δὲ παρὲξ ἅλα φῦκος ἔχευεν.

et alibi:

ὡς δ' Εὖρός τε Νότος τ' ἐριδαίνετον ἀλλήλοιιν
οὔρεος ἐν βήσσῃς βαθέην πελεμιζέμεν ὕλην
φηγόν τε μελίην τε τανύφλοιόν[140] τε κράνειαν,
αἵ τε πρὸς ἀλλήλας ἔβαλον τανυήκεας ὄζους
ἠχῇ θεσπεσίῃ, πάταγος δέ τε ἀγνυμενάων,
ὣς Τρῶες καὶ Ἀχαιοὶ ἐπ' ἀλλήλοισι θορόντες
δῄουν, οὐδ' ἕτεροι μνώοντ' ὀλοοῖο φόβοιο.

idem et hic[141] vitium quod superius incurrit, de duabus Graecis parabolis unam dilucidius construendo.

16. prosequitur surgens a puppi ventus euntis.

ἡμῖν δ' αὖ κατόπισθε νεὸς κυανοπρῴροιο
ἴκμενον οὖρον ἵει πλησίστιον, ἐσθλὸν ἑταῖρον.

139 et G, *om.* ω
140 τανύ- *Hom.*: βαθύ- α

41 The Virgilian passage is treated as an imitation of Ennius at 6.2.27.

the west wind, the south, and the east wind that delights
in the horses of the Dawn: the woods shriek, and foaming
Nereus rages with his trident, stirring the sea from its depths. (*A.* 2.416–19)

15. As two winds stir the sea that teems with fish,
the north wind and the west, arising in a sudden
storm from Thrace: at once the black wave crests and
spills wrack in heaps along the border of the sea. (*Il.* 9.4–7)

and elsewhere:

As the east wind and the south clash with one another
in mountain glens and make the deep wood tremble,
oak and ash and long-leafed cornel:
they batter each other as they toss their slender limbs
with a mighty noise, clattering as they split asunder.
So the Trojans and Akhaians charged each other and
cut each other down, no thought of deadly fear on either side. (*Il.* 16.765–71)

Here too is the same fault he encountered just above, by too baldy assembling a single comparison from two Greek models.[41]

16. Rising from astern the wind attends them as they go. (*A.* 3.130)

From behind our dark-prowed ship [Circe] sends
a favoring breeze that sped us on, a good companion. (*Od.* 11.6–7)

quod noster dixit κατόπισθε νεὸς, vester ait "surgens a puppi" satis decore: sed excellunt epitheta quae tot et sic apta vento noster imposuit.

17. visceribus miserorum et sanguine vescitur atro.
vidi egomet, duo de numero cum corpora nostro[142]
prensa manu magna medio resupinus in antro
frangeret ad saxum . . .

ἀλλ' ὅ γ' ἀναΐξας ἑτάροις ἐπὶ χεῖρας ἴαλλεν
σύν τε[143] δύω μάρψας ὥς τε σκύλακας ποτὶ γαίῃ
κόπτ'· ἐκ δ' ἐγκέφαλος χαμάδις ῥέε, δεῦε δὲ γαῖαν.
τοὺς δὲ διὰ μελεϊστὶ ταμὼν ὡπλίσσατο δόρπον·
ἤσθιε δ' ὥς τε λέων ὀρεσίτροφος, οὐδ' ἀπέλειπεν,
ἔγκατά τε σάρκας τε καὶ ὀστέα μυελόεντα.
ἡμεῖς δὲ κλαίοντες ἀνεσχέθομεν Διὶ χεῖρας.

narrationem facti nudam et brevem Maro posuit, contra Homerus πάθος miscuit et dolore narrandi invidiam crudelitatis aequavit.

18. hic et Aloidas geminos immania vidi
corpora, qui manibus magnum rescindere caelum

141 idem et hic *Bentley*: demet huic ω
142 nostro S: nostra ω

42 Cf. Serv. on A. 3.623.

For what our poet conveyed by the phrase "from behind the ship" your poet uses the phrase "rising from astern," handsomely enough: but the several apt epithets that our poet applied to the breeze come off better.

> 17. He dines upon the poor men's guts and black blood.
> I saw it with my own eyes, as his great hand caught up
> the bodies of two[42] of our crew and dashed them against the rock
> as he lay on his back in the cave. . . . (*A*. 3.622–25)

> But springing up he quickly snatched at my companions,
> grabbing two at once, and dashed them against the ground
> like puppies: their brains spilled to the floor and wet the earth.
> Butchering them limb by limb, he prepared them for his supper,
> then ate them like a lion raised in the mountain—innards,
> flesh, and bones full of marrow—leaving nothing.
> We wept and raise our hands in prayer to Zeus. (*Od*. 9.288–94)

Maro made his narrative bare and brief, whereas Homer added a touch of emotion and balanced the grief of the narrative with the righteous indignation that the cruelty inspires.

> 18. Here too I saw Otus and Ephialtes, monstrous,
> hulking, who with their own hands tried to tear

adgressi superisque Iovem detrudere regnis.

Ὦτόν τ᾽ ἀντίθεον τηλεκλειτόν τ᾽ Ἐπιάλτην,[144]
τοὺς[145] δὴ μηκίστους θρέψε ζείδωρος ἄρουρα
καὶ πολὺ καλλίστους μετά γε κλυτὸν Ὠρίωνα·
ἐννέωροι γὰρ τοί γε καὶ ἐννεαπήχεες ἦσαν
εὖρος, ἀτὰρ μῆκός γε γενέσθην ἐννεόργυιοι.
οἵ ῥα καὶ ἀθανάτοισιν ἀπειλήτην ἐν Ὀλύμπῳ
φυλόπιδα στήσειν πολυάϊκος πολέμοιο.
Ὄσσαν ἐπ᾽ Οὐλύμπῳ μέμασαν θέμεν, αὐτὰρ ἐπ᾽ Ὄσσῃ
Πήλιον εἰνοσίφυλλον, ἵν᾽ οὐρανὸς ἀμβατὸς εἴη.

19. Homerus magnitudinem corporum alto latoque dimensus est et verborum ambitu membra depinxit, vester ait "immania corpora" nihilque ulterius adiecit, mensurarum nomina non ausus attingere. ille de construendis montibus conatum insanae molitionis expressit, hic "adgressos[146] rescindere caelum" dixisse contentus est. postremo locum loco si compares, pudendam invenies differentiam.

20. fluctus uti primo coepit cum albescere ponto,
paulatim sese tollit mare et altius undas
erigit, inde imo consurgit ad aethera fundo.

ὡς δ᾽ ὅτ᾽ ἐν αἰγιαλῷ πολυηχέϊ κῦμα θαλάσσης
ὄρνυτ᾽ ἐπασσύτερον Ζεφύρου ὕπο κινήσαντος·
πόντῳ μέν τε πρῶτα κορύσσεται, αὐτὰρ ἔπειτα

143 σύν τε] σὺν δὲ *Hom.*
144 Ἐπιάλτην ([*Zon.*] E.790.6)] Ἐφι- *Hom.*

great heaven down and pitch Jupiter from his realm
above. (*A.* 6.582–84)

Godlike Otus and far-famed Epialtes,
the tallest men the fruitful earth has nurtured,
and much the fairest after glorious Orion:
at nine years old they were nine cubits
across, while in height they reached nine fathoms.
They threatened to raise the din of furious war
even against the immortal gods on Olympus.
They were frantic to set Ossa on Olympus, then leafy
Pelion on Ossa, and that way open a path to heaven.
(*Od.* 11.308–16)

19. Homer gave the dimensions of their breadth and height and with his phrasing set their limbs before you, but your poet says "monstrous, hulking" and no more, not daring to specify their dimensions. Homer made explicit their attempt to complete the insane project of setting one mountain on another, while Virgil was content to say "tried to tear down heaven." In short, if you compare the two passages, you'll find the difference embarrassing.

20. As when white-caps first start to appear on the
deep,
little by little the sea rises, making the swells mount
higher, then it surges up to heaven from its very
depths. (*A.* 7.528–30)

As when on the far-echoing shore the sea's swells
mount one after another, stirred by the west wind,
the first crests arise on the deep, then break on dry
land

*χέρσῳ ῥηγνύμενον μεγάλα βρέμει, ἀμφὶ δέ τ' ἄκρας*
*κυρτὸν ἐὸν κορυφοῦται, ἀποπτύει δ' ἁλὸς ἄχνην.*

21. ille cum marino motu et litoreos fluctus ab initio describit, hoc iste praetervolat. deinde quod ait ille, *πόντῳ μέν τε πρῶτα κορύσσεται*, Maro ad hoc vertit "paulatim sese tollit mare." ille fluctus in incremento suo ait in sublime curvatos litoribus inlidi et asperginem collectae sordis exspuere quod nulla expressius pictura signaret, vester mare a fundo ad aethera usque perducit.

22. dixerat idque ratum Stygii per flumina fratris
per pice torrentis atraque voragine ripas
adnuit et totum nutu tremefecit Olympum.

*ἦ καὶ κυανέῃσιν ἐπ' ὀφρύσι νεῦσε Κρονίων·*
*ἀμβρόσιαι δ' ἄρα χαῖται ἐπερρώσαντο ἄνακτος*
*κρατὸς ἀπ' ἀθανάτοιο· μέγαν δ' ἐλέλιξεν Ὄλυμπον.*

et alibi:[147]

*καὶ τὸ κατειβόμενον Στυγὸς ὕδωρ, ὅς τε μέγιστος*
*ὅρκος δεινότατός τε πέλει μακάρεσσι θεοῖσιν.*

23. Phidias cum Iovem Olympium fingeret, interrogatus

[145] *τοὺς*] *οὓς Hom.* [146] adgressos C: -sus *ω*

with a great roar, and towering, hollow billows
rise around the headlands and spew their salty spray.
(*Il.* 4.422–26)

21. Homer describes the surf on the shore along with the motion of the seas, but your poet is in too much of a hurry. Furthermore, Maro uses "little by little the sea rises" to express what Homer conveys by saying "the first crests arise on the deep." Homer says that as they grow the hollow swells rise high up, then break on the shore and spew a filthy spray—no painting could have shown more clearly—whereas your poet causes the sea to rise all the way up to heaven from its depths.

22. He finished speaking: to seal his word by the streams of his brother Styx,
by the banks seething with black eddies of pitch,
he nodded, and with that nod made all Olympus tremble. (*A.* 9.104–6†)

The son of Kronos spoke and with his dark brow nodded,
and his divine locks swept down from the lord's
immortal head: he made great Olympus tremble. (*Il.* 1.528–30)

and elsewhere:

. . . and the flowing water of the Styx, which is the greatest
and most dreadful oath for the blessed gods. (*Il.* 15.37–38)

23. When Phidias was fashioning his statue of Zeus at Olympus and was asked from what model he'd borrowed

de quo exemplo divinam mutuaretur effigiem, respondit archetypum Iovis in his se tribus Homeri versibus invenisse:

*ἦ καὶ κυανέῃσιν ἐπ' ὀφρύσι νεῦσε Κρονίων·*
*ἀμβρόσιαι δ' ἄρα χαῖται ἐπερρώσαντο ἄνακτος*
*κρατὸς ἀπ' ἀθανάτοιο· μέγαν δ' ἐλέλιξεν*
*Ὄλυμπον.*

nam de superciliis et crinibus totum se Iovis vultum collegisse. quod utrumque videtis a Vergilio praetermissum. sane concussum Olympum nutus maiestate non tacuit, ius iurandum vero ex alio Homeri loco sumpsit, ut translationis sterilitas hac adiectione compensaretur.

24. . . . ora puer prima signans intonsa iuventa.

*πρῶτον ὑπηνήτῃ, τοῦ περ χαριεστάτη*[148] *ἥβη.*

praetermissa gratia incipientis pubertatis—*τοῦ περ χαριεστάτη ἥβη*—minus gratam fecit Latinam descriptionem.

25. ut fera, quae densa venantum saepta corona
contra tela furit seseque haud nescia[149] morti
inicit et saltu supra venabula fertur.

*Πηλεΐδης δ' ἑτέρωθεν ἐναντίον ὦρτο λέων ὣς*
*σίντης, ὅν τε καὶ ἄνδρες ἀποκτάμεναι μεμάασιν*

147 et alibi N (*sed post μέγιστος in seq. versu*): *om.* PG$\beta_2$
148 *χαριεστάτη* (*codd. plerique Hom.*)] *-τος codd. aliquot Hom.*

43 For the anecdote cf. Strabo 8.3.30.

the god's likeness, he replied[43] that he'd found the basic pattern for Zeus in these three lines of Homer:

The son of Kronos spoke and with his dark brow nodded,
and his divine locks swept down from the lord's
immortal head: he made great Olympus tremble,

for (he said) he inferred the expression on Zeus' face from his brow and hair—both of which, you can see, Virgil omitted. Granted, he didn't pass over the jolt Olympus received from Zeus' awesome nod, but he took over the oath from another passage in Homer, using this addition to make up for his sterile borrowing.

24. . . . the boy with the first signs of youth on his unshaven cheeks. (*A.* 9.181)

. . . with a first growth of beard, his youth utterly alluring. (*Od.* 10.279)

By omitting the pubescent boy's winsomeness—"his youth utterly alluring"—he made his own Latin version less winsome.

25. As a wild beast, trapped by hunters' tight circle,
rages against their weapons: fully aware, it makes
a death-defying leap and bounds over the spears. (*A.* 9.551–53)

On the other side Peleus' son rose against him, like a lion
on the hunt, which men are frantic to slay when they have

ἀγρόμενοι, πᾶς δῆμος· ὃ δὲ πρῶτον μὲν ἀτίζων
ἔρχεται, ἀλλ' ὅτε κέν τις ἀρηϊθόων αἰζηῶν
<δουρὶ βάλῃ, ἐάλη τε χανών, περί τ' ἀφρὸς ὀδόντας>[150]
γίνεται, ἐν δέ τέ οἱ κραδίῃ στένει ἄλκιμον ἦτορ,
οὐρῇ δὲ πλευράς τε καὶ ἰσχία ἀμφοτέρωθεν
μαστίεται, ἑὲ δ' αὐτὸν ἐποτρύνει μαχέσασθαι,
γλαυκιόων δ' ἰθὺς φέρεται μένει, ἤν τινα πέφνῃ
ἀνδρῶν, ἢ αὐτὸς φθίεται πρώτῳ ἐν ὁμίλῳ·
ὣς Ἀχιλῆ' ὤτρυνε μένος καὶ θυμὸς ἀγήνωρ
ἀντίον ἐλθέμεναι μεγαλήτορος Αἰνείαο.

26. videtis in angustum Latinam parabolam sic esse contractam ut nihil possit esse ieiunius, Graecam contra et verborum et rerum copia pompam verae venationis implesse. in tanta ergo differentia paene erubescendum est comparare.

27. haud aliter Troianae acies aciesque Latinae
concurrunt: haeret pede pes densusque viro vir.

ὣς ἄραρον κόρυθές τε καὶ ἀσπίδες ὀμφαλόεσσαι.
ἀσπὶς ἄρ' ἀσπίδ' ἔρειδε, κόρυς κόρυν, ἀνέρα δ' ἀνήρ.

149 haud nescia $\beta_2$: n. h. ϵ (*corr.* C[2]), haud *om.* *a*
150 δουρὶ . . . ὀδόντας *suppl. ed. Paris. 1585* (*cf. iam ed. Basil.*

---

44 The lines are treated as an indirect imitation of Homer, via Ennius, at 6.3.5.

assembled, the whole people: at first the lion makes his way
unheeding, but when one of the sturdy youths, swift in battle,
strikes him with a lance, he's hemmed in, maw open, his teeth
awash in foam, and in his chest his noble heart groans,
his tail lashes his ribs and flanks, now on the right, now
on the left, and he urges himself on to make a battle of it,
and his rage carries him straight ahead, glaring, hoping
to kill one of the men or die himself in the first affray.
So his rage and heroic spirit drove Akhilleus on
to go and meet great-hearted Aineias. (*Il.* 20.164–75)

26. You see how the Latin comparison has been reduced to such narrow scope that nothing could be more jejune, whereas the Greek, with its rich diction and details, follows in full the vivid sequence of a real hunt. One must almost blush, then, to draw the comparison where the difference is so great.

27. Just so do the Trojan line and Latin line close at a run:
foot treads on foot, one man pressed to another. (*A.* 10.360–61*)[44]

So their helmets and bossed shields joined close together,
shield pressed against shield, helmet against helmet, man against man. (*Il.* 16.214–15)

quanta sit differentia utriusque loci lectori aestimandum relinquo.

28. utque volans alte raptum cum fulva draconem
fert aquila implicuitque pedes atque unguibus haesit:
saucius at serpens sinuosa volumina versat,
arrectisque horret squamis et sibilat ore
arduus insurgens, illa haud minus urguet obunco[151]
luctantem rostro, simul aethera verberat alis.

29. ὄρνις γάρ σφιν ἐπῆλθε περησέμεναι μεμαῶσιν
αἰετὸς ὑψιπέτης, ἐπ᾽ ἀριστερὰ λαὸν ἐέργων
φοινήεντα δράκοντα φέρων ὀνύχεσσι πέλωρον
ζωὸν ἔτ,᾽ ἀσπαίροντα, καὶ οὔ πω λήθετο χάρμης,
κόψε γὰρ αὖ τὸν ἔχοντα κατὰ στῆθος παρὰ δειρὴν
ἰδνωθεὶς ὀπίσω· ὃ δ᾽ ἀπὸ ἕθεν ἧκε χαμᾶζε
ἀλγήσας ὀδύνῃσι, μέσῳ δ᾽ ἐνὶ κάββαλ᾽ ὁμίλῳ,
αὐτὸς δὲ κλάγξας πέτετο πνοιῇς ἀνέμοιο.

30. Vergilius solam aquilae praedam refert, nec Homericae aquilae omen advertit, quae et sinistra veniens vincentium prohibebat accessum et accepto a captivo serpente morsu praedam dolore deiecit, factoque tripudio solistimo cum clamore dolorem testante praetervolat: qui-

*1535 in marg.), om. a*

I leave it to the reader to gauge the difference between the two passages.

28. And as a tawny eagle, soaring high, carries off a snake
it has snatched and wrapped about its feet, clinging with its talons:
but the wounded serpent writhes and twists its coils,
scales on edge, it bristles and hisses, rising up
to strike, yet the eagle still bears down on the struggling
snake with its hooked beak while it beats high heaven with its wings. (*A.* 11.751*–56)

29. For the bird swooped upon them as they were eager to cross,
a high-soaring eagle, hemming in the people on the left
as it carried a bloody serpent in its talons, a monster
still alive, writhing, still mindful of the joy of battle:
for it arched back and struck its captor in the chest
alongside the throat. Stung by the pain, the bird hurled
it to the ground, casting it down in the midst of the fray,
then with a cry flew off in a gust of wind. (*Il.* 12.200–7)

30. Virgil mentions only the prize the eagle carries off and takes no notice of the omen represented by Homer's eagle, which both hindered the victors' attack, by coming on the left, and threw down its prize out of pain, when the snake it had caught bit it; then, with the augury complete, it flew on with a cry that testified to its pain. All these elements indi-

bus omnibus victoriae praevaricatio significabatur. his praetermissis, quae animam parabolae dabant, velut exanimum in Latinis versibus corpus remansit.

> 31. parva metu primo, mox sese attollit in auras,
> ingrediturque solo et caput inter nubila condit.

> *ἥ τ' ὀλίγον*[152] *μὲν πρῶτα κορύσσεται, αὐτὰρ ἔπειτα*
> *οὐρανῷ ἐστήριξε κάρη καὶ ἐπὶ χθονὶ βαίνει.*

Homerus Ἔριν hoc est contentionem a parvo dixit incipere et postea in incrementum ad caelum usque succrescere. 32. hoc idem Maro de Fama dixit, sed incongrue. neque enim aequa sunt augmenta contentionis et famae, quia contentio etsi usque ad mutuas vastationes ac bella processerit, adhuc contentio est, et manet ipsa quae crevit; fama vero cum in immensum prodit, fama esse iam desinit et fit notio rei iam cognitae. quis enim iam famam vocet cum res aliqua a terra in caelum nota sit? deinde nec ipsam hyperbolen potuit aequare. ille caelum dixit, hic auras et nubila. 33. haec autem ratio fuit non aequandi omnia quae ab auctore transcripsit, quod in omni operis sui parte alicuius Homerici loci imitationem volebat inserere, nec tamen humanis viribus illam divinitatem ubique poterat aequare, ut in illo loco quem volo omnium nostrum iudicio in commune pensari.

34. 'Minerva Diomedi suo pugnanti dumtaxat flamma-

[151] obunco R[2]: ab- ω

cated that victory was being handed to the other side—and by leaving out the elements that gave the comparison its soul, the Latin verses were left, so to speak, with the lifeless corpse.

> 31. Small and timid at first, she soon rises high as the breezes
> and strides upon the earth, her head hidden among the clouds. (*A.* 4.176–77)

> She rises up but a little at first, but thereafter
> Her head is set fast in heaven as she walks upon the earth. (*Il.* 4.442–43)

Homer said that *Eris*—that is, Strife—is little at first and later continues growing until she reaches the heavens. 32. Maro gave the same account of Rumor, which it doesn't fit. Strife and rumor don't grow in the same way: even if strife reaches the point of mutual destruction in war, it is still strife—for all its growth, it remains itself—whereas when rumor grows beyond all bounds, it ceases to be rumor and becomes instead the awareness of a known fact. Who would call it "rumor" when some fact is known from the earth all the way up to heaven? Furthermore, he was not able to match Homer's exaggeration: the latter referred to "heaven," Virgil to "breezes" and "clouds." 33. However, he did not come up to the level of everything he borrowed from his model, because he wanted to insert imitations of Homeric passages in every part of his own work, and yet it was not within his human powers to match that godlike talent everywhere—for example, in the following passage, which I'd like us to evaluate together.

34. 'Minerva gives Diomedes, her favorite, the blazing

rum addit ardorem, et inter hostium caedes fulgor capitis vel armorum pro milite minatur:

> *δαῖέ οἱ ἐκ κόρυθός τε καὶ ἀσπίδος ἀκάματον*
> *πῦρ.*

35. hoc miratus supra modum Vergilius immodice est usus. modo enim ita de Turno dicit:

> tremunt sub[153] vertice cristae
> sanguineae clipeoque micantia fulmina mittunt;

modo idem ponit de Aenea:

> ardet apex capiti cristisque ac[154] vertice flamma
> funditur, et vastos umbo vomit aereus[155] ignis;

quod quam importune sit positum hinc apparet, quod necdum pugnabat Aeneas sed tantum in navi veniens apparebat. 36. alio loco:

> cui triplici crinita iuba galea alta Chimaeram
> sustinet Aetnaeos efflantem faucibus ignis.

quid quod Aeneas recens allatis armis a Vulcano et in terra positis miratur?

> terribilem cristis galeam flammasque vomentem.[156]

[152] ὀλίγον] *ὀλίγη Hom.*

[153] sub] in *Verg.*

[154] ac (*codd. plerique Verg., DServ.*)] a *codd. aliquot Verg., Tib., Non. 240.28, 313.10, edd.*

[155] aereus (*cod.* M *Verg.*)] aureus *codd. cett. Verg.*

[156] vomentem (*codd. plerique Verg.*)] micantem *codd.* Pγ

heat of fire, at least when in battle, and while he's cutting the enemy down, the glow of his head and armor is as daunting as the warrior himself. (*Il.* 5.4):

> an unwearying fire was blazing from his helmet and his shield.

35. Virgil admired this touch immoderately—and used it immoderately. For now he describes Turnus in these terms (*A.* 9.733–34),

> at his crown the blood-red
> crest quivers and flashing lightning bolts issue from his shield,

at another time Aeneas, also in the same terms (*A.* 10.270*–71):

> The crown of his head is ablaze, flame spills from the peak
> of his crest, his shield's bronze boss belches huge flames.

The poor timing of this description is evident from the fact that Aeneas is not yet in battle but is just coming into view while riding on his ship. 36. In another passage (*A.* 7.785–86),

> His helmet, with it high horse-hair crest arranged in three rows,
> supports a Chimaera the breathes the fires of Aetna from its maw.

Then there's Aeneas all agog at the arms just brought from Vulcan and set upon the ground (*A.* 8.620):

> the helmet belching flames, its crest awesome.

37. 'Vultis aliam fruendi aviditatem videre? loci cuius[157] supra meminimus fulgore correptus—

ἦ καὶ κυανέῃσιν ἐπ' ὀφρύσι νεῦσε Κρονίων,
ἀμβρόσιαι δ' ἄρα χαῖται ἐπερρώσαντο ἄνακτος
κρατὸς ἀπ' ἀθανάτοιο· μέγαν δ' ἐλέλιξεν
Ὄλυμπον—

38. sero[158] voluit loquenti Iovi adsignare parem reverentiam. nam cum et in primo volumine et in quarto et in nono loquatur quaedam Iuppiter sine tumultu, denique post Iunonis et Veneris iurgium,

infit (eo dicente deum domus alta silescit
et tremefacta solo tellus, silet arduus aether,
tum Zephyri posuere, premit placida aequora
pontus)—

tamquam non idem sit qui locutus sit paulo ante sine ullo mundi totius obsequio. 39. similis importunitas est in eiusdem Iovis lance quam ex illo loco sumpsit—

καὶ τότε δὴ χρύσεια πατὴρ ἐτίτηνε[159] τάλαντα—

nam cum iam de Turno praedixisset Iuno,

nunc iuvenem imparibus video concurrere fatis,
Parcarumque dies et lux[160] inimica propinquat,

*Verg., edd. nonnull.*

157 cuius *Willis*: huius cuius $\beta_2$, huius *α*
158 sero FC: servo *ω* 159 ἐτίτηνε] ἐτίταινε *Hom.*

45 Cf. §§22–23; the Virgilian passage is treated as an imitation of Ennius at 6.2.26.

37. 'Would you like to consider another example of the greedy pleasure Virgil takes in Homer? He was ravished by the brilliance of the passage I quoted earlier[45] (*Il.* 1.528–30)—

> The son of Kronos spoke and with his dark brow nodded,
> and his divine locks swept down from the lord's
> immortal head: he made great Olympus tremble—

38. and he wanted to show equal, if belated, respect for the speech of Jupiter. For though he has Jupiter speaking in Books 1, 4, and 9 without making a fuss about it, at long last, after the quarrel of Juno and Venus (*A.* 10.101–3),

> He speaks: and as he speaks the gods' lofty house is hushed,
> the earth is shaken to it foundation, high heaven is silent,
> then the west winds fall, the sea holds it calm surface in check—

as though it wasn't the same person who spoke just a little earlier without the whole world paying dutiful obeisance. 39. Similarly unseasonable is his use of the Jupiter's scale, which he borrowed from this passage (*Il.* 8.69 = 22.209),

> . . . and just then the father poised the golden scale:

for Juno had already made her prediction about Turnus (*A.* 12.149–50),

> Now I see the young man in conflict with a fate that is stronger,
> and his day of destiny approaches, the light that is his enemy,

manifestumque esset Turnum utique periturum, sero tamen

> Iuppiter ipse duas aequato examine lances[161]
> sustinet et fata imponit diversa duorum.

40. 'Sed haec et talia ignoscenda Vergilio, qui studii circa Homerum nimietate excedit modum. et re vera non poterat non in aliquibus minor videri, qui per omnem poesin suam hoc uno est praecipue usus archetypo. acriter enim in Homerum oculos intendit ut aemularetur eius non modo magnitudinem sed et simplicitatem et praesentiam orationis et tacitam maiestatem. 41. hinc diversarum inter heroas suos personarum varia magnificatio, hinc deorum interpositio, hinc auctoritas fabulosorum, hinc adfectuum naturalis expressio, hinc monumentorum persecutio, hinc parabolarum exaggeratio, hinc torrentis orationis sonitus, hinc rerum singularum cum splendore fastigium.

14 'Adeo autem Vergilio Homeri dulcis imitatio est ut et in versibus vitia quae a non nullis imperite reprehenduntur imitatus sit, eos dico quos Graeci vocant ἀκεφάλους, λαγαροὺς, ὑπερκαταληκτικούς, quos hic quoque heroicum stilum approbans non refugit; 2. ut sunt apud ipsum ἀκέφαλοι:

160 lux (*cf. A.* 9.355)] vis *Verg.*

---

46 "Headless" lines begin with a syllable that appears to be metrically short in place of the expected long (in the examples given, *arietat, abietibus*; in fact the *i* after *r* is consonantal, the syllable long); in the examples of "thin-waisted" and "hypermetric" lines (which M. himself defines just below) the relevant syllables are, respectively, *obice/pater* and *omnia/umorem/sulphura/horrida*.

and it is plain that Turnus is certainly going to die, yet we still find later on (*A.* 12.725*–26),

> Jupiter raises the scale's two pans, makes them
> balanced
> and level, then places on them the two men's
> divergent destinies.

40. 'But Virgil must be forgiven these lapses, and others like them, when he goes too far in his excessive fondness for Homer. He really could not help but appear the lesser of the two in some respects, seeing that he used this one model above all in his whole poetic oeuvre. He keeps his keen gaze fixed on Homer with the goal of imitating not just his grandeur but also his straightforwardness, the vividness of his speech, and his quiet majesty. 41. That is where he derives the varying degrees of lordliness that his heroes' different personalities display, that is where he derives the gods' interventions, the credibility of his mythical touches, the realistic expression of the emotions, his complete command of ancient history, the cumulative effect of his comparisons, the sound of his flowing speech, the dignity and brilliance he lends to every detail.

'Moreover, Virgil takes such great pleasure in imitat- 14
ing Homer that he even imitates flaws in versification that some people ignorantly criticize—I mean the lines that Greeks call "headless" [*akephaloi*], "thin-waisted" [*lagaroi*], and "hypermetric" [*hyperkatalêktikoi*], which Virgil does not avoid because he thinks them appropriate to the heroic style:[46] 2. "headless" lines in Virgil, for example,

arietat in portas . . .

abietibus[162] textum caecis iter . . .

et similia; 3. λαγαροὶ autem, qui in medio versu breves syllabas pro longis habent,

. . . et duros obice postes

concilium ipse pater et magna incepta Latinus;

4. ὑπερκαταληκτικοὶ syllaba longiores sunt:

. . . quin protinus omnia

<et>:[163]

. . . Vulcano decoquit umorem

et:

. . . spumas miscent argenti vivaque sulphura

et:

. . . arbutus horrida.

5. 'Sunt apud Homerum versus vulsis ac rasis similes et nihil differentes ab usu loquendi. hos quoque tamquam heroice incomptos adamavit:

*ἵππους δὲ ξανθὰς ἑκατὸν καὶ πεντήκοντα*
*πάσας θηλείας.*

161 lances *ed. Ven. 1472*: -cis *ω*

162 abietibus (*cf.* A. *9. 674*)] parietibus *ed. Ven. 1472 ex Verg.*

ramming against the gates . . . (*A.* 11.890)

a passageway crafted from fir-wood void of light . . . (*A.* 5.589)

and the like; 3. "thin-waisted" lines, which have short syllables in place of long syllables in the middle of a line,

. . . and against the doorways firmly bolted (*A.* 11.890)

the council and its great undertakings father Latinus himself . . . (*A.* 11.469);

4. "hypermetric" lines are too long by one syllable:

. . . indeed, the whole thing straightway (*A.* 6.33),

and

. . . boils down the liquid with fire (*G.* 1.295*),

and

. . . they mix in litharge and natural sulfur (*G.* 3.449*),

and

. . . bristling arbutus (*G.* 2.69*).

5. 'Homer has lines that are plucked and shaved, in no way different from ordinary speech, and Virgil had a great affection for these too, as though they are heroic in their unadorned state:

. . . sorrel horses, one hundred and fifty,
all mares. (*Il.*11.680–81)

omnia vincit Amor: et nos cedamus Amori.

nudus in ignota, Palinure, iacebis harena.

6. 'Sunt amoenae repetitiones quas non fugit:

. . . ἅ τε παρθένος ἠΐθεός τε,
παρθένος ἠΐθεός τ' ὀαρίζετον ἀλλήλοιιν.

Pan etiam Arcadia mecum si iudice certet,
Pan etiam Arcadia dicet[164] se iudice victum.

7. 'Homerica quoque epitheta quantum sit admiratus imitando confessus est:

. . . μοιρηγενὲς ὀλβιόδαιμον . . .

. . . χαλκεοθωρήκων· ἀτὰρ ἀσπίδες ὀμφαλόεσσαι . . .

. . . θωρήκων τε νεοσμήκτων . . .

. . . κυανοχαῖτα Ποσειδάων . . .

. . . Διὸς νεφεληγερέταο . . .

. . . οὔρεά τε σκιόεντα θάλασσά τε ἠχήεσσα . . .

. . . κύαμοι κυανόχροες[165] . . .

et mille talium vocabulorum, quibus velut sideribus micat divini carminis variata maiestas. 8. ad haec a vestro respondetur,[166]

[163] et *ed. Lugd. Bat. 1670, om.* ω
[164] dicet (*cod.* P2 *Verg.*)] dicat *Verg.*
[165] κυανό-] *μελανό- Hom.*

Love conquers all: let us too yield to Love. (*E*. 10.69)

You will lie naked, Palinurus, on an unknown shore. (*A*. 5.871)

6. 'There are pleasing repetitions that he doesn't avoid:

. . . things that a maiden and young boy,
a maiden and young boy whisper to one another. (*Il*. 22.127–28)

If Pan should compete with me, even before Arcadia as judge,
Pan will admit he's been beat, even before Aracadia as judge. (*E*. 4.58–59)

7. 'He acknowledged, through his imitations, how much he admired Homeric epithets:

. . . God-blessed child of destiny . . . (*Il*. 3.182)

. . . men of the bronze cuirass. But the boss-studded shields . . . (*Il*. 4.448 = 8.62)

. . . and of new-polished cuirasses . . . (*Il*. 13.342)

. . . dark-haired Poseidon . . . (*Il*. 13.563 = 14.390)

. . . Zeus cloud-gatherer . . . (*Il*. 5.631 = 5.736 *et al*.)

. . . both shadowy mountains and resounding sea . . . (*Il*. 1.157)

. . . dark-skinned beans . . . (*Il*. 13.589)

and a thousand other such words that, like stars, make the godlike poem glitter in its variegated majesty. 8. Your poet's answer to these touches runs to

... malesuada fames ...,

... auricomi rami ...,

... centumgeminus Briareus ...

adde et "fumiferam noctem" et quicquid in singulis paene versibus diligens lector agnoscit.

9. 'Saepe Homerus inter narrandum velut ad aliquem dirigit orationem:

ἔνθ' οὐκ ἂν βρίζοντα ἴδοις Ἀγαμέμνονα δῖον

<et>:[167]

φαίης κεν[168] ζάκοτόν τινα[169] ἔμμεναι ἄφρονά τ' αὔτως.

10. nec hoc Vergilius omisit:

migrantes cernas totaque ex urbe ruentes,

et:

... totumque instructo Marte videres
fervere Leucaten,

et:

... pelago credas innare revulsas
Cycladas,

166 respondetur *ed. Ven. 1472*: -dentur ω
167 et *suppl. ed. Basil. 1535*, om. ω
168 κεν] PEN α, κε *Hom.*

. . . evil-urging hunger . . . (*A.* 6.276),

. . . golden-haired branches . . . ,[47]

. . . hundred-fold Briareus . . . (*A.* 6.287),

to which you can also add "smoke-bearing night" (*A.* 8.255) and any others that present themselves to an attentive reader in almost every single verse.

9. 'Often in the course of his narrative Homer speaks as though to some individual listener:

you would not see brilliant Agamemnon napping there (*Il.* 4.223)

and

you might say that he was some surly fellow, or simply a fool (*Il.* 3.220).

10. Nor did Virgil miss this trick:

you could see them leaving, rushing from the entire city (*A.* 4.401*),

and

. . . you could have seen all of Leucate churning as they prepared for battle (*A.* 8.676–77),

and

. . . you might believe that the Cyclades had been torn up and left bobbing (*A.* 8.691†–92),

[47] Apparently an inexact recollection of *A.* 6.141 *auricomos . . . fetus* ("golden-haired growth" sc. of a tree).

et:

. . . studio incassum videas gestire lavandi.

11. 'Item divinus ille vates res vel paulo vel multo ante transactas opportune ad narrationis suae seriem revocat ut et historicum stilum vitet, non per ordinem digerendo quae gesta sunt, nec tamen praeteritorum nobis notitiam subtrahat. 12. Theben Asiae civitatem aliasque plurimas Achilles antequam irasceretur everterat, sed Homeri opus ab Achillis ira sumpsit exordium. ne igitur ignoraremus quae prius gesta sunt, fit eorum tempestiva narratio:

ᾠχόμεθ' ἐς Θήβην, ἱερὴν πόλιν Ἠετίωνος,
τὴν δὲ διεπράθομέν τε καὶ ἤγομεν ἐνθάδε πάντα,

et alibi:

δώδεκα μὲν[170] σὺν νηυσὶ πόλεις[171] ἀλάπαξ' ἀνθρώπων,
πεζὸς δ' ἕνδεκά φημι κατὰ Τροίην ἐρίβωλον.

13. item ne ignoraremus quo duce classis Graecorum ignotum sibi Troiae litus invenerit, cum de Calchante quaereretur,[172] ait:

καὶ νήεσσ' ἡγήσατ' Ἀχαιῶν Ἴλιον εἴσω
ἣν διὰ μαντοσύνην, τήν οἱ πόρε Φοῖβος Ἀπόλλων,

et ipse Calchas narrat omen quod Graecis navigantibus de

170 μὲν] δὴ *Hom.* 171 πόλεις] ΠΟΛΙC *a*
172 quaereretur *Davies* (*coll. Il. 1. 62*): quereretur *a*

and

> . . . you could see [seabirds] frivolously cavort in their
> eagerness to bathe (*G.* 1.387).

11. 'Similarly, that divine bard summons up events from the recent or distant past and applies them to his own narrative sequence, in a way that avoids falling into a historical mode—for he doesn't just arrange them in chronological order—but yet makes knowledge of the past available to us. 12. Before he withdrew in anger Achilles had sacked Thebe, a city in Asia, and very many others, but Homer begins his poem with the anger of Achilles. To make sure, then, that we know of those earlier exploits, he finds an appropriate moment to tell us of them (*Il.* 1.366–67):

> We went to Thêbê, Êëtiôn's sacred citadel,
> we sacked it and brought everything within it here,

and elsewhere (*Il.* 9.328–29):

> With my ships I sacked twelve cities of men, eleven
> I claimed with soldiers on foot in the fertile land of Troy.

13. Similarly, so that we might know under whose guidance the Greeks' fleet found the coast of Troy when it was unknown to them, he says, when an inquiry was being made of Calchas (*Il.* 1.71–72),

> and he led the Akhaians' ships to Ilium
> by his seer-craft, which Phoibos Apollo gave him.

Calchas himself also tells of the omen that the Greeks encountered on their voyage, the snake devouring the

serpente passerum populatore contigerit, ex quo denuntiatum est exercitum annos decem in hostico futurum. 14. alio loco senex, id est referendis fabulis amica et loquax aetas, res refert vetustas:

> ἤδη γάρ ποτ' ἐγὼ καὶ ἀρείοσιν ἠέ περ ὑμῖν
> ἀνδράσιν ὡμίλησα

et reliqua; et alibi:

> αἴθ'[173] ὣς ἡβώοιμι, βίη δέ μοι ἔμπεδος εἴη

et sequentia. 15. Vergilius omne hoc genus pulcherrime aemulatus est:

> nam memini Hesionae visentem regna sororis
> Laomedontiaden Priamum,

et:

> atque equidem memini Teucrum[174] Sidona venire,

et:

> qualis eram cum primam aciem Praeneste sub ipsa
> stravi,

et de furto vel poena Caci tota narratio. 16. nec vetustissima tacuit, quin et ipsa notitiae nostrae auctoris sui imitator ingereret:

[173] αἴθ'] εἴθ' *Hom.*
[174] memini Teucrum (*cod.* R[1] *Verg.*)]: T. m. *Verg.*

---

[48] It is Odysseus who "tells of" the omen, at *Il.* 2.284–332, though he quotes Calchas' interpretation (*Il.* 2.322–29) in the course of his narration.

sparrows, which revealed that the army would be ten years in the enemy's territory.[48] 14. In another passage old Nestor —being of an age that is garrulous by nature and loves telling tales—reports events long past (*Il.* 1.260–61):

> For once upon a time I was a man among men better
> even than you

and so on; elsewhere, too (*Il.* 7.157),

> Would that I were in my prime, and the might still in
> me,

and the lines that follow. 15. Virgil did a very fine job of imitating this sort of thing:

> For I recall that Priam, in the line of Laömedon,
> came
> to see his sister Hesione's realm (*A.* 8.157–58),

and

> And I for my part recall that Teucer came to Sidon
> (*A.* 1.619),

and

> such as I was when at the foot of Praeneste itself I
> laid low
> the enemy's first line (*A.* 8.561–62),

and the whole story about Cacus' theft and punishment (*A.* 8.185–275). 16. Nor did he pass by in silence events of very great antiquity—quite the opposite, he thrusts them upon our attention, in imitation of his model (*A.* 10.189):

namque ferunt luctu Cycnum[175] Phaëthontis amati
. . .

et similia.

15 'Vbi vero enumerantur auxilia, quem Graeci catalogum vocant, eundem auctorem suum conatus imitari in non nullis paululum a gravitate Homerica deviavit. 2. primum quod Homerus praetermissis Athenis ac Lacedaemone vel ipsis Mycenis, unde erat rector exercitus, Boeotiam in catalogi sui capite locavit, non ob loci aliquam dignitatem, sed notissimum promuntorium ad exordium sibi enumerationis elegit, 3. unde progrediens modo mediterranea, modo maritima iuncta describit, inde rursus ad utrumque situm cohaerentium locorum disciplina describentis velut iter agentis accedit, nec ullo saltu cohaerentiam regionum in libro suo hiare permittit, sed hoc viandi more procedens, redit unde digressus est; et ita finitur quicquid enumeratio eius amplectitur. 4. contra Vergilius nullum in commemorandis regionibus ordinem servat sed locorum seriem saltibus lacerat. adducit primum Clusio et Cosis Massicum; Abas hunc sequitur manu Populoniae Ilvaeque comitatus; post hos Asilan miserunt Pisae, quae in quam longinqua sint Etruriae parte notius est quam ut adnotandum sit. inde mox redit Caere[176] et Pyrgos et Graviscas,[177]

[175] Cycnum *ed. Ven. 1472* (Cygnum S, *cf. 5.16.4*): cynum ω
[176] Caere G: cerae ω
[177] Graviscas *ed. Ven. 1472*: oraviscas ω

---

49 Cosa (mod. Ansedonia) is on the coast while Clusium (mod. Chiusi) is nearly 100 km inland in NE Etruria; Populonia is on the coast about 90 km NW of Cosa, and Ilva (mod. Elba) is an island about 20 km SW of Populonia. Pisa is over 80 km N of Populonia.

For they say that Cycnus, in grief for his beloved
Phaëthon . . .

and that sort of thing.

'But when listing the allied forces in what Greeks call a 15
"catalogue," he tried to imitate the same model but in some respects fell short of the weighty effect that Homer achieved. 2. To start with, Homer bypassed Athens and Sparta and even Mycenae, home of the army's general, and set Boeotia at the head of his catalogue (*Il.* 2.494–510), not because of some special prestige attaching to the place but because he chose the best known headland to start off his list. 3. From there he goes on to describe now the inland settlements, now the neighboring coastal areas, then moves on to the inland and coastal sites of the adjacent territories, providing a description as systematic as he would were he making the journey. He makes no sudden jumps and allows no gaps to open in the territorial continuity of his book but progresses in the manner of a wayfarer until he comes back to the point where he began. That is how he rounds off all that his list comprises. 4. By contrast, Virgil observes no sequence in the places he mentions (*A.* 10.166*–212) but jumps around and cuts the sequence up. First he introduces Massicus from Clusium and Cosa; Abas follows, accompanied by troops from Populonia and Ilva; after these, Asilas with a detachment from Pisa—and how far distant a spot in Etruria *that* is is too well known to require comment.[49] Then he soon returns to Caere and Pyrgi and Graviscae, places very close to Rome led (in Vir-

loca urbi proxima, quibus ducem Asturem dedit. hinc rapit illum Cinirus ad Liguriam, Ocnus Mantuam. 5. sed nec in catalogo auxiliorum Turni, si velis situm locorum mente percurrere, invenies illum continentiam regionum secutum.

6. 'Deinde Homerus omnes quos in catalogo enumerat etiam pugnantes vel prospera vel sinistra sorte commemorat et, cum vult dicere occisos quos catalogo non inseruit, non hominis sed multitudinis nomen inducit et quotiens multam necem significare vult, "messem" hominum factam dicit, nulli certum nomen facile extra catalogum vel addens in acie vel detrahens. 7. sed Maro vester anxietatem huius observationis omisit. nam et in catalogo nominatos praeterit in bello et alios nominat ante non dictos. sub Massico duce "mille manus iuvenum" venisse dixit,

. . . qui moenia Clusi
quique Cosas liquere,[178]

deinde Turnus navi fugit,

qua rex Clusinis advectus Osinius oris,

quem Osinium numquam antea nominavit et nunc ineptum est regem sub Massico militare. 8. praeterea nec Massicus nec Osinius in bello penitus apparent, sed et illi quos[179] dicit "fortemque Gyam fortemque Serestum,"[180]

178 Cosas liquere C (*cf.* Cosis *recte* §4): c(h)oras l- $\alpha$, c(h)oros l- $\beta_2$, urbem liquere Cosas *Verg.*
179 quos C: quod $\omega$ 180 Serestum] Cloanthum *Verg.*

50 Cf. Serv. on *A.* 7.647.
51 Cf. Serv. on *A.* 10.166.

gil's account) by Astyr; after that, Cinirus hurries him off to Liguria, and Ocnus to Mantua. 5. But no more will you find that he followed an unbroken territorial sequence in the catalogue of Turnus' allies (*A.* 7.647–817), if you mentally review the places' locations.

6. 'Another point: all those whom Homer lists in his catalogue he also mentions in his account of the fighting, whether they fare well or ill, and when he intends to say that people he didn't include in the catalogue were killed, he uses the name of some large group, not an individual: whenever he wants to convey a scene of great slaughter, he says there was a "harvest" of men (cf. *Il.* 11.67ff.), neither naming anyone not in the catalogue nor failing to name anyone included. 7. But your Maro did not observe this finicky habit: some men named in the catalogue he passes over in battle, and then names in battle some not previously mentioned.[50] He said that "a thousand youthful hands" came to war under Massicus' leadership (*A.* 10.167–68),[51]

> . . . those who left the walls of Clusium
> and those who left Cosa,

then Turnus flees by the ship (*A.* 10.655*)

> that bore king Osinius from Clusium's shore:

it's clumsy for Osinius, whom he at no point previously named, now to be a king fighting under Massicus.[52] 8. Furthermore, neither Massicus nor Osinius plays any role in the war, and even those whom he calls "gallant Gyas and

[52] And clumsier still for the land-locked Clusium to be given a shore, cf. above.

"pulcher" quoque "Aquiculus . . . et Mavortius Haemon" et "fortissimus Vmbro" et Virbius "Hippolyti proles pulcherrima bello" nullum locum inter pugnantium agmina vel gloriosa vel turpi commemoratione meruerunt. 9. Astyr[181] itemque Cupavo[182] et Cinirus,[183] insignes Cycni[184] Phaethontisque fabulis, nullam pugnae operam praestant, cum Halaesus et Sacrator[185] ignotissimi pugnent et Atinas ante non dictus.

10. 'Deinde in his quos nominat fit saepe apud ipsum incauta confusio. in nono

> . . . Corynaeum sternit Asilas,

deinde in duodecimo Ebusum Corynaeus interficit:

> obvius ambustum torrem Corynaeus ab ara
> corripit et venienti Ebuso plagamque ferenti
> occupat os.

11. sic et Numam, quem Nisus occidit, postea Aeneas

> persequitur fortemque Numam . . .

181 Astyr (Astur *ed. Ven. 1472*): Antio ω (*obelo notat Willis*)
182 Cupavo C: pavo ω
183 Cinirus *Jan*: cinerus ω
184 Cycni] Cygni C, cigni P2, cynni ω
185 Sacrator *ed. Ven. 1472*: sacrato ω

gallant Serestus" (*A.* 1.612), and "fair Aquiculus and martial Haemon" (*A.* 9.684–85) and "most gallant Umbro" (*A.* 7.752) et Virbius, "Hippolytus' offspring, the fairest one in the war" (*A.* 7.761)—none of them merited a place in the ranks of fighting men by either a glorious notice or a disgraceful one. 9. Astyr and, similarly, Cupavo and Cinirus, marked out from the crowd by the story of Cycnus and Phaethon (*A.* 10.185–93), perform no service in battle, though utter unknowns like Halaesus[53] and Sacrator (*A.* 10.747–48) appear, and Atinas too (*A.* 11.869), without prior mention.

10. 'Then there's also the fact that he often becomes careless and confused about those whom he does name. In Book 9 (571)

> . . . Asilas lays Corynaeus low,

but then in Book 12 (298–300) Corynaeus kills Ebusus:

> Coming to meet him, Corynaeus snatches from the altar a scorched
> brand, and catches Ebusus square in the face as he charges, arm
> raised for the blow.

11. So too, Nisus kills Numa (*A.* 9.454), then Aeneas later (*A.* 10.562)

> chases gallant Numa. . . .

[53] A slip: Halaesus, who appears in battle at *A.* 10. 352–53, 411–25, is also featured as the leader of a contingent in the catalogue of Turnus' allies (*A.* 7.723–32).

Camerten in decimo Aeneas sternit, at in duodecimo[186] Iuturna:

. . . formam adsimulata Camertae.[187]

12. Chlorea[188] in undecimo occidit Camilla, in duodecimo Turnus. Palinurus Iasides et Iapyx Iasides quaero an fratres sint. Hyrtacides est Hippocoon, et Nisus,[189]

Hyrtacides <comitem Aeneae quem miserat Ida>,[190]

13. sed potuerunt duo unum nomen habuisse. ubi est illa in his casibus Homeri cautio? apud quem cum duo Aiaces sint, modo dicit Τελαμώνιος Αἴας, modo Ὀϊλῆος ταχὺς Αἴας, item alibi ἶσον θυμὸν ἔχοντες ὁμώνυμοι, nec desinit quos iungit nomine insignibus separare, ne cogatur lector suspiciones de varietate appellationis agitare.

14. 'Deinde in catalogo suo curavit Vergilius vitare fastidium, quod Homerus alia ratione non cavit eadem figura saepe repetita:

*οἳ δ' Ἀσπληδόνα ναῖον . . . ,*

*οἳ δ' Εὔβοιαν ἔχον . . . ,*

186 duodecimo C: undecimo ω (*an lapsu Macrob.*?)
187 Camertae (*Prisc. GL 2:393.5*)] -ti *Verg.*
188 Chlorea *Jan* (Clorea *ed. Ven. 1472*): h(a)eclorea ω
189 Nisus *Jan*: rursus ω
190 comitem . . . Ida *Jan concinne ex A. 9. 177*: Corynaeum sternit Asilas ω (*ex §10 repetita*)

Aeneas kills Camertes in Book 10 (562), but in Book 12 (224) Juturna

> . . . mimics the appearance of Camertes.

12. Chloreus is Camilla's victim in Book 11,[54] Turnus' in Book 12 (363). Palinurus the son of Iasus (*A.* 5.843) and Iapyx the son of Iasus (*A.* 12.391–92)—pray tell, are they brothers? Hippocoön is Hyrtacus' son (*A.* 5.492), and Nisus (*A.* 9.177)

> Hyrtacus' son, <whom Ida had sent to accompany Aeneas>—

13. though two men could have had the same name. Where in these cases is Homer's careful practice? Since there are in the *Iliad* two men named Aias, he speaks now of "Aias son of Telamôn" (*Il.* 2.528 *et al.*), now of "swift Aias, Oïleus' son" (*Il.* 2.527 *et al.*), and similarly elsewhere of the men "who have the same name and equal spirit" (*Il.* 17.720), and he continually uses specific markers to distinguish those he gives the same name, so the reader won't be forced to guess who is meant by the name at any given time.

14. 'Next I can point out that Virgil takes pains to avoid monotony in his catalogue, a precaution that Homer, basing himself on a different principle, does not take, but instead often repeats the same verbal arrangement:

> Those who dwelt in Asplêdôn . . . (*Il.* 2.511),
>
> Those who held Euboia . . . (*Il.* 2.536),

[54] A slip: at *A.* 11.768ff. Camilla tracks Chloreus but is killed before she can kill him.

οἳ δ' Ἄργός τ' εἶχον Τίρυνθά τε . . . ,

οἳ δ' εἶχον κοίλην Λακεδαίμονα κητώεσσαν.

15. hic autem variat velut dedecus aut crimen vitans repetitionem:

primus init bellum Tyrrhenis asper ab oris . . . ,

filius huic iuxta Lausus . . . ,

post hos insignem fama[191] per gramina currum . . . ,

tum gemini fratres . . . ,

nec Praenestinae fundator . . . ,

at Messapus, equum domitor . . . ,

ecce Sabinorum prisco de sanguine . . . ,

hic[192] Agamemnonius . . . ,

et te montosae . . . ,

quin et Marruvia venit de gente sacerdos,

ibat et Hippolyti proles . . . .

16. has copias fortasse putat aliquis divinae illi simplicitati praeferendas, sed nescio quo modo Homerum repetitio illa unice decet, et est genio antiqui poetae digna enumerationique conveniens quod in loco mera nomina relatu-

191 fama] palma *Verg.*
192 hic] hinc *Verg.*

Those who held Argos and Tiryns . . . (*Il.* 2.559),

Those who held hollow Lakedaimôn, land of ravines . . . (*Il.* 2.581).

15. Virgil, on the other hand, engages in variation, avoiding repetition as though it were a disgrace or crime:

First to come to war, a harsh man from Etruria's coast . . . (*A.* 7.647),

His son Lausus by his side . . . (*A.* 7.649),

After these over the grassy track a chariot marked by glory . . . (*A.* 7.655),

Then twin brothers . . . (*A.* 7.670),

Nor was Praeneste's founder . . . (*A.* 7.678),

But Messapus, tamer of horses . . . (*A.* 7.691),

Look, from the Sabines' primal stock . . . (*A.* 7.706),

Here the scion of Agamemnon . . . (*A.* 7.723),

And you, [sc. Ufens], mountainous [Nersae] . . . (*A.* 7.744),

Here too comes a priest from the people of Marrubia . . . (*A.* 7.750),

There passed Hippolytus' offspring too . . . (*A.* 7.761).

16. Perhaps some think this abundant invention preferable to Homer's divine simplicity, but that repetition is somehow uniquely becoming to Homer, a listing that is appropriate and worthy of the ancient poet's genius: in a passage where he was just going to recount names, he didn't do

rus non incurvavit se neque minute torsit deducendo stilum per singulorum varietates, sed stat in consuetudine percensentium tamquam per aciem dispositos enumerans, quod non aliis quam numerorum fit vocabulis. 17. et tamen egregie, ubi oportet, de nominibus ducum variat:

*αὐτὰρ Φωκήων Σχεδίος καὶ Ἐπίστροφος ἦρχον*
. . . ,

*Λοκρῶν δ' ἡγεμόνευεν Ὀϊλῆος ταχὺς Αἴας* . . . ,

*Νιρεὺς αὖ Σύμηθεν ἄγεν*[193] *τρεῖς νῆας ἐΐσας.*

18. illam vero enumerationis congestionem apud Homerum Maro admiratus ita expressit ut paene eum dixerim elegantius transtulisse:

*οἳ Κνωσόν τ' εἶχον Γόρτυνά τε τειχιόεσσαν,*
*Λύκτον Μίλητόν τε καὶ ἀργινόεντα Λύκαστον*
*Φαιστόν τε,*

et similia. 19. ad quod exemplum illa Vergiliana sunt:

agmina densentur campis Argivaque pubes
Auruncaeque manus, Rutuli veteresque Sicani;
stant Gauranae[194] acies et picti scuta Labici,
qui saltus, Tiberine, tuos sacrumque Numici

193 *ἄγεν* (*codd. Hom.*)] *ἄγε Aristarch., edd.*
194 stant Gauranae] et Sacranae *Verg.*

contortions or deviate the least bit from just drawing out the various details, but he stands there listing the arrayed forces as though he were conducting a military review, a subject that calls for no verbiage beyond the numbers. 17. And yet, when it's right to do so, he works some wonderful variations in presenting the leaders' names:

> Then Skhedios and Epistrophos lead the men of
> Phôkia . . . (*Il.* 2.517),

> Swift Aias, Oïleus' son, led the Lokrians . . .
> (*Il.* 2.527),

> Nireus led three balanced ships from Symê . . .
> (*Il.* 2.671).

18. In his admiration for the kind of heaped-up list found in Homer Virgil conveyed the effect in a way I would almost say is more elegant than his model (*Il.* 2.646–48):

> Those who held Knôsos and high-walled Gortyn
> Lyktos and Milêtos and shining white Lykastos
> and Phaistos . . .

and other passages like that. 19. Along the same lines one finds in Virgil (*A.* 7.794–801):

> The columns are marshaled thick on the plains, the
> Argive youth
> and platoons of Aurunci, the Rutuli and ancient
> Sicani;
> battle lines from Mount Gaurus are in place and the
> Labici
> with their painted shields, who work your glades,
> Tiberinus,

litus arant Rutulosque exercent vomere colles
Circaeumque iugum, quis Iuppiter Anxuris[195] arvis
praesidet

et cetera.

16 'Vterque in catalogo suo post difficilium rerum vel nominum narrationem infert fabulam cum versibus amoenioribus, ut lectoris animus recreetur. 2. Homerus inter enumeranda regionum et urbium nomina facit locum fabulis quae horrorem satietatis excludant:

*καὶ Πτελεὸν καὶ Ἕλος καὶ Δώριον, ἐνθάδε*[196] *Μοῦσαι*
*ἀντόμεναι Θάμυριν τὸν Θρήϊκα παῦσαν ἀοιδῆς*
*Οἰχαλίηθεν ἰόντα παρ' Εὐρύτου Οἰχαλιῆος—*
*στεῦτο γὰρ εὐχόμενος νικησέμεν, εἴ περ ἂν αὐταὶ*
*Μοῦσαι ἀείδοιεν κοῦραι Διὸς αἰγιόχοιο—*
*αἳ δὲ χολωσάμεναι πηρὸν θέσαν, αὐτὰρ ἀοιδὴν*
*θεσπεσίην ἀφέλοντο καὶ ἐκλέλαθον κιθαριστύν,*

3. et alibi:[197]

*τῶν μὲν Τληπόλεμος δουρικλυτὸς ἡγεμόνευεν,*
*ὃν τέκεν Ἀστυόχεια βίῃ Ἡρακληείῃ,*

[195] Anxuris S, anxiris A (aux- *ω*): Anxurus *Verg.*
[196] *ἐνθάδε*] *ἔνθά τε Hom.*
[197] et alibi P: *om. ω*

and the Numicus' sacred shore, plying with their
plows the Rutulian hills
and the ridges at Circeii, the fields where Jupiter
Anxur
holds sway,

and so on.

'When their catalogues have to include a passage filled with names or events that tax the reader, both poets insert a story in more attractive verse, to refresh the reader's mind. 2. Thus Homer, in listing the names of districts and cities, makes room for stories to forestall the repugnance that monotony brings (*Il.* 2.594–600): 16

Pteleos and Helos and Dôrion, where the Muses
met the Thracian Thamyris and put an end to his
singing
as he came from Oikahliê and Oikhaliê's king
Eurytos—
for boasting he undertook to best them, even if the
Muses
themselves should sing, daughters of Zeus who wields
the aegis—
but they in their wrath left him lamed, stripped him
of his
wondrous song, made him forget his skill with the
lyre,

3. and elsewhere (*Il.* 2.657–62):

These were led by Tlêpolemos, renowned with the
spear,
whom Astyokheia bore to the might of Hêraklês,

*τὴν ἄγετ' ἐξ Ἐφύρης ποταμοῦ ἄπο Σελλήεντος*
*πέρσας ἄστεα πολλὰ διοτρεφέων αἰζηῶν.*
*Τληπόλεμος δ' ἐπεὶ οὖν τράφ' ἐνὶ μεγάρῳ*
*εὐπήκτῳ,*
*αὐτίκα πατρὸς ἑοῖο φίλον μήτρωα κατέκτα,*

et reliqua quibus protraxit iucunditatem. 4. Vergilius in hoc secutus auctorem in priore catalogo modo de Aventino, modo de Hippolyto fabulatur, in secundo Cycnus ei fabula est. et sic amoenitas intertexta fastidio narrationum medetur. 5. in omnibus vero Georgicorum libris hoc idem summa cum elegantia fecit. nam post praecepta, quae natura res dura est, ut legentis animum vel auditum novaret, singulos libros acciti extrinsecus argumenti interpositione conclusit, primum de signis tempestatum, de laudatione rusticae vitae secundum, et tertius desinit in pestilentiam pecorum, quarti finis est de Orpheo et Aristaeo non otiosa narratio. ita in omni opere Maronis Homerica lucet imitatio.

6. 'Homerus omnem poesin suam ita sententiis farsit ut singula eius *ἀποφθέγματα* vice proverbiorum in omnium ore fungantur:

*ἀλλ' οὔ πως ἅμα πάντα θεοὶ δόσαν ἀνθρώποισιν,*

when he took her from Ephyrê, from the river Sellêeis,
after sacking the many cities of sturdy men nurtured by Zeus.
When Tlêpolemos was raised in his well-made hall,
he suddenly killed his father's mother's brother,

and so on with the rest of the tale used to draw out this pleasant interlude. 4. Virgil followed his model in his first catalogue, telling stories now about Aventinus (*A.* 7.657–63), now about Hippolytus (*A.* 7.765–80), while in the second catalogue Cycnus provides him with a tale (*A.* 10.189–93): by weaving in these pleasant interludes he provides an antidote to narrative monotony. 5. Indeed, he did the same thing in all the books of the *Georgics*, with supreme subtlety. For after the didactic material, which is naturally hard going, he ended each book by inserting extraneous material, to refresh the reader's intellect or aesthetic sense—the first book, with the excursus on weather-signs (351–468), the second, with praise of the rural life (458–540), while the third book ends with the plague that struck the farm animals (478–566), the fourth with the story of Orpheus and Aristaeus that is far from pointless (315–558). Thus in every aspect of his oeuvre Maro's imitation of Homer is clear as day.

6. 'Homer stuffed all his verse so full of epigrams that his individual sayings have the status of proverbs and are on everyone's lips:

But the gods do not give all at once to mortal men (*Il.* 4.320),

χρὴ ξεῖνον παρεόντα φιλεῖν, ἐθέλοντα δὲ πέμπειν,

μέτρον δ' ἐπὶ πᾶσιν ἄριστον,

οἱ πλέονες κακίους,

δειλαί τοι δειλῶν γε καὶ ἐγγύαι ἐγγυάασθαι,

ἄφρων θ' ὅς[198] κ' ἐθέλῃ πρὸς κρείσσονας ἀντιφερίζειν,

7. et alia innumerabilia, quae sententialiter proferuntur. nec haec apud Vergilium frustra desideraveris:

non omnia possumus omnes,

omnia vincit Amor,

labor omnia vincit[199]
improbus,

usque adeone mori miserum est?,

stat sua cuique dies,

dolus an virtus, quis in hoste requirit?,[200]

198 θ' ὅς] δ' ὅς *Hom.*
199 vincit] vicit *Verg.*
200 requirit] -at *Verg.*

Befriend a guest at your table, send him on his way when he wants to go (*Od.* 15.74),

Balance is the best in all things,[55]

The larger the number, the worse the men (*Od.* 2.277),

Even the pledges of worthless men are worthless to receive (*Od.* 8.351),

Witless the man who wishes to compete with his betters,[56]

7. and countless others that are cited as wise sayings. Nor would you look in vain for the like in Virgil:

We cannot all do all things (*E.* 8.63),[57]

Love conquers all (*E.* 10.69),

Relentless toil conquers all (*G.* 1.145–46),

Is death so utterly wretched? (*A.* 12.646),

For each man his day [of death] stands fixed (*A.* 10.467),

Who cares whether it's trickery or courage that works in the enemy's midst? (*A.* 2.390),

55 Not in Homer: *Od.* 15.71 conveys a related idea ("all things suitable are best," cf. also Hes. *Works and Days* 694), but the proverb appears in the form quoted only at Stob. 3.15.7, [Pythag.] *Golden Poem* 38, [Theano] p.198.27.

56 Not Homer, but Hesiod *Works and Days* 210.

57 Treated as an imitation of Lucilius at 6.1.35.

et quid quaeque ferat regio et quid quaeque recuset,

auri sacra fames.

8. et, ne obtundam nota referendo, mille sententiarum talium aut in ore sunt singulorum aut obviae intentioni legentis occurrunt.

'In non nullis ab Homerica secta haud scio casune an sponte desciscit. Fortunam Homerus nescire maluit et soli decreto,[201] quam *μοῖραν* vocat, omnia regenda committit, adeo ut hoc vocabulum *τύχη* in nulla parte Homerici voluminis nominetur. contra Vergilius non solum novit et meminit, sed omnipotentiam quoque eidem tribuit, quam et philosophi qui eam nominant nihil sua vi posse, sed decreti sive providentiae ministram esse voluerunt. 9. et in fabulis seu in historiis non numquam idem facit. Aegaeon apud Homerum auxilio est Iovi, hunc contra Iovem armant versus Maronis. Eumedes Dolonis proles bello praeclara animo manibusque parentem refert, cum apud Homerum Dolon imbellis sit. 10. nullam commemorationem de iudicio Paridis Homerus admittit. idem vates Ganymedem non ut Iunonis paelicem a Iove raptum, sed Iovialium poculorum ministrum in caelum a dis ascitum refert, velut *θεοπρεπῶς*. 11. Vergilius tantam deam, quod cuivis de honestis feminae deforme est, velut specie victam Paride iu-

[201] decreto *ed. Ven. 1472*: deoreto *ω*

---

[58] The judgment is mentioned at *Il.* 24.28–30, though the lines have been judged spurious both in antiquity and by modern editors.

Both what each region bears and what it refuses to bear (*G.* 1.53),

The accursed hunger for gold (*A.* 3.57).

8. And not to belabor the matter by quoting familiar tags, suffice it to say that you encounter countless epigrams of that sort either on people's lips or when you read with attention.

'In some cases he fails to follow Homer, whether accidentally or intentionally I'm not sure. Homer preferred to turn a blind eye to Chance and instead hands over everything to be guided solely by the ordinance that he calls *moira* ['destiny'], to the extent that the word *tykhê* ['chance'] is nowhere used in the Homeric corpus. Virgil, by contrast, not only knows and makes mention of chance but makes it all powerful, though even the philosophers who mention it claimed that it had no power of its own but was the agent of the ruling ordinance or providence. 9. He also sometimes departs from Homer in treating tales from myth or history. In Homer Aegaeon is Jupiter's ally (*Il.* 1.401–6), but Maro's verse makes him Jupiter's adversary (*A.* 10.565–68). He says that Eumedes, Dolon's son and a "distinguished warrior," "recalls his father with his deeds of courage" (*A.* 12.347–48), though in Homer Dolon is unwarlike (*Il.* 10.373–457). 10. Homer makes no mention of the judgment of Paris,[58] and he speaks of Ganymede, not as a sexual rival to Juno whom Jupiter kidnapped (cf. *A.* 1.28), but in terms that preserve the gods' dignity, as Jupiter's cup-bearer whom the gods received into heaven (*Il.* 20.234–35). 11. Virgil's account of the great goddess Juno would disgrace any honorable mortal woman: he says that she was aggrieved by Paris' judgment, when she lost the

dicante doluisse, et propter Catamiti paelicatum totam gentem eius vexasse commemorat.

12. 'Interdum sic auctorem suum dissimulanter imitatur, ut loci inde descripti solam dispositionem mutet et faciat velut aliud videri. 13. Homerus ingenti spiritu ex perturbatione terrae ipsum Ditem patrem territum prosilire et exclamare quodam modo facit:

*ἔδδεισεν δ' ὑπένερθεν ἄναξ ἐνέρων Ἀϊδωνεύς,*
*δείσας δ' ἐκ θρόνου ἆλτο καὶ ἴαχε, μή οἱ ἔνερθεν*[202]
*γαῖαν ἀναρρήξειε Ποσειδάων ἐνοσίχθων,*
*οἰκία δὲ θνητοῖσι καὶ ἀθανάτοισι φανείη*
*σμερδαλέ' εὐρώεντα, τά τε στυγέουσι θεοί περ·*

14. hoc Maro non narrationis sed parabolae loco posuit, ut aliud esse videretur:

non secus ac si qua penitus vi terra dehiscens
infernas reseret sedes et regna recludat
pallida, dis invisa, superque immane barathrum
cernatur, trepident immisso lumine Manes.

hoc quoque dissimulando subripuit; nam cum ille dixisset deos sine labore vivere, *θεοὶ ῥεῖα ζώοντες*, hoc idem dixit occultissime:

202 *ἔνερθεν*] *ὕπερθε Hom.*

---

59 Lat. Dis (cf. 1.7.30n.) ~ Gk. Hades.

beauty contest, and that because Ganymede was her rival she plagued his entire race (*A.* 1.26–28).

12. 'Sometimes he disguises his imitation, changing the arrangement of the passage he's borrowed and making it appear different. 13. Homer makes father Dis[59] himself give a great gasp, leap up in terror, and cry out when the earth is shaken (*Il.* 20.61–65):

> Beneath the earth Hades, the lord of those below, felt fear,
> leaping up from his throne and crying out in fear, lest
> Poseidon, earth-shaker, crack open his abode below the earth
> and reveal to mortals and immortals alike his dwelling,
> dreadful and dank, hated indeed by the gods.

14. Maro made this part of a comparison, not the narrative, giving it a different appearance (*A.* 8.243–46):

> Just as if some force should make the earth gape to its core,
> unlock the settlements of hell and disclose those realms—
> ghastly, hated by the gods—making the vast abyss visible
> from above, making the spirits of the dead tremble in a flood of light.

Here is another passage that he stealthily snatched: for whereas Homer said that "the gods live without toil" (*Il.* 6.138), Virgil said the same thing very indirectly (*A.* 10.758–59):

di Iovis in tectis casum[203] miserantur inanem
amborum et tantos mortalibus esse labores,

quibus ipsi scilicet carent.

17 'Quid Vergilio contulerit Homerus hinc maxime liquet quod, ubi rerum necessitas exegit a Marone dispositionem inchoandi belli, quam non habuit Homerus—quippe qui Achillis iram exordium sibi fecerit, quae decimo demum belli anno contigit—laboravit ad rei novae partum: cervum fortuito saucium fecit causam tumultus. 2. sed ubi vidit hoc leve nimisque puerile, dolorem auxit agrestium, ut impetus eorum sufficeret ad bellum. sed nec servos Latini, et maxime stabulo regio curantes atque ideo quid foederis cum Troianis Latinus icerit[204] ex muneribus equorum et currus iugalis non ignorantes, bellum generis domini oportebat inferre. 3. quid igitur? deorum maxima deducitur e caelo, et maxima Furiarum de Tartaris adsciscitur, sparguntur angues velut in scaena parturientes furorem, regina non solum de penetralibus reverentiae matronalis educitur, sed et per urbem mediam cogitur facere discursus; nec hoc contenta silvas petit accitis reliquis matribus in societatem furoris, bacchatur chorus quondam pudicus et orgia insana celebrantur. 4. quid plura? maluissem Maronem et in hac parte apud auctorem suum vel apud quemlibet Graecorum alium quod sequeretur habuisse.

203 casum] iram *Verg.* 204 icerit *ed. Ven. 1472*: iecerit *ω*

60 §§1–3 offer a remarkably tendentious account, not least in treating the intervention of Juno and Allecto as a "sequel" to the stag's "chance" wounding, which their intervention in fact precedes and which Allecto intentionally causes (A. 7.476–82).

The gods in Jupiter's hall take pity on the vain suffering
of both sides and grieve that mortals know such toils,

toils, that is to say, from which they themselves are free.

'Homer's contribution to Virgil is above all apparent 17
from the fact that when the course of events forced Maro to arrange the outbreak of war, which Homer did not treat—since he began with the anger of Achilles, in the tenth year of the war—he plainly struggled to produce the new material, making the chance wounding of a stag the cause of the upheaval.[60] 2. But when he realized that this was a trivial and exceedingly childish device, he exaggerated the peasants' emotional response, so that their attack would be a sufficient cause of war. It was just wrong, however, to have Latinus' slaves—especially those looking after the royal stable, who knew the sort of pact Latinus had struck with the Trojans because of the horses and yoked chariot he was giving the latter (cf. *A.* 7.274–83)—start a war against their master's in-laws. 3. What's the sequel? The greatest goddess is brought down from heaven, the greatest Fury is recruited from Tartarus, snakes are flung about to create a frenzy—like some theatrical turn—the queen is not just brought out from the private quarters that preserve her matronly honor but is even forced to go charging this way and that through the middle of town—no, not just that, she makes for the woods, calling on all the other matrons to be her allies in madness—and they go raving about, a chorus that's lost all sense of decorum, and celebrate insane rites. 4. Need I say more? I only wish that for this part, too, Maro had found material to follow in his mentor—or some other Greek author.

'"Alium" non frustra dixi, quia non de unius racemis vindemiam sibi fecit, sed bene in rem suam vertit quidquid ubicumque invenit imitandum; adeo ut de Argonauticorum quarto, quorum scriptor est Apollonius, librum Aeneidos suae quartum totum paene formaverit, ad Didonem vel Aenean amatoriam incontinentiam[205] Medeae circa Iasonem transferendo. 5. quod ita elegantius auctore digessit, ut fabula lascivientis Didonis, quam falsam novit universitas, per tot tamen saecula speciem veritatis obtineat et ita pro vero per ora omnium volitet, ut pictores fictoresque et qui figmentis liciorum contextas imitantur effigies, hac materia vel maxime in effigiandis[206] simulacris tamquam unico argumento decoris utantur, nec minus histrionum perpetuis et gestibus et cantibus celebretur. 6. tantum valuit pulchritudo narrandi ut omnes Phoenissae castitatis conscii, nec ignari manum sibi iniecisse reginam, ne pateretur damnum pudoris, coniveant tamen fabulae, et intra conscientiam veri fidem prementes[207] malint pro vero celebrari quod pectoribus humanis dulcedo fingentis infudit.

7. 'Videamus utrum attigerit et Pindarum, quem Flaccus imitationi inaccessum fatetur. et "minuta" quidem

[205] incontinentiam *ed. Lips. 1774*: conti- ω
[206] effigiandis *ed. Lugd. Bat. 1597*: efficiendis ω (effig- PR[1])
[207] prementes *ed. Colon. 1521*: frem- ω

'And it is not for nothing that I said "other," because he did not make his vintage wine from the grapes of only one source: he nicely adapted to his own purposes whatever he found that was worth imitating, from any and every source, going so far as to virtually shape the whole of the *Aeneid's* fourth book on the model of Book 4 of the *Argonautica* by Apollonius, assigning to Dido or Aeneas the unrestrained love that Medea bore for Jason.[61] 5. Our author treated that theme so subtly that the story of Dido lost in passion, which everyone knows is not true,[62] has for so many generations now maintained the appearance of truth, and so flits about on the lips of men as though it were true, that painters and sculptors and the weavers of tapestries use this above all as their raw material in fashioning their images, as though it were the unique pattern of beauty, and it is no less constantly celebrated in the gestures and songs of actors. 6. The story's beauty has had such power that though everyone knows of the Phoenician queen's chastity and is aware that she took her own life to avoid the loss of her honor, they nonetheless wink at the tale, keep their loyalty to the truth to themselves, and prefer to celebrate as true the sweetness that the artist instilled in human hearts.[63]

7. 'Now let us see whether he put his hand to Pindar too, who Horace admits (cf. *Odes* 4.2.1ff.) is beyond imitation. To be sure, I leave to one side the "small and dewy"

[61] Cf. Serv. on *A.* 4.1.

[62] Here and in §6 ("everyone knows of [Dido's] chastity") M. speaks, a bit oddly, as though there were a "true" story of Dido independent of the poetic version.

[63] The force of this beauty is implied in Augustine's recollection of weeping over the dead Dido, *Confessions* 1.21.

"atque rorantia" quae inde subtraxit relinquo, unum vero locum quem temptavit ex integro paene transcribere, volo communicare vobiscum quia dignus est ut eum velimus altius intueri. 8. cum Pindari carmen quod de natura atque flagrantia montis Aetnae compositum est aemulari vellet, eius modi sententias et verba molitus est ut Pindaro quoque ipso, qui nimis opima et pingui facundia existimatus est, insolentior hoc quidem in loco tumidiorque sit. atque uti vosmet ipsos eius quod dico arbitros faciam, carmen Pindari quod est super monte Aetna, quantulum mihi est memoriae, dicam:

9. *τᾶς ἐρεύγονται μὲν ἀπλάτου πυρὸς ἁγνόταται*
*ἐκ μυχῶν παγαί· ποταμοὶ δ' ἁμέραισιν*
*μὲν προχέοντι ῥόον καπνοῦ*
*αἴθων'· ἀλλ' ἐν ὄρφναισιν*[208]
*φοίνισσα κυλινδομένα φλὸξ ἐς βαθεῖ-*
*αν φέρει πόντου πλάκα σὺν πατάγῳ.*
*κεῖνο δ' Ἁφαίστοιο κρουνοὺς ἑρπετόν*
*δεινοτάτους ἀναπέμπει, τέρας μὲν*
*θαυμάσιον προσιδέσθαι,*
*θαῦμα δὲ καὶ παρεόντων ἀκοῦσαι.*

10. audite nunc Vergilii versus ut inchoasse eum verius quam perfecisse dicatis:

208 *πέτρας om. et ω et Gell.* (*cf. Marshall CR 1964, 170, Timpanaro Gnomon 1964, 788*)

---

64 Here and 7.9.1 M. borrows a metaphor used by Cicero (*On Old Age* 46) to describe the "small and dewy" cups used in a symposium: the point of the metaphor, which depends on knowledge

touches[64] that he drew from Pindar and instead want to share with you one passage that he tried to copy almost entirely, because it's worth our taking an unusually close look at it. 8. Since he wished to rival Pindar's poem on the nature of Mount Aetna and its eruption, he amassed figures of thought and speech of the sort that caused him to be even more *outré* and overdone in this passage than Pindar himself, whose style was thought too full and rich.[65] And to let you judge what I'm talking about, I'll recite Pindar's poem on Mount Aetna, to the extent that I can remember it (*P.* 1.21–26):

9. From its inmost recesses the holiest founts of unapproachable
fire belch forth: during the day rivers
pour forth a blazing stream
of smoke; in the dark times of night
a ruddy glow rolls forth and is borne rumbling
into the deep plain of the sea.
There that serpent[66] sends up most dread
streams of Hephaistos, a portent
wondrous to look upon,
a marvel even to learn from witnesses.

10. If you listen now to Virgil's version, you'll more truly say that he made a start than that he brought it off (*A.* 3.570–77):

of Cicero's source (Xen. *Symp.* 2.26, referring to small cups filled frequently, as opposed to large cups filled just once), is quite thoroughly obscure here.

65 §§8–14 are based on Gell. 17.10.8–19 (*pace* Jocelyn 1964, 288 n.2).

66 Variously identified with the rebel Giant Enceladus or Typhon.

portus[209] ab accessu ventorum immotus et ingens
ipse: sed horrificis iuxta tonat Aetna ruinis,
interdumque atram prorumpit ad aethera nubem,
turbine fumantem piceo et candente favilla,
attollitque globos flammarum et sidera lambit.
interdum scopulos avulsaque viscera montis
erigit eructans liquefactaque saxa sub auras
cum gemitu glomerat fundoque exaestuat imo.

11. in principio[210] Pindarus veritati obsecutus dixit, quod res erat quodque illic oculis deprehenditur, interdiu fumare Aetnam, noctu flammigare. Vergilius autem dum in strepitu sonituque verborum conquirendo laborat, utrumque tempus nulla discretione facta confundit. 12. atque ille Graecos quidem fontes imitatus[211] ignis eructare et fluere amnes fumi et flammarum fulva et tortuosa volumina in plagas maris ferre, quasi quosdam igneos angues,[212] luculente dixit, at hic vester atram nubem turbine piceo et favilla fumante *ῥόον καπνοῦ αἴθωνα* interpretari volens crasse et immodice congessit, globos quoque flammarum, quod ille *κρουνούς* dixerat, duriter posuit et *ἀκύρως*. 13. hoc vero vel inenarrabile est, quod nubem atram fumare dixit turbine piceo et favilla candente. non enim fumare solent neque atra esse quae sunt

[209] portus *ed. Ven. 1472 ex Verg.*: pontus *ω*

[210] iam principio *Gell.*

[211] Graecos . . . imitatus (*codd. Gell., cf. Marshall ibid.*): Graecus . . . imitus *Lipsius ad Gell.*

[212] angues *ed. Lugd. 1550, Gell.*: amnes *ω*

The harbor is unshaken by the winds' approach, and huge
in itself: but nearby Aetna thunders, a scene of dread destruction.
Now and again it blasts a black cloud up to heaven
in a smoking cyclone of pitch and blazing ash
and raises balls of fire that lick at the stars.
Now and again it belches straight up whole crags,
the mountain's guts, sends melting boulders with a groan
melding in the wind, and boils up from its very depths.

11. To start with, Pindar spoke with an eye on the facts when he said that Aetna smokes during the daytime and sends up flames at night, the actual situation that can be seen there on the ground. Virgil, on the other hand, puts his effort into devising verbal sound-effects and draws no temporal distinction but mixes the two periods together. 12. Furthermore, the former, taking Greek sources as his model, did a brilliant job of describing founts of fire belching from its depths and streams of smoke flowing and tawny, twisting coils of flame borne like fiery snakes into the sea's expanse, but this poet of yours, in trying to translate "blazing stream of smoke" went too far and made a coarse mess with "a cloud . . . in a smoking cyclone of pitch and blazing ash"; furthermore, his attempt to render "streams" [*krounoi*] with "balls of fire" entails a harsh and improper usage. 13. Indeed the effect he rendered as "a black cloud . . . in a smoking cyclone of pitch and blazing ash" really does not work as a description: things that are "blazing" are usually neither smoky nor black, unless he

candentia, nisi forte candenti dixit pervulgate et improprie pro ferventi, non pro relucenti: nam candens scilicet a candore dictum, non a calore. 14. quod autem scopulos eructari et erigi eosdemque ipsos statim liquefieri et gemere atque glomerari sub auras dixit, hoc nec a Pindaro scriptum nec umquam fando auditum, et omnium quae monstra dicuntur monstruosissimum est.

15. 'Postremo Graiae linguae quam se libenter addixerit de crebris quae usurpat vocabulis aestimate:

dius Vlixes[213]

spelaea ferarum,

daedala . . . tecta,

Rhodopeiae arces,
altaque Panchaea[214] . . .
atque Getae atque Hebrus et Actias[215] Orithya[216]

et:

16. Thyas[217] ubi audito stimulat[218] trieterica Baccho
orgia nocturnusque vocat clamore Cithaeron,

213 Ulixes C (Ulyxes S): -is $\omega$
214 Panc(h)aea (Panch- *et codd.* MR *Verg.*)] Pangaea *Verg.*
215 Actias *ed. Ven. 1472*: accias $\beta_2$, accia $\alpha$
216 Orithya] –thyia *Verg.*
217 Thyas] Thyias *Verg.*
218 stimulat] -lant *Verg.*

used "blazing" in a vulgar and improper way for "burning" rather than "glowing," for the verb "blaze" [*candere*] is obviously derived from the noun meaning "blazing bright light" [*candor*] not "heat" [*calor*]. 14. As for Virgil's other touches—the crags being belched straight up and also immediately melting and groaning and melding in the wind—they're not in Pindar and they're absolutely unheard of, the most monstrous of all things described as "monsters."

15. 'Finally, you can judge how eagerly he surrendered to the Greek language from his frequent borrowings of individual words:

> brilliant [*dius*] Ulysses[67]
>
> caves [*spelaea*] of beasts (*E.* 10.52*),
>
> intricate [*daedala*] . . . dwellings (*G.* 4.179),
>
> the summits of Rhodopê
> and lofty Panchaea . . .
> and the Getae and the Hebrus and Attic Orithyia (*G.* 4.461–63)

and (*A.* 4.302–3*)

> 16. As when a bacchant [*thyas*], hearing the god, urges on the biennial
> rites [*orgia*], and Mount Cithaeron calls out with a shout in the night,

[67] The topic of §§15–19—'borrowings from the Greek'—implies that M.'s text of Virgil (or his source's) did read *dius* (= Gk. *dîos*, cf., e.g., *Od.* 1.196 *dîos Odysseus*), a word that Virgil in fact nowhere uses; the phrase *dirus Ulixes* ("loathsome Ulysses") appears at *A.* 2.261 and 762.

et:

non tibi Tyndaridis facies invisa Lacaenae,

et:

ferte simul Faunique pedem Dryadesque puellae,

et:

hinc atque hinc glomerantur Oreades,

et:

pars pedibus plaudunt choreas,

et:

17. Milesia vellera nymphae
carpebant hyali saturo fucata colore
Drymoque Xanthoque Ligeaque Phyllodoceque

et:[219]

Nisaee Spioque Thaliaque[220] Cymodoceque[221]

et:

Alcandrumque Haliumque Noëmonaque
Prytaninque

et:

Amphion Dircaeus in Actaeo Aracintho,[222]

et:

. . . senior Glauci chorus Inousque Palaemon.

219 et *post* Phyllodoceque *coll. Holford-Strevens*, *post* colore ω (*secl. ed. Lips. 1774*)

220 Thaliaque *ed. Ven. 1472*: ethaliaque ω

221 *G. 4.338* (= *A. 5.826*) *om. codd. plerique Verg., Serv., secl. edd.*

222 Aracintho] -cyntho A, *Verg.*

and (*A.* 2.601)

> No concern of yours the hated face of the Spartan [*Lacaena*] daughter of Tyndareus [*Tyndaris*],

and (*G.* 1.11)

> Come along together, you Fauns and young wood-nymphs [*Dryades*],

and (*A.* 1.500*)

> Mountain-nymphs [*Oreades*] are massed on every side,

and (*A.* 6.644*)

> Some dance in a circle [*choreae*], feet pounding,

and (*G.* 4.334–36):

> 17. The nymphs [*nymphae*] were plucking the wool
> of Miletus [*Milesia*], deep dyed the color of glass [*hyalus*]—
> Drymo and Xantho and Ligea and Phyllodocê

and (*G.* 4.338)

> Nisaeê and Spio and Thalia and Cymodocê,

and (*A.* 9.767*)

> Alcandrus and Halius and Noëmon and Prytanis,

and (*E.* 2.24)

> Dircaean Amphion in Attic Aracinthus,

and (*A.* 5.823)

> . . . Glaucus' elder chorus and Palaemon born of Ino.

18. versus est Parthenii quo grammatico in Graecis Vergilius usus est:

Γλαύκῳ καὶ Νηρῆι καὶ Ἰνώῳ[223] Μελικέρτῃ,

hic ait:

Glauco et Panopeae et Inoo Melicertae.

et:

Tritonesque citi,

et:

immania cete.

19. adeo autem et declinationibus Graecis delectatur ut "Mnesthea" dixerit pro "Mnestheum," sicut ipse alibi:

nec fratre Mnestheo,[224]

et pro "Orpheo" dicere maluerit "Orphi" Graece declinando, ut:

Orphi[225] Calliopea, Lino formosus Apollo,

et:

vidimus o cives Diomede,[226]

223 Ἰνώῳ (*e Verg.*)] *εἰναλίῳ verius ap. Gell. 13.27.1*

224 Mnestheo (*codd. plerique Verg., Tib.*)] Menestheo *codd.* dehn *Verg., Serv., edd.*

225 Orphi (*codd.* Racnoγ[1] *Verg.*)] -phei *codd. plerique Verg., edd.*

226 Diomede *ed. Ven. 1472, cod.* f *Verg., agnosc. Serv.*: -den *ω* (*codd.* MPRabevγ *Verg., Tib.*)

18. There's a verse of Parthenius, who taught Virgil Greek language and literature (fr. 36):

To Glaukos and Nêreus and Melikertês born of Înô.

Virgil says (*G.* 1.437):

To Glaucus and Panopea and Melicertes born of Ino,

and (*A.* 5.824)

and swift Tritons,

and (*A.* 5.822*)

monstrous beasts of the sea [*cêtê*].

19. Furthermore, he was so taken with the declensional forms of Greek nouns that he used "Mnesthea" in place of "Mnestheum" (*A.* 4.288, 12.561), as he elsewhere says (*A.* 10.129)

nor with his brother Mnestheus [*Mnestheo*],[68]

and in place of "Orpheo" he preferred "Orphi," declining in the Greek fashion, as at (*E.* 4.57):[69]

Calliopea for Orpheus [*Orphi*], fair Apollo for Linus,

and (*A.* 11.243*)

my fellow citizens, we saw Diomede,

68 I.e., he uses the proper Latin ablative form, *Mnestheo*, as he could have used the proper Latin accusative form, *Mnestheum*, but chose not to.

69 Cf. Serv. on *G.* 4.545; at issue is the appropriate form of the dative case.

ut talium nominum accusativus Graecus est in $\eta$[227] desinens. nam si quis eum putat Latine dixisse "Diomeden,"[228] sanitas metri in versu desiderabitur. 20. denique omnia carmina sua Graece maluit inscribere "Bucolica" "Georgica" "Aeneis," cuius nominis figuratio a regula Latinitatis aliena est.

18 'Sed de his hactenus, quorum plura omnibus, aliqua non nullis Romanorum nota sunt. ad illa venio quae de Graecarum litterarum penetralibus eruta nullis cognita sunt, nisi qui Graecam doctrinam diligenter hauserunt. fuit enim hic poeta ut scrupulose et anxie, ita dissimulanter et quasi clanculo doctus, ut multa transtulerit quae unde translata sint difficile sit cognitu. 2. in exordio Georgicorum posuit hos versus:

> Liber et alma Ceres, vestro si munere tellus
> Chaoniam pingui glandem mutavit arista,
> poculaque inventis Acheloia miscuit uvis.

3. nihil in his versibus grammaticorum cohors discipulis suis amplius tradidit nisi illud opera Cereris effectum, ut homines ab antiquo victu desisterent et frumento pro glandibus uterentur; Liberum vero vitis repertorem praestitisse humano potui vinum cui aqua admisceretur. cur

227 $\eta$ *'fortasse rectius' Jan* (*qui* e *legit*), *cf. Serv. ad A. 11.243*: en PGC, em NRFA

228 Diomeden $\alpha$: -dem P$\beta_2$

---

70 In referring to the "Latin form" of the Greek name, with terminal *-n*, M. or his source is thinking, e.g., of *Aenean*, the objective case form that Virgil regularly uses for *Aeneas*; the true Latin form, *Diomedem*, is preferred by Virgil's modern editors.

since the Greek accusative of such names ends in -*ê*. For if someone supposes that he used the Latin form "Diomeden,"[70] the line will be metrically unsound. 20. Finally, he preferred to give Greek titles to all his works, the *Bucolica* and the *Georgica* and the *Aeneïs*, the last having a noun-form that's alien to regular Latin usage.[71]

18 'But enough about such things, most of which all Romans know, while others are known to at least some. I come now to things fetched from the inner sanctum of Greek literature, things no Roman knows, save those who have earnestly drunk a full draught of Greek learning. For this poet here was as evasive and secretive in his learning as he was diligent and finicky: as a result, the sources of many of his borrowings are difficult to recognize. 2. Here's what he wrote in the introduction to the *Georgics* (*G.* 1.7–9†):

> Liber and nourishing Ceres, if through your gift the earth
> exchanged the Chaonian acorn for the rich ear of grain,
> discovered the grape, and mixed it with cups of the Acheloüs.

3. The troupe of school teachers has taught its students nothing about these lines save that it is thanks to Ceres' efforts that humankind put aside their old means of sustenance and came to enjoy grain instead of acorns, and that Liber, who discovered the fruit of the vine, gave humankind wine to drink mixed with water. But no one asks why

[71] I.e., the forms of the name in cases other than the nominative (subject case) follow a Greek rather than a Latin pattern (e.g., genitive *Aeneïdos*).

autem Acheloum amnem potissimum Vergilius cum aquam vellet intellegi nominarit, nemo vel quaerit vel omnino subesse aliquid eruditius suspicatur. 4. nos id altius scrutati animadvertimus doctum poetam antiquissimorum Graecorum more (sicut docebit auctoritas) elocutum, apud quos proprie in aquae significationem ponebatur Achelous. neque id frustra. nam causa quoque eius rei cum cura relata est. sed priusquam causam propono, illud antiquo poeta teste monstrabo, hunc morem loquendi pervagatum fuisse, ut Acheloum pro quavis aqua dicerent. 5. Aristophanes vetus comicus in comoedia Cocalo[229] sic ait:

ἤμουν ἄγριον
βάρος—ἤπειγεν[230] γάρ τοι μ' οἶνος—
. . . [231]
οὐ μείξας πῶμ'[232] Ἀχελῴῳ.

gravabar, inquit, vino cui aqua non fuisset admixta, id est mero. 6. cur autem sic loqui soliti sunt Ephorus notissimus scriptor Historiarum libro secundo ostendit his verbis:

*τοῖς μὲν οὖν ἄλλοις ποταμοῖς οἱ πλησιόχωροι μόνοι θύουσιν, τὸν δὲ Ἀχελῷον μόνον πάντας ἀνθρώπους συμβέβηκεν τιμᾶν, οὐ τοῖς κοινοῖς ὀνόμασιν ἀντὶ τῶν ἰδίων <ὀνομάζοντας τοὺς*

229 Cocalo *ed. Basil. 1535* (Cacalo C): cot- ω

230 *ἤπειγεν Papabasileios* (*coll. βάρος antecedent. et* gravabar *sequent.*): ἤτειρεν N, ἤγειρεν P

231 *lac. inter vv. 2 et 3 stat. Kassel metri causa*

232 *οὐ μείξας πῶμ'*] *οὐ πόμα μίξας Jan*

Virgil named the Acheloüs, among all other rivers, when he intended "water" to be understood, and no one suspects that some more profound bit of learning might be present. 4. But after examining the matter more deeply I have found that the learned poet has spoken (as my evidence will show) in the manner of the most ancient Greeks, who used "Akheloös" as the proper term for "water"—nor did they do that to no purpose: rather, the reason has been carefully recorded. But before I explain the reason, I shall use the testimony of an ancient poet to show that this manner of speaking—using "Akheloös" to mean "water" in general—was pervasive.[72] 5. Aristophanes, a poet of the Old Comedy, says in his *Rooster* (fr. 365 *PCG* 3,2:205),

> I was puking up a nasty
> burden—for the wine was weighing me down—
> . . .
> I had not mixed the drink with Akheloös.

I was being weighed down (he says) by the wine that had not been mixed with water, that is, by pure wine. 6. Furthermore, Ephorus, the well known author, shows in Book 2 of his *Histories* why they adopted this usage (no. 70 fr. 20 *FGrH*):

> Now, only the inhabitants nearby sacrifice to other rivers; the Akheloös alone happens to be honored by all humankind, who refer to other rivers by their proper names, not by one or another common term,

[72] Cf. (D)Serv. on *G.* 1.8 (citing but not quoting Aristophanes and Ephorus).

ἄλλους ποταμούς, ἀλλὰ›[233] τοῦ Ἀχελῴου τὴν ἰδίαν ἐπωνυμίαν ἐπὶ τὸ κοινὸν μεταφέροντας. 7. τὸ μὲν γὰρ ὕδωρ ὅλως, ὅπερ ἐστὶν κοινὸν ὄνομα, ἀπὸ τῆς ἰδίας ἐκείνου προσηγορίας Ἀχελῷον καλοῦμεν, τῶν δὲ ἄλλων ὀνομάτων τὰ κοινὰ πολλάκις ἀντὶ τῶν ἰδίων ὀνομάζομεν τοὺς μὲν Ἀθηναίους Ἕλληνας, τοὺς δὲ Λακεδαιμονίους Πελοποννησίους ἀποκαλοῦντες. τούτου δὲ τοῦ ἀπορήματος οὐδὲν ἔχομεν αἰτιώτατον εἰπεῖν ἢ τοὺς ἐκ Δωδώνης χρησμούς· 8. σχεδὸν γὰρ ἐν ἅπασιν αὐτοῖς προστάττειν ὁ θεὸς εἴωθεν Ἀχελῴῳ θύειν, ὥστε πολλοὶ νομίζοντες οὐ τὸν ποταμὸν τὸν διὰ τῆς Ἀκαρνανίας ῥέοντα, ἀλλὰ τὸ σύνολον ὕδωρ Ἀχελῷον ὑπὸ τοῦ χρησμοῦ καλεῖσθαι, μιμοῦνται τὰς τοῦ θεοῦ προσηγορίας. σημεῖον δὲ ὅτι πρὸς τὸ θεῖον ἀναφέροντες οὕτω λέγειν εἰώθαμεν· μάλιστα γὰρ τὸ ὕδωρ Ἀχελῷον προσαγορεύομεν ἐν τοῖς ὅρκοις καὶ ἐν ταῖς εὐχαῖς καὶ ἐν ταῖς θυσίαις, ἅπερ πάντα περὶ τοὺς θεούς.

9. potestne lucidius ostendi Acheloum a Graecis veteribus pro quacumque aqua dici solitum? unde doctissime Vergilius ait vinum Acheloo Liberum patrem miscuisse. ad quam rem etsi satis testium est, cum Aristophanis comici et Ephori historici verba prodiderimus, tamen ultra progrediemur. Didymus enim grammaticorum omnium facile

233 *post* ἰδίων *lacunam stat.*, ὀνομάζοντες [sic]. . . ἀλλὰ *exempli gratia coniec. Jacoby*

whereas they adopt the Akheloös' proper name as the common term. 7. For we generally call "water" (as the common term has it) "Akheloös," from the river's proper name, whereas in the case of other names we often use the common terms in place of the proper, for example calling Athenians "Hellenes" or Spartans "Peloponnesians." As the best explanation of this puzzle I can offer only the oracles from Dodona. 8. For in nearly all his pronouncements the god was accustomed to enjoin sacrifice to Akheloös, with the result that many people came to believe that by "Akheloös" the oracle meant, not the river that flows through Akarnania,[73] but "water" *tout court*, and so they imitate the terms of address used by the god. As a token of this, there's the fact that we usually speak that way in referring to the divine: for we call water "Akheloös" above all in oaths and in prayers and in sacrifices, all the things that concern the gods.

9. Can there be any clearer demonstration that the ancient Greeks were in the habit of using "Acheloüs" to refer to water of any sort? That's how Virgil came to make the very learned statement that father Liber mixed wine with Acheloüs. And though I think that in quoting the comic poet Aristophanes and the historian Ephorus I've given enough testimony on this point, we will nonetheless go a step further. For Didymus—easily the most learned of

[73] Acarnania lay on the Ionian Sea in NW Greece: the Acheloüs marked the boundary with Aetolia to the east, the Ambracian Gulf the boundary with Epirus on the north.

eruditissimus, posita causa quam superius Ephorus dixit, alteram quoque adiecit his verbis:

10. *ἄμεινον δὲ ἐκεῖνο λέγειν ὅτι διὰ τὸ πάντων τῶν ποταμῶν πρεσβύτατον εἶναι Ἀχελῷον τιμὴν ἀπονέμοντας αὐτῷ τοὺς ἀνθρώπους πάντα ἁπλῶς τὰ νάματα τῷ ἐκείνου ὀνόματι προσαγορεύειν. ὁ γοῦν Ἀγησίλαος*[234] *διὰ τῆς πρώτης ἱστορίας δεδήλωκεν ὅτι Ἀχελῷος πάντων τῶν ποταμῶν πρεσβύτατος. ἔφη γαρ· Ὠκεανὸς δὲ γαμεῖ Τηθὺν ἑαυτοῦ ἀδελφήν, τῶν δὲ γίνονται τρισχίλιοι ποταμοί, Ἀχελῷος δὲ αὐτῶν πρεσβύτατος καὶ τετίμηται μάλιστα.*

11. licet abunde ista sufficiant ad probationem moris antiqui, quo ita loquendi usus fuit ut Achelous commune omnis aquae nomen haberetur, tamen his quoque etiam Euripidis nobilissimi tragoediarum scriptoris addetur auctoritas, quam idem Didymus grammaticus in his libris quos *τραγῳδουμένης λέξεως* scripsit posuit his verbis: 12. *Ἀχελῷον πᾶν ὕδωρ Εὐριπίδης φησὶν ἐν Ὑψιπύλῃ. λέγων γὰρ περὶ ὕδατος ὄντος σφόδρα πόρρω τῆς Ἀκαρνανίας, ἐν ᾗ ἐστιν ὁ ποταμὸς Ἀχελῷος, φησὶν:*

*δείξω μὲν Ἀργείοισιν Ἀχελῴου ῥόον.*

13. 'Sunt in libro septimo illi versus quibus Hernici po-

[234] Ἀγησίλαος] Ἀκουσίλαος *ed. Lugd. Bat. 1670*

all grammarians—cited the explanation given by Ephorus above and added a second, as follows (*Tragic Diction* fr. 2):

> 10. Better to say that humankind honors Akheloös for being the oldest of all rivers by addressing simply all rivers with his name; Agêsilaos,[74] at any rate, in Book 1 of his History, makes it plain that the Akheloös is the oldest river, saying, "Ôkean wed his own sister, Têthys, and from them were born 3,000 rivers, with Akheloös oldest among them and much the most honored.

11. Though all that is more than enough to establish the customary ancient turn of phrase whereby "Acheloüs" was treated as a common term for "water" in general, let the following verse of Euripides, the most noble tragic poet, add still further authority, as the same Didymus cites it, in his books on *Tragic Diction*, in these words (ibid.): 12. "Euripides, in his *Hypsipylê, uses 'Akheloös' to mean water of every sort: for in speaking about water located quite far from Akarnania, home of the river Akheloös, he says (fr. 753 TGrF* 5,1:758):

> I shall show the Argives Akheloös' stream.[75]

> 13. 'The following lines are found in Book 7, where the

[74] Didymus surely cited Acusilaus of Argos (= no. 2 fr. 1 *FGrH* = fr. 1 *EGM*), not "Agesilaos" (a common confusion): I assume with past editors that the error was made by M. (or his source), not his scribes.

[75] Cf. also Hesych. A.8841, Σ Vet. *Il.* 21.194, 24.616b, Σ Eur. *Andromache* 167, Σ Aesch. *Persians* 869, Eustath. *Comm. Il.* 1:553.16–19, 793:4–6, 3:491.21–23, 4:484.12–14, *Etym. Mag.* p. 181.10–15.

puli et eorum nobilissima,[235] ut tunc erat, civitas Anagnia enumerantur:

> . . . quos dives Anagnia pascit,[236]
> quos Amasene pater: non illis omnibus arma
> nec clipei currusve sonant, pars maxima glandis
> liventis plumbi spargit, pars spicula gestat
> bina manu fulvosque lupi de pelle galeros
> tegmen habent capiti, vestigia nuda sinistri
> instituere pedis, crudus tegit altera pero.

14. hunc morem in Italia fuisse ut uno pede calceato, altero nudo iretur ad bellum, nusquam adhuc quod sciam repperi; sed eam Graecorum non nullis consuetudinem fuisse locupleti auctore iam palam faciam. 15. in qua quidem re mirari est poetae huius occultissimam diligentiam. qui cum legisset Hernicos, quorum est Anagnia, a Pelasgis oriundos, appellatosque ita a quodam Pelasgo duce suo, qui Hernicus nominabatur, morem quem de Aetolia legerat Hernicis adsignavit, qui sunt vetus colonia Pelasgorum. 16. et Hernicum quidem hominem Pelasgum ducem Hernicis fuisse Iulius Hyginus in libro secundo urbium non paucis verbis probat. morem vero Aetolis fuisse uno tantum modo pede calceato in bellum ire ostendit clarissimus scriptor Euripides tragicus, in cuius tragoedia quae Meleager inscribitur nuntius inducitur describens quo quisque habitu fuerit ex ducibus qui ad aprum capiendum convenerant. in eo hi versus sunt:

235 nobilissima G: -mi ω

236 pascit (*codd. fere omnes Verg., Tib., edd. nonnull.*)] pascis *cod.* V *Verg., Serv. ad 7.685, edd. nonnull.*

---

76 The story of Meleager and the Calydonian boar, sent by

Hernici and Anagnia, their best known city (as it was then), are listed in the catalogue (*A.* 7.684–90):

> . . . those whom rich Anagnia sustains,
> or you, father Amasenus: none has arms that clash
> and clatter, no shields or chariots, but most spray shot
> of dull dark lead, some carry light spears,
> two in each hand; tawny caps of wolf's hide
> cover their heads, they plant the tracks
> of their left feet unshod, a rawhide boot covers the right.

14. So far as I know, it is nowhere attested that there was in Italy the custom of going to war with one foot shod, the other bare; but I shall now adduce abundant authority to show that some Greeks had this custom. 15. Here indeed we can marvel at the care the poet took while making no display of it at all: having read that the Hernici, whose city is Anagnia, were Pelasgians by origin and derived their name from a certain Pelasgian king named Hernicus, he attributed to the Hernici, who were an ancient colony of the Pelasgi, a custom that he had read about in connection with Aetolia. 16. Julius Hyginus, in Book 2 of his *Cities*, demonstrates at length that a certain Pelasgian named Hernicus was the leader of the Hernici (fr. 8 *HRR* 2;74 = fr. 13 *GRF* 1:533–34). That it was the Aetolians' custom to go to war with only one foot shod is shown by Euripides, the most brilliant of tragic poets, in his tragedy *Meleager*, when a messenger enters to describe the dress of each of the leaders who had assembled to capture the boar.[76] Here are the lines (fr. 530 *TGrF* 5,1:563):

Artemis to plague the land after she was slighted in cult by Meleager's father, is first told at *Il.* 9.529ff.

17. Τελαμὼν δὲ χρυσοῦν αἰετὸν πέλτης ἔπι,
πρόβλημα θηρός, βότρυσι δ' ἔστεψεν κάρα,
Σαλαμῖνα κοσμῶν πατρίδα τὴν εὐάμπελον.
Κύπριδος δὲ μίσημ', Ἀρκὰς Ἀταλάντη, κύνας
καὶ τόξ' ἔχουσα, πελέκεως δὲ δίστομον
γένυν ἔπαλλ' Ἀγκαῖος.[237] οἱ δὲ Θεστίου
παῖδες τὸ λαιὸν ἴχνος ἀνάρβυλοι ποδός,
τὸ δ' ἐν πεδίλοις, ὡς ἐλαφρίζον γόνυ
ἔχοιεν, ὃς δὴ πᾶσιν Αἰτωλοῖς νόμος.

18. animadvertitis diligentissime verba Euripidis a Marone servata? ait enim ille:

. . . τὸ λαιὸν ἴχνος ἀνάρβυλοι ποδός,

et eundem pedem nudum Vergilius quoque dixit:

vestigia nuda sinistri instituere pedis.

19. in qua quidem re quo vobis studium nostrorum magis comprobetur, non reticebimus rem paucissimis notam, reprehensum Euripiden ab Aristotele, qui ignorantiam istud Euripidis fuisse contendit, Aetolos enim non laevum pedem nudum habere sed dextrum. quod ne adfirmem potius quam probem, ipsa Aristotelis verba ponam ex libro quem de poetis secundum scripsit,[238] in quo de Euripide loquens sic ait:

20. τοὺς δὲ Θεστίου κόρους τὸν μὲν ἀριστερὸν

[237] Ἀγκαῖος *Schneidewin*: ΑΚΤΑΙΟϹ α

[238] secundum scripsit *Eyssenhardt*: secundo subscripsit α, secundo supra scripsit $\beta_2$

17. Telamôn had a golden eagle on his shield,
a defense against the beast, grape clusters crowned
his head to honor Salamis, his home, land rich in
vines.
Arcadian Atalantê, whom the Cyprian goddess hates,
had hounds and bow, while Ankaios brandished
an axe's two-edged bite. The children of Thestios
had the left foot's track unshod,
the other sandaled, that they might keep
their step unfettered, the custom all Aetolians keep.

18. Do you see how carefully Maro followed Euripides' wording? The latter says,

. . . had the left foot's track unshod,

and Virgil too said that the left foot is bare:

. . . they plant the tracks
of their left feet unshod.

19. To show you more plainly still how attentive he was to Greek practice in this matter, I will tell you something that very few know: Euripides was criticized by Aristotle, who claimed that Euripides statement, quoted above, was uninformed, since the Aetolians have their right foot bare, not their left. To demonstrate this, and not merely assert it, I shall quote Aristotle's exact words, from Book 2 of his *On Poets*, where he says, with reference to Euripides (fr. 74 Rose):

20. Euripides claims that the sons of Thestios ad-

πόδα φησὶν Εὐριπίδης ἐλθεῖν ἔχοντας ἀνυπόδετον· λέγει γοῦν ὅτι[239]

> . . . τὸ λαιὸν ἴχνος ἦσαν[240] ἀνάρβυλοι ποδός,
> τὸ δ' ἐν πεδίλοις, ὡς ἐλαφρίζον γόνυ
> ἔχοιεν,

ὡς δὴ πᾶν τοὐναντίον ἔθος τοῖς Αἰτωλοῖς· τὸν μὲν γὰρ ἀριστερὸν ὑποδέδενται, τὸν δὲ δεξιὸν ἀνυποδετοῦσιν. δεῖ γὰρ οἶμαι τὸν ἡγούμενον ἔχειν ἐλαφρόν, ἀλλ' οὐ τὸν ἐμμένοντα.

21. cum haec ita sint, videtis tamen Vergilium Euripide auctore quam Aristotele uti maluisse, nam ut haec ignoraverit vir tam anxie doctus minime crediderim. iure autem praetulit Euripiden: est enim ingens ei cum Graecarum tragoediarum scriptoribus familiaritas, quod vel ex praecedentibus licet vel ex his quae mox dicentur opinari.

19 'In libro quarto in describenda Elissae morte ait quod ei crinis abscisus esset his versibus:

> nondum illi flavum Proserpina vertice crinem
> abstulerat Stygioque caput damnaverat Orco.

deinde Iris a Iunone missa abscidit ei crinem et ad Orcum refert. 2. hanc Vergilius non de nihilo fabulam fingit, sicut vir alias doctissimus Cornutus existimat, qui adnotationem eius modi adposuit his versibus: "unde haec[241] historia ut crinis auferendus sit morientibus, ignoratur: sed adsuevit poetico more aliqua fingere ut de aureo ramo." haec Cor-

239 λέγει γοῦν ὅτι *secl. Eyss.*
240 ἦσαν *ab Arist. addit.* (*cf.* §*17*), *si quidem verum*
241 haec A: hac *ω*

vance with their left feet unshod. Here is what he says:

> . . . went with the left foot's track unshod,
> the other sandaled, that they might keep
> their step unfettered,

when in fact the Aetolian's custom is just the opposite: their left foot is shod, the right unshod, for the lead foot (I believe) should be unfettered, not the one that's planted.[77]

21. For all that, you still see that Virgil preferred to follow Euripides' authority, not Aristotle's—for I can scarcely believe that a man of such finicky learning was unaware of all this. And he was right to prefer Euripides. That he had a vast knowledge of the Greek tragedians can be inferred either from what I've just said or from what I'm about to say.

'When describing Dido's death in Book 4, he says in 19
these lines that a lock of her hair was cut off (*A.* 4.698–99):

> Proserpina had not yet stolen away the golden lock
> from her crown and consigned her life to Stygian
> Orcus.

Then Iris is dispatched by Juno, cuts off the lock, and brings it to Orcus. 2. Virgil did not just make this story up, as that otherwise deeply learned man Cornutus supposes in commenting on these lines (fr. 29 *GRF* 2:200–1): "No one knows the source of the story that a lock of hair must be taken from those on the point of death; but he was accustomed to making some things up, as poets do, for exam-

[77] Cf. Serv. on *A.* 7.689.

nutus. 3. sed me pudet quod tantus vir, Graecarum etiam doctissimus litterarum, ignoravit Euripidis nobilissimam fabulam Alcestim. 4. in hac enim fabula in scaenam Orcus inducitur gladium gestans quo crinem abscidat Alcestidis et sic loquitur:

*ἡ δ' οὖν γυνὴ κάτεισιν εἰς Ἅιδου δόμους.*
*στείχω δ' ἐπ' αὐτήν, ὡς κατάρξωμαι ξίφει·*
*ἱερὸς γὰρ οὗτος τῷ κατὰ χθονὸς θεῷ*[242]
*ὅτῳ*[243] *τόδ' ἔγχος κρατὸς ἁγνίσῃ τρίχα.*

5. proditum est, ut opinor, quem secutus Vergilius fabulam abscidendi crinis induxerit. *ἁγνίσαι* autem Graeci dicunt dis consecrare, unde poeta vester ait ex Iridis persona,

. . . hunc ego Diti
sacrum iussa fero teque isto corpore solvo.

6. 'Nunc quia pleraque omnia quae supra dixi instructa auctoritate tragicorum probavi, id quoque quod a Sophocle tractum est adnotabo. 7. in libro enim quarto Vergilius Elissam facit, postquam ab Aenea relinquitur, velut ad sacricolarum sagarumque carmina et devotiones confugientem et inter cetera ait sedandi amoris gratia herbas quaesitas quae aëneis falcibus secarentur. 8. haec res nonne quaestione digna est, unde Vergilio aëneae falces in mentem venerint? ponam itaque Vergilianos versus mox et inde[244] Sophoclis quos Maro aemulatus est:

242 *τῷ κ. χ. θεῷ*] *τῶν κ. χ. θεῶν Eur.*
243 *ὅτῳ*] *ὅτου Eur.*
244 mox et inde] exinde et *Eyss.*

ple in the case of the golden bough." 3. But I'm deeply embarrassed that such a great man, and one with a scholar's deep knowledge of Greek literature, did not know Euripides' very famous play, *Alcestis*.[78] 4. In this play Orcus enters holding a sword to cut off Alcestis' lock, and he says (73–76):

> This woman, then, will go down to Hades' house.
> I come to her, to dedicate her with my sword:
> whoever has a hair of his head consecrated by this
> sword
> is set apart for the god who dwells below the earth.

5. I trust this makes it clear whom Virgil followed when he introduced this story of the severed lock. The Greeks use the verb *hagnisai* to mean "consecrate to the gods," and that is why your poet says, about the character Iris (*A.* 4.702–3),

> . . . I bear this sacred offering
> to Dis, as I was bid, and release you from your body.

6. 'Now, since nearly everything I've said to this point has been informed by the tragedians' authority, I'll also draw attention to what he borrowed from Sophocles. 7. After Aeneas abandons Dido in Book 4, Virgil has her take refuge, as it were, in the spells and curses of witches and the sort of folk who lurk about altars, and in the course of her remarks she says that she's sought out herbs to calm her passion, cut with a bronze blade. 8. Don't you think it's worth asking how Virgil came to think of blades made of bronze? I'll quote Virgil's lines first, then the lines of Sophocles that Maro imitated (*A.* 4.513–14):

[78] Cf. Serv. on *A.* 3.46, 4.694, DServ. on *A.* 4.703.

9. falcibus et messae ad lunam quaeruntur aënis
pubentes herbae nigri cum lacte veneni.

Sophoclis autem tragoedia id de quo quaerimus etiam titulo praefert: inscribitur enim Ῥιζοτόμοι. in qua Medeam describit maleficas herbas secantem, sed aversam, ne vi noxii odoris ipsa interficeretur, et sucum quidem herbarum in cados aeneos refundentem, ipsas autem herbas aëneis falcibus exsecantem. 10. Sophoclis versus hi sunt:

ἡ δ' ἐξοπίσω χερὸς ὄμμα τρέπουσ'[245]
ὀπὸν ἀργινεφῆ στάζοντα τομῆς
χαλκέοισι κάδοις δέχεται . . .

et paulo post:

. . . αἱ δὲ καλυπταὶ
κίσται ῥιζῶν κρύπτουσιν[246] τομάς,
ἃς ἥδε βοῶσα ἀλαλαζομένη
γυμνὴ χαλκέοις ἤμα δρεπάνοις.

11. haec Sophocles, quo auctore sine dubio Vergilius protulit aëneas falces. omnino autem ad rem divinam pleraque aënea adhiberi solita, multa indicio sunt, et in his maxime sacris quibus delinire aliquos aut devovere aut denique exigere morbos volebant. 12. taceo illud[247] Plautinum cum ait:

245 τρέπουσα *plene scriptum a nostro; similiter* βοῶσα, 5.21.6 τινα, 5.21.13 ἀναψυκτῆρα, 7.15.22 πνεύμονα.
246 κρύπτουσιν (*contra metrum*)] κρύπτουσι *edd. Soph.*
247 illud PG: illum N$\beta_2$

9. I've sought out, too, herbs full of sap; bronze
   blades cut
them down by moonlight, juicy with black poison.

Sophocles' tragedy even has in its title the subject of our inquiry: for it's called *Herbalists*. In this play he describes Medea cutting poisonous herbs with head averted, lest she herself be killed by the force of their noxious odor: she pours the herbs' juice into bronze casks and cuts the herbs themselves with bronze blades. 10. These are Sophocles' lines (fr. 534 *TGrF* 4:410):

Keeping her gaze averted behind her hand,
she receives in bronze casks the cloudy white juice
that drips from the cutting . . .

and a little after that:

. . . These covered
baskets hide the roots' cuttings,
which she reaped with a bronze blade,
with a cry and a shout, naked.

11. So Sophocles, whom Virgil doubtless took as his model in producing the bronze blades. Now there are plenty of indications that bronze implements are generally used for sacrifice, and above all in sacrifices that aim either to soothe people, or curse them, or (finally) heal them of illnesses. 12. I say nothing of that line where Plautus says (*fab. inc.* 60 Goetz):

me<di>cum[248] habet patagus[249] morbus aes,

et quod alibi Vergilius,

Curetum sonitus crepitantiaque aera,

13. sed Carminii, <viri>[250] curiosissimi et docti, verba ponam, qui in libro de Italia secundo sic ait: "prius itaque et Tuscos aëneo vomere uti cum conderentur urbes solitos in Tageticis[251] eorum sacris invenio et in Sabinis ex aere[252] cultros quibus sacerdotes tonderentur." 14. post haec Carminii verba longum fiat si velim percensere quam multis in locis Graecorum vetustissimi aeris sonos tamquam rem validissimam adhibere soliti sunt. sed praesenti operi docuisse nos sufficit falces aëneas Maronis exemplo Graeci auctoris inductas.

15. 'In libro nono Vergilius posuit hos versus:

stabat in egregiis Arcentis filius armis
pictus acu chlamydem et ferrugine clarus Hibera,
insignis facie, genitor quem miserat Arcens
eductum matris luco Symaethia circum
flumina, pinguis ubi et placabilis ara Palici.

248 medicum *Bücheler*: mecum ω
249 patagus *Canter* (pet- A): p(a)eagus ω
250 viri *suppl. Willis*
251 Tageticis S: taiet- ω
252 aere AC[2]: ea re ω

---

79 Plautus' *patagus* = Gk. *patagos*, which denotes a range of harsh sounds, including the clatter of arms, the crash of thunder, and the rumbling of flatulence (*LSJ*[9] s.v.).

80 Cf. Tages fr. 14.

81 In Etruscan myth, a child endowed with divine wisdom who

The disease of flatulence[79] is healed by bronze,

and what Virgil elsewhere says (*G.* 4.151),

the Curetes' cries and clattering bronze,

13. but I will quote the words of Carminius, a most careful and learned man, who in Book 2 of his *Italy* says:[80] "Thus I find that previously both the Etruscans used to use a bronze ploughshare in their rites of Tages,[81] when they were founding cities, and among the Sabines priests had their hair clipped with bronze blades." 14. After this quotation from Carminius I would be drawing things out too long should I choose to review all the places in which the most ancient among the Greeks used to use the sound of bronze as a very effective device. For the present purpose it's enough to have shown that Maro's bronze blades are based upon a Greek model.

15. 'In Book 9 Virgil wrote (*A.* 9.581*†–85):[82]

Arcens' son was standing firm, conspicuous in his arms,
with an embroidered cape of brilliant Spanish russet,
a man of signal beauty sent by his father Arcens
after he'd been raised in his mother's grove near Symaethus'
stream, where stands Palicus' rich altar that brings conciliation.

revealed the practices of divination: Cic. *On Divination* 2.50–51, Fest. p. 492.6–8, Lucan 1.635–37, Serv. on *A.* 2.781, Mart. Cap. 2.157.

[82] With the account in (D)Serv. ad loc. cf. Lact. Plac. on Statius *Theb.* 12.156–57.

16. quis hic Palicus deus vel potius qui di Palici—nam duo sunt—apud nullum penitus auctorem Latinum quod sciam repperi, sed de Graecorum penitissimis litteris hanc historiam eruit Maro. 17. nam primum ut Symaethus fluvius, cuius in his versibus meminit, in Sicilia est, ita et di Palici in Sicilia coluntur, quos primus omnium Aeschylus tragicus, vir utique Siculus, in litteras dedit, interpretationem quoque nominis eorum, quam Graeci *ἐτυμολογίαν* vocant, expressit versibus suis. sed priusquam versus Aeschyli ponam, paucis explananda est historia Palicorum.

18. 'In Sicilia Symaethus fluvius est. iuxta hunc nympha Thalia compressu Iovis gravida metu Iunonis optavit ut sibi terra dehisceret. factum est. sed ubi venit tempus maturitatis infantum quos alvo illa gestaverat, reclusa terra est, et duo infantes de alvo Thaliae progressi emerserunt appellatique sunt Palici *ἀπὸ τοῦ πάλιν ἱκέσθαι*, quoniam prius in terram mersi denuo inde reversi sunt. 19. nec longe inde lacus breves sunt sed in immensum profundi, aquarum scaturrigine semper ebullientes, quos incolae crateras vocant et nomine Dellos appellant fratresque eos Palicorum aestimant, et habentur in cultu maximo praecipueque circa exigendum iuxta eos ius iurandum praesens et efficax numen ostenditur. 20. nam cum furti negati vel cuiuscemodi rei fides quaeritur, et ius iurandum a suspecto

83 Some of the lore that M. is about to recount was evidently known to Ovid (*Met*. 5.405–6, *Pont*. 2.10.25) and Silius Italicus (14.219–20), independently of Virgil.

84 Aeschylus died in Sicily (456/455 BCE) but was born in Attica (ca. 525 BCE).

85 The relation between §§18–22 and §§24–30 is curious: the etymology in §18 anticipates Aeschylus quoted in §24, §19 antici-

16. So far as I know, absolutely no Latin author attests who this god Palicus is, or rather the gods Palici (for there are two), but Maro unearthed this lore from the most recondite Greek sources.[83] 17. First of all, just as the river Symaethus mentioned in this passage is in Sicily, so too the gods Palici are worshipped in Sicily and are first attested in the work of the tragedian Aeschylus—who was of course a Sicilian[84]—in lines that also provide an explanation of their name, what the Greeks call an "etymology." But before I quote Aeschylus' lines, I should briefly set out the history of the Palici.[85]

18. 'On the banks of the river Symaethus in Sicily the nymph Thalia was impregnated by Jupiter and then, out of fear of Juno, prayed that the earth would open up to receive her. And it did. But when the infants that she had carried in her womb came to term, the earth opened up again, and the two babies who came forth from Thalia's womb were named the Palici, from "coming back again" (*palin hikesthai*), seeing that they were first buried in the earth and then came back out again. 19. Not far from that spot are pools that are not far across but immeasurably deep, their boiling surface always bubbling. The inhabitants refer to them as the "Mixing Bowls"[86] and give them the name "Delli," taking them to be the brothers of the Palici: they are a very important cult center, where the divine power is shown to be especially effective in enforcing oaths in their presence. 20. For when a person's credibility is being tested—in the case of a theft that has been denied,

pates Callias in §25, and §§20–22 essentially paraphrase Polemon and Xenagoras quoted in §§26–30; yet not all the details found in §§18–22 reappear in the sources subsequently quoted.

[86] Gk. *krâtêr* > Engl. "crater."

petitur, uterque ab omni contagione mundi ad crateras accedunt, accepto prius fideiussore a persona quae iuratura est de solvendo eo quod peteretur, si addixisset eventus. 21. illic[253] invocato loci numine testatum faciebat esse iurator de quo iuraret. quod si fideliter faceret discedebat inlaesus, si vero subesset iuri iurando mala conscientia, mox in lacu amittebat vitam falsus iurator. haec res ita religionem fratrum commendabat ut crateres quidem implacabiles, Palici autem placabiles vocarentur. 22. nec sine divinatione est Palicorum templum. nam cum Siciliam sterilis annus arefecisset, divino Palicorum responso admoniti Siculi heroi cuidam certum sacrificium celebraverunt, et revertit ubertas. qua gratia Siculi omne genus frugum congesserunt in aram Palicorum, ex qua ubertate ara ipsa pinguis vocata est.

23. 'Haec est omnis historia quae de Palicis eorumque fratribus in Graecis tantum modo litteris invenitur, quas Maro non minus quam Latinas hausit. sed haec quae diximus auctoritatibus adprobanda sunt. 24. Aeschyli tragoedia est quae inscribitur Aetna. in hac cum de Palicis loqueretur, sic ait:

— *τί δῆτ' ἐπ' αὐτοῖς ὄνομα θήσονται βροτοί;*
— *σεμνοὺς Παλικοὺς Ζεὺς ἐφίεται καλεῖν.*
— *ἦ καὶ Παλικῶν εὐλόγως μένει φάτις;*

253 illic *ed. Ven. 1513*: ille *ω*

---

87 Actually, *Women of Aetna*, written to celebrate the city's founding by Hieron of Syracuse in 461 BCE.

or anything of that sort—and the suspect is asked to swear an oath, both parties approach the Mixing Bowls in a state of ritual purity, after the party who is going to swear the oath has provided a surety to see that the claim will be paid should the outcome find him liable. 21. After the divinity of the site has been invoked, the party swearing the oath testifies to the matter that the oath concerns: if he has acted in good faith, he departs unharmed, but if the oath rests upon bad faith, the perjurer soon loses his life in the pool. This fact so confirmed the religious awe attaching to the brothers that the Mixing Bowls came to be called "those beyond conciliation," the Palici "those easily reconciled." 22. The precinct of the Palici is also used for divination: when a barren year had left Sicily parched, the inhabitants were advised by an oracle of the Palici to offer a specific sacrifice to a certain hero, and when they did, the island's fertility returned. In thanks, the Sicilians heaped every sort of produce on the altar of the Palici, which came to be called the "rich altar" because of that abundance.

23. 'This is the whole account of the Palici and their brothers that is found—exclusively—in Greek sources, which Maro exhausted no less than he did Latin sources. But the account I've given must now be corroborated from authoritative sources. 24. There is a tragedy by Aechylus called *Aetna*,[87] in which he speaks about the Palici in these terms (fr. 6 *TGrF* 3:127–28):

— What, then, is the name that mortals shall give them?
— Zeus bids us to call them the awesome Palikoi.
— And does the name of the Palikoi abide for a sound reason?

— *πάλιν γὰρ ἵκουσ'*[254] *ἐκ σκότους τόδ' εἰς φάος.*

haec Aeschylus. 25. Callias autem in septima historia de rebus Siculis ita scribit:[255] *ἡ δὲ Ἐρύκη τῆς μὲν Γελῴας ὅσον ἐνενήκοντα στάδια διέστηκεν, ἐπιεικῶς δὲ ἐχυρός*[256] *ἐστιν ὁ τόπος καὶ * * **[257] *τὸ παλαιὸν*[258] *Σικελῶν γεγενημένη πόλις· ὑφ' ᾗ καὶ τοὺς Δέλλους καλουμένους εἶναι συμβέβηκεν. οὗτοι δὲ κρατῆρες δύο εἰσὶν οὓς ἀδελφοὺς τῶν Παλικῶν οἱ Σικελιῶται νομίζουσιν, τὰς δὲ ἀναφορὰς τῶν πομφολύγων παραπλησίας βραζούσαις ἔχουσιν.* hactenus Callias. 26. Polemon vero in libro qui inscribitur *Περὶ τῶν ἐν Σικελίᾳ θαυμαζομένων ποταμῶν* sic ait:

> *οἱ δὲ Παλικοὶ προσαγορευόμενοι παρὰ τοῖς ἐγχωρίοις αὐτόχθονες θεοὶ νομίζονται. ὑπάρχουσιν δὲ τούτοις*[259] *ἀδελφοὶ κρατῆρες χαμαίζηλοι. προσιέναι δὲ ἁγιστεύοντας χρὴ πρὸς αὐτοὺς ἀπό τε παντὸς ἄγους καὶ συνουσίας, ἔτι δὲ καί τινων ἐδεσμάτων.* 27. *φέρεται δὲ ἀπ' αὐτῶν ὀσμὴ βαρεῖα θείου καὶ τοῖς πλησίον ἱσταμένοις καρηβάρησιν ἐμποιοῦσα δεινήν. τὸ δὲ ὕδωρ ἐστὶ θολερὸν αὐτῶν καὶ τὴν χρόαν ὁμοιότατον χαλαιρύπῳ*[260] *λευκῷ· φέρεται δὲ κολπούμενόν τε καὶ παφλάζον, οἷαί εἰσιν αἱ δῖναι τῶν ζεόντων ἀναβολάδην ὑδάτων. φασὶν δ' εἶναι καὶ τὸ βάθος ἀπέραντον τῶν κρατήρων τούτων, ὥστε καὶ βοῦς εἰσπεσόντας ἠφανίσθαι καὶ ζεῦγος ὀρικὸν ἐλαυνόμενον, ἔτι δὲ*

[254] *ἵκουσ'* *ed. Basil. 1535*: HK- *α*

— Yes: they come back [*palin hikousi*] from darkness into the light.

So Aeschylus. 25. Callias, however, in Book 7 of his *History of Sicily* writes (no. 564 fr. 1 *FGrH*): "Erykê is as much as ninety stades from Gela; the location is tolerably secure and . . . long ago was a city of the Sicilians. At its base, it happens, are the so-called Delloi, two craters that the Sicilians regard as the brothers of the Palikoi: from them a bubbling arises that resembles boiling water." So Callias. 26. But Polemon, in his book titled *On the Miraculous Rivers of Sicily*, says (fr. 83 *FHG* 3:140–41):

> The so-called Palikoi are believed by the inhabitants to be gods native to the region. They have as brothers craters sunk in the ground: those who approach them must be free of pollution and abstain from sexual intercourse, and also from certain foods. 27. The heavy odor of brimstone rises from them and produces a strange drowsiness in bystanders; their water is foul, with a color very like white soapsuds, and rises in frothing waves, like the swirling and bubbling of water on a high boil. They say that these craters are unfathomably deep, so that cattle that fall into them and a mule-team driven into them disappear, as do grazing mares that jump in them.

---

255 *Graec. litt. in §§25–30 perquam corrupt. habet* α

256 ἐχυρός *Schneidewin*: -ΤΟϹ α 257 *post* καὶ *lacunam statuit Eyss.*, ἡ Παλικὴ *suppl. Schneidewin*

258 παλαιὸν] παλικόν *Valckenaer* 259 τούτοις *Willis dubitanter*: -των α, τοὺτων δύο *G. Hermann, alii alia*

260 χαλαιρύπῳ *Jan*: ΧΑΜΑΙΡΥΠΩ α

*φορβάδας ἐναλλομένας.* 28. *ὅρκος δέ ἐστι τοῖς Σικελιώταις μέγιστος καθηραμένων τῶν προκληθέντων· οἱ δὲ ὁρκωταὶ γραμματεῖον*[261] *ἔχοντες ἀγορεύουσιν τοῖς ὁρκουμένοις περὶ ὧν ἂν χρῄζωσιν τοὺς ὅρκους· ὁ δὲ ὁρκούμενος θαλλὸν κραδαίνων, ἐστεμμένος, ἄζωστος καὶ μονοχίτων, ἐφαπτόμενος τοῦ κρατῆρος, ἐξ ὑποβολῆς δίεισιν τὸν ὅρκον.* 29. *καὶ ἂν μὲν ἐμπεδώσῃ τοὺς ῥηθέντας ὅρκους, ἀσινὴς ἄπεισιν οἴκαδε· παραβάτης δὲ γενόμενος τῶν θεῶν ἐμποδὼν τελευτᾷ. τούτων δὲ γινομένων ἐγγυητὰς ὑπισχνοῦνται καταστήσειν τοῖς ἱερεῦσιν, ἐπὴν νεαρόν τι*[262] *γένηται, κάθαρσιν ὀφλισκάνουσιν τοῦ τεμένους. περὶ δὲ τὸν τόπον τοῦτον ᾤκησαν Παλικηνοὶ πόλιν ἐπώνυμον τούτων τῶν δαιμόνων Παλικήν.*

haec Polemon. 30. sed et Xenagoras in tertia historia sua de loci divinatione ita scribit: *καὶ οἱ Σικελοὶ τῆς γῆς ἀφορούσης ἔθυσαν Πεδιοκράτει*[263] *τινὶ ἥρωι, προστάξαντος αὐτοῖς τοῦ ἐκ Παλικῶν χρηστηρίου, καὶ μετὰ τὴν ἐπάνοδον τῆς εὐφορίας πολλοῖς δώροις τὸν βωμὸν τῶν Παλικῶν ἐνέπλησαν.* 31. absoluta est, aestimo, et auctoribus idoneis adserta explanatio Vergiliani loci, quem litteratores vestri nec obscurum putant, contenti vel ipsi

261 *γραμματεῖον*] –ΤΙΟΝ *α*

262 *ἐπὴν νεαρόν τι*] *ἐπὴν ἐπάρατον Jan, ἐπὴν δ' ἄρα τι G. Hermann, ἐάν τι νεαρὸν ed. Basil. 1535*

263 Πεδιοκράτει (ΠΕΔΕΙΟ- *α*)] Πεδια- *Diod. Sic. 4.23.5*

> 28. For the Sicilians the craters provide the most powerful oath, when opponents who have issued a challenge have been ritually purified. With a writing tablet in hand, the persons administering the oath address the parties to the oath about whatever matter it is for which the oath is being sought. Then one party to the oath, garlanded and waving a green bough, ungirt and wearing only a tunic, dips his hand in the crater and repeats the words of the oath after the person administering it. 29. Should he make good the oath taken, he departs for home unscathed; but if he is shown to have transgressed against the gods, he dies on the spot. In the course of the ritual the parties promise that they will provide bondsmen for the priests, who are liable for purifying the shrine should anything untoward happen.[88] Near this spot the Palikênoi founded the city Palikê, named after the gods.

So Polemon. 30. Xenagoras too, in Book 3 of his inquiry into the site's standing as an oracle, writes (no. 240 fr. 21 *FGrH*): "The Sicilians too, when their land was barren, sacrificed to a certain hero named Pediokratês at the direction of an oracle they received from the Palikoi, and after the land's fertility was restored they heaped the altar of the Palikoi with many gifts." 31. I think this should round off my interpretation of the Virgilian passage, complete with the support of suitable authorities, though your school-

[88] A euphemism, referring to the perjurer's death, which would cause pollution; for a similar account cf. [Arist.] *Marvels Heard* 57 834b.

scire vel insinuare discipulis Palicum dei esse cuiusdam nomen. quis[264] sit autem deus iste vel unde sic dictus tam nesciunt quam scire nolunt, quia nec ubi quaerant suspicantur, quasi Graecae lectionis expertes.

20 'Nec illos versus relinquemus intactos qui sunt in primo Georgicon:

> umida solstitia atque hiemes orate serenas,
> agricolae: hiberno laetissima pulvere farra,
> laetus ager. nullo tantum se Mysia cultu
> iactat et ipsa suas mirantur Gargara messes.

2. sensus hic cum videatur obscurior pauloque perplexius quam poetae huius mos est pronuntiatus, tum habet in se animadvertendam quaestionem ex Graeca antiquitate venientem, quae sint ista Gargara quae Vergilius esse voluit fertilitatis exemplar. 3. Gargara haec igitur sunt in Mysia, quae est Hellesponti provincia. sed significatio nominis et loci duplex est. nam et cacumen montis Idae et oppidum sub eodem monte hoc nomine vocantur. 4. Homerus significationem cacuminis ita ponit:

> Ἴδην δ' ἵκανεν πολυπίδακα, μητέρα θηρῶν,
> Γάργαρον.

264 quis $R^2$: quid *ω*

---

89 This could well be the authentic voice of M., who knew Greek exceptionally well at a time when education in Greek was in decline in the Latin-speaking parts of the empire; but for similar criticism of Roman grammarians, cf. Athen. 160C.

90 §§3–16: cf. DServ. on *G.* 1.102 (citing Serenus Sammonicus).

teachers do not even think the passage is difficult, being content themselves with the knowledge—which they pass along to their students—that Palicus is the name of some god. As to who the god is or how he got his name, their ignorance is as complete as their indifference, since they don't even know where to begin to look, being as good as Greek-less.[89]

'Nor will we fail to touch on the following lines from 20
Book 1 of the *Georgics* (100–3):

> Pray for damp solstices and calm winters,
> farmers: emmers grow best in the dust of winter,
> the fields are fertile. Mysia can make no such boast
> about its tillage nor Gargara itself so marvel at its
> harvests.

2. Not only is the meaning here rather obscure and the expression a bit more tangled than usual for this poet, but the passage involves a question derived from ancient Greece that deserves notice: what is that "Gargara itself" that Virgil held out as a model of fertility? 3. The Gargara in question is in Mysia, a province on the Hellespont, but the name has two different meanings, referring to two different places: Gargara is the name of both the top of Mount Ida and the town at foot of the mountain.[90] 4. Homer uses the name of the mountain-top here (*Il.* 8.47–48):

> He came to Ida, rich in springs, mother of beasts,
> Gargaron.

hic Gargarum pro excelsissimo montis loco accipi convenire et ipse sensus indicium facit, nam de Iove loquitur. 5. sed et alibi eodem Homero teste manifestius exprimitur:

*ὣς ὃ μὲν ἀτρέμας εὗδε πατὴρ ἀνὰ Γαργάρῳ ἄκρῳ*

et Epicharmus vetustissimus poeta in fabula quae inscribitur Troes ita posuit:

*Ζεὺς ἄναξ, ναίων ἀν' Ἴδαν*[265] *Γάργαρα*[266] *ἀγάννιφα.*

6. ex his liquido claret Gargara cacumen Idae montis appellitari. 7. pro oppido autem Gargara qui dixerint enumerabo. Ephorus, notissimus historiarum scriptor, in libro quinto sic ait: *μετὰ δὲ τὴν Ἄσσον ἐστὶν τὰ Γάργαρα πλησίον πόλις*. nec Ephorus solus, sed etiam Phileas vetus scriptor in eo libro qui inscribitur Asia ita meminit: *μετὰ Ἄσσον πόλις ἐστὶν ὄνομα Γάργαρα· ταύτης ἔχεται Ἄντανδρος*. 8. Arati etiam liber *ἐλεγείων* fertur in quo de Diotimo quodam poeta sic ait:

*αἰάζω Διότιμον, ὃς ἐν πέτραισι κάθηται*
*Γαργαρέων παισὶν βῆτα καὶ ἄλφα λέγων.*

ex his versibus etiam civium nomen innotuit, quia Gargares vocantur. 9. cum igitur constet Gargara nunc pro montis cacumine, nunc pro oppido sub eodem monte posito ac-

265 *ναίων ἀν' Ἴδαν Schneidewin*: ΑΝ ΑΔΑΝ ΝΑΙΩΝ *α*, *ἀν' ἄκρα ναίων Kaibel* 266 *Γάργαρα* (*contra metrum*)] *Γάργαρ' ἔνθ' Schneidewin*, *Γαργάρων Meineke*

Here the very meaning shows that it's appropriate to take "Gargarum" to denote the highest point on the mountain, since he's speaking about Jupiter. 5. But elsewhere, too, Homer's testimony makes the point more plainly (*Il.* 14.352):

> Thus the father slept untroubled on highest
> Gargaron;

and Epicharmus, a very ancient poet, wrote as follows in the play titled *Trojans* (fr. 130 *CGF* 1,1:115):

> Lord Zeus, dwelling on Ida, the place of snow-capped
> Gargara.

6. From these lines it's clear as day that "Gargara" is the name of Mount Ida's peak. 7. But now I'll list those who used "Gargara" as the name of a town. Ephorus, the very well-known historian, says in Book 5 (no. 70 fr. 47 *FGrH*): "Not far beyond Assos is the city of Gargara." And not just Ephorus: the ancient author Phileas, in his book titled *Asia*, recalls, "After Assos is a city named Gargara, which is bordered by Antandros." 8. Aratus' book of *Elegies* is in circulation, in which the poet says of a certain Diotimus (*Anth. Gr.* 11.437),

> I wail in grief for Diotimus, who sits upon a rocky
> perch,
> teaching the Gargareans' children their ABCs.

From these lines we also learn the name of the town's citizen, because they're named as "Gargareans." 9. Since, then, it is well established that "Gargara" at one time has to be understood as the name of the mountain-top, at another

cipienda, Vergilius non de summo monte sed de oppido loquitur. cur tamen Gargara posuerit ut locum frugum feracem requiramus.

10. 'Et omnem quidem illam Mysiam opimis segetibus habitam satis constat scilicet ob umorem soli. unde et Vergilius in supra dictis versibus, cum dixisset "umida solstitia," intulit "nullo tantum se Mysia cultu iactat," ac si[267] diceret, omnis regio quae opportunos habuerit umores aequiperabit fecunditates arvorum Mysiae. 11. sed Homerus cum ait *Ἴδην . . . πολυπίδακα*, umidum designat subiacentem monti agrum. nam *πολυπίδακα* significat fontibus abundantem. unde[268] haec Gargara tanta frugum copia erant ut qui magnum cuiusque rei numerum vellet exprimere pro multitudine immensa "Gargara" nominaret. 12. testis Alcaeus, qui in *κωμῳδοτραγῳδίᾳ*[269] sic ait:

*ἐτύγχανον μὲν ἀγρόθεν †πλείστους†*[270] *φέρων*[271]
*εἰς τὴν ἑορτὴν †ὅσον οἶον†*[272] *εἴκοσι,*
*ὁρῶ δ' ἄνωθεν γάργαρ' ἀνθρώπων κύκλῳ.*

Gargara, ut videtis, manifeste posuit pro multitudine. nec aliter Aristomenes *ἐν* Μύθοις:[273]

*ἔνδον γὰρ ἡμῖν ἐστιν ἀνδρῶν γάργαρα.*

267 ac si *Willis* (atque si *ed. Lugd. 1550 in marg.*): atque ω

268 unde R: inde ω

269 *κωμῳδοτραγῳδίᾳ Fabricius*: caedo(*vel* coedo-)tragoedia ω

270 *πλείστους*] *πλεκτούς* Herwerden, *πελάνους* Kock

271 *φέρων ed. Basil. 1535*: -ΡΩ α

272 *ὅσον οἶον*] *ὡς ἄν, οἴομ' Schneidewin*, *ὄψον, οἶον εἰκὸς ἦν Herwerden*

273 Μύθοις (*lapsu Macrob.*): Βοηθοῖς *Fabric. ex* Σ *Acharn. 3*

as the name of a town at that mountain's foot, Virgil is speaking not about the former but about the latter. Now, though, let's investigate why he named Gargara as a productive place for crops.

10. 'And indeed, we can take it as settled that all of Mysia is thought to have excellent harvests, no doubt because the soil is moist. That's also why when Virgil used the phrase "damp solstices" in the lines quoted above he adduced the statement, "Mysia can make no such boast about its tillage," as if to say that every region that has a ready supply of moisture will match the fertility of Mysia's fields. 11. But when Homer says that Ida is *polypîdax* ["rich in springs"] (*Il.* 8.47 *et al.*), he indicates that the land lying at the mountain's foot is damp. Accordingly, this city of Gargara had such abundant crops that someone who wanted to convey a large number of any sort of objects would use the named "Gargara" to mean "an immeasurable number." 12. Alcaeus gives evidence of this, when he says in his *Comic-tragedy* (fr. 19 *PCG* 2:9),

I happened to be carrying . . . from the country
to the festival . . . twenty,
when I see from on high a heap [*gargara*] of people
in a circle.

As you see, he plainly used *gargara* to denote a large number, just as Aristomenes does in his *Myths* (fr. 1 *PCG* 1:415):

For we have within a heap [*gargara*] of men.

13. Aristophanes autem comicus composito nomine ex harena et Gargaris innumerabilem, ut eius lepos est, numerum conatur exprimere. in fabula enim Acharneusin ait,

ἃ δ᾽ ὠδυνήθην, ψαμμακοσιογάργαρα.

ψαμμακόσια autem seorsum pro multis Varro saepe in Menippeis suis posuit, sed Aristophanes adiecit γάργαρα ad significationem numerositatis innumerae. 14. est ergo secundum haec sensus horum versuum talis: cum ea sit anni temperies ut hiems serena sit, solstitium vero imbricum, fructus optime proveniunt. haec autem adeo agris necessaria sunt ut sine his nec illi natura fecundissimi Mysiae agri responsuri sint opinioni fertilitatis quae de his habetur. 15. addit Mysiae nominatim Gargara, quod ea urbs posita in imis radicibus Idae montis defluentibus inde umoribus inrigetur possitque videri solstitiales imbres non magnopere desiderare. 16. hoc in loco ad fidem sensui faciendam quod uliginosa sint non sola Gargara pro vicinia montis, sed et universae Mysiae arva, adhiberi potest testis Aeschylus:

ἰὼ Κάϊκε Μύσιαί τ᾽ ἐπιρροαί.

17. 'Quid de Graecis in hoc loco traxerit diximus. addemus praeterea hoc iucunditatis gratia et ut liqueat Vergilium vestrum undique veterum sibi ornamenta traxisse, unde hoc dixerit, "hiberno laetissima pulvere farra": 18. in

13. Moreover, the comic poet Aristophanes, true to his charming manner, tries to convey an infinite number by forming a compound from the nouns "sand" and "Gargara," saying in his *Acharnians* (3),

> What pains I had, a sand-hundred-heaps' worth
> (*psammakosiogargara*).

In his *Menippean satires* Varro often used "sand-hundred" [*psammakosia*] by itself to mean "many" (fr. 585 Cèbe), but Aristophanes added "heaps" [*gargara*] to signify an infinite number. 14. It follows, then, that the sense of Virgil's passage is this: when the season is so mild that the winter is mild and the solstice rainy, a bumper crop is produced; moreover, these conditions are so necessary for the fields that without them not even the fields of Mysia, which are naturally very productive, will correspond to the opinion that's entertained about their fertility. 15. To Mysia he adds Gargara by name, because that city, placed as it is at the very base of Mount Ida, is kept wet by all the moisture that flows down from the mountain and could appear not to need rainy solstices. 16. Here Aeschylus can be brought on as a witness to corroborate the view that not only is Gargara wet, because of the neighboring mountain, but the farmlands of Mysia as a whole are, too (fr. 143 *TGrF* 3:258):

> Hail Kaïkos and Mysia's streams!

17. 'I've finished my account of Virgil's borrowing from the Greeks, but let me add—as a pleasant footnote, and to make plain that your Virgil derived his ornaments from every antique nook and cranny—the source he relied on for "emmers grow best in the dust of winter": 18. in a book of

libro enim vetustissimorum carminum, qui ante omnia quae a Latinis scripta sunt compositus ferebatur, invenitur hoc rusticum vetus canticum:

hiberno pulvere, verno luto,
grandia farra, camille, metes.

21 'Nomina poculorum Vergilius plerumque Graeca ponit, ut carchesia, ut cymbia, ut cantharos, ut scyphos. de carchesiis ita:

". . . cape Maeonii carchesia Bacchi,
Oceano libemus," ait,

et alibi:

hic duo rite mero libans carchesia Baccho.

de cymbiis:

inferimus tepido spumantia cymbia lacte;

de cantharo:

et gravis attrita pendebat cantharus ansa;

de scyphis:

et sacer implevit dextram scyphus.

2. ea autem cuius figurae sint quisve eorum fecerit mentionem nemo quaerit, contenti scire cuiuscemodi esse pocula. et scyphos quidem cantharosque, consueta vulgi nomina, ferendum si transeant; sed de carchesiis cym-

---

[91] Cf. Paul. Fest. p. 82.18–22, DServ. on *G.* 1.101.

the most ancient poems, which is said to have been put together before the Romans had a literature, this ancient peasant's chant is found (fr. 16 p. 419 *FPL*³),[91]

From winter's dust, spring's mud
bushels of emmer, my boy, you'll reap.

'For the most part Virgil uses Greek names of vessels, like *carchesia* ["drinking cups"], like *cymbia* ["small cups"], like *canthari* ["large-handled cups"], like *scyphi* ["cans"]. About *carchesisa* (*G.* 4.380): 21

". . . take up carchesia of Maeonian Bacchus,"
he says, "and lets pour a libation to Ocean,"

and elsewhere (*A.* 5.77*):

hereupon pouring two carchesia of unmixed Bacchus
in customary libation . . . ;

about *cymbia* (*A.* 3.66*):

we bring in cymbia foaming with warm milk;

about the *cantharus* (*E.* 6.17):

and a heavy *cantharus* was hanging by its well-worn
handle;

about *scyphi* (*A.* 8.278):

and a holy scyphus filled his right hand.

2. But people do not ask what shape these vessels are or what author mentioned them, being content to know that they are cups of a certain sort. Now, it's tolerable for them to ignore the *scyphi* and *canthari*, labels that everyone's used to. But in the case of *carchesia* and *cymbia*—terms

biisque, quae apud Latinos haud scio an umquam reperias, apud Graecos autem sunt rarissima, non video cur non cogantur inquirere quid sibi nova et peregrina nomina velint. 3. est autem carchesium poculum Graecia tantum modo notum. meminit eius Pherecydes in libris historiarum aitque Iovem Alcmenae pretium concubitus carchesium aureum dono dedisse. sed Plautus insuetum nomen reliquit aitque in fabula Amphitryone pateram datam cum longe utriusque poculi figura diversa sit. 4. patera enim, ut et ipsum nomen indicio est, planum ac patens est, carchesium vero procerum et circa mediam partem compressum, ansatum mediocriter, ansis a summo ad infimum pertingentibus. 5. Asclepiades autem, vir inter Graecos adprime doctus ac diligens, carchesia a navali re existimat dicta. ait enim navalis veli partem inferiorem *πτέρναν* vocari, at circa mediam ferme partem *τράχηλον* dici, summam vero partem carchesium nominari et inde diffundi in utrumque veli latus ea quae cornua vocantur. 6. nec solus Asclepiades meminit huius poculi sed et alii illustres poetae ut Sappho, quae ait,

*κῆνοι δ' ἄρα πάντες*
*καρχάσια ἔσχον,*[274]
*κἄλειβον . . . ,*

Cratinus *ἐν Διονυσαλεξάνδρῳ,*

[274] *καρχάσια ἔσχον* (*ἔχον Athen.*)] *καρχάσι' ἦχον Lobel-Page*, *καρχάσια τ' ἦχον Bergk*

---

[92] *carchesia* is first used by Rome's earliest poet, Livius Andronicus (fr. 30 *SRPF*[3] 1:5), but is found commonly only in poets

that I don't think any Latin authors use, and precious few Greeks[92]—I don't see why they aren't forced to investigate the meaning of these strange, foreign terms. 3. Be that as it may: the *carchesium* is a cup known only in Greece: it's mentioned by Pherecydes in the books of his *Histories*, where he says that Jupiter gave Alcmena the gift of a golden *carchesium* as a reward for lying with him (no. 3 fr. 13 *FGrH* = fr. 13a *EGM*).[93] But Plautus abandoned the unfamiliar name, saying in his play *Amphitryo* (534) that he gave her a *patera*, though the shapes of the two vessels are very different. 4. For a *patera*, as its very name indicates, is flat and open [*patens*], while a *carchesium* is tall, with a pinched waist and handles of middling heft that extend from lip to base. 5. But Asclepiades, one of the most learned and careful of the Greeks, thinks that the name *carchesia* was drawn from the nautical sphere:[94] for he says that the lower part of a ship's sail is called the *pterna* ["heel"], the middle part the *trachêlos* ["throat"], and the upper part the *carchesium*, from which the so-called horns [*cornua* = yard-arms] extend into either side of the sail. 6. Not only does Asclepiades mention this cup but so do other famous poets like Sappho, who says (fr. 141b),

All of them, then,
held *karkhâsia*
and were pouring libations . . . ;

Cratinus, in his *Dionysalexandros* (fr. 40 *PCG* 4:142),

writing after Virgil; *cymbia* is not attested in poetry before Virgil and Prop. 3.8.4.

93 §3 is based on Athen. 474F.

94 §§5–6 are based on Athen. 474F–475A.

—στολὴν δὲ δὴ τίνα[275] εἶχε; τοῦτό μοι φράσον.
—θύρσον, κροκωτόν, ποικίλον, καρχήσιον,

Sophocles in fabula quae inscribitur Τύρῳ,

πρὸς τήνδ' εἶμι[276]
τράπεζαν ἀμφὶ σῖτα καὶ καρχήσια.

7. 'Haec de carchesiis ignoratis Latinitati et a sola Graecia celebratis. sed nec cymbia in nostro[277] sermone reperies: est enim a Graecorum paucis relatum. Philemon, notissimus comicus, in Phantasmate[278] ait,

ἔπιεν ἡ Ῥόδη
κυμβίον ἀκράτου,

8. Anaxandrides etiam comicus in fabula Ἀγροίκοις:[279]

προπινόμενα καὶ μέστ' ἀκράτου κυμβία
ἐκάκωσεν[280] ὑμᾶς.

meminit eius et Demosthenes in oratione quae est in Midiam: ἐπ' ἀστράβης δὲ ὀχούμενος ἐξ Ἀργουρᾶς τῆς Εὐβοίας,[281] χλανίδας δὲ καὶ κυμβία[282] ἔχων, ὧν ἐπελαμβάνοντο οἱ πεντηκοστολόγοι. 9. cymbia autem haec, ut ipsius nominis figura indicat, diminutive a cymba dicta,

275 τίνα (*plene scriptum*)] τίν' *Porson*

276 πρὸς τήνδ' εἶμι (*contra metrum*)] προστῆναι μέσην *Athenaeus 11 475A*, προσβῆναι μέσην Hartung

277 nostro (*lapsu Macrob., cf. §9 inf.*)] vestro *ed. Lips. 1774*

278 Phantasmate] Phasmate *ed. Lugd. 1532 ex Athen.*

279 Ἀγροίκοις *ed. Basil. 1535*: a grecis ω (*versus sequentes Athenaeo duce edd. resarciunt*)

280 ἐκάκωσεν] ἐκάρωσεν *Athenaeus 11.63 481f*

— What sort of outfit did he have? Tell me.
— A thyrsos, a saffron gown, an embroidered robe, a *karkhêsion*;

Sophocles, in his play titled *Tyrô* (fr. 660 *TGrF* 4:469):

I will approach this
table for the sake of [?] bread and *karkhêsia*.

7. 'So much for *carchesia*, unknown to Latin and common only in Greece. But neither will you find *cymbia* mentioned in our tongue—in fact, only a few Greeks mention them. Philemon, the very well known comic poet, says in his *Ghost* (fr. 87 *PCG* 7:272),

Rhoda drank
a *kymbion* of wine neat;

8. Anaxandrides, another comic poet, in his *Peasants* (fr. 3 *PCG* 2:239):

Toasts made from *kymbia* of unmixed wine
have left all of you wasted.

Demosthenes too mentions it in his speech against Midias (21.133): "riding on a padded saddle from Argoura in Euboia, with fine-spun woollen stoles and *kymbia*, which the customs officers seized." 9. But *cymbia*, as the form of the word suggests, is a diminutive of *cymba*, a terms

---

281 *ἐξ Ἀργουρᾶς τῆς* Εὐβοίας (*codd.* AF *Dem., Herodian*)] *ἀργυρᾶς τῆς ἐξ* Εὐβοίας *cod.* S *Dem., ἀργυρᾶς Menand. Rhet.*
282 *κυμβία*] *κυμβία καὶ κάδους Dem.*

quod et apud Graecos et apud nos[283] ab illis trahentes navigii genus est. ac sane animadverti ego apud Graecos multa poculorum genera a re navali cognominata, ut carchesia supra docui, ut haec cymbia, pocula procera ac navibus similia. 10. meminit huius poculi Eratosthenes, vir longe doctissimus, in epistula ad Hagetorem Laecdaemonium his verbis: *κρατῆρα γὰρ ἔστησαν*[284] *τοῖς θεοῖς, οὐκ ἀργύρεον*[285] *οὐδὲ λιθοκόλλητον, ἀλλὰ γῆς*[286] *Κωλιάδος. τοῦτον δ' ὁσάκις ἐπιπληρώσαιεν,*[287] *ἀποσπείσαντες τοῖς θεοῖς ᾠνοχόουν ἐφεξῆς*[288] *βαπτιστῷ κυμβίῳ.*[289] 11. fuerunt qui cymbium a cissybio per syncopam dictum existimarent. cissybii autem, ut de Homero taceam qui hoc poculum Cyclopi ab Vlixe datum memorat, multi faciunt mentionem, voluntque non nulli proprie cissybium ligneum esse poculum ex hedera id est *κισσοῦ*. 12. et Nicander quidem[290] Colophonius in primo *Αἰτωλικῶν*[291] sic ait: *ἐν τῇ ἱεροποιήσει*[292] *τοῦ Διδυμαίου Διὸς κισσῷ σπονδοποιέονται,*[293] *ὅθεν τὰ ἀρχαῖα ἐκπώματα κισσύβια φωνέεται.* sed et Callimachus meminit huius poculi:

283 nos] vos *ed. Lips. 1774 (cf. §7 sup.)*
284 *ἔστησαν*] *ἵστασαν Athen. 11 482b*
285 *ἀργύρεον*] *ἀργυροῦν Athen.*
286 *γῆς Athen.*: THC *α*
287 *ἐπί τι πληρώσαιεν Athen.*
288 *ᾠνοχόουν ἐφεξῆς*] *ἐκ τῆς φιάλης ᾠ. ἐ. Athen.*
289 *βαπτιστῷ κυμβίῳ*] *τὸν νεοκρᾶτα βάπτοντες τῷ κ. Athen.*
290 quidem *ed. Paris. 1585*: quidam *ω*
291 *Αἰτωλικῶν Athen. 11 477 B* (Aetolicon *ed. Lugd. 1532*): italicon *ω*
292 *ἱεροποιήσει*] *ἱεροποιίῃ Athen.*
293 *πετάλοισιν post σπονδοποιέονται Athen.*

that the Greeks—and we, borrowing from them—use for a kind of sailing vessel.[95] Indeed, I've noticed that the Greeks have many kinds of cups that derive their name from the nautical sphere, like *carchesia*, as I noted above, and like these *cymbia*, which are tall cups similar to ships. 10. Eratosthenes, an extremely learned man, mentions this cup in a letter to the Spartan Hagetor, saying (*Philosophical Books* fr. 14):[96] "They set up a mixing bowl for the gods, not silver nor set with precious stones but of clay from Kôlias.[97] As often as they filled it, they made a libation to the gods and then poured servings one after the other, using a *kymbion* as a ladle." 11. There have been those who thought that *cymbium* was derived from *kissybium*, a syllable having fallen out.[98] But many writers mention the *kissybium*—to say nothing of Homer, who says that Ulysses gave this cup to the Cyclops (*Od.* 9.347)—and some claim that the *kissybium* is properly a wooden cup made of ivy, that is, *kissos*. 12. And in fact Nicander of Colophon, in Book 1 of his *History of Aetolia*, says (no. 271–72 fr. 2 *FGrH*): "In the festival of Zeus at Didyma they pour libations from ivy-wood, whence *kissybia*, the old-fashioned drinking cups, get their name." Callimachus too mentions this cup (*Aetia* fr. 178.11–12 Pf.):

[95] The *cymba* (or *cumba*, Gk. *kymbê*) was what we would call a "skiff"; *kymbion* is in fact the Greek diminutive form.

[96] §10 is based on Athen. 482A.

[97] A cape in Attica where there were beds of especially fine white clay.

[98] §§11–13 are based on Athen. 476F–477E.

καὶ γὰρ ὁ Θρηϊκίην μὲν ἀνήνατο[294] χανδὸν ἄμυστιν
ζωροποτεῖν,[295] ὀλίγῳ δ᾽ ἥδετο κισσυβίῳ.

13. qui autem cissybium ex hedera factum poculum οἷον εἰ κίσσιον dici arbitrantur Euripidis auctoritate niti videntur, qui in Andromeda sic ait:

πᾶς δὲ ποιμένων ἔρρει λεώς,
ὁ μὲν γάλακτος κίσσινον φέρων σκύφον,[296]
πόνων ἀναψυκτῆρα,[297] ὁ δ᾽ ἀμπέλων γάνος.

14. 'Haec de cymbio. sequitur ut quando cantharum et poculi et navigii genus esse supra diximus, probetur exemplis. et pro poculo quidem nota res est vel ex ipso Vergilio, qui aptissime proprium Liberi patris poculum adsignat Sileno: sed id, ut supra polliciti sumus, etiam pro navigio poni solitum debemus ostendere. 15. Menander in Nauclero:

— ἥκει λιπὼν Αἰγαῖον ἁλμυρὸν βάθος
Θεόφιλος ἡμῖν. ὦ Στράτων, ὡς εἰς καλὸν·
‹τὸν υἱὸν εὐτυχοῦντα καὶ σεσωμένον›[298]
πρῶτος λέγω σοι τόν τε χρυσοῦν κάνθαρον.
— ποῖον; τὸ πλοῖον;
— οὐδὲν[299] οἶσθας, ἄθλιε.

294 ἀνήνατο (*ex Athen. 11 477C*)] ἀπέστυγε *pap. Callim., Athen. 10 442F* 295 ζωροποτεῖν (*ex eodem*)] οἰνοποτεῖν *pap. Callim., Athen. 10 442F, 11 781D*

296 σκύφον] σκύφος *Athen. 11 477A*

297 ἀναψυκτῆρα (*plene scriptum*)] ἀναψυκτῆρ᾽ *edd. Eur.*

298 τὸν . . . σεσωμένον *suppl. ed. Basil. 1535 ex Athen.* (*iam ed. Colon. 1527,* υἱόν *om.*), om. *α* 299 οὐδὲν *Meineke*: -ΔΕΜ *α*

And indeed he refused to greedily knock back the Thracian wine
neat in one gulp, but he took his pleasure with a small *kissybion*.

13. But those who think that the *kissybium* is a cup made of ivy-wood—a *kission*, so to say—seem to rely on the authority of Euripides, who in his *Andromeda* says (fr. 146 *TGrF* 5,1:256),

The whole throng of herdsmen came streaming,
one carrying an ivy-wood cup [*kissinos skyphos*] of milk
to revive him from his toil, another the vine's refreshing joy.

14. 'So much for the *cymbium*. Next I should adduce examples to prove my earlier statement that the *cantharus* is both a kind of cup and a kind of ship.[99] The word's use to denote a kind of cup is in fact familiar even from Virgil himself, who very aptly attributes to Silenus (*E*. 6.17) the cup that's the property of father Liber; but I ought to show that it's also used to mean "ship," as I promised above. 15. Menander, in his *Ship's Captain* (fr. 286 Sandbach):

— Theophilos has arrived, leaving the Aegaean's
salty deep. O, Strato, you come just in time:
let me be the first to tell you that your son
is here safe and sound, and his golden *kantharos*.
— What kind of *kantharos*? A ship?—Unhappy man, you know nothing.

[99] A slip: cf. §9 above.

16. Et sacer implevit dextram scyphus.

scyphus Herculis poculum est, ita ut Liberi patris cantharus. Herculem vero fictores veteres non sine causa cum poculo fecerunt—et non numquam cassabundum et ebrium—non solum quod is heros bibax fuisse perhibetur, sed etiam quod antiqua historia est Herculem poculo tamquam navigio vectum[300] immensa maria transisse. 17. sed de utraque re pauca ex Graecis antiquitatibus dicam. et multibibum heroa istum fuisse, ut taceam quae vulgo nota sunt, illud non obscurum argumentum est quod Ephippus in Busiride inducit Herculem sic loquentem:

*οὐκ οἶσθά μ' ὄντα πρὸς θεῶν Τιρύνθιον*
*Ἀργεῖον, οἳ μεθύοντες ἀεὶ τὰς μάχας*
*πάσας μάχονται;*
*—τοιγαροῦν φεύγουσ' ἀεί.*

18. est etiam historia non adeo notissima nationem quandam hominum fuisse prope Heracleam ab Hercule constitutam Cylicranorum composito nomine ἀπὸ τῆς κύλικος, quod poculi genus nos una littera immutata calicem dicimus. 19. poculo autem Herculem vectum ad Ἐρύθειαν,[301] id est Hispaniae insulam, navigasse et Panyassis,[302] egregius scriptor Graecorum, dicit et Pherecydes auctor est, quorum verba subdere supersedi, quia propiora sunt fa-

[300] vectum *cod. Laurent. 65.36, Bentley ex coniect.*: ventis *ω*
[301] vectum ad Ἐρύθειαν *ed. Basil. 1535*: ductum ΑΔΕΓΥΤΗΡΑ *vel sim. α*
[302] Panyassis *ed. Basil. 1535, Athen.*: -astis *ω*

16. And a holy scyphus filled his right hand (*A.* 8.278*).

The *scyphus* is Hercules' cup, as the *cantharus* is father Liber's. In olden days sculptors fashioned Hercules with a cup—and sometimes stumbling drunk—with good reason: not just because the hero is said to have been fond of drink but also because of the old tale that he crossed the limitless seas in his drinking vessel, as though it were a sailing vessel. 17. I'll say a few words based on ancient Greek texts about both of these reasons. To say nothing of what's common knowledge, the hero's great fondness for drink is plainly shown by the fact that Ephippus, in his *Busiris*, brings Hercules onstage saying (fr. 2 *PCG* 4:132):

> Are you unaware, by the gods, that I am from Tiryns
> in the Argolid, where the people always fight all
> their battles drunk?
> — No doubt that's why they always run away.

18. There's also a story—not terribly well known—that there was a certain tribe near Heraclea, a city founded by Heracles, whose name, "Kylikrani," is formed from the word *kylix*, which is a kind of cup that we, with the change of a single letter, call the *calix*.[100] 19. However, the story that Hercules was borne along in a cup when he sailed to Erytheia—that is, an island off Spain—is told both by Panyassis, an outstanding Greek author (fr. 9 *PEGr* 1:176–77), and by Pherecydes (no. 3 fr. 18*a* *FGrH* = fr. 18a *EGM*):[101] I have refrained from appending them, because

[100] For the Kylikrani cf. Athen. 461E–462A.
[101] §19 is based on Athen. 469D, 470C–D.

bulae quam historiae. ego tamen arbitror non poculo Herculem maria transvectum sed navigio cui scypho nomen fuit ita ut supra cantharum et carchesium et a cymbis derivata cymbia, omnia haec asseruimus esse navigiorum vocabula.

22 'Nomina quoque Vergilius non numquam ex antiquissimis Graecorum historiis mutuatur. scitis apud illum unam ex comitibus Dianae "Opin" vocari, quod nomen vulgo fortasse temere impositum vel etiam fictum putatur ab ignorantibus insidiosum poetam cognomen, quod a veteribus Graecis scriptoribus ipsi Dianae fuerat impositum, comiti eius adsignare voluisse. 2. sed Vergilius sic ait:

velocem interea superis in sedibus Opin,
unam ex virginibus sociis sacraque caterva,
compellabat et has tristis Latonia voces
ore dabat;

et infra:

at Triviae custos iam dudum in montibus Opis.

3. Opin inquit comitem et sociam Dianae. sed audite unde Vergilius hoc nomen acceperit qui, ut dixi, quod epitheton ipsiusce legerat sociae eius imposuit. 4. Alexander Aetolus, poeta egregius, in libro qui inscribitur Musae, refert quanto studio populus Ephesius dedicato templo Dianae curaverit, praemiis propositis ut qui tunc erant poetae ingeniosissimi in deam carmina diversa componerent. in his

---

[102] There appears to be no parallel for such a usage.

what they say is closer to myth than to history. Still, *I* think that Hercules was carried across the seas, not in a cup, but in a ship that was called a *scyphus*,[102] just like the *cantharus* above, and the *carchesium*, and the *cymbia* that are named after the *cymba*, all of which I have shown to be terms for sailing vessels.

'Virgil sometimes borrows proper names, too, from ancient Greek history. As you know, he calls one of Diana's companions "Opis," a name people commonly think Virgil perhaps used at random or even made up: they don't know that the sly poet chose to give the name to the companion because ancient Greek authors had given it to Diana herself. 2. But here is what Virgil says (*A.* 11.532†–35): 22

> Meanwhile in their resting place on high Latonia
> was addressing swift Opis, one of her maiden allies,
> one of her holy troupe, and with her lips she spoke
> these sad words;

and further on (*A.* 11.836†):

> but for a long while now in the mountain Trivia's
> guardian, Opis. . . .

3. He says that Opis is Diana's companion and ally. But now hear how the name came to be used by Virgil, who (as I said) gave it to the goddess' companion because he had read that it was an epithet of the goddess herself. 4. Alexander of Aetolia, an outstanding poet, reports in his book titled *Muses* that the people of Ephesus cared for the temple dedicated to Diana so zealously that they posted rewards for the cleverest poets of the day to write different kinds of poems in the goddess' honor. In the lines I'm about to quote "Opis" is the name given, not to Diana's

versibus Opis non comes Dianae, sed Diana ipsa vocitata est. 5. loquitur autem, uti dixi, de populo Ephesio:

ἀλλ' ὅγε πευθόμενος πάγχυ Γραικοῖσι μέλεσθαι
 Τιμόθεον, κιθάρης ἴδμονα καὶ μελέων,
υἱὸν Θερσάνδρου †τὸν†[303] ἤνεσεν ἀνέρα σίγλων
 χρυσείων ἱερὴν δὴ τότε χιλιάδα
ὑμνῆσαι ταχέων τ'[304] Ὦπιν βλήτειραν ὀϊστῶν,
 ἥ δ'[305] ἐπὶ Κεγχρείῳ τίμιον οἶκον ἔχει

et mox:[306]

μηδὲ θεῆς προλίπῃ Λητωΐδος ἀκλέα ἔργα.

6. apparuit, ni fallor, Opin Dianam dictam, et Vergilium de nimia doctrina hoc nomen in eius comitem transtulisse.

7. Excessere omnes adytis arisque relictis
di . . .

'Hoc unde Vergilius dixerit nullus inquirit, sed constat illum de Euripide traxisse, qui in fabula Troadibus inducit Apollinem cum Troia capienda esset ista dicentem:

λείπω τὸ κλεινὸν Ἴλιον, <βωμούς τ' ἐμούς·
ἐρημία γὰρ πόλιν ὅταν λάβηι κακή,
νοσεῖ τὰ τῶν θεῶν οὐδὲ τιμᾶσθαι θέλει,> [307]

303 τὸν] κλυτὸν *Schneidewin* 304 τ' *add. Meineke, om.* α
305 δ'] τ' *Meineke* 306 et mox P, *om.* ω
307 βωμούς τ' . . . θέλει *add. ed. Colon. 1521* (*recte, cf.* qui versus docent), *om.* α

---

103 Contrast 3.9, where the same lines are attributed not to Greek inspiration but to traditional Roman ritual.

companion, but to Diana herself. 5. He is speaking about the people of Ephesus, as I said (fr. 4 *CA* p. 124):

> But when the people learned that the Greeks cared deeply
> for Timotheos, virtuoso of the lyre and lyric songs,
> they bade the man, Thersander's son, in return for shekels
> of gold, to celebrate in song the golden millennium then being
> marked and Opis, she who shoots swift arrows, who has her honored house on Kenkhreion;

and soon thereafter (ibid.),

> nor leave without renown the deeds of the goddess, Leto's daughter.

6. It has been made plain, if I'm not mistaken, that Diana was called Opis and that Virgil, relying on his extraordinary learning, transferred the name to her companion.

> 7. They all departed, abandoning their shrines and altars,
> the gods . . . (*A.* 2.351†–52)

'No one bothers to ask how Virgil came to say this,[103] but it is beyond question that he derived it from Euripides, who in his play *Trojan Women* brings Apollo[104] onstage when Troy is about to be captured, saying (25–27),

> I am leaving famous Ilion <and my altars:
> when wretched desolation takes a town,
> worship of the gods wilts and has no honor,>

104 A slip: the speaker is Poseidon.

qui versus docent unde Vergilius usurpaverit discessisse deos a civitate iam capta. 8. Nec hoc sine auctoritate Graecae vetustatis est quod ait:

> ipsa Iovis rapidum iaculata e nubibus ignem.

Euripides enim inducit Minervam ventos contra Graecorum classem a Neptuno petentem dicentemque debere illum facere quod Iuppiter fecerit, a quo in Graecos fulmen acceperit.

9. 'Apud Vergilium Pan niveo lanae munere Lunam inlexisse perhibetur, "in nemora alta vocans" "munere sic niveo lanae, si credere dignum est" et reliqua. in hoc loco Valerius Probus, vir perfectissimus, notat nescire se hanc historiam sive fabulam quo referat auctore. 10. quod tantum virum fugisse miror. nam Nicander huius est auctor historiae, poeta quem Didymus, grammaticorum omnium quique sint quique fuerint instructissimus, fabulosum vocat. quod sciens Vergilius adiecit, "si credere dignum est": adeo se fabuloso usum fatetur auctore.

11. 'In tertio libro cursim legitur, neque unde translatum sit quaeritur:

> quae Phoebo pater omnipotens, mihi Phoebus Apollo
> praedixit

et cetera. 12. in talibus locis grammatici excusantes imperitiam suam inventiones has ingenio magis quam doctrinae

lines that tells us the source from which Virgil took over the idea that the gods abandoned a city that had been captured. 8. This line also has the authority of Greek antiquity behind it (*A*. 1.42†):

> With her own hand she hurled Jupiter's swift bolt
> from the clouds;

for Euripides brings Minerva onstage asking Neptune to send winds against the Greeks' fleet and saying that he ought to do what was done by Jupiter, from whom he got a lightning bolt to use against the Greeks (*Tro*. 77–86).

9. 'In Virgil Pan is said to have lured the Moon with a snow-white gift of wool: "calling her into the deep groves" (*G*. 3.393) "with a snow-white gift of wool, if that deserves our credit" (*G*. 3.391†), and so on. Here Valerius Probus, a most accomplished man, remarks that he does not know on whose authority Virgil relates this anecdote or myth (fr. 9). 10. I am amazed that this escaped the great man: for Nicander is the source of this anecdote, a poet whom Didymus—the best trained of all grammarians who are or have been—calls a "myth-monger" (*Strange Tales* fr. 5). Aware of this, Virgil added "if that deserves our credit," thus acknowledging that he had used a myth-monger as his source.

11. 'In Book 3 (251–52) people hurriedly read—without asking the source of the borrowing—

> things the father almighty declared to Phoebus, and
> Phoebus
> Apollo to me,

and so on. 12. In such passages grammarians excuse their own ignorance by attributing these discoveries to Maro's

Maronis adsignant, nec dicunt eum ab aliis mutuatum, ne nominare cogantur auctores. sed adfirmo doctissimum vatem etiam in hoc Aeschylum, eminentissimum tragoediarum scriptorem, secutum 13. qui in fabula quae Latina lingua *Sacerdotes*[308] inscribitur sic ait:

> στέλλειν ὅπως τάχιστα· ταῦτα γὰρ πατὴρ
> Ζεὺς ἔνθα καθίει[309] Λοξίᾳ θεσπίσματα,

et alibi:

> πατρὸς προφήτης ἐστὶ Λοξίας Διός.[310]

14. ecquid clarum factum est inde sumpsisse Vergilium quod Apollo ea vaticinetur quae sibi Iuppiter fatur? probatumne vobis est Vergilium, ut ab eo intellegi non potest qui sonum Latinae vocis ignorat, ita nec ab eo posse qui Graecam non hauserit extrema satietate doctrinam? 15. nam si fastidium facere non timerem, ingentia poteram volumina de his quae a penitissima Graecorum doctrina transtulisset implere: sed ad fidem rei propositae relata sufficient.'[311]

308 Sacerdotes *ed. Basil. 1535*: -tis ω

309 ἔνθα καθίει (*contra metrum*: *v. Kaster 2010, 83*)] ἐγκαθίει *ed. Basil. 1535*

310 πατρὸς . . . ἐστὶ . . . Διός] Διὸς . . . δ' ἐστὶ . . . πατρός *Aesch.*

311 *post* sufficient *add.* FINIT DE HIS QVAE VIRGILIVS A GRECIS TRAXT/DE HIS QVAE A VETERIBVS LATINIS MARO TRANSTVLIT NGFA (quae sunt quae sumsit virgilius ab antiquis Latinorum poetis P, *om.* RC)

own wit, not his learning, nor do they say he borrowed them from others, to avoid being forced to name his sources. But I say confidently that in this detail too the most learned bard followed Aeschylus, the pre-eminent tragedian. 13. In his play titled (in Latin) *Sacerdotes* ["Priests"], he says (fr. 86 *TGrF* 3:209),

> Make ready as quickly as possible: for father
> Zeus entrusts these oracles to Loxias,

and elsewhere (*Eum.* 19),

> Loxias is the one who speaks for father Zeus.

14. Does that make plain the source of Virgil's statement that Apollo prophesies the things that Jupiter says to him? Have I persuaded you that the person who does not know the sound of Latin and the person who has not drained the fullest possible draught of Greek learning are both equally incapable of understanding Virgil? 15. If I didn't fear repelling you with still more, I could fill great volumes with the things he borrowed from the most arcane sources of Greek learning. But what I've said will be sufficient to convince you of my original thesis.'